BOYS DON'T CRY?

Boys Don't Cry?

Rethinking Narratives of Masculinity and Emotion in the U.S.

Edited by

Milette Shamir and Jennifer Travis

COLUMBIA UNIVERSITY PRESS

NEW YORK

COLUMBIA UNIVERSITY PRESS
Publishers Since 1893
New York   Chichester, West Sussex

"The Politics of Feeling: Men, Masculinity, and
Mourning on the Capital Mall" © 2002 Judith Newton.

"The Law of the Heart: Emotional Injury and Its
Fictions" by Jennifer Travis is a modified version of
"Sexual Evidence and the Scope of Injury: Willa Cather's
A Lost Lady" © Overseas Publishers Association N.V.,
1999. Reprinted by permission of Gordon and Breach
Publishers.

Library of Congress Cataloging-in-Publication Data
Boys don't cry? : rethinking narratives of masculinity and
emotion in the U.S. / edited by Milette Shamir and
Jennifer Travis.
p.   cm.
ISBN 0–231–12034–6 (cloth : alk. paper)—
ISBN 0–231–12035–4 (pbk. : alk. paper)
1. American literature—History and criticism.
2. Men in literature.   3. Men—United States—Attitudes.
4. Masculinity in literature.   5. Emotions in literature.
6. Narration (Rhetoric)   7. Men—Psychology.
I. Shamir, Milette.   II. Travis, Jennifer.
PS173.M36 B69 2002
810.9'352041—dc21

2001047444

To Avi and to Mike

Contents

Elizabeth Barnes is Associate Professor of English at the College of William and Mary and author of *States of Sympathy: Seduction and Democracy in the American Novel* (Columbia University Press, 1997). She is currently working on a project exploring the relationship between love and violence in American literature and culture, tentatively titled *The Whipping Boy of Love: Violence and Emotion in Nineteenth-Century America*. Her chapter in this book is a part of that project, as are articles she has recently published in *Modern Language Studies* and *University of Mississippi Studies in English*.

Evan Carton is Professor of English at the University of Texas, Austin. He is the author of *The Rhetoric of American Romance* (Johns Hopkins University Press, 1985) and *The Marble Faun: Hawthorne's Transformations* (G.K. Hall &Co., 1992), and a co-author of *The Cambridge History of American Literature*, Volume 8, *Poetry and Criticism: 1940–1995* (1996).

Stephen Davenport teaches American Literature at the University of Illinois. He is currently working on a book entitled *Jack Kerouac, Men's Studies, and the Wounded Male: Repositioning the Positional Son in American Literature* and has published several articles on the Beat movement, postmodernism, African American culture, and men's movements.

Eric Haralson teaches in the Department of English at SUNY Stonybrook. He is the author of several essays that have appeared in such journals as *Arizona*

Quarterly, American Literature, and *The Henry James Review.* His latest book is *Henry James and Queer Modernity* (Cambridge University Press, 2002).

Thomas Lutz is the author of *Crying: A Natural and Cultural History of Tears* (Norton, 1999), *These 'Colored' United States* (Rutgers University Press, 1996), and *American Nervousness* (Cornell University Press, 1991). He has published articles in *A History of Clinical Psychiatry, Black Music Research Journal, American Literary History,* and elsewhere. He is Associate Professor of English at the University of Iowa.

Judith Newton is Professor and Director of Women and Gender Studies at U.C. Davis. Her most recent book is *Starting Over: Feminism and the Politics of Cultural Critique* (University of Michigan Press, 1994). She is currently working on masculinities and is completing a book on men's movements.

Sally Robinson is an Associate Professor of English at Texas A & M. She has published articles in *Cultural Critique, Contemporary Literature, Genders,* and *Modern Fiction Studies,* among other journals. She is also the author of *Engendering the Subject* (1991) and *Marked Men: White Masculinity in Crisis* (Columbia University Press, 2000).

Ryan Schneider is an Assistant Professor in the Department of English and Comparative Literature at San Diego State University. His research focuses on comparative approaches to the discourse of emotion in canonical and non-canonical nineteenth-century American writers. He is currently completing a book entitled *Prophetic Emotion: Emerson, Du Bois, and the Invention of the American Public Intellectual.*

Milette Shamir lectures on American literature at Tel Aviv University. She has published articles on antebellum literature, gender, and law and literature, and is working on a book entitled *The Cult of Privacy: Space and Gender in Antebellum Fiction.*

Thomas Strychacz is Professor of American Literature at Mills College. He is the author of *Modernism, Mass Culture, and Professionalism* (Cambridge University Press, 1993) and *Hemingway's Theaters of Masculinity* (Louisiana State University Press, forthcoming).

Jennifer Travis is Assistant Professor in the Department of English at St. John's University (New York). She has published articles on masculinity and emotions, law and literature, and turn-of-the-century U.S. literature in such journals as *Arizona Quarterly, Women's Studies,* and *Modern Fiction Studies.* She is currently completing a book entitled, *"The Soul has Bandaged Moments": Emotional Injury and U.S. Culture.*

Acknowledgments

We are grateful to those friends and colleagues who gave their support at various stages of this project, particularly Ashley Cross, Naomi Fry, Cathy Jurca, Jean Lutes, Susannah Mintz, Nancy Schnog, and Rebecca Saunders. We wish to thank the contributors to this collection for their hard work, cheerful patience, and general willingness to put up with the many turns this project took along the way. Special thanks to Tom Lutz for his wise advice at several crossroads. Thanks also to Ann Miller, Jennifer Crewe, Leslie Bialler, and the anonymous readers at Columbia University Press for their guidance and insight. This work was partially made possible by financial support from the Newberry Library, Illinois State University, St. John's University, and Tel Aviv University.

BOYS DON'T CRY?

Introduction

MILETTE SHAMIR AND JENNIFER TRAVIS

Do U.S. men have an emotional history? To be sure, libraries are filled with literature detailing men's feelings about men's deeds; in fact, we are currently witnessing an astonishing array of studies on what men may feel "as men." Yet the emotional life of men in much of this work is surprisingly stiffed, to borrow from the title of one recent critique. As the American male is increasingly on display and under analysis, particularly he to whom Erving Goffman has referred as "the complete unblushing male"—white, heterosexual, middle-class, Protestant, northern, urban—we tend to cling hard to some of the most well-entrenched truisms about masculinity: that it connotes total control of emotions, that it mandates emotional inexpressivity, that it entraps in emotional isolation, that boys, in short, don't cry.[1]

Such truisms form the core of critical master narratives about U.S. masculinity. Studies of the literary canon have often taken the form of what Nina Baym termed pejoratively "melodramas of beset manhood," the paradigm that reads American culture, especially through the nineteenth century, as insistently reiterating man's escape from the sphere of sentiment to produce masculinities marked precisely by its rejection: the rugged and hyperindividualistic romantic hero, the alienated and ill-understood writer, the emotionally repressed marketplace man. "Men try to *control themselves*," as historian Michael Kimmel writes, ". . . and when feeling too pressured, they attempt an *escape*."[2] Twentieth-century melodramas have been cast in slightly different terms. In studies of modernism, for instance, the Code Hero epitomizes the strong, silent and emotionally stifled prototypical "Real Man," while more recently scholars have begun to describe "American Cool," the "distinctly

American" twentieth-century emotional code of restraint and disengagement, "an emotional mantle, sheltering the whole personality from embarrassing excess." It is an affective freeze whose avatars are decidedly masculine.[3] What is remarkable about this master narrative and its variations is not simply its historical resilience, but the extent to which it has survived its own critique. Feminist and gender studies, for instance, while reevaluating canonized masculinity through a historically informed understanding of the separate spheres ideology (working mostly on the nineteenth century but projecting their conclusions on the twentieth as well) have tended until recently to perpetuate the very cultural division that gave rise to "beset manhood" in the first place. Such work continued, that is, to divide cultural products into separate traditions along the line of emotional expressivity: a feminine mode marked by effusion of sentiment and its representational conventions, in contrast to a masculine mode where affect is presented negatively, in terms of disavowal and repression or—in such instances where men "betray" emotions—in terms of parody or "feminization."[4]

As Baym's rubric itself suggests, however, this division is an oversimplification. To call the definition of masculinity and its negation of sentiment a "melodrama" is to recognize that sentiment is often incited precisely at the moment of its announced disavowal. It is to appreciate, for example, that intense (male) readerly sentiment has congealed over the years around (male) antisentimental romances, thus endowing them with their canonical status. It is to acknowledge that sentiment and antisentiment have always been closely knit, even from the moment of their inception in the eighteenth century, as June Howard reminds us; neither sentiment nor antisentiment exist independently, she cautions, nor do they "belong" to one gender alone.[5] It is to grant, moreover, that it is an affective economy where masculine emotion is "scarce" and feminine emotion "excessive" that endows the slightest expression of masculine feeling with inflated value (from the staged tears of otherwise tough politicians to the climactic breaking of masculine emotional floodgates in Hollywood films such as *Magnolia*). Indeed, such accounting informs the recent collection of essays entitled *Sentimental Men: Masculinity and the Politics of Affect in American Culture*. Its editors affirm that "by constructing American masculine types such as the anti-domestic American Adam or the individual loner/revolutionary, critical master narratives . . . have masked the continued presence of sentimental men in American culture and letters." Their collection issues a response to Cathy Davidson's question in *American Literature*'s special issue *No More Separate Spheres!* that "if emotion is sentiment and sentiment is female, then what do we do with the canonical literature of and by emotional men—Cooper, Hawthorne, Melville, Douglass, Dreiser, Chesnutt, and Crane, to name just a few?" "Any literary evaluation that tries to keep rigid binaries intact," she writes, "is clearly in trouble."[6]

It is time, in other words, to remap what Davidson calls the "affective geography of gender."[7] *Boys Don't Cry?* joins this project of remapping. Its essays analyze the alignment of masculinity and emotion in literary narratives, offering revisionary readings of canonical texts by Crevecoeur, Brockden Brown, Thoreau, Lowell, and Du Bois. It redraws the cartography of twentieth-century affect as well by analyzing both literary narratives, by Cather, Hemingway, Kerouac, Irving, and more, and other kinds of narrative, including political theory, legal history, film melodramas, popular men's studies texts, academic discourse, and oral interviews. By contributing to the emotional history of American masculinity, the volume reproves the second part of the equation paraphrased above by Davidson that "emotion is sentiment and sentiment is female." But, perhaps as important, by replacing the key term "sentiment" with "emotion," it also critically recasts the first part of Davidson's equation; in other words, *Boys Don't Cry?* suggests that sentiment is only one among several epicenters from which to explore emotional gendering. The essays included stand against the self-evidence of sentiment, countering the tendency, summarized by June Howard in "What is Sentimentality?" to regard sentiment as "cultural" and "spurious" and emotion as "natural" and "authentic." Using the work of anthropologists and psychologists, Howard shows that both sentiment and emotion should be construed as at once physiological, cognitive, and social phenomena, "embodied thoughts," as Michelle Rosaldo put it.[8] Yet this does not mean they are coterminous. While neither one can be reduced to cultural constructions or to effects of the body, sentimentality "mark[s] moments when the discursive processes that construct emotion become visible."[9] Sentimentality, that is, is visibly crafted, self-conscious, conventionally stylized emotion. Thus whereas every instance of sentimentality evokes an emotion (itself discursive), not every emotional articulation is sentimental: "emotional men" are not necessarily "sentimental men." Furthermore, while the term "sentiment" is anchored in Enlightenment and Victorian discourses of feeling, "emotion" is a term that calls to mind more contemporary accounts. This volume chooses to utilize the latter term in its title, since many of its essays are concerned with emotional tropes that exceed sentimental convention, while over half of them interpret twentieth-century emotionologies.[10]

In extending chronologically and characterologically the affective mapping of gender, we are not motivated by the desire to "save" the "complete unblushing male" from a narrative that describes him as heartless by uncovering his latent emotional life. Indeed, as we will discuss shortly, a debate over the very possibility of producing change through the unmasking of suppressed emotions forms one of this volume's main axes. Rather, the chapters are allied by a set of interrelated questions: How did the master narrative of the emotionally stifled U.S. male come into being in the first place, and at what price? How did its lineaments change over time? What kind of emotions surrounded or, rather, were incited by this narrative? Why do constructions of emotionally alienated male subjects continue to dominate narratives about white, middle-class masculinity and what is at stake in the repeated announcement that men are emotionally stiffed? What are the cultural uses of representing male feelings in light of this alienated subjectivity?

Such questions seem particularly relevant at the present moment, when big bookstore chain shelves continue to be lined with titles such as *The Culture of Complaint* (Robert Hughes) and *A Nation of Victims* (Charles J. Sykes), which collectively lament what they see as a culture of criers, whiners, victims, predominantly women, men of color, gays, lesbians, and immigrants. Such books decry that "minorities" have begun to pervert the stoicism and self-sufficiency of the American tradition, as they seek to demean feminist and antiracist politics by treating charges of inequality as merely the apotheosis of overblown emotional wounds. "As our 15th-century forebears were obsessed with the creation of saints and our 19th-century ancestors with the production of heroes, from Christopher Columbus to George Washington, so are we with the recognition, praise and, when necessary, the manufacture of victims," writes Robert Hughes, adding that those victims' "one common feature is that they have been denied parity with that Blond Beast of the sentimental imagination, the heterosexual, middle-class white male."[11] Hughes's argument exemplifies the danger lurking in a dichotomous reading of emotion: it can lead to the view that women and other disenfranchised groups are the sole bankers of emotion, thus naturalizing victimization and then placing blame on the injured by mocking what Hughes calls their "whiny" status. All the while, the "heterosexual, middle-class white male" 's own access to emotional capital (including Hughes's) remains largely undertheorized and ignored.

Consider, by contrast, another group of best-selling books, those that call upon men to get in touch with their feelings, to cultivate precisely what

Hughes ridicules as a "sentimental imagination." From Warren Farrell's *The Liberated Man,* through various popular twelve-step programs, to Robert Bly's *Iron John,* men's "liberation" has been tied to the release of the emotive self, whether by creating a space for sharing feeling with other men, as in the Bly-inspired mythopoetic movement, or by calling upon men to embrace the "female" component of their psyches, as some profeminists do.[12] What much of this work shares is, first, the assumption that man is victimized by the strict gender codes of emotional restraint, and, second, the reading of signs of emotion, such as tears, as in themselves evidence for social transformation. Of course, such assumptions are not the exclusive domain of the men's movement. Cultural critic Stanley Aronowitz, for instance, in an article entitled "My Masculinity," closes his own sophisticated self-exploration by reiterating the well-worn "cost" of maleness: men have become "victims of the emotional plague by the imperative of having to be always in control. . . . Male power comes at the price of emotional isolation."[13] As David Savran and others have argued, this sense of victimization is certainly symptomatic of a culture enamored by narratives of disadvantage: for some white, heterosexual, middle-class men, a metaphorical emotional wound has come to substitute for social disenfranchisement; with its aid, manhood can once again be described as beset.[14] While wary of the dangers that such a position holds for women's struggles, mainstream feminism has sometimes subscribed to the view that men are victims of their own masculinity. Susan Faludi, for instance, has written with sympathy for a large portion of American men who are trapped by unbending codes of emotional control and expressed nostalgia for a lost brand of masculine bonding that at least offered men some emotional respite.[15] If men were only to get in touch with, "release," their emotions, some brands of feminist thought posits, patriarchy could be radically reformed.

At present, then, the narrative of emotionally controlled masculinity functions in multiple ways: as a strategy for reinstating the traditional power shaken by the assault of those wielding a "sentimental imagination," as a way to redefine the precarious position of mainstream masculinity through self-proclaimed victimization, as part of a political symbolic that equates emotional release with structural change. While it is perhaps easy to brush aside some of the positions outlined above, it is important to recognize that they are representative of a larger debate about the politics of affect and the political efficacy of emotions. One version of this debate is very familiar to students of U.S. culture by now. In 1977 Ann Douglas published her landmark *The Feminization of American Culture,* in which she criticized antebellum feminine sentimentalism as an inherently reactionary cultural expression that joined forces with both political conservatism and anti-intellectual consumerism. This argument was countered most famously by Jane Tompkins's 1985 important feminist study, *Sensational Designs,* where she rejoined that sentimentalism was a tool of resistance and political subversion. We cannot chart here all the interesting turns that this debate has since taken. Particularly useful for our purposes, however, is Lora Romero's contribution in the recent *Home Fronts,* where she argues, employing the work of Michel Foucault, that either/or constructions of the dynamics of power and subversion distort readings of sentimental texts and misconstrue the cultural work they perform. "We seem unable to entertain the possibility that traditions, or even individual texts, could be radical on some issues . . . and reactionary on others," she writes; "Or that some discourses could be oppositional without being outright liberating. Or conservative without being outright enslaving."[16]

The essays gathered in this collection stage another version of the debate over the politics of emotions, one produced not by feminine sentimentalism but by the narrative of masculinity as emotional restraint. For, as we have seen in relation to the popular feminist call for men to get in touch with their feelings, one way to read this narrative is dialectically: on the one hand, to highlight the way social control, oppressive gender codes, and mechanisms of internalization eclipsed men from their emotions in the course of history; while on the other, to regard emotion as capable, once recovered, of resisting the very power structures dedicated to its control. In tethering emotion to resistance, this position risks two major fallacies. The first is described by Lila Abu Lugoud and Catharine Lutz as the "essentializing" approach to emotion, the assumption that emotions are internal psychic or psychobiological energies, wholly distinct from society and language.[17] This position easily slides to a version of the repressive hypothesis, i.e., the viewing of the emotional subject as preceding the social, and the ensuing desire to liberate emotion as an act of political liberation. Some of the problems of this approach have been recently explored at length in Joel Pfister and Nancy Schnog's influential anthology, *Inventing the Psychological.* Pfister, through the Foucauldian concepts of implantation and incitement, discusses the ways in which seemingly "internal" emotions are in fact generated and naturalized by the mechanisms of power that seem to "externally" control them.[18] The second fallacy, evoked in Romero's argument above, is the belief that every oppositional stance is necessarily a liberating one, that every "liberation" of masculine emotion, for our purposes, would produce the desired political effect. A number of essays in this volume caution against this fallacy. Chapter 2, Elizabeth Barnes's essay on familicide, for instance, shows how the promotion of the affective family man in the late eighteenth century resulted in new forms of murderous domestic violence. And chapter 5, Ryan Schneider's essay on the racial politics of masculine sentimentalism, argues, along with Susan Mizruchi, that "reliance on sentiment also holds the potential to further alienate the races from each other," and that sentiment can be "suspect, even dangerous, as a means for launching a radical restructuring of race relations."

Yet, reading emotion as socially transformative *need* not slide into these fallacies. One of the important contributions to the theorization of affective politics has been Raymond Williams's analysis of "structures of feeling" as sites of social change. In *Marxism and Literature,* Williams eschews essentialization by discussing feeling not *against* thought but *as* thought, not as *preceding* the social but *as* social. The importance of feeling for Williams (in his definition, feeling is imbricated with "experience" and "subjectivity") is that it occupies a temporal present, an emergent or preemergent state before the procedure of classifying, defining, and fixing as cultural products (and relegating to the past) sets in. He is interested in feeling in its "embryonic phase before it can become fully articulate and defined exchange," a phase in which it is still a process and hence able to manifest change. Indeed, social change for him is "changes in structures of feeling."[19] Williams accords a special relevance to literature as an available articulation of changes in structures of feeling, and it is therefore not surprising that some of the more successful recent analyses of emotion as potentially transformative have taken place in the context of literature, books, and reading. In *Strange Fits of Passion: Epistemologies of Emotions, Hume to Austen,* for example, Adela Pinch is concerned not with structures but with discourses of feeling, illustrating how late-eighteenth-century aesthetic philosophers and writers produced an understanding of feelings as circulating, transpersonal entities capable of radically undermining concomitant claims to integrity of personhood and authentic individuality. Pinch intervenes in feminist discourse by denaturalizing the link between women and emotions; in the material she analyzes "women have no special place [in sympathy] as either objects or subjects of feeling."[20] Emotion, she shows, was understood as neither natural nor internal, but as performative and "extravagant," as constituting persons in social relations, from the *outside.* Janice Radway, in *A Feeling for Books: The Book-of-the-Month Club, Literary*

Taste, and Middle-Class Desire, describes a book culture filled with the "language of emotional and bodily response" that "may have nurtured a self potentially open to engagement with the social world in new ways, a subject not sealed off and autonomous but desiring and dependent, a subject therefore open to the possibility of fostering unprecedented connections and forging surprising alliances." As Christopher Newfield points out, Radway is not providing a simplified view of feeling as wholly escaping or wholly subverting the market system within which it is produced, but rather as constituting a form of "negative relation" to the social that makes, if not resistance, at least the search for resistance, possible.[21]

While some of the essays in *Boys Don't Cry?* subscribe to the potential use of emotion for resistance, others are more skeptical as to this promise and thus join the voices of scholars such as Wendy Brown and Lauren Berlant, whose work on pain and political identity in recent years has consistently problematized such political deployments. Brown analyzes the "wounded character of politicized identity" in late-modern liberalism, the subject's investment in pain and a history of suffering, as self-subverting and impassable. Using the Neitzschian term *ressentiment,* she describes a late-capitalist society in which subjects are seething with feelings of exclusion, powerlessness, and failure, feelings that are translated into a therapeutic politics, a politics of "anaesthetizing" pain by "moralizing revenge" and inflicting guilt on others. While her emphasis on the politics of identity may suggest that Brown is referring to everyone *but* the "white, middle-class, masculinist expression" of the liberal ideal, she in fact argues that "*all* liberal subjects, and not only markedly disenfranchised ones [are] vulnerable to *ressentiment.*" Indeed, to the extent that *ressentiment* is bred by the subject's failure of self-making, a failure acutely felt in the postindustrial corporate world, to the extent that it is bred by a sense of accountability coupled with a feeling of impotence, we feel that it is immensely useful in describing white masculine subjects and phenomena such as men's self-description as victims of their own power.[22] Berlant's critique of liberal sentiment pursues a similar line of thought to Brown's. She charts the appearances in the U.S. of a politics anchored in universalized pain and suffering, deployed to promote identification through empathy (and its earliest example: the Victorian women sentimentalists about whom Douglas and Tompkins debated). Such a sentimental politics, Berlant argues, relegates instances of social disenfranchisement to a purportedly preideological realm of feeling, imagining that the preideological can pose a radical challenge to existing institutions. In fact, sentimental politics thwarts its own political goals. The emphasis on universal, preideological feeling allows a "civic-minded but passive ideal of empathy" to stand for the "ethical imperative toward social transformation," and the privatized narrative of suffering, pain, and survival (*ressentiment*, if you will) comes to replace public action toward social freedom.[23] Both Brown and Berlant are concerned that a politics based on the recovery and articulation of feeling can fortify rather than dissolve distinction and result in stasis rather than promote social transformation.

Can white, middle-class masculine emotion, and a discourse of white, middle-class masculine emotion, then, remake existing forms of power, or will it necessarily reinforce them? In his contribution to this volume, Tom Lutz (chapter 9) suggests a path for rethinking emotion as both promoting change *and* causing resignation. Lutz, like Howard, finds that research in cognitive psychology and physiology can enrich our understanding of how emotions function socioculturally and politically. He cites research, for instance, that shows that tears are produced by two functions of the nervous system: the sympathetic and the parasympathetic, the former in charge of preparing the body to respond to exceptional situations (as in the "fight or flight" response to fear), the latter in charge of returning the body to homeostasis. Tears, then, operate on an "emotional arc" that includes both rise to action and return to stasis. Lutz draws sophisticated connections between this dual physiological function of tears and the complex social and political function of emotion, arguing, finally, that melodramatic narratives incite emotion that pressures toward social disruption *as well as* toward recovery and normalization. The conservatism of such narratives, he argues, "is exactly that which can help make it a tool of social critique and social change even as it makes us weep for traditional roles." Indeed, the essays collected in *Boys Don't Cry?* point to diverse positions on this emotional arc, at times expressing guarded optimism, at times judicious skepticism, as they analyze expressions of masculine emotion from the American Revolution to the present.

From its earliest moments, U.S. national symbolic deployed a discourse of emotion to define, shape, and articulate both subject and nation. Eighteenth-century philosophers often regarded feelings and selves as mutually constitutive: feelings express and evince the self, which, in turn, validates the very feelings that rendered it self-evident. As Evan Carton explains in the inaugurating essay of this volume, however, the ontological instability that characterized the transition from late colonial to early national America meant that this reassuring circuit of selfhood and feeling was not merely assumed but also reassessed. When shifts in traditional social structures rendered the self potentially alienable, the anchor of ostensibly inalienable feelings stabilized it; yet, at the same time, feelings themselves proved "riven," regarded as both inalienable and alienable (or even alien): "at once an effusion of nature and an object of art, a site of personal agency and of passive instrumentality, a mode of expressing and of overcoming the self." This ontological knot of selfhood and feeling is dramatized by Carton through the diametrically opposed reactions of Jonathan Edwards and Benjamin Franklin to the revivalist George Whitfield, whose mid-century tour of the American colonies left crowds "drenched in tears." Carton characterizes Edwards's reaction as "affective subjection": the residual use of emotion (as the word's etymology itself preserves) for the "moving out of or away from the self" toward subsumption in the collective or divine. By contrast, for the emergent "representative man" Franklin, personal identity had to resist the pull of emotion, to rewrite affective subjection as "strategic subjectivity," i.e., as self-sovereignty achieved through emotional control. But American men, Carton claims, did not entirely welcome this rewriting. Replacing J. Hector St. John de Crevecoeur's oft-quoted question, "What is an American?" with his own "What feels an American?" Carton produces an innovative reading of Crevecoeur's "farmer of feeling" as a "hybrid product of a Franklinian economy of rational and material self-reliance and an Edwardsian economy of affective communion," a hybrid for whom feelings occasion the acquisition of property and independence, which, in turn, produce the soil for cultivating familial and communal affective ties. This ideal reciprocity gradually reaches its limit as the book progresses, until the farmer's final letters, like Crevecoeur's own life amidst the violence of the revolution, confirm the triumph of strategic subjectivity and the "internment" of the American man as the "farmer of feeling," at the precise moment of national birth. This interment, Carton crucially suggests, "signifies not a death, necessarily, but an underground life," as the chapters that follow indeed demonstrate.

The "farmer of feeling" 's mingling of affective subjection and strategic subjectivity, implicitly lauded by Carton, produces very different, even fatal, results in Elizabeth Barnes's account of early national manhood. Indeed, it is the religious model of affective subjection, prescribing male submissiveness, sensitivity, and loving protectiveness, that in her analysis serves to bolster (and not contradict) individual masculine self-reliance and potency, even to the point of pathology. Through a cultural history of familicide, beginning with Mark Barton's recent killing spree in Atlanta but focusing on the wave of domestic murders that marked the early national period, Barnes shows how affective manhood could trigger, rather than prevent, violence. "Counterintuitive as it seems," Barnes provocatively claims, "love becomes the motive for murder." Familicide's skewed logic is traceable in Puritan theology: if feelings were crucial for religious salvation, and if God was figured by writers such as Edwards as violent and vindictive to inspire subjection, it became possible for men to project their anger and frustration onto God, recast them as fatherly love, and then identify themselves with that divine emotion. In case after case detailed by Barnes, husband and father perpetrators legitimated their act by appealing to God's will, at once ceding responsibility to him and appropriating his power as the consummate patriarch. Barnes engages this historical analysis in her reading of Charles Brockden Brown's *Wieland,* a novel that chooses to stage U.S. national and subject formation through the narration of an act of familicide: "Wieland fails," she concludes, "not because he is too blind to distinguish between good and evil, or too flawed to act on the difference, but because good and evil, love and aggression, are inextricably intertwined in the world Brown has created." A grotesque, gothic version of the farmer of feeling, "Wieland moves toward a telos of autonomy, but in such a way that affirms his participation in the equally powerful [and, in this case, especially dangerous] ethos of sensibility and sympathy."

Both Carton and Barnes, then, analyze the early national clash between affective patriarchy and what Dana Nelson calls a "series of affective foreclosures" that characterized the newly fashioned marketplace man.[24] Within the next few decades, through the antebellum "ideological and organizational separation of gendered spheres," this clash appeared outdated, seemingly resolved, as "emotion, involuntary response, and other-directedness were enshrined as the evidence—and the condition—of *female* identity."[25] Both Milette Shamir in chapter 3 and Eric Haralson in chapter 4 insist in their essays, however, that the separate spheres ideology offers too rigid and limited a grid for the nuanced analysis of antebellum manhood and affect. Shamir's essay recasts the collision of strategic subjectivity and affective subjection in the more Victorian language of "masculine" privacy and "feminine" intimacy. This gendered bifurcation, as many have shown, promoted the censuring of male intimacy, particularly homosocial intimacy, regarded by Victorian culture as harmful to the self, potentially feminizing, and tainted with sexual transgression. But does then bounded, private manhood always signal a decisive break from intimacy? Reading Henry David Thoreau as a representative example, Shamir replies that antebellum romantic writers developed an alternative logic of intimacy, one that avoids the "dangers" of femininity and homoeroticism. Throughout his career—in texts such as *Walden, A Week on the Concord and Merrimack Rivers,* and the lesser-known essay, "The Landlord"—Thoreau repudiated the conventional definition of intimacy as the exchange of concrete stories about the self, regarding such relations as dangerous to personal sovereignty and hence unable to sustain "the manliest relations to men." He developed instead a mode of intimacy based on abstraction rather than embodiment, on concealment rather than revelation, on distance rather than physical proximity, on silence rather than speech. Shamir demonstrates that this "depersonalizing intimacy" is not merely thematized but also *performed* by Thoreau's texts, which idealize intimacy between (male) writer and (male) reader, an idealization found also in the writing of Hawthorne, Melville, and Emerson. Shamir urges us, that is, to resist reading Thoreau's depersonalized relations and spare revelations simply as "affective foreclosures" but, rather, to see that given liberalism's (often misogynist and homophobic) construction of the masculine self, such relations might satisfy a desire for equal, reciprocal, and fraternal affection. This version of intimacy, moreover, offers a valid critique of antebellum as well as contemporary theories that too quickly laud self-exposure as political ethics, reminding us of Berlant's caution that empathy does not necessitate in social justice.[26]

Given the anxiety that attends masculine friendship described by Shamir, it is hardly surprising that most of the essays in this volume either touch or fully focus upon a different venue of masculine emotion: fatherhood. "Intimacy with children does not so easily evoke the anxiety over homosexuality that often haunts men's intimacy with each other," suggests Judith Newton in her essay collected here, nor the "anger and anxiety [that] inhibit[s] men's very interest in, not to mention their performance of, the love work involved in being open and intimate with women"; in other words, men find in fatherhood "a privileged site for exploring, celebrating, and encouraging greater feeling." Yet in a patriarchal culture, particularly one in which fatherhood has been a primary *public* trope, paternal affection is always already fraught with complex political, social, and psychological tensions. Some such ambiguities are traced by Eric Haralson and Ryan Schneider. In his essay on masculine elegies of dead children, Haralson issues a corrective to the still prevalent view (a view we have inherited from late-nineteenth-century writers such as Twain) that the domestic elegy—unlike the grand elegy of, say, Milton, Shelley, or Tennyson—is female-authored and "feminine" in style. Exploring over a dozen domestic elegies written by men, Haralson suggests that "if nineteenth-century paternal elegies . . . were sentimentally 'tender,' like kindred verses by women, the different social conditioning and political position of masculinity abridged and modified such emotionalism." Like Shamir, that is, Haralson finds that white, middle-class men did not forgo but rather *refashioned* emotional expressivity to accommodate codes of affective restraint. In elegeiac poetry this remodeling took various forms. Male-authored elegies, for example, often instantiated the cohabitation of sentimentalism and anti-sentimentalism, as when they waxed emotional over men's *flight* from feminizing grief, finding in mourning an occasion for further discipline of masculine affect. For paternal elegies the gender of the child is of importance: the most intense emotion congeals around the loss of the firstborn son, who is destined under patriarchy to carry on the father's name, trade, and legacy. In treating their child's death, male elegists tended to be more angry, more defiant against divine providence than their female counterparts, refusing the solace of resignation, the consolation of reunion in heaven, and the relief offered by open communication. However, like the male homosocial intimacies described by Shamir, paternal elegies nonetheless found in absence an occasion for emotional connectedness, precisely through depersonalizing emotions; through regarding the pain of loss as intensely private, inconsolable, and incommunicable; or through deploying personal grief for public goals. Mourning fathers might be said, then, to have occupied a liminal space, their private loss, as Haralson puts it, "rationalized for purposes of public consumption," their grief stretching, without breaking, strictures against "excessive" masculine feeling.

The major conventions that characterize white paternal poems of mourning similarly mark W. E. Du Bois's prose elegy, "On the Passing of the First-Born." In Schneider's reading in chapter 5 in this volume, Du Bois laments his son Burghardt's death in terms akin to Emerson or Lowell: he mourns the passing of a firstborn who was to succeed his father publicly and intellectually (in Du Bois's case, as "race man"), and, like his white counterparts, deploys his personal grief in the service of the larger public goal (in his case, of reforming race relations). Thus the boy's passing is an occasion for Du Bois's own "passing," as he assumes the guise of the white sentimentalist and his/her strategic use of the "sacred child" for a politics of recuperative transracial empathy. The strength of Schneider's essay, however, lies in its recognition that this sentimental mimicry is by necessity self-conflicted and incomplete. As gender shapes sentiment in Haralson's reading of paternal elegies, so does race interrupt the workings of the politics of sentiment according to Schneider: "structured around a complex advance-and-retreat from the sentimental elegy," Du Bois's essay employs "a strategy based on [his] recognition of both its potential as a form for the expression of masculine feeling and its cost in relation to his project of critiquing the status of race relations." Carefully analyzing the implication of another "passing" in the essay—the belief that had Burghardt lived, his "dark gold ringlets" and "eyes of mingled blue and brown" would have allowed him to physically pass as white—Schneider concludes that it is "the powerfully disruptive and intellectually unnerving force of his public confrontation with his son's body—a confrontation that cannot, finally, be categorized as either rescue or betrayal, resistance or complicity—which lies at the heart of Du Bois's elegy and which, ultimately, stands as a metaphor for his own dual status as a sentimental writer and a race man in the public sphere."

As Schneider notes, Du Bois's mimicry of sentimental fatherhood was often brushed aside by critics as awkwardly personal or embarrassingly emotional. Indeed, the neglect, if not derision, of masculine emotional expressivity in literary criticism and history is raised by almost every contributor to this collection. It is symptomatic of the phenomenon described by Peter Stearns and Jan Lewis in answer to the question of why we have no history of emotions: "from the moment history became a profession in the nineteenth century, it has usually aimed at objectivity and attempted to purge itself of the irrational."[27] This purging of emotion, constitutive to the process of professionalization itself, is the focus of Jennifer Travis's and Thomas Strychacz's chapters. In chapter 6 Travis turns our attention to the history of "criminal conversation" torts in the nineteenth and early twentieth centuries, a domain in which emotional injuries suffered by husbands of adulterous wives were recognized and compensated. The courts taking heed of narratives of emotional pain in such cases, Travis shows, is a fascinating instance of the law belying its own "deep structure," since a suspicion of emotional narratives and, indeed, the insistent disavowal of emotions, subtends the law's account of itself as objective, impartial, and gender-neutral. Claims of emotional injury suffered by men, therefore, "indicate the extent of the law's participation in what might be called the historical gendering of injury," explains Travis. Through a juxtaposition of a work of fiction—Willa Cather's *A Lost Lady*—and the "factual" history of tort law, Travis tells how male injuries uncompensated in the public sphere of corporate economy were displaced onto domestic relations, where male emotional distress (but not female) was given legal substance. Contrary to what some legal scholars assume today, then, the law's recognition of emotion often worked historically to reconsolidate rather than to challenge masculine hegemony. In basing this argument partially on Cather's novel, Travis's essay performs the work of revising another prevalent dichotomy: that of law as "rational" and literature as "emotional." Travis proposes that literature should be read not simply in contrast to law, as that which can "humanize" its cold procedures, but also "as a forum from which to analyze the kinds of fictions that the law employs in order to present itself as fully rational, fully neutral, fully unmediated and, largely, emotionless in its representations."

Fictions of gender not only fundamentally challenge the law's self-presentation, as Travis contends, they also expose, according to Thomas Strychacz in chapter 7, the deeply rhetorical practices of professional readers themselves. Revisiting a critical narrative of institutionalized antiemotionality—the making of Hemingway's modernist aesthetics—Strychacz argues that the deployment of emotional restraint as a "real" aesthetic, "true" to modernity and self-avowedly masculine, belies a counteraesthetic at work virtually everywhere in Hemingway's oeuvre, what Strychacz calls the "ethos of emotional disarray." Reading *Death in the Afternoon* as a representative example, Strychacz shows how Hemingway's "allegedly tough-minded pursuit of the 'real thing' constantly yields to a plangent sense of linguistic freeplay" and even emotional excess. Such reading disrupts the presumed link between Hemingway's "iceberg" style and taciturn masculinity, a link established in responses to Hemingway from his early career to the present. Strychacz notes that scholars in fact found this masculine aesthetics in very few of Hemingway's works; yet, rather than reexamine their tenet, scholars "began to treat the principle of a restrained masculine style as an ideal from which Hemingway had fallen," thus "stabilizing the very principle so often put in question by Hemingway's work." Why have scholarly audiences so insisted on modernism as an aesthetic of restraint? Strychacz shows that this insistence is evidence (largely underexamined) of an early struggle among newly professionalized scholars, who sought to refinance their "feminized life of contemplation" with new symbolic capital; in other words, speaking about tough, active masculinity, and speaking about it as an "aesthetic," became a way to ground their social authority in light of the apparent "weightlessness" of academic discourse itself. Strychacz's account of academic professionalization urges us to reconsider not only the hegemonic ideals of masculinity that are attributed to Hemingway but also the critical and cultural genealogies that portend it.

Such a reconsideration guides Stephen Davenport's analysis in chapter 8 of the next generation's critical master narrative, that of man's escape from society, family, and history. This critical master narrative, Davenport shows, reduces the interpretation of male flight in mid-century literature to a contrast of inevitable failures: failure to act as a responsible adult and family man or failure to escape from the conventions and emotional guilt that society deploys to tie a man down. The "American type," that is, "fails because he is not enough son (he abandons his family) or because he is too much son (he cannot help but return to it)." Such "melodramas of beset sonhood," argues Davenport, disable and flatten our reading of mid-century masculine literature and obscure the possibility that they might be read "profitably as expressions, not evasions, of woundedness and grief"; that "the abandoned or grieving male takes to the road, or lives in the fantasy of doing so, not to escape family in Adamic or revolutionary flight, but to encounter it in a recuperative space." Davenport reads Jack Kerouac's autobiographical series of novels, alongside Arthur Miller's "Death of a Salesman" and Tennessee Williams's "The Glass Menagerie," isolating the figure of the "second male" (son or younger brother) whose "road work" is motivated by the wounding loss of a father or older brother, a loss for which the road then functions as a space of "reconstructive surrogacy and emotional fulfillment." In flight, that is, the hero does not renege but, rather, renegotiates the relationship between family and freedom, "career" and "careening," the responsibilities of "place" and the openendedness of "space," always careful not to stray from the liminal position of second male, a position that allows him to continue the emotional work made possible by flight itself.

Like Davenport, Thomas Lutz locates a space where intense emotional work is performed, a space where masculine social roles are worked through. He locates it not in literary narratives of masculine escape, however, but in "male weepies," Hollywood melodramas created to induce male tears. Lutz's essay aims to resolve an ongoing debate in film studies over the ideological function of melodrama—whether it reinforces or subverts the patriarchal gender regime—by supplementing an analysis of social fantasy with data from the physiology of tears. As outlined earlier in this introduction, Lutz garners the fact that tears are a mix of excitatory and relaxing biological responses to prove that the genre of melodrama involves both the acceptance and transformation of social gender roles. We cry, that is, over "the character's recovery of his or her proper social role after an exciting foray into social disruption, but that return is always a notably compromised or transformed version of the role." This structural argument is then used for and reinforced by Lutz's analysis of a series of films from the 1950s, the heyday of the "male weepie." The 1950s witnessed "World War II veterans, men in gray flannel suits, Hollywood cowboys, rebels, beatniks, swingers, and upright suburban husbands" all competing over center stage. The "male weepies" flooded this scene with twofold effect: arousing tears of relief when protagonists finally returned to their appropriate male roles, while emotionally convincing their audiences that the terms of role fulfillment required at least some rewriting. Male melodramas, then, represented men as " 'within and against' their own worlds, as rebels without fully articulated causes."

Two decades later, in response to the continuing demands of "role fulfillment" and obliquely inspired by the insights of feminism, a movement for "male liberation" emerged among straight white professional men. With such titles as *The Liberated Man: Beyond Masculinity* (Warren Farrell) and *The Hazards of Being Male* (Herb Goldberg), this movement of the nineteen-seventies, Sally Robinson shows in chapter 10, represented men as "both literally and metaphorically wounded," wounded not by women or by feminism but "by their power, their responsibilities, and indeed, by patriarchy itself." Central to this self-proclaimed masculine crisis was the notion that men are denied emotional expressivity, a notion habitually metaphorized in the sexualized terms of a "flow," that is painfully "blocked," and must be "released" in order to set men free. At the same time, however, male liberationists as well as feminists recounted the dangers involved in such a release ("Every man is a potential rapist," wrote Marilyn French in 1977), imagining masculinity as a volcano always on the verge of violent explosion. Men, that is, were strangely encouraged to simultaneously restrain and release their impulses. Robinson traces this paradox not only through the laments of male liberationists but through two popular novels of the period: John Irving's *The Water-Method Man* and Leonard Michael's *The Men's Club*. Her reading of these novels illustrates that the "therapeutic value of male release," aimed at inspiring individual growth, is not easily translated into the social and political; in other words, the "unblocking" of the emotive self results in the psychological-therapeutic *standing in for* political change. The release of tears, Robinson argues, leaves an empty and ultimately depoliticized "liberated man," one who, in the final analysis, blocks the pursuit of social justice.

While Robinson doubts that the rhetoric of male liberation has been (or can be) liberatory at all, Judith Newton has more faith that organized men's movements and their politics of affect may, in fact, "resist, even as they are complicitous with, patriarchal and other structural inequalities." Newton turns our attention in chapter 11 to the 1990s, when the well-worn foundations of self-made manhood have seemingly expired, and from every direction masculinity was called "in crisis." As an effort to restore "moral identity" to men, the 1990s witnessed some spectacular gatherings of black and white men in the nation's capital, gatherings that epitomized new male efforts at "reenchanting" masculinity through "utopian dramas of tears and atonement." Newton's careful ethnographical reading of the Promise Keepers Stand in the Gap Assembly, the Million Man March, and the mass movements that propelled them, finds their call for masculine affect not a substitute but a facilitator of structural change. While Newton joins voices who worry that such movements may ultimately work to reinstate traditional patriarchal power, she sees in them the potential fulfillment of some important feminist aspirations, and she cautions feminists against the need to fully control "what counts as antisexist change"; in other words, the dramatic release of tears must not blind us to the promise of men's self-fashioned ideals, including efforts to replace competitive manhood not only with generative fatherhood and affective companionhood but also with a foundation of antiracism. The call for "compassion, community, and civility" bespeaks a serious strategy, one in which a politics of feeling is meant to ground rather than to obstruct substantive political action.

The men's movements of the late twentieth century may be one of the latest versions of the melodrama of beset manhood with which we have begun this introduction. The Promise Keepers' assembly, for instance, patterned itself on male romance narrative, featuring white men who leave women behind to celebrate emotional bonds with black men, as they affirm their own power and chart new terrain for themselves. The melodrama of beset manhood has proven, after all, one of the most historically stubborn narratives in the U.S. Yet, as Newton's essay cogently reminds us, male romance is also a "variable genre," one that is open to "continu[ed] reconstruction and a range of political uses."[28] *Boys Don't Cry?* narrates some of the turns male romance has taken throughout its history and some ways of reading the uses it has made of emotions along the way. Granted, the volume contains a far from complete narrative. It casts very few black, Indian, Latino, or Chicano men in leading roles.

It does not contain the counternarratives of gay, immigrant, or working-class men. It has only little to say on the perspective of Southerners or women. Its goal, however, is not to be comprehensive but, rather, to challenge a dominant view of white, middle-class heteromasculinity, a view that has proven extremely tractable in American literary, cultural, and gender studies.[29] It is important to note that such categories as race and sexuality are by no means absent as analytical categories from this collection. They are present, for instance, in Carton's analysis of affective manhood, shown to reach its limits when encountering a black slave, later to revive itself by projecting feelings onto Indians. They are present, to offer another example, in Davenport's recounting of "male flight" as a narrative of surrogacy wherein heterosexual men use homosexual relations to work through the wounds of family romances. Indeed, the volume conceives itself in relation to important work already done on sexuality, race, and class in male romance narratives by critics such as Joseph Boone, Robert Martin, Christopher Newfield, Julie Ellison, Robyn Wiegman, and Philip Harper, to name only a few.[30] By joining what is sure to be a long conversation about the politics of emotion and its constitutive role in narratives of gender, this collection insists that we think not only between analytic categories but also beyond conventionally stylized expressions of emotion, including sympathy and sentiment, emotional release, and male escape. Thus we may draw into critical view what happens when boys, indeed, do cry.

Notes

1. This first paragraph is a riff on Michael Kimmel's opening of *Manhood in America*, pp. 1–2. While the bibliography on masculinity is enormous (and far too lengthy to archive here), sustained critique of emotive men remains quite small by comparison, as this introduction will address. It is worth noting, however, that two recent and popular studies of masculinity, Susan Faludi's *Stiffed*, and Christine Hoff Sommer's *The War Against Boys*, revisit these truisms, albeit from different perspectives. Faludi argues that men in modern America are betrayed, their "superdominance" and stoicism merely a cruel facade for their powerlessness, and she presents the promise of some change if men are willing to revive virtues such as trust, loyalty, and compassion. Sommers alternatively argues that U.S. culture wrongly pathologizes male children for characteristics that should rightly be called admirable: competitiveness, tempered aggression, and so forth. Like Faludi, Sommers sees boys as increasingly dispossessed, and she cautions against what she calls throwing the ever popular "gender switch," demanding that boys behave more like girls.

Goffman's description is quoted in Kimmel, *Manhood in America*, p. 5.

2. Baym, "Melodramas of Beset Manhood"; Kimmel, *Manhood in America*, p. 9 (emphasis in original).

3. "Code Hero" was termed by Philip Young; see Thomas Strychacz's essay in this volume. "American Cool" is analyzed most extensively by Peter Stearns in a book by that title. While the book does not emphasize "coolness" as a particularly masculine emotional style, recent work insists on gendering it. Susan Fraiman, for instance, analyzes performances of coolness in academia in terms of a masculine disavowal of femininity/feminism. See her forthcoming *Cool Men and the Second Sex: Reading Left Intellectuals*.

4. For a summary of the tendency in feminist literary history to cling to the "too crude . . . too rigid and totalizing" (445) separate spheres binary and its gendering of sentiment see Cathy Davidson's preface to *No More Separate Spheres!* Two works on literature and gender that pioneered the study of manhood and emotions in American literature bear explicit mention here. Both rely on the middle-class separate spheres ideology as a basis from which to launch their argument, but both also go beyond its rigidity as a tool of analysis to produce more nuanced and complex versions of antebellum emotionologies. Leverenz's *Manhood and the American Renaissance* analyzes the feelings—of rage, alienation, anxiety—that accompany the transition from older paradigms of manhood to that of entrepreneurial, competitive individualism. Herbert's *Dearest Beloved* reads the lives of the Hawthornes as embodiments of the separate spheres ideology, pausing on the emotional conflicts and tensions that attend ideal middle-class manhood as captured in Hawthorne's life and his fiction.

5. Howard, "What is Sentimentality?" pp. 69–73.

6. Chapman and Hendler, *Sentimental Men*, p. 5. Davidson, "Preface," p. 456.

7. Davidson, "Preface," p. 444.

8. Rosaldo, "Toward an Anthropology of Self and Feeling," p. 143.

9. Howard, "What is Sentimentality?" p. 69.

10. Emotionology is a term coined by Peter N. Stearns and Carol Z. Stearns in their article "Emotionology: Clarifying the History of Emotional Standards" to denote the "collective emotional standards of a society," standards that they distinguish from emotional experience, the transferable and changeable shape of emotions over time. "We may never be able to know with certainty whether men and women in the past have felt the same emotions that we experience today," write Lewis and Stearns, but emotionology enables us to study "the way other people's emotions, and one's own, are perceived and evaluated." Quoted in Lewis and Stearns, "Introduction," pp. 7, 1, 5.

11. Hughes, *The Culture of Complaint*, pp. 22–23.

12. See Kimmel and Kaufman, "Weekend Warriors."

13. Aronowitz, "My Masculinity," p. 320.

14. Savran, *Taking it Like a Man*. See also Sally Robinson in this volume.

15. Faludi, *Stiffed*. For another perspective, see Christopher Newfield's discussion of "male femininity" in "The Politics of Male Suffering," pp. 63–67. Here Newfield describes the danger of assuming that the mere comingling of gender stereotypes will signal progressive change, arguing, in effect, that while "hegemonic patriarchy can survive without male assertion," it thrives with male "feminization" and the various forms that such "feminization" may take, including, for our purposes here, the enduring demands for emotional res-

cue (66). For more on profeminist men see Judith Newton in this volume.

16. Romero, *Home Fronts,* p. 4. See also Ann Cvetkovich, *Mixed Feelings.*

17. Lutz and Abu-Lughod, *Language and the Politics of Emotion,* pp. 2–3.

18. Pfister, "On Conceptualizing the Cultural History of Emotional and Psychological Life," pp. 25–34.

19. Williams, *Marxism and Literature,* pp. 128–35.

20. Pinch, *Strange Fits of Passion,* p. 25.

21. Radway, *A Feeling for Books,* pp. 44, 360; Newfield, "Middlebrow Reading and Feeling Good," pp. 912–13.

22. Brown, "Wounded Attachments," pp. 211, 214 (emphasis in original).

23. Berlant, "Poor Eliza," p. 641. See also her "The Subject of True Feeling: Pain, Privacy, and Politics," and *The Queen of America Goes to Washington,* especially pp. 1–22.

24. Dana Nelson, *National Manhood,* p. ix.

25. Carton in this volume, p. 000 (emphasis added).

26. Berlant, "Subject of True Feeling," p. 77.

27. Lewis and Stearns, "Introduction," p. 1.

28. See Newton in this volume, pp. 000, 000.

29. The term "heteromasculinity" is borrowed from Bryce Traister, whose recent article in *American Quarterly* analyzed some of the shortcomings that characterize the rise of American masculinity studies. Traister takes scholarship on straight white manhood to task for habitually excluding other masculinities from its analysis, thus reproducing in its methodology the act of historical exclusion it aims to critique. It remains unclear, however, what alternative Traister would propose to replace this methodology. He certainly does not mean to suggest that the project of studying heteromasculinity be abandoned altogether, nor that those replacing it could lay out a fully representative map of U.S. masculinities (and why settle for the U.S.?) and still claim any kind of analytical depth. It is necessary, in our view, not to conflate too easily democratic politics and the politics of academic representation.

30. In *American Anatomies,* Robyn Wiegman points to another risk that attends the project of analyzing privileged masculinity: "the oppositional framework for articulating power," she writes, "depends on a homogenization of identities into singular figurations, the 'straight-white-monied man' becoming the composite, fixed figure for defining social hierarchies. While one does not want to abandon the ability to talk about the cultural hegemony of this category the logic of 'majority' reaches an impasse when the social subject cannot be aligned, without contradiction, on one side or the other of the minority-majority divide. Where, for instance, is the straight, black, working class man or the gay, white, monied woman?" (6–7). While our collection's emphasis on both emotion and masculinity as historical variables, and ones that are variably imbricated, is meant to resist the homogenization of the straight-white-monied man, we nonetheless acknowledge a certain artificiality in limiting the discussion of emotional restraint to that figure, an artificiality that is the result of our goal to rethink a narrative of American masculinity that itself reduces the multiplicity of identity. Our hope is that subsequent work would register the ways in which emotional restraint as a form of cultural power is capitalized upon, and produces contradictions within, more complex subject positions.

1

What Feels an American?

Evident Selves and Alienable Emotions in the New Man's World

EVAN CARTON

The plain Truth is, an enlightened Mind, not raised Affections, ought always to be the guide of those who call themselves Men.

—Charles Chauncy, *Seasonable Thoughts on the State of Religion*, 1743

To the European, the American is first and foremost a dollar-fiend. We tend to forget the emotional heritage of Hector St. John de Crevecoeur. We tend to disbelieve, for example, in Woodrow Wilson's wrung heart and wet hanky. Yet surely these are real enough. Aren't they?

—D. H. Lawrence, *Studies in Classic American Literature*, 1923

The struggle for American political independence, as Jay Fliegelman has observed, coincided with and made use of "a new affective understanding of the operations of language, one that reconceives all expression as a form of self-expression, as an opportunity as well as an imperative to externalize the self, to become self-evident."[1] For Common Sense philosopher Thomas Reid and other prominent eighteenth-century intellectuals, this "natural language" of feeling—an expression not of words "but of all the muscles of the body"—substantiated its author, evidenced his essential self, even in the case (writing) of his physical absence.[2] Reciprocally, the self thus evidenced authenticated the feelings and language that gave it expression.

The Declaration of Independence is just such a reciprocal linguistic operation in which a represented state of feeling and a represented state of the self authorize and naturalize one another. It is, in Jefferson's opening sentence, the felt "[necessity] for one people to dissolve the political bands which have connected them with another" that constitutes Americans as "one people" in the first place and warrants their assumption of "the separate & equal station to which the laws of nature and of nature's god entitle them."[3] In turn, this expression of national entitlement, of "separate & equal" identity, certifies that the felt necessity of separation from Britain is no vagary or artifice but rather an inevitable and unerring "affective understanding" (in Fliegelman's phrase) of "the laws of nature and of nature's god." Thus, ingeniously, the feeling and the fact of Americanness declare one another here and affirm one another to be united, natural, evident—ingeniously, because outside the constitutive circuit of this declaration, neither the affective nor the political state of The United States fits any of these descriptions.

The special appeal to eighteenth-century Americans of natural language theory's understanding of verbal expression "as an opportunity as well as an imperative to externalize the self, to become self-evident," arose from their experience of personal identity—let alone, in the revolutionary years, of national identity—as anything but stably grounded or securely possessed. That is why, for many, the promise of natural self-expression seemed not only opportune but, as Fliegelman writes, "imperative," a chance "to *become* self-evident." Both in their respective internal conflicts and in their relational dialectic, the careers and writings of Jonathan Edwards and Benjamin Franklin, those most expressive of colonial Americans, lay out many of the grounds of ontological instability for men of this time and place. Was selfhood given or made, founded in the family or forged in the marketplace, discovered in community and in faithful subjection or invented in autonomous and experimental subjectivity, realized in seasons when one is deeply moved or plotted across spaces that one deftly moves through? (As passages of especial poignancy in both Edwards and Franklin intimate, each of these alternative models of identity may confer upon its adherent both a felt plenitude and a felt lack of being.)

The very alienation or alienability of identity at a moment when its traditional anchors—religion, family structure, local community, economic system, nationality—seemed shifting and insecure gave rise to the massive and multifaceted effort of eighteenth-century writers and thinkers to anchor the self in the ostensible immediacy and inalienability of feeling. Indeed, such an effort, as Claudia Johnson puts it, represented a "commanding imaginative response to a world riven with crisis."[4] Yet, in various ways that literary historians continue to map, feeling's self in this period was also riven.[5] One particular rift in feeling provides the occasion for this essay: it is feeling's double identification on the one hand as a property and a characterological signature of individuals and, on the other, as a site of resistance not only to secure personal possession but to the very establishment of a regime of individual autonomy.

In her recent study, *Strange Fits of Passion: Epistemologies of Emotion, Hume to Austen,* Adela Pinch describes this tension as follows: "If feelings at times seem to be their own evidence and proof, and to belong infallibly to the self, they often seem at times impossible to know or to claim as one's own."[6] Eighteenth-century writers, Pinch argues, are concerned "to pin feelings down," to account for their origins and essences; yet they tend to find, with Hume, that "feelings spread about freely and fluidly," that "they do not know the boundaries of individuals," and, most unsettlingly, that these "alien influences" raise the question whether "the claims of individuals are subordinate to the feelings that visit them from without."[7] Thus emotions, crucial exhibits of the self's case and intimate agents of its externalization, are at once, scandalously, "alien influences" that undermine the individual's claim to self-possession. In its circumvention of the will and its transportation of foreign affairs into the deepest precincts of the individual, sensibility, commonly understood as one's "natural and involuntary ability . . . to be responsive to the pain, pleasures, and needs of other[s]," alienates the very self it evidences.[8]

By the middle of the nineteenth century, this identity crisis had been eased, at a cost that we continue to tally and pay, through the ideological and organizational separation of gendered spheres. Emotion, involuntary response, and other-directedness were enshrined as the evidence—and the condition—of female identity. This revisionist containment of the transgender "cult of sensibility" as "the cult of true womanhood" putatively freed "the man of feeling" to become "the self-made man." And this independent and proprietary individualist is (stereo)typically invoked by historians and critics in response to the question that Michel-Guillaume (also known as J. Hector St. John) de Crevecoeur asked at American identity's moment of truth, which is to say American manhood's and American nationhood's moment of fabrication: "What is an American?"

A project of this volume, however, is to indicate how the gendered containment of emotion in America failed; where men as well as women resisted or transgressed the conventional bounds of feeling; and what encumbrances upon men the cult of *in*sensibility entailed—among them, the burden that Tocqueville, surveying American individualism in 1831, described as "a strange melancholy which often haunts the inhabitants of democratic countries in the midst of their abundance."[9] In inaugurating this collective project, I wish to return to the cultural, political, and affective context in which Crevecoeur posed his question—that is, to a moment that precedes, or occurs at the outset of, feeling's binding and gendering—in order to challenge its answer's (anachronistic) self-evidence. Indeed, to return to Crevecoeur's question in this context is to consider American (male and national) identity before it became "self-evident" precisely through its alienation, and feminization, of emotion. This essay proposes to effect such a return in order, first, to trace the process of such self-becoming and, second, to explore its internal resistances and perhaps to gather their residues. I attempt the former by means of a preliminary comparison of Jonathan Edwards's and Benjamin Franklin's personal encounters with the celebrated revivalist, George Whitefield, and a brief return to Jefferson's Declaration; I pursue the latter in a reading of Crevecoeur's *Letter from an American Farmer* that is more affected than most modern readings are (willing to be) by Crevecoeur's narrator's self-designation as "the farmer of feelings."[10]

Learning early in 1740 of George Whitefield's plan to tour the American colonies that fall, Jonathan Edwards sent the young English revivalist a humble and beseeching letter. "I apprehend, from what I have heard, that you are one who has the blessing of heaven attending you wherever you go," Edwards wrote to the newly famous twenty-five-year-old, "and I have a great desire, if it may be the will of God, that such a blessing as attends your person & labors may descend on this town, and may enter mine own house, and that I may receive it in my own soul."[11] At thirty-six, Edwards himself could reasonably lay claim to preeminence among American ministers, having increased the congregation and perhaps even eclipsed the reputation of his magisterial grandfather, Solomon Stoddard, in the decade since he had succeeded "the Pope of the Connecticut Valley" as pastor at Northampton. Moreover, Edwards's leadership and stirring account of the Northampton religious awakening of 1735–36 had won him international renown and helped energize the English Nonconformist movement that produced Whitefield. Yet Edwards approaches the younger man as a supplicant, entreating him—if not to visit—at least to pray "for me among others," and closes: "I am, reverend sir, unworthy to be called your fellow laborer, Jonathan Edwards."[12]

When Whitefield preached in Boston some months later, he left his crowds of twenty to thirty thousand "affected and drenched in tears," according to contemporary witnesses, "like persons that were hungering and thirsting after righteousness."[13] Whitefield's histrionic, free-form sermons little re-sembled the more controlled, text-centered discourses that Edwards preached and preferred. Even in his first authenticating account of Northampton's re-cent awakening, a 1735 letter to the Boston minister Benjamin Colman, Ed-wards had expressed uneasiness about the workings of mass psychology and about the susceptibility of some, under the sway of powerful feelings, to mis-take these for conversion. Still, subordinating whatever personal preferences or reservations he may have had, Edwards welcomed the revivalist that Octo-ber into his home and church; indeed, a member of the Northampton con-gregation reported that, when Whitefield presided there, "dear Mr. Edwards wept during almost the whole time of the exercise."[14]

Soon afterward, and almost as eagerly as Edwards had done, colonial America's other representative man seized his opportunity to experience Whitefield's presence. Benjamin Franklin, however, did not weep. "The Mul-titudes of all Sects and Denominations that attended his Sermons were enor-mous," Franklin reports, in the first of a surprisingly extended series of encounters between himself and Whitefield that he does not just mention but stages in *The Autobiography,* "and it was matter of Speculation to me who was one of the Number, to observe the extraordinary Influence of his Oratory on his Hearers."[15] Here, Franklin establishes the paradigmatic form and purpose of all his contacts with Whitefield: amidst "Multitudes" engaged in affective communion, in the ecstatic erasure or transcendence of the boundaries of their individual (and mortal) selves under Whitefield's "extraordinary Influ-ence," Franklin stands in detached "Speculation," performing a private exer-cise.

Were this merely an exercise in sociological curiosity or in religious indif-ference, it doubtless would have sufficed Franklin to perform it once. But Franklin's insistence that he "often" attended Whitefield's sermons and his dramatization of his mode of attendance suggest that, for him, these were ritual occasions to test, protect, and refortify the boundaries of personal iden-tity by resisting the collective emotion that threatened them, by refusing re-ceptivity and sensation in favor of productivity and calculation.[16] Such a purpose is discernible throughout Franklin's treatment of Whitefield in *The Autobiography,* but it is exemplified in the extraordinary image of himself among the rapt congregation that Franklin evokes in the following passage:

He preach'd one Evening from the Top of the Court House Steps, which are in the Middle of Market Street, and on the West Side of Second

Street which crosses it at right angles. Both Streets were fill'd with his Hearers to a considerable Distance. Being among the hindmost in Market Street, I had the Curiosity to learn how far he could be heard, by retiring backwards down the Street towards the River, and I found his Voice distinct till I came near Front Street, when some Noise in that Street obscur'd it. Imagining then a Semicircle, of which my Distance should be the Radius, and that it were fill'd with Auditors, to each of whom I allow'd two square feet, I computed that he might well be heard by more than Thirty Thousand.[17]

In their respective encounters with Whitefield, Edwards and Franklin both confront the vexed relationship between affect and identity that Pinch's book describes. Edwards, working within the logic and vocabulary of Christian identity-in-communion, embraces a subjectivity not only compatible with but dependent on "alien influences,"[18] "involuntary . . . responsive[ness],"[19] and transgression of "the boundaries of individuals"[20]—a subjectivity, indeed, neither freestanding nor self-evident but predicated on a kind of self-alienation. Franklin, by contrast, takes Whitefield and the "strange fits of passion" that his preaching elicited "as an opportunity as well as an imperative to externalize the self, to become self-evident," an opportunity that for him entails the alienation of emotion.

As the word itself suggests, emotion—a moving out of or away from (the self)—offers Edwards a means of overcoming the "lust for selfhood"[21] to which, in Edwards's view, the Arminian tendency of eighteenth-century American religion and the commercial and entrepreneurial tendencies of eighteenth-century American society pandered. For Edwards, the most authentic of human emotions are those "affections of the soul"[22] that, in Eliza New's elegant summary of his position, "affiance us to Being at the expense of self-love."[23] Such affections, Edwards indicates, are both alien and intimate, involuntary and desired, self-decentering and self-defining: "effects of God's Spirit which . . . are entirely above nature, altogether of a different kind from anything that men find within themselves by nature,"[24] they nonetheless comprise "actings of the will and inclination of the soul."[25]

Thus, at its most sublime, feeling is the vehicle by which one may discover and exercise a will beyond and against one's natural, self-serving inclination. This is the will adumbrated for Edwards in his youth in "the wondrous and curious works of the spider," which, "doubtless with abundance of pleasure," airily propels itself to the sea to be consumed.[26] Later, it is the will by means of which the awakened Abigail Hutchinson, consenting to her inability to swallow, transcends "her long strugglings and stranglings" and her "raging appetite to food" and becomes "as perfectly contented without it, as if she had no appetite to it."[27] And it is the affectionate will by which Edwards himself overcomes his intellectual "objections against the doctrine of God's sovereignty, in choosing whom he would to eternal life, and rejecting whom he pleased," and discovers in place of these objections "not only . . . a conviction, but a *delightful* conviction" of this "sweet doctrine"; for "absolute sovereignty is what I love to ascribe to God."[28]

The most striking and significant contrast between Edwards's "Personal Narrative" and Franklin's autobiography is the pervasiveness of the language of emotional and sensory experience in the former and its virtual absence, except as an object (lesson) of containment, in the latter. This vivid difference arises from a similarity: like Edwards, Franklin understands feeling to occasion a kind of self-alienation, to undo personal sovereignty. In fact it might be said that the quintessential rhetorical and psychological move of *The Autobiography*, a move that motivates and links its author's repeated portrayals of religious believers and of the various "alter egos" whose fates he escapes, is Franklin's rewriting of affective or sensational subjection as strategic subjectivity. It is not, for example, passionate Protestantism that distinguishes Franklin's great-great-grandfather, who risked his life to worship secretly during Queen Mary's reign, but his ingenuity in rigging the Geneva Bible to the underside of a joint stool cum lectern. As for the ascetic "Maiden Lady of 70" who lives on unboiled watergruel in the garret of Franklin's boardinghouse in London and whose only regular visitor is the priest who daily confesses her, Franklin finds her worthy of remark as "another Instance on how small an Income Life and Health may be supported."[29] Similarly, Franklin corrects, in his own life, the errata of such masters, mentors, and associates as Keimer, Collins, Ralph, and brother James, learning to exercise affective and sensory control over what they variously indulge—disputatiousness, anger, gluttony, poetry, wanderlust, libido. Even at its most self-ironizing, Franklin's narrative bolsters the sovereign self by rationalizing and voluntarizing any and all susceptibilities to or expenditures of feeling. Repeatedly exposing his own ungovernable tendency toward vanity, Franklin in a sense finally masters it by thoroughly textualizing it. Along similar lines, we may see something more than a witty confession of the arbitrariness and interestedness of the reign of reason in the incident in which Franklin observes a small cod taken from the belly of a large one and promptly reconsiders his ethical vegetarianism in time to partake of a succulent fish fry. This famous episode does not just illustrate Franklin's ironic awareness that reason is easily manipulated to warrant desire ("So convenient a thing it is to be a *reasonable Creature,* since it enables one to find or make a Reason for everything one has a mind to do"[30]); it also epitomizes Franklin's need to convert affection and sensation (his great love of fish; the frying cod's enticing aroma) into cognitive principle (something he "has a mind to do") before he can so much as taste, or—as his father's principle of improving dinner conversation taught—not taste, food.

As even the Northampton congregationalists would show, when they dismissed "dear Mr. Edwards" for challenging the individual's autonomous authority to certify his own experience of grace, emergent American manhood more typically entailed what I've called the rewriting of affective or sensational subjection as strategic subjectivity than the inclination to affiance oneself to Being—or to other beings—at the expense of self-love. Indeed, to return to it briefly, the most resonant words of the Declaration of Independence may be seen to comprise the locus classicus of precisely such rewriting. The "self-evident" truth asserted at the outset of the Declaration's second sentence—"that all men are created equal"—echoes, as it follows from, the claim of its first to a "separate & equal station" for Americans, who, as "one people," are logically (as well as naturally and divinely) entitled "to dissolve the political bands which have connected them with another."[31] Here, the rhetoric of self-evident national and personal subjectivity is marshaled not just against British arguments for the colonists' political subjection but against the powerful and complex affective connections to Britain, to local communities, or to both that, in 1776, most Americans themselves felt— connections that rendered them neither "one people" nor "separate & equal" individuals. Thus to found American identity, personal and national, on the principle of "inalienable rights" was at the same time to found it on the principle of alienable emotions.

This insight prompts what is perhaps an uncommon perspective on Jefferson's famous trinity of rights, "life, liberty, and the pursuit of happiness"— one that views "the pursuit of happiness" differently than in its relations to Lockean property rights, to moral sense philosophy, or to the rhetorical precedents that, as Garry Wills has shown, established "public happiness [as] a secular and scientific term" and "a political norm" for Enlightenment thinkers.[32] What this perspective makes visible, rather, is the construction of happiness here not as a feeling to which one is subject but as an object of will and of pursuit whose very alienability is a crucial piece of the self's evidence.[33]

Alienable emotions are the price of evident selves in revolutionary America's new (man's) world, my reading of "the pursuit of happiness" suggests. And, if this is so, then the questions "What is an American?" and "What feels an American?" might evoke significantly different answers from the inhabitants of this world. The man who writes this difference most dramatically, and whose identity it most powerfully inscribes, is Michel-Guillaume J. Hector St. John de Crevecoeur.

Feeling—at once an effusion of nature and an object of art, a site of personal agency and of passive instrumentality, a mode of expressing and of overcoming the self—figures centrally and problematically in *Letters from an American Farmer,* and, as we have seen, in other eighteenth-century American formulations of individual and collective identity. Modern critics of Crevecoeur, however, have tended to deny, deflect, or diminish the central importance of his narrator's self-description, in the early chapter that proposes to situate the American farmer, as "the farmer of feelings" (26). Like Franklin at a George Whitefield revival, they have not accorded emotion a place in their reckonings, or they have accorded it a Lawrencian dismissal: "Hector St. John, you are an emotional liar."[34]

Philip D. Beidler, for instance, compares the narrators of Franklin's *Autobiography* and of Crevecoeur's *Letters* in order to nominate Franklin the model American man for his "ability to measure [both his] individual and representative identities by expectations no more permanent . . . than the self-consciously articulated fictions they sustain."[35] While Franklin's moral account book is fitted with "erasable pages," Crevecoeur cannot so facilely adapt to the assaults of slavery, capitalism, and revolution on his "cherished design" of a life and a society; thus, Beidler scornfully concludes, he "[commits] himself at the last to the specious rigidities of a mind hopelessly trapped within the mythic designs of its own imaginings."[36] Franklin, to put Beidler's point differently (and unsympathetically), is exemplary because he is unencumbered by affective ties to any particular "fiction" of the self or nation. Crevecoeur is tied by and to the facticity of his feelings (affective subjection), yet, since Beidler's model of identity (strategic subjectivity) provides no place for feelings, he can only represent Crevecoeur as the victim of "specious rigidities of mind" and of "designs" that, impractically "cherished," must be "mythic."

Another approach to *Letters* ratifies Beidler's commitment to strategic subjectivity and affectless intellection yet rescues Crevecoeur from his attack by means of the common disciplinary assumption of a clear distinction between the text's affectionate narrator and its ostensibly disillusioned author.

Such an assumption, observes a recent challenger of the reading it affords, is grounded in "the modern notion that ironic distance is—a priori—more 'literary' than emotional engagement, thus allowing the critic to cite the book's literary' character as evidence that its sentimental portions must have been meant ironically."[37] Accordingly, Mary E. Rucker understands *Letters* as a masked satire by a "knowledgeable, rational, and essentially pessimistic" author on the "self-indulgent sentimentality" and " 'very limited power of mind' " of his "strictly emotional" narrator.[38] Rucker's contempt for Crevecoeur's "farmer of feelings" is downright alarming in its virulence: "a man of mere sensibility," Rucker's Farmer James is a bundle of "psychic and moral inadequacies," an hysteric who "irrationally accepts his children's nightmares" as prognostications and whose inability to choose sides in the Revolution bespeaks "his moral cowardice."[39] What actually appalls Rucker, though, is her Franklinian association of emotional susceptibility with abject uncontrol. Of James's delight and astonishment by natural phenomena, Rucker remarks: "Incapable of penetrating phenomena to discover either scientific or spiritual laws, James responds to nature as a man of feeling."[40] And, she asserts, in a parallel and still more revealing comment on James's social plight: "incapable of *comprehending phenomena rationally and thereby mastering them,* James . . . [is rendered] susceptible to traumatic onslaughts of the unfamiliar."[41]

Myra Jehlen treats feeling in *Letters* far more sensitively and productively in the context of her interest in Crevecoeur's "problem of reconciling individual independence with mutuality"—a problem, she adds, that "was not Crevecoeur's alone . . . [but] occupied his entire century and, for that matter, the next."[42] (And, for that matter, the next—the twentieth—as well.) But Crevecoeur's emotions ultimately reduce, in Jehlen's reading, to epiphenomena of his proprietary security, or its abridgement; she does not consider them to be essential properties of identity or objects of value for Crevecoeur in themselves. Crevecoeur "defined personal identity entirely in terms of self-possession and property," she writes, arguing too that "personal worth for him was measured by autonomy" and that a land in which "everyone had complete control of his life, and none had power over another's" comprised his American ideal—an ideal that, in the end, he found less threatened by a distant monarchy than by marketplace democracy.[43] An alternative and a fuller understanding of *Letters from an American Farmer,* however, would take property, and even self-possession, not as the ultimate objects of Crevecoeur's affections but only, as Crevecoeur's own metaphor would have it, as the soil in which feelings may be most freely cultivated.

Such is decidedly the case in the passage that surrounds and contextualizes a sentence Jehlen cites as evidence of Crevecoeur's central commitment to proprietary individualism: "The instant I enter on my own land, the bright idea of property, of exclusive right, of independence, exalt my mind" (27). Occurring near the middle of the opening eight-page paragraph of Letter II, a paragraph almost entirely devoted to detailed, empirical description of the farmer's labors and loves, this sentence is atypical in its ideational abstraction and its sublimation of feeling in general conceptual objects, bright ideas. Indeed, the sentence is marked by the one that immediately precedes it as a self-conscious effort to sublimate familial affections and sensory pleasures that Crevecoeur's narrator has indulged so effusively and with such abandon as, momentarily, to embarrass him and prompt him to explain himself in more practical and "manly" terms. Here is the excerpted sentence again, restored to its circumambient meditation:

> When I contemplate my wife, by my fire-side, while she either spins, knits, darns, or suckles our child, I cannot describe the various emotions of love, of gratitude, of conscious pride, which thrill in my heart, and often overflow in involuntary tears. I feel the necessity, the sweet pleasure, of acting my part, the part of a husband and father, with an attention and propriety which may entitle me to my good fortune. It is true these pleasing images vanish with the smoke of my pipe, but, though they disappear from my mind, the impression they have made on my heart is indelible. When I play with the infant, my warm imagination runs forward, and eagerly anticipates his future temper and constitution. I would willingly open the book of fate, and know in which page his destiny is delineated. Alas! where is the father, who, in those moments of paternal extacy, can delineate one half of the thoughts which dilate his heart? I am sure I cannot. Then again I fear for the health of those who are become so dear to me; and, in their sicknesses, I severely pay for the joys I experienced while they were well. Whenever I go abroad it is always involuntary. *I never return home without feeling some pleasing emotion, which I often suppress as useless and foolish.* The instant I enter on my own land, the bright idea of property, of exclusive right, of independence, exalt my mind. Precious soil, I say to myself, by what singular custom of law is it that thou wast made to constitute the riches of the freeholder? . . . Often, when I plough my low ground, I place my little boy on a chair which screws to the beam of the plow. Its motion and that

of the horses please him: he is perfectly happy, and begins to chat. As I lean over the handle, various are the thoughts which croud into my mind. I am now doing for him, I say, what my father formerly did for me: may God enable him to live that he may perform the same operations for the same purposes when I am worn out and old! (27–28)

Property and independence are not the objects that Crevecoeur exalts here; at best, they are means to more desired ends. "The riches of the freeholder," for Crevecoeur, are largely affective ones; the conventions of the cult of sensibility and of the fictional epistolary narrator are at once vehicles and screens for the nonetheless difficult, suspect, and "often suppress[ed]" articulation of male emotion. Indeed, the lines quoted recall or anticipate notable attempts to overcome the separate sphere of the dispassionate male self by American writers decades removed from Crevecoeur. When Farmer James writes of "the necessity, the sweet pleasure, of acting my part . . . with an attention and propriety which may entitle me to my good fortune," his words echo Edwards' consent in "Personal Narrative" to the "pleasant, bright and sweet" necessity of God's sovereign design and to his own small part in it. When he partly veils the intensity of his affections by likening his domestic images to ephemeral pipe smoke, even as he confesses their engravement on his heart, he prefigures Hawthorne's ambivalent accommodation of emotional and domestic masculinity in his trope of romance. And when he depicts himself leaning over his plow handle, his mind crowded with thoughts in which personal identity is dissolved and perpetual self-renewal is attained in a genealogy of physical and emotional retracings of his course by others, Crevecoeur's farmer adumbrates Whitman's amative, transgenerational body politic in "Crossing Brooklyn Ferry."

The feelings that James farms here and elsewhere in the narrative are not exclusively domestic ones. If, for James, familial bonds justify proprietary independence—"I married; and this perfectly reconciled me to my situation. . . . I felt that I did not work for myself alone, and this encouraged me much" (25)—that same independence paradoxically facilitates the farmer's affective, rather than exploitative, connections to the land and to the other inhabitants of his natural and social environments. Such connections comprise the profits and pleasures that the early letters enumerate: the farmer's first "astonish[ing]" encounter, upon his "return home through my low grounds" after a day of fieldwork, with "the myriads of insects which I perceive dancing in the beams of the setting sun" (28); his collaboration with a "bold phalanx" of bees that, so long as they work in concert, succeed in defending themselves against a predatory kingbird (29); the "neighborly excursions" to other farms, from which he returns "extremely happy, because there I see good living almost under every roof" (67). Even in Crevecoeur's widely anthologized "What is an American?," a letter generally viewed as an archetypal instance of the liberal individualism that would become America's dominant ideology, the satisfactions of Farmer James's American identity are more often affective than acquisitive, collective or mutual than autonomous and competitive: "a share of national pride" (40); "attachment" to a country that affords him "land, bread, protection, and consequence" (43); "mixture of blood" and "[incorporation] into one of the finest systems of population which has ever appeared" (44); and "not . . . gold and silver" but "a better sort of wealth; cleared lands, cattle, good houses, good clothes, and an increase of people to enjoy them" (55).

The "new man" (44) of *Letters from an American Farmer*, then, is a hybrid product of a Franklinian economy of rational and material self-reliance and an Edwardsian economy of affective communion.[44] For Crevecoeur, the former economy accommodates the latter, which, in turn, accords the first meaning and virtue. One discursive indicator of the book's mixed imaginative economy is its amalgamation of two opposing rhetorics, each positively freighted: a rhetoric of mobility and volition and one of rootedness and involuntariness. Feeling is what grounds, environmentally and socially, the potentially placeless and insular self, and Crevecoeur's narrator typically aligns it with the force and pleasure of involuntary obligation, as in the quoted passage from Letter II in which James's survey of his domain elicits "involuntary tears" that make him "feel the necessity, the sweet pleasure, of acting my part, the part of a husband and father, with an attention and propriety which may entitle me to my good fortune" (26). As for the farmer's legal and historical entitlement to his estate, it is significant that Crevecoeur affords his alter ego deeper American roots than his own and imagines James's property in his farm to derive not from purchase or independent labor but from inheritance.[45] Crevecoeur's farming of feeling, his rhetoric of rootedness and affective necessity, is central to his vision of American selfhood yet it also functions as imaginative and imaginary compensation for the actual shallowness of the new man's geographical and communal roots. Thus, it relegates *Letters'* perception of American atomism and acquisitive antagonism to the margins ("What is an American?" literally locates and contains these conditions on the western frontier) as it veils, until the final chapters, some of the new world's less savory structures of social connection and compulsion.

The narrator's encounter in Letter IX with a caged, blinded slave in the woods near Charleston at once traumatically unveils the most brutal of these structures and begins to reconfigure feeling, once an effective motive and vehicle of democratic communion, as a state of alienation from society and from the self. Earlier, James had shot a predatory kingbird and rescued fifty-four surviving bees ("tenants of my farm" [28]) from his craw; here, on his way to dine with a Carolina planter, he comes upon a tree in which hovering birds of prey obscure an immobilized victim. "Actuated by an involuntary motion of my hands, more than by any design of my mind," James recalls, "I fired at them" (164), but this spontaneous gesture plays out differently than any of his previous extensions of sympathy. Whereas the bees "licked themselves clean, and joyfully went back to the hive; where they probably informed their companions of such an adventure and escape, as I believe had never happened before" (29), the immediate effect of James's shot here is to scatter the birds "to a short distance" and to reveal a doomed, disfigured black man who, momentarily relieved of the vultures, is set upon by "swarms of insects . . . eager to feed on his mangled flesh and to drink his blood" (164). Moreover, James's emotional impulse, which exhausts his ammunition, turns out to deprive him of the means of relieving the sufferer by ending his life: "finding [himself] unable to perform so kind an office," James can only stand "convulsed" and "motionless, involuntarily contemplating the fate of this negro in all its dismal latitude" (164).

The language of this haunting episode insistently aligns involuntary affect with incapacity, paralysis, and even self-disintegration (convulsion) as its content refuses James any genuine fellowship with the slave. Though he is not himself a member of the Southern planter class who, "by habit, . . . neither see, hear, nor feel for, the woes of their poor slaves, from whose painful labours all their wealth proceeds" (153), James is clearly implicated by his race, by his own possession of slaves (however "faithful and healthy" [26] he has blithely attested them to be), and by his dinner plans. Helplessly relegating the caged slave to the category of "shocking spectacle," the farmer musters "strength enough to walk away, and soon reached the house at which I intended to dine" (165). There, informed that the torture of the black man, who had killed an overseer, is required and justified by "the laws of self-preservation" (165), James abruptly closes the letter without reporting what he responded or whether he ate.

The unwritten, yet powerfully implied conclusion of Letter IX—in which the farmer sits down to his "intended" meal with his planter host—

may be viewed as a ghostly figuration of the particular despair that suffuses the entire letter. For such a dinner—a barely social scene of consumption without communion—epitomizes the fate of feeling both here and in the final letters of Crevecoeur's book. Emotional indulgence and spectatorial consumption without communion define James's encounter with the caged man and render it a variant of the multiform cannibalism that seems, with this letter, to take dominion everywhere. From the narrator's opening observation on a "climate [that] renders excesses of all kinds very dangerous, particularly those of the table" (152); to his depictions of planters insensibly battening on the fruits of fields watered by "showers of sweat and of tears which from the bodies of Africans daily drop" (153); to his bitter judgment that "man, an animal of prey, seems to have rapine and the love of bloodshed implanted in his heart" and to esteem most highly "the most successful butchers of the world" (159); to his own convulsed presence as birds and insects feast on the "mangled flesh" and "drink [the] blood" of a living man (164); to the simultaneous dinner at the plantation house that proceeds undisturbed on the grounds of "self-preservation" (165); and on into the enthralled observations of feeding and fighting snakes and hummingbirds in the next letter (166–72), cannibalism emerges as a governing trope, a grotesque synthesis of the dialectical principles of unrestricted self-interest and intimate interpersonal connection in Crevecoeur's America.

In the concluding Letter XII, "Distresses of a Frontier-Man," this trope is extended to convey what the narrator experiences as the self-consuming revolutionary frenzy of the entire Anglo-American body politic. The letter's title itself suggests that a violent margin has swallowed up the center, as the former cultivator of the "middle settlements" (45) involuntarily finds himself a "frontier-man," the inhabitant of a region whose denizens, as described from a safe distance in Letter III, "are often in a perfect state of war; that of man against man" (46) and "appear to be no better than carnivorous animals, of a superior rank" (47). Now, this state is general. Crevecoeur's narrator, moreover, unwilling to sever his affective bonds either to England or to his anticolonial neighbors, risks violent assault by both sides and conceives himself, his family, and, indeed, the society itself to be in a position reminiscent of that of the ravaged slave in Letter IX.

Must I with meekness wait for that last pitch of desolation, and receive, with perfect resignation, so hard a fate from ruffians, acting at such a distance from the eyes of any superior; monsters, left to the wild impulses of the wildest nature? Could the lions of Africa be transported here and let loose, they would, no doubt, kill us in order to prey upon our carcasses; but their appetites would not require so many victims. Shall I wait to be punished with death, or else to be stripped of all food and raiment, reduced to despair without redress and without hope? Shall those, who may escape, see everything they hold dear destroyed and gone? Shall those few survivors, lurking in some obscure corner, deplore in vain the fate of their families, mourn over parents either captivated, butchered, or burnt? (195)

Under these circumstances, as the frenzied rhetoric of Letter XII makes plain, emotion itself joins the attack. Farmer James's feelings—for the community's and the country's plight as well as his own—feed on the atmosphere of dissolution and menace until they become his most immediate assailants, as if they were infiltrators in the service of an enemy. "When I consider myself as connected in all these characters, as bound by so many cords, all uniting in my heart, I am seised with a fever of the mind" (188). His instinctive yet lamented recourse is to contain emotion by turning it resolutely inward, to force his faculty of spontaneous affective connection with place, with the objects of his physical environment, and with others to consume itself in his private interest. "A man who exquisitely feels for the miseries of others as well as for his own" (188), he grimly sacrifices "his political maxims" and the title of "citizen" under whose banner he has "glow[ed] so warmly with the glory of the metropolis" to turn "all his wishes . . . toward the preservation of his family" (194). "Self-preservation," he resolves, echoing the brutal planter of the earlier letter, "the rule of nature, seems to be the best rule of conduct" (193).

That this willful atomism is itself the principal "distress" of the last letter is evidenced by the fact that the plan of self-preservation James undertakes in its name reconstitutes his original communal and affective ideal. A man "cannot live in solitude, he must belong to some community, bound by some ties, however imperfect" (187), he insists at the letter's outset. Accordingly, as his community is "convulsed and . . . half-dissolved" (187), the farmer seeks not just his family's survival but their social reincorporation, their "adoption" as "naturalised" citizens of an Indian village, whose organization he now perceives to be "more congenial to our native dispositions than the fictitious society in which we live" (202). What makes it so is precisely the Indians' affective economy. Only roused passions and "the stings of vengeance . . . can impel them to shed blood: far superior in their motives of action to the Europeans, who, for sixpence per day, may be engaged to shed that of any people on earth" (206). "On their hospitality," James avers, he can "rely more securely . . . than on the witnessed compacts of many Europeans" (207), and in exchange for it he contemplates his family's humble assimilation to Indian ways.

> As soon as possible after my arrival, I design to build myself a wigwham, after the same manner and size with the rest. . . . According to their customs we shall likewise receive names from them, by which we shall always be known. My youngest children shall learn to swim, and to shoot with the bow . . . [and] my wife, . . . like the other squaws, . . . must learn to bake squashes and pompions under the ashes [and] . . . cheerfully adopt the manners and customs of her neighbors. (208–9)

James's plan, of course, may be disdained as an expression of the romance of noble savagery that took root in the Euro-American imagination in the eighteenth century and that, as many scholars have noted, proved perfectly compatible in the nineteenth with what Melville would dub "the metaphysics of Indian-hating."[46] Even in this early version, the romance is vitiated by the narrator's racialist revulsion at the prospect of his family's sexual amalgamation with its native hosts ("however I respect the simple, the inoffensive, society of these people in their villages, the strongest prejudices would make me abhor any alliance with them in blood" [211]). Yet, in the context of this examination of the function and value of emotion in early American models of male selfhood, what is important about Crevecoeur's romance is that it constitutes a way of saving feeling, of sustaining affective communion, at a moment when events seem to dictate its self-interested abandonment.

As if in illustration of the social and psychic schism of the Revolutionary moment, however, Crevecoeur's own biographical course of action diverges sharply from the course he imagines for his literary alter ego. Refusing partisanship, like James, Crevecoeur does not gather his family and push further westward in search of a more perfect union, a cooperative and affection-bound society "more congenial to our native dispositions." Rather, he takes the practical, self-preservative step of returning to monarchical France, after a quarter-century absence, to resecure property and inheritance rights there for himself and his children. Whereas James rejects any response to the crisis that would entail his separation from his family ("That I could never submit to!" [212]), Crevecoeur leaves his on the farm, which—in a grim instance of life (or, in this case, death) imitating art—is burnt by Indian allies of the British during the war, killing his wife and leaving his children refugees.

Like Beidler's ideal Franklinian man, the actual multinational Michel-Guillaume J. Hector St. John de Crevecoeur—American farmer, Parisian salon intellectual, London literary celebrity, ambassador of Louis XVI, New York import-export businessman, fellow of the American Philosophical Society and the Académie Française—appears to free himself, in the postwar years, from "specious rigidities" of identity and feeling. Doubtless, such liberation, such mobility, entailed in some measure his alienation from the emotions of Farmer James and suppression of the affective economy that informs his *Letters.* Yet, at the dangerous and uncertain outset of his journey, when he left his farm amidst escalating Revolutionary hostilities and sought passage back to France, the property that Crevecoeur most jealously guarded was his manuscript. Poignantly, and symbolically, he buried (or planted) his text, as a precaution against its confiscation, beneath the soil of American botanical samples that he proposed to exhibit in Europe, and he preserved it throughout his long detainment on suspicion of spying, his subsequent nervous collapse, and a blockade that further delayed his transatlantic crossing. It is an apt figure: the interment of the American man as "farmer of feeling" at the moment of national independence—an interment, however, that signifies not a death, necessarily, but an underground life. A seeding: indigenous, germinant, cultivatable.

Notes

1. Fliegelman, *Declaring Independence: Jefferson, Natural Language, and the Culture of Performance,* p. 2.

2. Ibid., p. 47.

3. Wills, *Inventing America: Jefferson's Declaration of Independence,* p. 374.

4. Johnson, *Equivocal Beings: Politics, Gender, and Sentimentality in the 1790s: Wollstonecraft, Radcliffe, Burney, Austen,* p. 2. Johnson's remark specifically refers to the emotion-saturated sentimental and gothic fiction of the 1790s and its response to the crisis of revolutionary social and political change in Europe. A related inquiry into "the plight of feeling" in postrevolutionary American sentimental and gothic fiction is Stern's *The Plight of Feeling: Sympathy and Dissent in the Early American Novel.* But the crisis to which "the cult of sensibility," the popular eighteenth-century character type of "the man of feeling," and the flood of sentimental literature respond long predates the revolutions in the Ameri-

can colonies and in France and—as I elaborate in n. 5—pertains to "riven" or, in the recurrent and resonant locution of the era, "convulsed" personal identities as well as political ones.

5. In "Suggestions Toward a Genealogy of the 'Man of Feeling', " Crane finds this pervasive figure of eighteenth-century social thought to have originated in the efforts of Restoration Latitudinarian divines to overcome the residual influence of the Puritan doctrine of innate depravity and to advance a thesis of sociability—partly in compensation for the loosening of the Puritan bond of Christian communion—that might withstand the challenge of Hobbes's vision of the instinctive, savage, and atomistic struggle of each against all (*The Idea of the Humanities* 190–91, 204). At the same time, as Leon Howard has noted, the impulse to elevate feeling and to posit its elementality reflected the era's free-floating anxiety about the denaturing and demoralizing implications of its emergent scientific and philosophical orthodoxies: instrumental reason, Lockean empiricism, Humean skepticism ("The Late Eighteenth Century: An Age of Contradictions," in *Transitions in American Literary History* 68–72). Pronouncing "the cult of sensibility"—the celebration of the intrinsic (if unequally developed) human capacity for refined emotion and quick compassion—to be the dominant ideology of Anglo-American fiction from the 1740s through the 1770s in England and the 1790s in the United States, Todd outlines feeling's function as a disciplinary and self-disciplinary regime: a means of defining social identity and regulating sexual morality in an age of great and confusing physical and social mobility (*Sensibility: An Introduction* 4, 7, 17). But, Todd points out, the faculty of feeling is often portrayed as failing in its regulatory office and partaking in the very confusion it would resist, as quick compassion quickens passion. Thus, while Adam Smith and Lord Shaftesbury held emotion to be central to moral identity and community, many of their contemporaries wondered whether it might rather be fatal to these.

6. Pinch, *Strange Fits of Passion: Epistemologies of Emotion, Hume to Austen*, p. 164.

7. Pinch, pp. 3, 2, 2, 15, 2.

8. Fliegelman, *Declaring Indepedence*, p. 148.

9. Tocqueville's remark is quoted in Delbanco's *The Death of Satan*, p. 103. Delbanco's book is a suggestive meditation on the historical processes by which a particular feeling—the sense of evil—was rendered alien or inarticulable as a condition of modern selfhood.

10. Crevecoeur, *Letters from an American Farmer*, p. 26. Page numbers of subsequent quotations from Crevecoeur's work refer to this edition and will be cited parenthetically in the body of the essay.

11. Edwards, *A Jonathan Edwards Reader*, p. 300.

12. Ibid., p. 302

13. Miller, *Jonathan Edwards*, p. 133.

14. Ibid., p. 142.

15. Franklin, *Benjamin Franklin's Autobiography*, ed. Lemay and Zall, p. 87.

16. Ibid., p. 90.

17. Ibid., p. 90.

18. Pinch, *Strange Fits of Passion*, p. 15.

19. Fliegelman, *Declaring Independence*, p. 148.

20. Pinch, *Strange Fits of Passion*, p. 2.

21. Miller, *Edwards*, p. 124.

22. Edwards, *Reader*, p. 144.

23. New, *The Line's Eye: Poetic Experience, American Sight*, p. 24.

24. Edwards, *Reader*, p. 160.

25. Ibid., p. 142.

26. Ibid., pp. 1–2.

27. Ibid., pp. 81–82.

28. Ibid., p. 283, italics in original.

29. Franklin, *Autobiography*, p. 38.

30. Ibid., p. 28.

31. Wills, *Inventing*, p. 374.

32. Ibid., pp. 254–55.

33. Wills, in accordance with the analyses by Fliegelman, Pinch, Todd, and others of the ambivalent connection between feeling and identity in the eighteenth century, takes the idea of "the pursuit of happiness" to signify both "the ground of human right and the goal of human virtue. It is the basic drive of the self, and the only means of transcending the self" (247). Although, as Wills argues, this phrase commonly connoted a natural and involuntary impulse to which man was bound as well as a freedom to which he was entitled, it functions in the Declaration not, I think, as a mark of what I've called "affective subjection" but as a vehicle of "strategic subjectivity."

34. Lawrence, *Studies in Classic American Literature*, p. 34.

35. Beidler, "Franklin's and Crevecoeur's 'Literary' Americans," p. 62

36. Ibid., p. 61.

37. Holbo, "Imagination, Commerce, and the Politics of Associationism in Crevecoeur's *Letters from an American Farmer*," p. 21.

38. Rucker, "Crevecoeur's *Letters* and Enlightenment Doctrine," pp. 193–94.

39. Ibid., pp. 199, 195, 204, 206.

40. Ibid., p. 196.

41. Ibid., p. 195. Rucker's pervasive implication that emotion renders Farmer James effeminate (childish, fearful, incapable of penetration or mastery) remains current in one of the most recent published interpretations of *Letters*, Carew-Miller's "The Language of Domesticity in Crevecoeur's *Letters from an American Farmer*." Carew-Miller writes that Crevecoeur and his narrator feel that Farmer James "has been overdomesticated and [has] . . . lost his virility in the process" (250), yet I see this reading as an instance of a contemporary critic, writing within a now dominant paradigm and myth of masculinity that is sometimes as coercive for feminists as for their antagonists, projecting onto Crevecoeur what she claims "he perceives as effeminacy" (252). As Holbo points out: "A number of researchers have shown that the literature of sensibility was not yet, in the eighteenth century, considered a 'low,' feminized genre; exploration and cultivation of sensibility was as much the domain of the male *philosophe* as of the bourgeois female" (24).

42. Jehlen, "J. Hector St. John Crevecoeur: A Monarcho-Anarchist in Revolutionary America," p. 207.

43. Ibid., pp. 218, 207, 206.

44. Kolodny takes a similar view of this new man's position and reflects on its ultimate

insupportability: "What now, with hindsight, appear to us as mutually exclusive attitudes—the rights of personal possession and the dream of communal brotherhood—are never explicitly recognized as such by Crevecoeur; rather, they stand side by side, in unresolved and unstated tension." *The Lay of the Land,* p. 65.

45. Crevecoeur's narrator represents his father as the immigrant from Europe who established the family farm. In the author's case, he was himself the first-generation American farmer.

46. The phrase constitutes the topic of a chapter, "Containing the Metaphysics of Indian-Hating, According to the View of One Evidently not so Prepossessed as Rousseau in Favor of Savages," in Melville's *The Confidence Man: His Masquerade,* pp. 124–31. For a suggestive account of the compatibility of the romance of the noble savage with the metaphysics of Indian-hating, see Rogin's *Fathers and Children: Andrew Jackson and the Subjugation of the American Indian,* especially pp. 113–25.

2

Loving with a Vengeance:

Wieland, *Familicide and the Crisis of Masculinity in the Early Nation*

ELIZABETH BARNES

When Mark Barton killed his wife, his eight year-old daughter, and his twelve year-old son with a hammer in July, 1999, then proceeded to shoot nine people at two different brokerage houses before shooting himself, his murderous "rampage" was attributed by the press to his newfound habit of day trading. Although little was known about this man, who one fellow trader claimed was "one of the nicest guys you ever met," Barton's reasons for murdering his children on that Wednesday night, and his wife the night before, appeared self-evident to journalists: as a *Newsweek* article summed up the case, "His debts going up, his marriage going bad, an Atlanta day trader bludgeons his family to death and goes on a shooting spree, a tragedy with a twist of cyber-greed."[1] Rather than "husband," "father" or even "man," Barton is characterized simply as "day trader," rendering his "shooting spree" the predictable outcome of an acquisitive, impulsive, and undisciplined nature.[2]

Such a reading has the advantage of giving what at first appears an inexplicable act the reassuring moral of a cautionary tale. But this moral addresses only part of the story. Familicide, the killing of one's spouse and children, has been increasingly documented by psychologists for the past ten years, and as these professionals attest, it is a peculiarly male crime.[3] To a certain extent, then, we might say that Barton suffered most from being a man, and an emotional one at that. At a time when men are expected to be more sensitive as husbands and more devoted as fathers, the expectations for them to provide ever more material goods for their families has also risen. In Barton's case, as in the cases that follow, the confluence of these expectations produces a masculine crisis resulting in an act of termination of responsibility for family but performed in such a way that the man's absolute devotion to wife and children is, psychologically at least, reinforced. Counterintuitive as it seems, love becomes the motive for murder. Add to this Barton's stated belief that God would take better care of his family than Barton himself had, and we have a formula for familicide reaching back two hundred years. In case after case of family murder in America's early republic, purportedly "pious" men report their belief that God sanctioned—even, in some cases, demanded—their actions. They submitted to His will. What becomes clear through these stories is the extent to which Christian paradigms can invigorate "sensitive" male characteristics—relationality, submissiveness, loving protectiveness— with masculine potency. Ultimately, religion provides a type of spiritual male bonding in which the earthly father's submission to God is translated into a(nother) form of power.

The press's attempts to reduce Barton's actions merely to greed, or even mental instability, misses the cultural significance of the fact that for Barton, violence was a legitimate expression both of extreme love *and* extreme hatred. As his letter of confession attests, he murdered his children in an entirely different spirit, and with a different motive, than he murdered his fellow traders at the brokerage firms. The latter were those who, according to Barton, deserved to die, because they "greedily sought [his] destruction." His children, on the other hand, were killed to spare them having to suffer what he himself had suffered. While one murder represented an act of vengeance, the other represented an act of intimacy and of paternal care. In killing his children, Barton was to play the role, finally, of the consummate father, who, by killing his family, saved them from disgrace (of his financial collapse), from loss (of the head of the family, when he committed suicide), and from inevitable heartache: "I killed the children to exchange for them five minutes of pain for a lifetime of pain. I forced myself to do it to keep them from suffering so much later. No mother, no father, no relatives. . . . The fears of the father are transferred to the son. It was from my father to me and from me to my son. He already had it. And now to be left alone. I had to take him with me."[4] These words speak not only to Barton's confused and confusing state of mind but to the double-edged nature of family bonds: i.e., family attachments can destroy you equally by their absence ("No mother, no father, no relatives . . . now to be left alone"), and by their presence ("The fears of the father are transferred to the son. It was from my father to me and from me to my son").

Such a double bind was, according to Barton, the curse his own son would inevitably inherit. His wife and daughter would suffer, by contrast, from their dependence on a man who could never truly protect them. Some years before, after his first wife's death, Barton had been suspected of sexually molesting his daughter.[5] Whether it was that which Barton was attempting to spare his son (the ambiguous reference to the fact that his son "already had it" would in this case mean the son, like Barton, had already been the victim of incest and might one day pass it on to his own children), or whether his anxiety was a more generalized, though acute, symptom of depression, will never be known. What is clear is that Barton believed the curse was hereditary, and male-oriented. His only hope of saving the family, and his own expiring masculinity, was in sending them to a better, or at least more effectual, Father: "I know that Jehovah will take care of them all in the next life. . . . If Jehovah is willing I would like to see them all again in the resurrection. To have a second chance." Though a failed father in this life, Barton hoped to resurrect the domestic dream through an act of violence that would ultimately wipe out the past and usher in a new, and different, future. It is an act that evinces at once Barton's power and his impotence. For though self-willed, Barton represents the consequences of the murders as beyond his control. He submissively places himself and his family in the hands of God. By doing so, Barton attempts to fulfill the role of both good father and obedient son to make his own male identity meaningful once again by surrendering himself to a paternal figure whose omnipotence promises stability, security, and, perhaps most important, unimpeachable male prowess.

The media spin on Barton's multiple murders reflects a society deeply ambivalent about the implications of technological advancement, specifically in this case, the power of the internet. But though day trading is a recent phenomenon, Barton's extreme response to personal and professional failure is not. Familicide reached a high point during America's revolutionary and early national periods, when a burgeoning capitalist economy put increasing pressure on men to prove their manliness through market savvy. Between 1781 and 1836 an unprecedented eleven cases of familicide were reported. The last of these marks the end of such crimes recorded until the twentieth century.[6] "Though the number of cases is much too small to venture any sort of quantitative argument," Daniel Cohen notes, "yet the concentration of publicized familicides in the early republic is certainly suggestive."[7] My essay attempts to address the cultural significance of this seeming epidemic, as well as the particular rendition of the crime in one of the first American novels, Charles Brockden Brown's gothic tale, *Wieland, or The Transformation* (1798). An ambitious author committed to establishing a new, distinctly "American" (as opposed to British) literature, Brown chose familicide as the subject of his national novel. In doing so, he complicated the already charged relation between metaphorical "fathers" and "sons" during the revolutionary and postrevolutionary periods (embodied first in the relationship between Britain, the "parent" country, and America, then in the relationship between the Founding Fathers and their republican sons).[8] Based on two specific cases in the early 1780s, those of James Yates and William Beadle, *Wieland* tells the story of a man who, having heard what he believes to be the voice of God, murders his family to prove his obedience and devotion to God.[9] As with recent readings of the Barton murders, critics of *Wieland* have tended to focus on *why* Brown's eponymous protagonist suffers such a breakdown. I am interested, however, in the particular *form* the breakdown takes: i.e., the man's eradication of those who are legally, financially, and, most important, emotionally tied to him and in whom he has an emotional investment. Brown's novel helps give some perspective on what is at stake for men in this act of "loving" murder. At a time of particular crisis in the history of American masculinity, familicide perpetrators sought to exemplify manhood by asserting absolute sovereignty over their wives and children. In Wieland's case, masculinity is equated with deity and with the autonomy and independence that identification with the Almighty Father embodies and engenders.

Although the subject of this essay is familicide of the eighteenth, rather than the twentieth, century, Barton's case is relevant for its striking similarities to such cases two centuries earlier. For example, Barton's breakdown was precipitated by the same local crisis facing four out of the seven men for whom we have documented histories: the perceived threat of economic ruin. Moreover, Barton's justification for the crime echoes, sometimes word for word, rationalizations given by the majority of men whose narratives we have in hand. In six out of seven cases religious convictions motivated or justified the deed in the perpetrator's mind. The significant difference is that in these earlier histories the religious component is far more inflammatory, probably because the majority of Americans were more sensitized to its rhetoric and more susceptible to its implications. James Yates (1781) responded to a vision whose voice ordered him to kill all of his idols; he began with his sleigh and his horses and ended with his wife and children. Once arrested, Yates refused to repent and, addressing himself to God, declared, "my father, thou knowest that it was in obedience to thy commands, and for thy glory that I have done this deed."[10] William Beadle (1782) suffered a reversal of fortune during the Revolutionary war. Refusing to give in to poverty, however, he continued to live beyond his means. When persuaded that he would be found out by neighbors, Beadle decided to kill himself. "Unwilling any of his family should stay behind to encounter its troubles," writes Stephen Mix Mitchell in 1783, "and since 'tis a father's duty to provide for his flock, he chose to consign [his children] over to better hands."[11] He took an axe to his wife as well, so as not to leave her behind. Though Beadle struggled with the decision for three years, eventually he convinced himself that familicide was God's will: "I seem to be convinced in a steady, calm and reasonable way, that it is appointed for me to do it—that it is my duty and that it must be done. That it is God himself that prompts and directs me, in all my reflections and circumspection, I really believe."[12] Matthew Womble (1784) attacked his wife with an axe out of anger during an argument. He then proceeded to slay his four sons. In explanation of the deed, Womble claimed that he slew his family in obedience to the divine command of a supernatural emissary, "Satan in disguise."[13] Able Clemmens (1805), who for years labored under the idea that his "misery" had arisen from neglected obedience to his "maker," was eventually overcome by the idea that his failure to please God and to provide adequately for his family would result in his being "torn from them." His solution was to take them all to heaven with him.[14] Depressed by the advent of a drought, James Purrinton (1806) confided to his neighbors that he feared "his family would suffer for want of bread." Purrinton resolved to kill himself, but when his wife and children got wind of the plan, Purrinton changed his strategy and decided to kill his family as well. They would "suffer a momentary pang," he reasoned, but once in heaven they would "lose their sorrows . . . and be with him eternally happy."[15] Isaac Heller (1836) experienced "frequent strong temptations" to kill his wife and children and was taken with the idea of beheading his favorite child, John Wesley, after the manner of John the Baptist; eventually he succumbed to his temptations.[16] Thus two of the men believed that God condoned the murders, while three affirmed that God directly ordered their families to be killed. All six expressed the opinion that their families should not be left alone on earth and looked forward to the time when they and their families would be reunited in heaven.[17]

Like Mark Barton, Yates, Purrinton, Beadle, Clemmens, and Heller were described as gentle, sober, industrious, kind, tender, and affectionate. There was no history of domestic abuse. Thus one of the startling aspects of the crime is the seeming anomaly between the man's character and his deed. According to Karen Halttunen, it was exactly the mysterious, alien, and inexplicable nature of the crime that so disturbed and thrilled eighteenth-century readers of murder narratives.[18] Addressing such readers, Stephen Mix Mitchell (author of *A Narrative of the Life of William Beadle*) concedes, "'Tis very natural for you to ask, whether it was possible a man could be transformed from an affectionate husband and an indulgent parent to a secret murderer, without some previous alteration, which must have been noticed by the family or acquaintance? Yet this was the case . . . there was no visible alteration in his conduct."[19] So how do we account for the fact that otherwise mild-mannered, "family men" turned homicidal? Or that the majority attributed their actions to a divine imperative? One explanation offered by Cohen is that these men of the new republic suffered from the "radical new 'conditions of freedom' " and self-determination with which they found it impossible to cope. In order to "evade and annul" that freedom, they "constructed internal imperatives" that took choice and, ultimately, responsibility out of their hands.[20] Conditions in the new republic, as Cohen acknowledges, include not only freedom but political and economic instability, "the otherwordly individualism"[21] of the Great Awakening, and a growing emphasis on affective ties between family members. The latter helped legitimate the model of the sensitive man, the "affectionate husband and indulgent parent" that describes men such as Beadle. But an ethos of increased male sensitivity, exemplified in and encouraged by numerous eighteenth-century sentimental novels such as Henry MacKenzie's *The Man of Feeling* (1768) and Laurence Sterne's *A Sentimental Journey* (1781), may actually have contributed to rather than discouraged the violence inflicted on these families. As Cohen observes, "the very intensity of the new affective ties between men and their wives and children may have helped to transform simple suicides into mass murders," because husband-fathers were now determined not to leave their families behind.[22] The all-too-loving father's hold on the family was further strengthened by a spirit of individualism in the economic sphere that helped domesticate the once feudal model of the "lord of the manor"; in essence, it put patriarchy in the home. As Juliet Mitchell has argued, the rise of capitalism in the eighteenth century was coeval with the rise of the autonomous, affective family, as the latter became the focal point of the idea of private property.[23] The image of the lord of the manor is superseded by the common man whose "home is his castle," and though the latter lacks the political and economic control of the former, that lack is reassuringly obscured by the image of the father's *personal* control over the members of his family.[24] In the extreme case of familicide, one could say that the authority given to male emotion, combined with the authority men were deemed to have in their homes, proved a fatal mix.

Emphasis on individualism and the power of personal feeling had made its way into the religious realm as well. Men and women alike were told that their salvation, i.e., their success in the life hereafter, was dependent upon their ability to *feel* God's presence and thereby discover his will. Emotion thus became one index to truth. This poses a particular problem for men, who potentially identify with God as patriarch. The question becomes, What is to keep a man from projecting onto God his own feelings and frustrations and calling them divine? Various writers tried to address just this problem through sermons and didactic essays designed to delineate the bounds of appropriate feeling and response. Publishers often issued these moral commentaries alongside murder narratives in order to help guide readers to a proper interpretation of the material. The *New-York Weekly Magazine,* for example, included an essay entitled "The Fatal Effects of Indulging the Passions" in their 1796 issue reprinting the account of James Yates's murder of his family. Various editions of Mitchell's *Narrative of the Life of William Beadle* published from 1783 to 1805 concluded with extracts from the sermon preached at the Beadle family funeral, "The Great Sin and Danger of Striving with GOD." *Sketches of the Life of James Purrinton* (1806) was published with "remarks on the fatal tendency of erroneous principles, and Motives for receiving and obeying the pure and salutary precepts of the gospel." In their attempts to contradict these men's "erroneous principles" about the deity, however, these writers tend to depict God as just as emotionally volatile as the men who supposedly misunderstood His plan. As early as Jonathan Edwards's "Sinners in the Hands of an Angry God" (1741), for example, that urtext of the Great Awakening, God is figured as jealous, bitter, and capricious: "O sinner! Consider the fearful danger you are in: it is a great furnace of wrath, a wide and bottomless pit, full of the fire of wrath, that you are held over in the hand of that God, whose wrath is provoked and incensed as much against you, as against many of the damned in hell." Granted, Edwards is preaching to the unconverted, but in the context of Edwards's belief that salvation, or "election," is preordained ("However you may have reformed your life in many things, and may have had religious affections . . . it is nothing but His mere pleasure that keeps you from being this moment swallowed up in everlasting destruction"), these words are daunting indeed.[25]

Edwards takes as his text for "Sinners" verse 32:35 of Deuteronomy:

"Vengeance is mine, and recompense, for the time when their foot shall slip; for the day of their calamity is at hand, and their doom comes swiftly." His sermon underscores the problematic theology of a patriarch who would let his creations drop into the burning fires of hell without a moment's notice simply because he can. The idea that God has the right to destroy what he has made is echoed in a sermon given forty years later, at the funeral for William Beadle's wife and children. There the Reverend John Marsh proclaims the incontrovertible right of God to do with humankind what he deems best, for "having made them [God] has an absolute propriety in them."[26] Like father, like son, we might say: Beadle reasons in just this way in justifying the destruction of his own children.[27] What is principally at stake for Marsh in this sermon is a repudiation of Beadle's self-proclaimed deist principles—Beadle's assertion that men are powerless to change what God has created, including themselves, and that God does not require them to do so.[28] To refute Beadle's theology, Marsh strives to show that God does indeed care about the actions of men: "this Being, on whom we depend for our existence, and who has a sovereign authority over us . . . requires our submission" to the laws he has given to protect us. Marsh attempts to reinstitute the hierarchy that Beadle's "pride" as a man has abrogated. But though God, "the Father of mankind," disciplines us in order to save us from our own "irregular and vicious inclinations," God's way of doing so appears equally vicious: "they, who strive with their Maker . . . are continually liable to be exposed to his vindictive pleasure, and will finally be made the monuments of his eternal vengeance, if they persist in opposing his compassionate efforts to save them from perishing." In his efforts to make God *personal*, Marsh makes Him *emotional*, and vindictive: i.e., because Beadle failed to believe utterly in the Father's wisdom and love, the Father destroyed him (and his family as well). "[God] will not fail to make all, who persist in opposing him," warns Marsh, "to feel, sooner or later, the direful effects of his righteous vindictive resentment."[29]

As with so many familicide cases, it was crucial for Beadle to believe that he was acting not out of anger but out of love. Therefore, though his anger with his neighbors, who he believed would "laugh at" his fall from prosperity, could be articulated, his *expression* of that anger, which was turned on himself and his family, had to be recast as ideal paternal love: "I mean to close the eyes of six persons thro' perfect humanity, and the most endearing fondness and friendship; for mortal father never felt more of their tender ties than myself."[30] Marsh's portrayal of God paints a similarly disturbing picture of violence wedded to love. Read in the context of Calvinist theology, the "transformation" of a man such as Beadle once "affectionate" and "indulgent" into one violent and controlling may come to appear less a transformation than an identification, an identification with the emotionally volatile, masculine godhead American culture has promulgated. Having been revealed as at once protective, controlling, and unpredictably malicious, God provides the perfect figure for the projected fears and frustrations of mortal men. His reputation proves Him capable of such feelings even as His ultimate "sovereignty" fully justifies them.

The significance of God as able to command the absolute obedience of His creations, even to the point where they sacrifice their own children, is epitomized in the Old Testament story of Abraham and Isaac. Tellingly, this story is one of the foremost sources for *Wieland*. Brown's patrilineal line for his fictional Wieland family goes back to the eighteenth-century German poet, Christoph Martin Wieland, and as Alan Axelrod has documented, this popular poet's early work, *Der Gepryfte Abraham* (*The Trial of Abraham,* 1754) served as an important influence on Brown's concept of *Wieland*. "Like Theodore Wieland and James Yates," writes Axelrod, "C. M. Wieland's Abraham consciously subdues 'natural affection' to the command of the divine will." In the father's willing sacrifice of his beloved son, we have a model for the absolute obedience required to prove absolute faith. What takes this biblical story out of the realm of the universal and allows it to be used in a particular American context, argues Axelrod, is the poet's foregrounding of the wilderness as a symbol of epistemological uncertainty. Wilderness becomes, in Brown's hands, a condition of American life that prompts fanaticism in the absence of healthy social intercourse. Both Yates and Wieland live in secluded areas, far from city or from an established church. For Brown, wilderness signifies both a historical and moral condition; it represents the void that religious certitude and a personal relationship to the Deity must fill.[31]

At the beginning of the novel, we discover that Wieland's father suffered such a lack in his early life. After an oppressive seven years' service as apprentice to a London merchant, however, he experienced a spiritual awakening, though one, according to his daughter, Clara, who narrates the story, which had its foundation in "hasty" and inconsistent constructions of biblical precepts. He became convinced that God wanted him to move to America to preach to the Indians. He bought a farm on the Schuylkill river, outside Philadelphia; eventually he married and, in time, became prosperous. Though his missionary work to the Indians failed, his religious devotion increased, and it became his practice to spend several hours each day in solitary worship in the temple he built for his Deity. When the Wieland children were still young, the father became obsessed by a conviction that there was "a command which had been laid upon him, which he had delayed to perform." There had been given him a time for hesitancy, he told his wife, but that time had passed, and now "the duty assigned to him was transferred, in consequence of his disobedience, to another." All that remained for him "was to endure the penalty" (13). What this penalty was he couldn't say, but some days later, alone at midnight while worshiping in the temple, the elder Wieland met his demise by suddenly and inexplicably bursting into flame.

The elder Wieland's death arguably causes an emotional void in the young son, a void that is only temporarily filled by the son's devotion to "science . . . and literature" (23). Read in its political context, *Wieland*'s staging of the son's need for an absolute father figure to love and obey has signified for some critics the loss of patriarchal authority in the wake of revolution. As Jay Fliegelman has shown, the father-son relation symbolized political conflict for Americans in the revolutionary era. In its bid for independence, America cast itself as the abused son of a tyrannical parent, England, who refused to recognize the son's maturity. In the years that follow, however, the break with England was ambivalently marked by literature that attempted, in Julia Stern's words, "to address and work through the unprecedented sense of loss."[32] According to Jane Tompkins, Brown was less concerned with loss than chaos. In her view the absence of Wieland's father (the young children are raised by their aunt) contributes to Wieland's future collapse. In political terms, too much "independence" is revealed by Brown to have "horrifying consequences."[33] Although they approach the text from different angles, both Axelrod and Tompkins ultimately interpret *Wieland* as an indictment of Enlightenment optimism that identifies reason as an antidote to superstition, including religious superstition. For Axelrod, Wieland's fall into murder reveals "the frailty of human perception," while Tompkins interprets the disintegration of the Wielands' "miniature society" as a "more or less direct reflection of Federalist skepticism about the efficacy of religion and education in preparing citizens to govern themselves."[34] These readings are seemingly substantiated by Brown himself. At the opening of the novel, Clara Wieland, sole survivor of the Wieland family massacre and sister to the man who eradicated the family, offers her interlocutor a nicely packaged moral by which to understand the fantastic tale that follows: "[My narrative] will exemplify the force of early impressions, and show the immeasurable evils that flow from an erroneous or imperfect discipline."[35] I believe, however, that Brown's novel is darker than either its narrator or its twentieth-century critics give it credit for being. *Wieland* certainly casts doubt on the power of reason or sympathy to curb the baser human passions; however, Theodore Wieland fails not because he is too blind to distinguish between good and evil, or too flawed to act on the difference, but because good and evil, love and aggression, are inextricably intertwined in the world Brown has created. Wieland suffers as much from his father's presence as he does from his absence: it is implicit in the story that the duty the elder Wieland has "delayed to perform" has devolved onto his son. And Clara herself acknowledges that Wieland has most likely inherited the father's religious mania, if not his divine obligation. What we learn from this moral tale is that, however much sons need fathers, fathers inevitably betray their sons, either wittingly or unwittingly. Paternal love is no defense against the world's evil. In fact, quite the contrary: it magnifies the violence.

The threatening aspects of paternal love recall us to the devastating emotional logic of familicide: the notion that violence is to function as an expression of *love* as well as hatred. Such logic allows a man to (re)gain a sense of self-reliance (by eliminating his family) without abdicating his position as devoted family man. Brown takes us through this complicated and perverse process by offering us a protagonist whose love for his family becomes the basis for his destruction of them. Unlike the historical cases cited above, however, Brown makes more explicit the competitive impulse underlying the attack. In an age preoccupied with the political ramifications of feeling—the ways in which compassion and, more important, empathy, were believed to form the emotional foundation of an egalitarian republic—Wieland's actions take on the appearance of an ideological revolt. However, Wieland is acting both *on* as well as *against* the transsubjective nature of love. Through murder, Wieland moves toward a telos of autonomy, but in such a way that affirms his participation in the equally powerful ethos of sensibility and sympathy.

As we have seen, the crisis of masculinity experienced by familicide perpetrators from Beadle to Barton can be attributed in part to radical economic shifts that put pressure on fathers to prove their manhood by providing ever better for their families. As Dana Nelson notes, tests of masculinity were increasingly located in competitive market relations after the war, and the strain affected men from all economic strata: "From privileged merchants to farmers, shifts of authority, affiliation, and capital in the early nation seem to have reconfigured men's experience of and intensified their focus on manliness.

Fears over masculine identity as experienced in the family, and about masculine rivalry" were "foregrounded in the market transition."[36] Failure to become prosperous was no longer attributed to social forces or political upheaval, but to a personal lack of character.[37] Brown takes up the crisis of masculinity present in his time but disengages it from its economic moorings. Instead he locates that crisis squarely in the family, and by focusing on issues of identity, addresses the *repercussions* of sociopolitical and economic changes, manifested for Wieland in a crisis of epistemology. This epistemological crisis becomes inflected with the very issues facing men in the marketplace: issues of masculinity, hierarchy, and competition. These issues are manifested in Wieland's longing for absolute knowledge and in his desire, as Axelrod puts it, for an "original relation to the absolute."[38]

As Clara herself attests, she, her brother Wieland, Wieland's wife, Catherine, and Catherine's brother, Henry Pleyel, live together in edenic bliss: "Every day added strength to the triple bonds that united us. We gradually withdrew ourselves from the society of others, and found every moment irksome that was not devoted to each other. My brother's advance in age made no change in our situation. . . . His fortune exempted him from the necessity of personal labour" (21). But although Wieland lacks for nothing materially, he suffers, as his father did before him, from a "thirst for knowledge of [God's] will" (165). Wieland's bond with his family does not fully satisfy him. It is an even more perfect union that he seeks. And he eventually finds it with God. On the night of the murders, he prays to God: "O! That I might be admitted to thy presence; that mine were the supreme delight of knowing thy will, and of performing it! The blissful privilege of direct communication with thee, and of listening to the audible enunciation of thy pleasure!" (167). Wieland seeks direct access to the Father. He looks for a sign, not only of God's presence but of his own status as God's especial son. Wieland's prayers are seemingly answered, and through a disembodied voice, he is granted the "knowledge" he seeks: he is ordered first to "sacrifice" his wife, and then later his children, to show his devotion to God. As with James Yates, who testified that a spirit ordered him to "destroy all [his] *idols*" (including his family), Wieland imagines a Father whose love is founded on the slain bodies of all who compete for Wieland's attention.

Ostensibly, Wieland's love for his family makes them a more valuable sacrifice to God, but it is clear that he also gains a more earthly reward. In murdering his family, he murders their emotional power over him as well. When

Wieland finds Catherine at Clara's house (Clara is not home) and hears God's decree, he proceeds to strangle Catherine. A change then takes place; Catherine's emotional hold over Wieland begins to fade along with her beauty: "Grimness and distortion took place of all that used to bewitch me into transport, and subdue me into reverence." When she is finally dead, he is at first assaulted by "desperate and outrageous sorrow": "The breath of heaven that sustained me was withdrawn, and I sunk into *mere man*" (173). But a few moments later his confidence returns, and he is elated by his masterful handling of the situation: "This was a moment of triumph. Thus had I successfully subdued the stubbornness of human passions" (172). So successful is Wieland in subduing "human passion" that after she is dead, Catherine becomes unrecognizable to him: "I asked myself who it was whom I saw? Methought it could not be Catherine. . . . Where was her bloom! These deadly and blood-suffused orbs but ill resemble the azure and exstatic [sic] tenderness of her eyes" (173). He then returns to his own house where he murders all of his children, including his attractive young ward, Louisa Conway. Of the latter's face, Clara is horrified to report, *"not a lineament remained"* (157). Wieland not only takes these women's lives, he obliterates their identities, and with the destruction of their faces, he destroys beauty's power.

What family affections fail to effect, Wieland finds in his "supreme passion" (165). Through murder Wieland is lifted up out of the democratic mass of men and put on a par with God. Thus after he is arrested, Wieland refuses any longer to be judged by human standards and addresses himself directly to God: "Thou, Omnipotent and Holy! Thou knowest that my actions were conformable to thy will. I know not what is crime; what actions are evil in their ultimate and comprehensive tendency or what are good. Thy knowledge, as thy power, is unlimited. I have taken thee for my guide, and cannot err. To the arms of thy protection, I entrust my safety. In the awards of thy justice, I confide for my recompense" (176). Wieland's rhetoric of submission to God is a disavowal of his own feelings in the matter, but in fact, those feelings are of paramount importance to his actions. As Clara herself surmises, had Wieland not loved her with "a passion more than fraternal" (185), he would never have felt the need to kill her: "In vain should I endeavour to stay his hand by urging the claims of a sister or friend: these were his only reasons for pursuing my destruction. Had I been a stranger to his blood; had I been the most worthless of human kind; my safety had not been endangered" (189). Clara, it seems, has gotten to the heart of the matter. The intensity of

Wieland's love is matched only by the intensity of the violence that expresses it: "I was hunted to death . . . by one . . . whose implacability was proportioned to the reverence and love he felt for me" (189). Wieland does not kill his family *despite* the fact that he loves them but *because* he loves them. Once again, emotional attachment proves not the cure but the motive for murder.

The strength of Wieland and Clara's attachment arguably renders Clara's death the most necessary to Wieland's deification. Critics have noted with interest the incestuous attraction between Wieland and Clara and have offered various interpretations as to its meaning.[39] For our purposes, Wieland's passion, "more than fraternal," raises the stakes of familial bonding and offers another angle from which to view Wieland's violent attempts at constructing a powerful, autonomous self. Wieland has already acknowledged to Clara that "There is no human being whom [he] love[s] with more tenderness" (109). Clara, for her part, seems to feel the same way, but she intuits that the closeness of their relationship will eventually destroy her. For example, one night, in a state of depression, Clara takes a walk and falls into a dreamlike state on a bench. "I at length imagined myself walking," she records,

> to my brother's habitation. A pit, methought, had been dug in the path I had taken, of which I was not aware. As I carelessly pursued my walk, I thought I saw my brother, standing at some distance before me, beckoning and calling me to make haste. He stood on the opposite edge of the gulph. I mended my pace, and one step more would have plunged me into this abyss, had not some one from behind caught suddenly my arm, and exclaimed, in a voice of eagerness and terror, "Hold! Hold!" (62)

As David Brion Davis concludes, "This dream suggested that Carwin [the someone who apprehended her] had saved Clara from an incestuous relation with her brother."[40] The notion is not far-fetched. Days later Clara has a premonition that someone is lying in wait in her bedroom closet (it is Carwin), and she is overcome with the idea that the "ruffian" therein is her brother, Wieland (87–88). Norman Grabo suggests that Clara's fear of her brother's murderous/incestuous desires is actually projection. He sees in Clara's narrative the "movement toward a kind of identity with Theodore attainable only over the bodies of Theodore's wife and children."[41] In either case it is clear that incestuous desire ends in death. We reach the climax of Clara and Wieland's unconsummated romance on the night of the murders.

Wieland is on the way to Clara's house when he hears God's voice and, finding his wife, Catherine, instead of Clara, kills Catherine *in Clara's bed*, connecting the themes of murder and sex that have preoccupied Clara from the beginning of her narrative.

Even before Clara discovers that Wieland is the culprit in Catherine's murder, she senses that, in Stern's words, "some massive displacement of forbidden desires has occurred" (28). Upon finding Catherine's body, she observes: "I was the object of [the murderer's] treason; but by some tremendous mistake, his fury was misplaced" (151). Misplaced emotion and misrecognition are the cornerstones of the text. Catherine initially feels an attraction to the grotesque stranger Carwin, and he is attracted to her; yet when he hides in her closet, she mistakes him for Wieland. Though Wieland has actually murdered his wife and children, Clara initially comes to the conclusion that the deed is Carwin's. Clara falls in love with Wieland's best friend, Henry Pleyel, brother to Catherine, but Pleyel is tricked into believing that Clara has sacrificed her virtue to Carwin. In fact, Carwin has seduced Clara's maid. Clara's desires come to appear free floating, fixing on different male characters at different times. Her erotic disorientation is matched only by the mutable emotions passing through Wieland and Pleyel. Though Pleyel has previously worshiped Clara as the feminine ideal, the "certainty" that she has engaged in illicit acts with Carwin transforms her into the object of his fury; he verbally attacks her and she faints. His only justification for the sudden "phrenzy" of his emotion, he says, is his desire to help her: "Should I see you rushing to the verge of a dizzy precipice, and not stretch forth a hand to pull you back?" (129). His metaphor recalls the very service that Carwin had earlier performed for Clara. As we discover in the next chapter, while Pleyel has been warning Clara of God's "vengeance," his eagerness to "exterminate" her for her (alleged) promiscuity, Wieland is at Clara's house, murdering her substitute (118).

Clearly, doubling and displacement abound in *Wieland*. This may be accounted for in part by the novel's genre; as Eve Sedgwick observes, in the Gothic view, individual identity is relational and transactional rather than original or private.[42] But Brown's ubiquitous narrative displacements of identity and desire speak to more than the "transferential logic," to use Dana Luciano's phrase, of the Gothic genre.[43] They signal emotional and psychological dislocations that Wieland's act of familicide both exemplifies and attempts to repair. Sacrificing his family to God, with whom he now identifies, Wieland seeks simultaneously to rise above his family and to bring them home to himself. According to Clara, his goal is realized. After Wieland escapes from prison and tracks Clara down at her home, Carwin intervenes and, through his unique skill of ventriloquism, keeps Wieland from murdering Clara. Feigning the voice of God, Carwin convinces Wieland that he has been laboring under a delusion of the senses (to which this voice, apparently, is an exception). Now aware of his (ostensible) error, Wieland falls "from his lofty and heroic station" and, "weighed to earth by the recollection of his own deeds," is, claims Clara, "transformed at once into the *man of sorrows!*" (230). Taking a penknife, Wieland stabs it into his own neck and dies instantly. Clara's rendition of this scene "transforms" the man into his myth. Recounting Wieland's last moments on earth, Clara (mis)represents him as Jesus Christ, the figure who most fully embodies the mortal and the divine, the submissive and the powerful, the relational and the original.

After a three-year recovery from her grief, Clara offers her reader a final moral lesson: evil deeds owe their existence as much to the "errors" of the victims as to the malice of the authors of such deeds. Curiously, Clara includes Wieland in the list of victims rather than authors (thereby further victimizing Wieland's wife and children, who, already murdered, have their memories obliterated as well by their exclusion from Clara's final ruminations).[44] She saves the author role for Carwin, whose ventriloquism has produced, to her mind, these disastrous results. It must have been Carwin's voice, Clara reasons, rather than God's that Wieland heard and obeyed when killing his family. In Clara's reading, Wieland suffers the same "imperfect discipline" with regard to religion as their father had. Had the son been less susceptible, less inclined to believe in supernatural agency, or at least in a God who would authorize such acts, Carwin would never have succeeded in deluding him (244). The trouble with this interpretation is that Carwin, though he admits to having used ventriloquism for malicious purposes, denies any part in Wieland's previous delusions. Furthermore, Wieland, having arrived at Clara's house to kill her, hears the voice of God when Carwin is nowhere around and while Clara is still in the room. She hears nothing. And finally, the discovery of Carwin's ventriloquism does nothing to solve the earlier mystery of the father's "disobedience" and death. Though it is tempting to read *Wieland* as a story of the Fall, where the evil seducer, Carwin, upsets the edenic but fragile harmony of the Wieland community, Brown himself has made it impossible to believe in Clara's reading by leaving open the possibility that God really *did* speak to Wieland—and to his father before him. Brown may be attempting, through Clara, to moralize on human nature's capacity to be equally susceptible to evil and to good, but the moral falls flat. After all, the Author of Goodness, God, has himself been portrayed, in popular sermons, murder narratives, and this novel specifically, as a jealous, vindictive, murderous father.

Though Mark Barton arguably lived in a different world from those in the early nation, his psychological response to the expectations of American manhood in some sense bridges the gap. From the new republic to the new millennium, novels, newspapers, and magazines confront us with gothic tales of fathers whose love is indistinguishable from hatred. We might theorize that in a culture preoccupied simultaneously with the power of feeling and with patriarchal power, men are created who conflate the two and who seek to express themselves through violence. The violence is then obscured, in their own minds at least, by the strength of emotion that both produces and excuses it. Leslie Fiedler has observed that the eighteenth-century gothic novel, sinister sibling to the domestic novel, substitutes terror for love, and ends in death rather than romance.[45] Thus many readers have been disturbed by what appears to be an "inconsistent" ending to Brown's gothic "American Tale"—his substitution of romance for destruction and death. In the added final chapter, we learn that Clara has moved to Europe and has married Henry Pleyel. Her resumption of a quiet, domestic life has struck some readers as a capitulation to the "happy ending" Brown believed his audience was looking for. I suggest that Brown's conclusion is disturbing for the opposite reason: its ability to shade death as romance and vice versa. *Wieland* reminds us that in constructions of American masculinity—fictional and nonfictional, "gothic" and "domestic," eighteenth-century and twenty-first—love and violence come bound together in a patriarchal, Gordian knot whose strands we are, as yet, still powerless to untie.

Notes

1. Cohen, "It's a Bad Trading Day," p. 22.

2. Other reports told a similar story: "Day Trading: It's a Brutal World" read one section of *Time* magazine's coverage of the serial murders, and the *San Francisco Chronicle's* *Nation* section headlined its article, "Volatile Business of Day Trading," explicitly correlating the financial volatility of active stock trading with the psychological volatility of this man who practiced it. Unsure whether to blame Barton himself or a financial market that had cooler heads spinning, magazines and newspapers consistently linked the two, thereby reducing Barton and his actions to the level of a foregone conclusion: i.e., only a man already unstable would participate in a venture that was itself the symbol of instability; con-

versely, the only payoff for high stakes trading in today's mercurial market is insanity and death. See Thomas and Gegax, "The Atlanta Massacre," p. 26; *San Franscisco Chronicle,* July 31, 1999.

3. See Ewing, *Fatal Families,* p. 134. According to statistics in the national archives of Canada and Wales, from the 1970s to 1990 men were responsible for 95 percent of all familicides. See Wilson, Daly, and Daniele, "Familicide," pp. 279–80.

According to Ewing, the typical familicide perpetrator is a white male in his thirties or forties, controlling yet dependent on family; he views himself as the center of the family and comes to believe that only he can satisfy the family's needs. These men typically have an idealized or romanticized notion of the family and they strive to make the family fit that image. For many of the men Ewing profiled, the crisis came when they experienced a significant financial reversal that threatened to alter their regular style of living. As Ewing sums it up, the familicide perpetrator is "a man who, in his own eyes, is, or is about to become, a failure. . . . Ultimately, he convinces himself that familicide followed by suicide is not just the only way out but the honorable and right thing to do" (134–36).

4. The entire letter of confession is reprinted in *Newsweek,* August 9, 1999, p. 27.

5. In fact, his daughter, Mychelle, accused him herself in 1994, at the age of two, but authorities decided that she was probably experiencing trauma from her mother's death. See Cohen, "Bad Trading Day," p. 27; Thomas and Gegax, "Atlanta Massacre," p. 25; "Volatile Business of Day Trading," *San Francisco Chronicle.*

6. Nelson, *National Manhood,* p. 61. Nelson and Cohen both cite Neil King Fitzgerald for an account of the eleven cases. See Fitzgerald, "Toward an American Abraham."

7. Cohen, "Homicidal Compulsion and the Conditions of Freedom," p. 725. See also Wilson, Daly, and Daniele, "Familicide."

8. For a discussion of the former, see Burrows and Wallace, "The American Revolution," and Fliegelman, *Prodigals and Pilgrims.* For an account of the latter, see Rogin, *Fathers and Children.*

9. Brown in his preface reminds skeptical readers of a recent historical case on which his story is based. His reference is almost certainly to the 1781 Yates case. However, his novel bears a striking resemblance to the Beadle case as well, as Shirley Samuels notes in *Romance of the Republic,* pp. 52–54.

10. "An Account of a Murder Committed by Mr. J— Y—, upon his Family, in December, A.D. 1781," pp. 20, 28.

11. Mitchell, *A Narrative of the Life of William Beadle,* p. 16.

12. Quoted from Beadle's note of confession in "The Great Sin and Danger of Striving with GOD, A SERMON Preached . . . at the Funeral of Mrs. Lydia Beadle," in Marsh, *The Great Sin and Danger of Striving with GOD,* p. 24.

13. See Leland, *A True Account of how Matthew Womble Murdered his Wife.*

14. *A Succinct Narrative of the Life and Character of Abel Clemmens,* quoted in Cohen, "Homicidal Compulsion," pp. 732–36. As Cohen records in a footnote, neither the original Morgantown edition, nor its reprint, *Cruel Murder!! A True Account of the Life and Character of Abel Clemmens* is available on the microcard edition of *Early American Imprints.* The only known copy of *Cruel Murder!!* is at the American Antiquarian Society in Worcester, Massachusetts.

15. *Horrid Massacre! Sketches of the Life of Captain James Purrinton,* p. 8.

16. *The Life and Confession of Isaac Heller, Alias Isaac Young.*

17. For an accurate and detailed summary of each of these histories, see Cohen, "Homicidal Compulsion."

18. Halttunen, *Murder Most Foul,* especially chap. 5.

19. Stephen Mitchell, *Narrative of the Life of William Beadle,* p. 14.

20. Cohen, "Homicidal Compulsion," p. 753.

21. The phrase is Berthoff's: "Independence and Attachment," p. 103.

22. Cohen makes a similar claim when he offers that "the very intensity of the new affective ties between the men and their wives and children may have helped to transform simple suicides into mass murder" ("Homicidal Compulsion" 748).

23. Juliet Mitchell, *Women's Estate,* p. 154.

24. Sedgwick's summary of Mitchell's argument. See *Between Men,* p. 14.

25. Edwards, "Sinners in the Hands of an Angry God," 561–562. Benjamin Trumbull reports that during Edwards's sermon, "there was such a breathing of distress, and weeping, that the preacher was obliged to speak to the people and desire silence, that he might be heard," p. 145.

26. Marsh, *The Great Sin,* p. 6.

27. Beadle suffered doubts about whether he had the right to kill his wife, since he "had no hand in bringing her into existence and consequently had no power over her life." Stephen Mitchell, *Narrative of the Life of William Beadle,* p. 13.

28. Marsh, *The Great Sin,* p. 21.

29. Ibid., pp. 6, 16, 5.

30. Ibid., p. 19.

31. Axelrod, *Charles Brockden Brown: An American Tale,* pp. 61, 57.

32. Stern, *The Plight of Feeling,* p. 31.

33. Tompkins, *Sensational Designs,* p. 44.

34. Axelrod, *Charles Brockden Brown,* p. 63; Tompkins, p. 53.

35. Brown, *Wieland,* p. 5. All citations will hereafter appear in parentheses following quotations.

36. Nelson, *National Manhood,* p. 37. See also Ditz, "Shipwrecked; or, Masculinity Imperiled."

37. Ditz, p. 58.

38. Axelrod, *Charles Brockden Brown,* p. 57.

39. Leslie Fiedler reads the incest motif as an integral part of the Gothic genre, a genre born of a revolutionary age preoccupied with its oedipal sins. Brother-sister incest displaces the son's desire for the mother, theorizes Fiedler, but it produces the same guilt, "the guilt of the revolutionary haunted by the (paternal) past which [the son] has been striving to destroy" (129). More recently, Shirley Samuels has read the incest plot as corroboration that threats to the virtue of the republic actually come from within the new nation rather than from forces external to it: "Published while the fear of contagion by the alien was at its height, the novel both blames Carwin for introducing sexuality, disorder, and violence into the Wieland family, and explains that introduction as nothing more than an enhancement of sexual and familial tensions already present" (49). Stern concurs, adding that "un-

der the incestuous pressures of the inverted world of Wieland, a future based on identity proves impossible" (*The Plight of Sympathy* 247n.).

40. Davis, *Homicide in American Fiction*, p. 90.

41. Grabo, *The Coincidental Art of Charles Brockden Brown*, p. 27.

42. Sedgwick, *The Coherence of Gothic Conventions*, p. 142.

43. Luciano, "Perverse Nature," p. 17.

44. This gesture is akin to John Marsh's in *The Great Sin and Danger of Striving with GOD*, where he interprets Beadle's familicide as the result of God's personal vengeance against him, never addressing the implications of his theory for Beadle's wife and children, who, though also dead, seemed to have escaped God's notice. One could argue that, even in their crimes, men remain in the privileged position of attention.

45. Fiedler, *Love and Death in the American Novel*, p. 134.

3

"The Manliest Relations to Men"

Thoreau on Privacy, Intimacy, and Writing

MILETTE SHAMIR

> You are the fact in a fiction. . . . This is what I would like,—to be as intimate with you as our spirits are intimate,—respecting you as I respect my ideal. Never to profane one another by word or action, even by a thought. Between us, if necessary, let there be no acquaintance.
>
> —Henry D. Thoreau, *A Week on the Concord and Merrimack Rivers*

> Some thirty inches from my nose
> The frontier of my Person goes.
> And all the untilled air between
> Is private pagus or demesne.
> Stranger, unless with bedroom eyes
> I beckon you to fraternize,
> Beware of rudely crossing it:
> I have no gun, but I can spit.
>
> —W. H. Auden, *About the House*

In the first epigraph to this essay the speaker yearns for intimacy unprofaned by physical violation; in the second the speaker yearns for privacy violated only by physical intimacy. Privacy and intimacy: these two concepts are central to the analysis of manhood and emotion. But what is the relationship between the two? Are these concepts interdependent, the one constituting a prerequisite for the other, or are they in conflict, even mutually threatening? To the extent that intimacy is understood in terms of the emotional exchange of affairs of the self, privacy has often been imagined as its savings account, as the reservoir where personal information is accumulated to be expended in intimate relations. As Charles Fried imagines it, "privacy creates the moral capital which we spend in friendship and love."[2] But even by the same logic intimacy can be seen as privacy's violation and depletion. Richard Sennett, for instance, while sharing Fried's liberal view of the self as constituted first in privacy and only then in relation to the other, has argued that the "market exchange of confession," an attribute of modernity's "tyranny of intimacy," erodes the personal boundaries upon which both privacy and public life rely. Originating with the Victorian ideology of the separate spheres, the modern stress on pouring out feelings, desires, experiences, robs the self of its privacy and hence also of meaningful sociability.[3]

The ideology of the separate spheres grappled with the ambivalences of privacy and intimacy in a characteristic way: through gendering. For the antebellum, white, Northern U.S. middle class, intimacy was figured by the "true woman" and her "natural" capacity for emotional expressivity and self-denial. The "cult of true womanhood" not only placed women in charge of the domestic sphere and its intimate relations but also encouraged them to cultivate a world of intimate bonds with each other through confessional exchanges and outpourings of sentiment. Thus, while symbolizing the private, middle-class womanhood was construed in contradistinction to privacy: ideally, the "true woman" thrived in intimate society, kept little or nothing from her family and confidantes, and was never alone.[4]

Meanwhile, the same market realities that "feminized" the middle-class home bolstered an affianced but opposite masculine ideal of stringent individualism and aggressive competitiveness. As scholars (including Evan Carton in this volume) have shown, this ideal highlighted an ethos of privacy, bounded self-containment, affective restraint and reticence, at the expense of emotional expressivity and intimacy. Notably, antebellum manhood was associated with a public sphere that allowed for little or no intimacy between men: since middle-class ideology carefully channeled affection into heterosexual courtship, marriage, and the family, and by opposition to the (now described as "heartless") masculine world of competitive work, laissez-faire economy, and hard-core politics, any sentiment between men became a prima facie violation of boundaries, a leaking of affection out of its designated sphere. As Nathaniel Hawthorne put it, "between man and man, there is always an insuperable gulf. They can never quite grasp each other's hands; and therefore man never derives any intimate help . . . from his brother man, but from woman—his mother, his sister, or his wife."[5] Masculine intimacy threatened the "insuperably engulfed" man with erosion of boundaries and de-individualization; it was perceived—and disavowed—as feminizing, infantilizing, and sexually transgressive. Social historians have shown that becoming a man in antebellum America meant shedding the male intimacies of childhood and early adolescence and replacing them with the more distant, ritualized, and rigidly hierarchical relations of the place of business, the club, or the political party. The competitive regime of such masculine spaces triggered anxiety about intimate friendship between men and, indeed, had homophobia built into it.[6] Moreover, as Christopher Newfield has recently argued, other, more open kinds of public spaces—streets, urban crowds—likewise provoked fears of erasure of boundaries and loss of self-differentiation, closely linked to anxieties over sodomy. It is hardly surprising, then, that writers of conduct manuals lured their middle-class readers away from spaces of potential male intimacy—barrooms, lodges, streets—and carefully directed their steps from the daytime workplace to an evening of marital and familial bliss.[7]

This gendered separation of intimacy and privacy was both thematized in and performed by the dominant fictional forms of the antebellum period. The form most often associated with "true womanhood," the sentimental/domestic novel, evolved from nonfictional and confessional modes such as journals, diaries, and personal letters, and, like them, was designed to be read aloud, in intimate social or familial settings. Mimicking a conversational tone of voice, and based on sharing anecdotes from personal life, the sentimental novel found its natural habitat in the middle-class parlor, where an assemblage of family and friends, engaged in activities such as sewing, conversing, or learning and presided over by the figure of the domestic woman, was united by the experience of shared reading. This "parlor literature," as one critic termed it, relied upon a sense of proximity between writer and reader and, like the domestic woman on whom it so often centered, saw it as its purpose to advance emotionally laden intersubjective bonds.[8]

A very different mode of writing and reading was cultivated across the hall from the parlor, in the study of the bourgeois paterfamilias. While the parlor constituted a space of sociability and intimacy, the governing principles of the study were privacy and seclusion, marking the limit of woman's reign of the home. As masculine sanctum sanctorum, the study encouraged individualized self-fashioning through solitary reading and writing. Ralph W. Emerson wrote that it was "a matter of vital importance to all book reading and book writing men, to be at night the autocrat of a chamber be it ever so small . . . wherein to dream, write, & declaim alone," and declared that he "shun[s] father and mother and wife and brother when [his] genius calls [him]" there.[9] Like Fried, Emerson regarded privacy as essential for the production of that "moral capital" which can then be exchanged with others. But his words reveal that even as privacy was regarded as essential and primary to the (masculine) self, as preceding intimacy, it was in fact achieved by the (often immoral) shunning of intimacies that precede *it*. The space of the study was carved out by the rejection of the emotional world of the parlor.

And if the parlor constituted the ideal setting for the sentimental/domestic novel, the study was linked to masculine romantic literature, perhaps most explicitly in Hawthorne's prefaces to his tales and romances, where it is described as a masculine enclave, freed from the strains of social intimacies and familial chores and thus serving as the ideal setting for the production and consumption of romance. Whereas the sentimental novel relied on conventions of intimacy between reader and writer, romantic literature helped produce the antebellum masculine ethos of boundedness, individualization, and reticence by developing an aesthetic code of elusive symbolism, ambiguity, and multiplicity of interpretations. Whereas the former capitalized on the sharing of personal life, the latter strove, in Hawthorne's famous phrase, "to keep the inmost Me behind its veil," to foster a desire for privacy, social invisibility, and withdrawal and to mark a clear boundary between the writer and his public.[10]

In its emphasis on boundedness and privacy, then, American romanticism has been read as a melodrama wherein the hero/romancer flees the coercive intimacies and intrusive sentiments of the domestic woman/novelist.[11] And perhaps no writer is more closely associated with that melodrama than Henry David Thoreau. Thoreau, who fled "civilization" to explore the wilderness, who chose pond over mother and sister, who loved a "broad margin to life," and wrote silently and reservedly, is often seen as a particularly distilled prototype of the masculine cult of privacy and rejection of intimacy. It was he, after all, who penned such lines as: "Pathless the gulf of feeling yawns— / No trivial bridge of words / Or arch of boldest span, / Can leap the moat that girds / The sincere man" (*Week* 235), lines that portray the "sincere man" as an impenetrable bulwark, surrounded by an emotional gap, one unbridgeable by "trivial" words or deeds.

But, precisely because of his representative status, I wish to reread Thoreau in order to interrogate some of the assumptions we make about manhood, emotion, intimacy, and privacy. Does bounded, privatist manhood always signal a decisive break from intimacy? Must male intimacy always connote the dangers of invasion, de-individualization and loss of self? In the lines above, for instance, do we have to read Thoreau as *celebrating* unfeeling manhood or could he be expressing a *yearning* for an emotional bond, albeit such that would not compromise "sincerity"? The metaphor of the "pathless gulf of feeling," after all, could signal the typically romantic desire to explore an uncharted terrain, particularly as it is embedded in *A Week on the Concord and Merrimack Rivers,* a narrative devoted to the art of navigating the pathless wilderness. In *A Week*—which recounts Thoreau's travels with a beloved brother—and particularly in its "Wednesday" chapter, Thoreau repeatedly expresses a desire for intimacy with other men of his class and race and actively seeks a path of emotional connectedness that will bypass the strictures imposed on bounded manhood, the pitfalls of femininity, and the obstacles of homoeroticism. The escape to the wilderness, then, is not necessarily a flight from intimacy; as Thoreau states a few lines after the ones above: "There's nothing in the world I know / That can escape from love" (235).

In what follows I will first argue that throughout his writing Thoreau busily imagines and articulates what he calls in *Walden* "the manliest relations to man," a consistent logic of manly intimate relations. In making that argument, I will not be suggesting, as some critics have, that Thoreau is at times "feminized," nor that he posits a "queer" alternative to the "grand narrative of connubiality" of his (and our) time. Such arguments sometimes seem to be not only decontextualized but also needlessly reproductive of Victorian gender and sexuality binarisms.[12] I argue that Thoreau, as well as other antebellum romantic writers, while tacitly accepting (by escaping from it) the hegemonic, confessional, "feminine" definition of intimacy of the separate spheres ideology, simultaneously creates, from *within* that ideology and its prescriptions, an alternative, contesting logic of intimacy, thus complicating the familiar binary of womanhood\intimacy vs. manhood\boundedness. Thoreau's logic, I will claim, is based on physical distance rather than proximity, on concealment rather than revelation, on silence rather than speech. It may be termed, following Candace Vogler, "depersonalizing intimacy." Perhaps the fact that this logic has been largely ignored is testimony to our own culture's at times monolithic understanding of intimacy as capital exchange of affairs of the self. But, as Vogler claims, "not all intimacies are affairs of the self and . . . the fact that some intimacies are *not* affairs of the self is what makes people want them."[13]

The second part of my argument will be that Thoreau's writing does not merely contain but stylistically performs this logic of intimacy, fixing the relationship between (male) writer and (male) reader as an ideal. The intimate merger between writer and reader is for him not predicated on the kind of transgressive and bodily identification highlighted in the sentimental/domestic novel, but on the obfuscation of personal experience and the production of an unmediated space, at once transsubjective and intensely private, at once masculine and beyond gender, sexuality, and the body. Thus, while writing versions of the liberal self as constituted first in privacy and only then in intimacy, Thoreau nonetheless finds potential for intersubjective affect at the core of the private, masculine self.

Thoreau's most famous melodrama of beset manhood is, of course, *Walden*. But readers sometimes overlook the fact that what impels this melodrama is rejection of public men rather than of domestic women. Concord appears to Thoreau as a "great news room" where men examine each other "with their bodies inclined forward and their eyes glancing along the line this way and that . . . with voluptuous expression," and it is from the "dangers" of such open proximities that he "escaped wonderfully."[14] "What do we want most to dwell near to?" he asks; "Not to many men surely, the depot, the post-office, the barroom, the meeting-house, the school-house, the grocery, Beacon Hill, or the Five Points, where men most congregate" (428). As "the value of a man is not in his skin, that we should touch him" (431), manly life is defined negatively, via distance from the spaces of "many men." Thoreau's individualism qua privacy is based upon a foreclosure of physical male proximity, understood as violation and forced exposure. This foreclosure lies at the core of American Transcendentalism: recall Emerson's famous dictum that "Union is only perfect when all the uniters are absolutely isolated. Each man being the Universe, if he attempts to join himself to others, he instantly is jolted, crowded, cramped, halved, quartered, or on all sides diminished of his proportion."[15] Union between men must rely on their isolation from each other, since proximity threatens with collision, or the loss of whole, self-contained manhood; any sign of intimacy between men is thus, counterintuitively, destructive to the creation of a community of men. Emerson's embodiment of ideal manhood, that "autocrat of the study" who shuns the company of others in order to read and write alone, serves, curiously, as the basis for masculine union. Echoing Emerson's "jostling, crowding, cramping, halving, and quartering" of manhood in association, Thoreau warns in *Walden* that "we live thick and are in each other's way, and stumble over one another" (428) and re-moves himself to the quintessential private study, a cabin a mile away from any other man.

But Thoreau begins exploring the problems of masculine intimacy much earlier in his writing career. In a lesser-known essay entitled "The Landlord," he imagines a homosocial utopia in the space of the tavern, the public an-tithesis of the private Walden Cabin. That this "public house," "where espe-cially men congregate"[16] is a haven of fraternal love and intimacy is due to the figure that presides over it: the landlord or "publican." The landlord is the closest approximation to the "perfect man," since he abandons private inter-est for the sake of an all-inclusive masculine friendship. Because he is "gen-eral," "open," of "universal sympathies" and "general sympathies," "public and inviting," "open and public," "wide," "broad" (188–90), he stands for the possibility of a masculine bond at once inclusive and democratic: "while na-tions and individuals are alike selfish and exclusive, he loves all men equally, and if he treats his nearest neighbor as a stranger . . . the farthest traveler is to some measure kindred to him" (189).

The problem is that the intimacies of the tavern render individual differ-ence fungible. In the world of the publican, where the distinction between kin, neighbor, and stranger is erased, the "tender but narrow ties of private friendship" are sacrificed "to a broad, sunshiny, fair-weather-and-foul friend-ship for his race" (188). What the landlord loves, then, is mankind, not indi-vidual men. Indeed, as the essay progresses, the landlord becomes more of a comic, or even monstrous, caricature, than a viable ideal. Unable to see the other as particular, he is likewise unable to maintain a differentiated self: "His sentiments on all subjects will be delivered as freely as the wind blows; there is nothing private or individual in them . . . but they are public" (192). Unlike the "man of genius," who "says, by all possible hints and signs, I wish to be alone,—good-by,—farewell," the Landlord "can afford to live without pri-vacy. He entertains no private thought" (193). The publican is, in fact, "ab-stractly offensive" (192). In his open and unbounded exhibitionism, both his house and his body cease to function as barriers. All his secrets are "exhibited to the eyes of men, above and below, before and behind," and while "there can be no *pro*fanity where there is no fane behind," one senses that Thoreau is somewhat disturbed by the fact that "the whole world may see quite round him" (193). And if his behind is exposed, so are his insides: "when he eats, he is liver and bowels and the whole digestive apparatus to the company, and so all admit the thing is done" (192). The imagery shifts from democratic equality to mastery: whosoever "steps across the threshold" of the tavern (imagined as a huge body with "heart," "left ventricle," and "vital part") becomes its "master" (190–91). What initially seemed a paradise of intimate fraternalism turns out to be a problematic vision of servitude and loss of privacy to the dissolution of both self and other.

The view that intimacy with the male—rather than female—other is the principle threat to the masculine self of course predates and exceeds American romanticism and can be traced back at least to the appearance of autonomy and privacy as preconditions to selfhood in the founding texts of Liberalism. What its early annals reveal, in Seyla Benhabib's lucid summary, is "the fear of being engulfed by the [male] other" or the "brother," "the anxiety that the other is always on the look to interfere in your space and appropriate what is yours." This anxiety makes imperative the construction of the "disembedded and disembodied" generalized other, the view of the other solely on the basis of the nonconcrete and universal. Such a view allows the individual to relate to other individuals without interfering with their privacy or risking interference with his own. The invention of the generalized other relies, therefore, on the suppression and concealment of private differences, an "epistemological blindness" to the particulars of private affairs of the self, now deliberately hidden behind a "veil of ignorance" (recall Hawthorne's "so far as I am a man of really individual attributes, I veil my face"). The veiled, generalized other is what allows for the existence of a public despite liberal individualism's emphasis on privacy, by allowing men to relate to each other from an epistemological distance that obscures vision into embodied and private existences. Moreover, the disembodiment of the generalized other, while masculine in its motivation, tends to marginalize gender differentiation (as even the androgynous metaphor of the veil suggests), and hence relaxes the rigid codes that forbid masculine proximity.[17]

In light of this description, Thoreau's "abstractly offensive" landlord makes sense: as the principle of public fraternity, the landlord cultivates the universal but fails to patrol his own boundaries, resulting in deterritorialization and (literal) disembodiment. The "publican" has generalized himself out of existence. For Benhabib and other feminist theorists, such fantasies reveal the inadequacies of the liberal model, its inability to comaintain private self and human connectedness. Benhabib thus suggests an alternative, "feminine" mode of relations, one that highlights the empathic knowledge of the concrete facts of the other's private life—the removal of the veil of ignorance—as its basis. If we refuse to generalize the other, but view her/him instead as a "coherent narrative" or as "the protagonist of a life's tale," human bonds could depend on the reciprocal reading and mutual sharing of stories of the concrete, embodied self.[18] Benhabib thus recalls the conception of privacy with which we have begun, as a reservoir of affairs of self, there only to be consumed in intimate relations. She also recalls the separate spheres ideology from which this definition evolved: it is once again in the hands of women—who are putatively uniquely endowed with the capacity to feel for and know the other—that the role of maintaining intimacy is placed. But she wishes to expand that model, from parlor to public as it were, believing that the sharing of affairs of self could guarantee the coexistence of equality, difference, and an ethics of care. For Thoreau, however, nothing could be further from the truth. The model whereby the self is constantly emplotted in "coherent narratives" and "life tales" and exhibited to others results, in his view, in the demise of intimacy, in the eradication of difference, and in potential tyranny.

The verb "to intimate," to which "intimacy" is etymologically linked, connotes two seemingly conflicting actions: "to make known," to "notify," "to communicate openly," in its older use, "to signify indirectly," "imply," "hint at," in its more current; a lavish impulse to publicize on the one hand, a frugal sparseness of signs on the other.[19] This duality is interlaced in Thoreau's meditations on intimacy in "Wednesday." Close to the chapter's middle, Thoreau tells of his relationship with a woman who embodies the "feminine" or self-exposure principle of intimacy: "I know a woman who possesses a restless and intelligent mind," he writes, "Yet our acquaintance plainly does not attain to that degree of confidence and sentiment which women, which all, in fact, covet" (227). Women like her, he explains, expect acts of mutual confiding to which he refuses to yield, opting for a different, more impersonal mode of exchange. He explains that he "feel[s] as if [he] appeared careless, indifferent, and without principle to her," because she fails to recognize that his model of *"true though incomplete intercourse"* is "infinitely better than a more unreserved but falsely grounded one, without the principle of growth in it" (227, emphasis added). Intimacy based on an unreserved revelation of the private is falsely grounded, partially because it is destined to a short life span: once the parties to the exchange deplete their reservoir of personal stories intimacy exhausts itself. Moreover, while his "true though incomplete" mode of intimacy makes "equal demand" on both parties, the confessional mode connotes a surrendering of self to other. "We often forbear to confess our feelings, not from pride, but for fear that we could not continue to love the one who required us to give such proof of our affection" (226–27): the one who demands confession, according to Thoreau, exercises undue power.

The shorthand term that Thoreau habitually uses to describe this "unreserved" type of intimacy is "sympathy." In his journal he describes sympathy as a "loosening" of emotional "gates," as begetting "a certain softness to which [he is] otherwise and commonly a stranger."[20] Sympathy is the "loose," "softening," "diseased" emotion that characterizes, for instance, social reformers, who loosen the gates of privacy in the name of doing good. "If I knew for a certainty that a man was coming to my house with the conscious design of doing me good," Thoreau writes, "I should run for my life, . . . for fear that I should get some of his good done to me, some of its virus mingled with my blood." Such sympathy is "dyspepsia": it comes not from the head or heart, but from the "bowels"—"for that is the seat of sympathy" (*Walden* 381–83). As Donald Yacovone has shown, antebellum reform societies rebelled against contemporaneous definitions of bounded manhood by emphasizing close male bonding, Christian androgyny, and interpersonal merger ("You are mine and I am yours. God made us one from the beginning," is an example of their rhetoric).[21] For Thoreau, interventions into his private space, however benevolent, are analogous to (passive) molestation: reformers "would not keep their distance," he complains, "but cuddle up and lie spoon-fashion with you, no matter how hot the weather nor how narrow the bed. . . . It was difficult to keep clear of [the reformer's] slimy benignity, with which he sought to cover you before he swallowed you and took you fairly into his bowels" (*Journal* 5:264–65). Michael Warner has brilliantly analyzed such passages in terms of Thoreau's simultaneous strict abhorrence of and luxurious pleasure in erotic anality, an instance of his ability to forcefully bring forth the tension inherent to liberal capitalism between ascesis and waste, self-integration and self-dissolution. I wish to stress the degree to which self-integration, imagining the self in terms of a coherent bounded space, is inherent to the discourse on middle-class masculinity. Where masculinity is defined as bounded, sympathy, as erosion of boundaries, triggers fantasies of bodily consumption and subsumption that resonate with unfulfillable desire, with gender anxiety, and with sexual panic.[22]

Thoreau's "true though incomplete" intimacy, by contrast, "consists with a certain disregard for men and their erections, the Christian duties and humanities, while it purifies the air like electricity" (*Week* 224). How is such antiseptic intimacy to be construed? Consider a poem Thoreau wrote in 1839 (apparently for his eleven-year-old star student, Edmund Sewall[23]). The poem was first entitled "Sympathy" but later reproduced in *A Week* without the title (perhaps because "sympathy" has by then acquired its dyspeptic connotations for Thoreau). It begins by describing "a gentle boy," whom "virtue," figured (despite its etymological roots) as a woman, "manned . . . for her own strong-hold" and who "On every side . . . open was as day" (211–12). This is a portrait of childhood: the boy is enfolded by virtue's "strong-hold" as a child by his doting mother and has not yet developed the "walls and ports" of adult manhood. But, though passive, the gentle boy is by no means weak: he is so appealing, in fact, that his power of attraction is unlimited; as "Caesar was victorious," so "this youth was glorious . . . No strength went out to get him victory / when all was income of its own accord." Not even the speaker can resist this imperial, alluring force, and is "taken unawares by this," as "each moment . . . we nearer drew to each." But, like the Emersonian collision of universes, this intimacy produces unhappy results: "I might have loved him had I loved him less," the speaker says, "We two were one while we did sympathize, / So could we not the simplest bargain drive." The merger of two into one, the too thorough knowledge of each other brought about by the boy's magnetic openness, demolishes intimacy because it prevents what Thoreau metaphorizes as "driving the simplest bargain," the distance required for equal commerce.[24] Indeed, as the speaker is sucked into the gentle boy's realm (not unlike being swallowed by the reformer), the two seem "less acquainted than when first we met" (212). Soon the poem drifts into an elegiac mode: the boy is "irrevocably gone," ringing "knell of departure," and the speaker is left to "celebrate [his] tragedy" by singing this "elegy" (213), hinting that the boy is dead (young Sewall simply left Thoreau's school). The poem can be read, then, as a lament over the impossibility of male intimacy, which momentarily surfaces in childhood but cannot survive beyond.

And yet the poem does not end there. Two more stanzas are added:

Is't then too late the damage to repair?
Distance, forsooth, from my weak grasp hath reft
The empty husk, and clutched the useless tare,
But in my hands the wheat and kernel left.

If I but love that virtue which he is,
Though it be scented in the morning air,
Still shall we be truest acquaintances,
Nor mortals know a sympathy more rare. (213)

These lines suggest why the gentle boy's tragic absence may indeed be celebrated, and what "true though incomplete" intimacy could mean. It is plau-
sible that the boy did not die after all, but simply grew up: no longer in
infantile "virtue's strong-hold," he now holds virtue *within* him, as his
"wheat" or "kernel"; no longer "open as the day," but walled-off and distant,
he can now engage in mutual, equal commerce with the speaker. (A friend,
Thoreau writes in the next pages, is he "we give the best to, and receive the
best from"; friendship is "the state of the just dealing with the just, the magnanimous with the magnanimous, the sincere with the sincere, man with
man" [218, 217].) What friends exchange is not the concrete affairs of the embodied self—the "empty husk" or "useless tare"—but a universal, transsubjective, metaphysical "kernel" that is imagined to constitute the self's innermost,
essential core. This kernel, because abstract and universal, resists the codes of
restrained masculinity (recall that "virtue" is feminine) and seems to tend
toward gender neutrality. Physical separation, disembodiment, platonic abstraction are thus the conditions upon which "truest acquaintance" can be
constructed. As Thoreau says to an imaginary friend: "I love thee not as
something private and personal which is *your own,* but as something universal
and worthy of love, *which I have found*" (219, emphasis in original).

The "gentle boy" poem thus falls under the rubric of what Dana Nelson
recently called the "melancholy of white manhood." Nelson points to the fact
that, at least in the nineteenth century, "white men seem able to achieve the
equalitarian reassurance of unmediated brotherhood only with dead or imagined men." The distancing and generalizing impulses of white brotherhood,
she argues, while appearing to promote democracy, instead "entail[] a series of
affective foreclosures that block those men's more heterogeneous democratic
identifications and energies."[25] As I hope is by now clear, Thoreau's logic of
intimacy is no exception. He seems only interested in intimacy with "the
brother" of his own color and class, and his understanding of fraternal bonds
is predicated upon the disavowal of femininity and homoeroticism, both seen
as threats to masculine privacy.

I am wondering, though, whether by dismissing this logic on the basis of
its "affective foreclosures" we do not thereby foreclose our own reading of the
text and its potentialities. Take, for example, the way Thoreau binds his logic
of intimacy together with an implicit critique of expansionism. In an extended and well-worn metaphor of bounded manhood that runs throughout
"Wednesday," Thoreau imagines the self as "some fair floating isle of palm"
containing "richer freights . . . than Africa or Malabar." But although

"Prince and monarchs will contend" who will first "call [this] distant soil their own," this territory of the self forever eludes the violence of the conquering other: "Columbus has sailed westward of these isles . . . but neither he nor his successors have found them" (214): as in the "gentle boy" poem, the distance that thwarts imperial ambition is metonymically that which safeguards male intimacy. Nowhere is this metonymy more fully instantiated than in the story of the friendship between the Indian Wawatam and Henry the fur trader, "Wednesday's" most elaborate example of male intimacy. Adapted from William Henry's *Travels and Adventures in Canada and the Indian Territories,* the story opens with the "imperturbable" Wawatam, who "after fasting, solitude, and mortification of body, comes to the white man's lodge and affirms that he is the white brother whom he saw in his dream." The two become great friends, "and they hunt and feast and make maple-sugar together." Moreover, "If Wawatam would taste the 'white man's milk' with his tribe, or take his bowl of human broth made of the trader's fellow countrymen, he first finds a place of safety for his Friend." Finally, "after a long winter of undisturbed and happy intercourse" the two must part. " 'We now exchanged farewells,' says Henry, 'with an emotion entirely reciprocal. . . . All the family accompanied me to the beach; and the canoe had no sooner put off than Wawatam commenced an address to the Kichi Manito, beseeching him to take care of me, his brother . . .' We never hear of him again" (223–24). Thoreau's version of the story, torn from its original context and embedded in a chapter of abstract thoughts on friendship, infuses his logic of intimacy with a fantasy of complete and affective equality between races. Once again, it is based on disembodiment: Wawatam's "fasting" and "mortification of body" precondition the friendship, not to mention his symbolic transformation into a "white brother" (problematically: whiteness signaling perhaps, as it so often does in American literature, racial neutrality and *dis*embodiment). That the two men are able to develop a bond "entirely reciprocal" depends upon an abstention from a cannibalistic appetite for bodily merger on behalf of the Indian (he would not taste this "white man's milk") and on restraint of the white man's appetite for colonization on the other (this white man leaves rather than settles). Unlike that of more famous nineteenth-century interracial male couples, this fantasy, disembedded from its original narrative context, manages to escape the narratives of conquest, empire, and slavery and cultivate instead a vision of complete equality based on disembodiment, respect for boundaries, and, ultimately, territorial isolationism.

All that aside, Thoreau's interest is indeed in friendship with his social and racial equal, and only metaphorically with men of color. Wawatam is there to illustrate the notion that intimate knowledge of the other can amount to subjugation whereas "incomplete intercourse" promotes equality.[26] This precisely counters the notion promoted by Benhabib that listening to the other's concrete, "coherent narratives" and "life tales" necessitates empathy, equality, and respect for difference. (It is enough to consider the contemporary culture of confessional talk shows to put that idea in question.) Indeed, Thoreau's logic of intimacy through distance prescribes a mistrust of *any* speech, since speech is the medium of physical proximity and of self-exposure. Speech is by definition antithetical to the principles of privatist masculinity: it is the "commonly transitory" and "almost brutish" language of the public sphere, the parlor, and the mother and does not withstand the test of man's private space; "what is commonly called eloquence in the forum is commonly found to be rhetoric in the study," Thoreau writes (*Walden* 404). Rather than serve as a masculine adhesive, speech endangers intimacy, because it tends to drift to the concrete facts of personal life rather than to the universal, to the "husk" rather than "kernel." "All words are gossip," Thoreau writes in his journal, "what has speech to do with [friendship]. When a man approaches his friend who is thus transfigured to him, even his own hoarse salutation sounds prosaic and ridiculous and makes him least happy in his presence. . . . There is friendship—but without confession—in silence as divine—" (2:380). Speech transfigures the other precisely by embedding him in a concrete narrative, by reducing him to "gossip." In "Wednesday" Thoreau explains: "persons, when they are made the subject of conversation, though with a Friend, are commonly the most prosaic and trivial of facts. The universe seems bankrupt as soon as we begin to discuss the character of individuals. Our discourse all runs to slander, and our limits grow narrower as we advance." Speech is by definition slanderous, because discussing persons empties them of universal truths and reduces them to a trivial and conventionalized prose. "I say," Thoreau concludes, "let us speak of mushrooms and forest trees rather" (211).

Mushrooms and trees: tolerable speech between men displaces the personal and unites the speakers in an impersonal, exterior, third subject such as nature. This displacement of speech from the personal to the neutral was recently described by Julie Ellison as an important aspect of the relationship between antebellum middle-class men. Emerson, for example, to protect what he called the "metaphysical isolation" of the individual man, supported a taboo on personal remarks, and encouraged conversation on topics such as "culture." Indeed, Ellison argues, "culture was required so that people may talk about things other than themselves."[27] For Thoreau, nature was the topic of choice capable of sustaining intimacy through speech. But even such impersonal conversation, we learn in *Walden,* is still framed by too close a physical proximity between men: "One inconvenience I sometimes experienced in so small a house," he writes, was

> the difficulty of getting to a sufficient distance from my guest when we began to utter the big thoughts in big words. . . . Individuals, like nations, must have suitable broad and natural boundaries, even a considerable neutral ground, between them. I have found it a singular luxury to talk across the pond to a companion on the opposite side. . . . If we speak reservedly and thoughtfully, we want to be farther apart, that all animal heat and moisture may have a chance to evaporate. If we would enjoy the most intimate society with that in each of us which is without, or above, being spoken to, we must not only be silent, but commonly so far apart bodily that we cannot possibly hear each other's voice in any case. . . . As the conversation began to assume a loftier and grander tone, we gradually moved our chairs farther apart till they touched the wall in opposite corners, and then commonly there was not room enough. (434–35)

"Intimate society," then, is predicated not only on speaking "reservedly" on "big thoughts" and "loftier" subjects; it could only be freed from the threat of the contaminating bodily proximity, from "animal heat and moisture," if it is protected by physical distance. And more: paradoxically, intimate conversation is only possible through silence, as real speech between friends is about that which is "above being spoken to."

Indeed, if speech is "mother's tongue," silence for Thoreau is a constitutive of manhood. "It takes a man to make a room silent," he writes (*Journal* 2:67), and again: "For where man is there is silence, and it takes a man to make any place silent" (2:112). Sentiment between men is best expressed through the withholding of any speech altogether: "silence is the ambrosial night in the intercourse of Friends," Thoreau explains in "Wednesday," "in which their sincerity is recruited and takes deeper root" (221). If speech tends to always violate boundaries by exposing and trivializing the personal and by demanding closeness, silence allows men to bond without the threat of merger. Friends, Thoreau explains, "will be most familiar, they will be most unfamiliar, for they will be so one and single that common themes will not have to be bandied between them, but in silence they will digest them as one mind; but they will at the same time be two and double, that each will be to the other as admirable and as inaccessible as a star" (*Journal* 2:7). Silence, then, allows for sentiment without deforming mediation; it allows both familiarity and unfamiliarity, both oneness and doubleness, both metaphysical proximity and physical separation; it allows for consumption (for digesting the "common") without depletion of self. It is the medium, that is, of the intimate generalized other.

The only full dramatization in *Walden* of an encounter between two middle-class men of equal social position appears in "Brute Neighbors," where Thoreau dramatizes a meeting between the "Poet" and himself, the "hermit." This encounter is striking because it never really happens: it is both an evasion of an encounter and a hint of an encounter yet to happen. It begins with the hermit, rapt in private reverie, only to be interrupted by the arrival of the poet. The former tenderly asks him to "leave [him] alone, then, for a while," but his line of thought is irreparably damaged by the intrusion. When the poet returns, they leave the scene together to go fishing, and the rest of the scene happens in the realm of our own imagination. This scene, more a conjoining of two separate monologues than a dialogue, encapsulates Thoreau's ideal intimacy: always intrusive on one's privacy, approximated only to be immediately shunned, when it finally takes place, it takes place in silence, outside the boundaries of the text (501–2).

Thoreau's writing often centers, then, on the problem of generating sentiment between men despite a gender ideology that imagined the ideal man, in Clinton Rossiter's words, as "the private man, the man who keeps some of his thoughts and judgments entirely to himself, who feels no overriding compulsion to share everything of value with others, not even those he loves and trusts."[28] If mutual self-revelation according to Thoreau is not only unnecessary for intimacy but destructive to it, then his own "reserved" and "deliberate" writing style performs this idea as well as presents it. In that sense, I would argue, books such as *Walden* may be described as affective, or even "sentimental," despite a long critical tradition of drawing a thick borderline between "classic," romantic American literature and the sentimental novel. One need only consider the deep affections triggered by *Walden* in enthusiastic Thoreauvians from F. O. Blake to Stanley Cavell to acknowledge that the book creates an intimate emotional tie with its (particularly male) readership that is perhaps no less powerful than that of, say, *Little Women* with generations of women readers. This not because it follows any of the conventions of the sentimental novel: on the contrary, Thoreau poses his writing in contradistinction to this genre. The sentimental novel conforms to a specific understanding of sentiment that we have seen Thoreau refer to as "sympathy," the kind of identification that blurs the boundaries between public and private, highlights bodily-ness, consumption, and physical proximity, and aspires to arouse empathy by narrativizing human *sameness.* Conversely, the kind of "masculine" sentiment that Thoreau propagates and *Walden* exemplifies is such that forges a bond between men not through the cancellation but the concealment of private differences, through the displacement of affairs of the self, through *intimation.* The "reservedness" with which Thoreau says he wrote the book and urges us to read it is the aesthetic equivalent of what I have described as Thoreau's depersonalizing intimacy. The relationship between the male writer and the male reader, each ensconced in his solitary study, epitomizes that mode of intimacy.

Cavell's reading of Thoreau in *The Senses of Walden* provides a good example. Cavell acknowledges the feeling shared by *Walden*'s readers that Thoreau has withdrawn "from the words on which he had staked his presence," the feeling of his "words' indifference to us, their disinterest in whether we choose to stay with them or not." He attributes this sense to the fact that "every new clarity makes the writer's existence obscurer to us" and to "his willingness to remain obscure." Cavell describes the experience of reading *Walden* as an "almost unbearable sense of his isolation" since "we find ourselves, perhaps, alone with a book in our hands, words on a page, at a distance." But this feeling is overcome—or, rather, accepted—once we realize that in the world of Thoreau "what is most intimate is what is furthest away" and that separateness is the very condition of kinship, an idea that Cavell is able to embrace. His sentiments toward Thoreau grow not in spite of this obfuscation of the personal but *because* of it, since this obfuscation points to the text's "sincerity," defined as "the capacity to live in one's own separateness, to sail the Atlantic and Pacific Ocean of one's being alone." Only in isolationist writing, in that sense, one can be sincere.[29]

We have seen that Thoreau mistrusts speech (and regards it as feminine and maternal) because, immediate and transitory, it always risks exposing on the personal and slipping into "slander" and "gossip." Writing, on the other hand, is "our father tongue, a reserved and select expression" (*Walden* 403).

Writing—indeed, "silent" speech—is paternal and masculine because of the writer's control over its contents, his ability to check and edit himself rather than be swayed by the personal contingencies of the moment. These qualities allow writing and reading to bring men closer together. Writing "speaks to the intellect and heart of mankind" and is "at once more intimate with us and more universal than any other work of art" (*Walden* 404), Thoreau claims, because, through reservedness and self-control, it can be at once universal and personal, at once general and intimate.

But not all writing, of course. Thoreau warns against the way sentimental novels contaminate the private by invading, publicizing, and conventionalizing it, the way "the happy novelist rings the bell for all the world to come together and hear" (406). Men read novels out of a sickened intrusiveness, not for genuine "universal intimacy." Like the men in Concord's street who gaze at Thoreau with "voluptuous" expression, they read "with saucer eyes, and erect primitive curiosity, and with unwearied gizzard," not to form a bond between "the heart and intellect of mankind" but for bodily pleasure (407). In a language similar to that used by contemporaneous conduct manuals to describe the effects of masturbation on youth, Thoreau describes the result of reading novels as the "dulness of sight, a stagnation of the vital circulations, and a general deliquium and sloughing off of all the intellectual faculties" (407). Like the intrusiveness of social reformers, the conventions of sentimental fiction are based on false, sickly, bodily sympathy. "I laughed at myself the other day to think that I cried while reading a pathetic story," Thoreau writes in his journal; "I was no more affected in spirit than I frequently am, methinks. The tears were merely a phenomenon of bowels, and I felt that . . . I should be ashamed to have the subject of it understand" (4:176–77). The problem of sentimental fiction, like that of speech, is that by publicizing and narrativizing private life, it turns it into type, into a conventionalized story. It reifies the private into an artificial, typecast plot, denies idiosyncrasy, and thus turns both itself and its readers into affective "machines" (406). And the same is true of newspapers: "To a philosopher," Thoreau writes, "all news, as it is called, is gossip, and they who edit and read it are old women over their tea" (397). News, like novels and speech, is "effeminate" because it conventionalizes the private by mechanical repetition: "if we read of one man robbed, or murdered, or killed by accident, or one house burned, or one vessel wrecked, or one steamboat blown up . . . we never need read of another. One is enough. If you are acquainted with the principle, what do you care for a myriad instances and applications?" (397). "Reserved" writing and reading, conversely, are such that displace individual instances and applications, the particularized stuff of personal life, in favor of abstraction. Precisely because Thoreau's own essays and books reject the conventions and types of sentimentalism and news in favor of depersonalization they are capable of triggering the sentiments of the reader and striking a genuine emotional cord.

We might say, then, that Thoreau's economy of friendship and attendant aesthetic of intimation, or economy of words, mirror the kind of extramarket economy idealized by him in *Walden*. Intrusive, confessional intimacy is homologous to relations in the capitalist marketplace: using personal stories, rather than money, as its currency (recall Fried's definition of privacy as "moral capital"), it has the effect of enslaving and deessentializing the self and robbing it of its autonomy and privacy. The narrating of concrete stories is analogous to the consumption and reification of self in a capitalist economy. Depersonalizing intimacy, by contrast, reflects the self-reliance and unmediated relations of the Walden experiment. In "driving the simple bargains" of friendship, one does not rely on the mediation of speech and life stories as one's affective currency. Instead, silence or the sparest exchange creates a relatively unmediated economy of friendship that, like the alternative economy of *Walden*, preserves privacy, essence, and equality. Counterintuitively, then, writing is seen by Thoreau as a *less* mediated form of communication than speech: it is precisely its reservedness that enables direct and intimate identification.[30]

Walden, therefore, famously refrains from self-exposure and self-emplotting. As autobiographical works go, it relates surprisingly few facts about its subject's daily existence. Throughout the book Thoreau insists on describing his private "business" as his own, for himself only to mind, and he uses private incidents only to generalize on what he regards as universal truths. For *Walden* to be successful under Thoreau's terms, it must be like the cabin/study in which it was produced: defying clear visibility, protected by wide boundaries, and shielding its own interiority. For *Walden* to bond writer and readers, it must conceal as well as reveal or, through partial revealing, suggest that much remains concealed. In his journal (itself even less of a "life tale" and more of a series of generalized fragments than the books based upon it) he writes that "Men should hear of your virtue only as they hear the creaking of the earth's axle and the music of the spheres. It will fall into the course of nature and be effectually concealed by publicness" (1:263). The obscuring of the personal in *Walden,* its "concealment by publicness," is a mode of communication, not the end to communication.

This deliberate obfuscation of the private has informed Barbara Johnson's assertion that *Walden* "delights because it baffles." Johnson has argued that Thoreau's language is characterized by catachretic symbolism that deliberately obscures its own tenors. She cites as an example Thoreau's famous and poignant passage: "I long ago lost a hound, a bay horse, and a turtle dove, and am still on their trail. . . . I have met one or two who had heard the hound, and the tramp of the horse, and even seen the dove disappear behind a cloud, and they seemed as anxious to recover them as if they had lost them themselves" (336), to argue convincingly that any attempt to fill the symbolic "hound," "horse," and "dove" with concrete meanings destroys the passage's affective power. What is symbolized is loss itself, rather than anything specific for which it stands. The obscurity of the passage is thus its very purpose, as well as the key to our affective identification with it. The power of Thoreau's prose lies in its ability to "wake us up to our own lost losses, to make us participate in the transindividual movement of loss in its infinite particularity."[31]

This link between intimacy and intimation is not limited to Thoreau but is representative of American romanticism more generally. It finds an accurate articulation, for instance, in Melville's description of his experience reading Hawthorne's romances in "Hawthorne and his Mosses." To read Hawthorne, Melville writes, a reader would ideally be positioned, like his narrator, within "a papered chamber in a fine old farm-house—a mile from any other dwelling, and dipped to the eaves in foliage." Such Thoreauvian isolation is the kind of space that the narrator imagines Hawthorne himself to occupy, and, moreover, to *embody:* he describes the "enchanting landscape in [Hawthorne's] soul," bound by an "intervening hedge" that blocks this interior space from the view of the other.[32] That both writer and reader are thus fixed in private isolation and separated by distance is what allows Hawthorne to "seize" the reader in his "seclusion" (1154), whereas physical proximity and personal acquaintance would have prevented a bond between them. Books must be "foundlings," he claims; "on a personal interview no great author has ever come up to the idea of his reader. But that dust of which our bodies are composed, how can it fitly express the nobler intelligences among us?" (1154). Disembedded, disembodied, and separated in space, the writer penetrates the very depth of the reader's being: "I feel that this Hawthorne has dropped germinous seeds into my soul. He expands and deepens down, the more I contemplate him; and further, and further, shoots his strong New-England roots into the hot soil of my Southern soul" (1157). Replacing Thoreauvian kernels with Hawthornian seeds, Melville fantasizes of complete and eroticized intimacy between men, made possible only on condition that a map of isolated studies, intervening hedges, and nationwide distances has been formerly guaranteed. His erotic language would have perhaps repelled Thoreau, but the principle of intimacy through separation is nonetheless similar.

Perhaps no passage in *Walden* captures the contours of this masculine transsubjective merger better than that which appears in "Solitude":

> I only know myself as a human entity; the scene, so to speak, of thoughts and affections; and am sensible of a certain doubleness by which I can stand as remote from myself as from another. However intense my experience, I am conscious of the presence and criticism of a part of me, which, as it were, is not a part of me, but spectator, sharing no experience, but taking note of it; and that is no more I than it is you. When the play, it may be the tragedy, of life is over, the spectator goes his way. It was a kind of fiction, a work of the imagination only, so far as he was concerned. This doubleness may easily make us poor neighbors and friends sometimes. (429–30)

The lingering sense of what is here described as "doubleness" makes *Walden* such a precise articulation of romantic masculine intimacy. Thoreau imagines himself as leading a schizophrenic existence, simultaneously operating within the hermetically circumscribed theater of his personal life, the realm of his thoughts and affections, and outside it, where the contingencies of personal life appear a mere fiction—a "coherent narrative" or "life tale" in Benhabib's terms—not more important, in the final analysis, than the "husk," or a fleeting theater performance. A certain remoteness from this fiction is precisely what allows Thoreau to be a writer: to universalize the particular and thus make it meaningful to others across time and space. And although this "doubleness may easily make us poor neighbors and friends sometimes," because it denies the significance of the "concrete other," it nonetheless produces a transsubjective space where intimate bonds are forged, despite individual difference. The writerly part of Thoreau is no more "I" than it is "you": removed from the affairs and burdens of the particularized self, it allows, finally, for an intimate merger between man and men, between Thoreau and his readers. Within his romantic construction of bounded masculinity, then, lies a domain that is at once its core and external to it, at once private beyond concrete articulation and fully nonsubjective, a domain where privacy and intimacy are reconciled.

Acknowledgment

A version of this chapter was presented at an NEH seminar on "The Question of Privacy" at Dartmouth College. I would like to thank the participants for their comments, particularly Don Pease, Lou Renza, and Jeff Weintraub.

Notes

1. Thoreau, *A Week on the Concord and Merrimack Rivers,* p. 220 (subsequent references are given parenthetically); Auden, *About the House,* p. 4.

2. Fried, "Privacy [A Moral Analysis]," p. 211. See also Rachels, "Why Privacy is Important," pp. 290–99. Another good example of this rhetoric is provided by Krattenmaker, who sees intimacy as "mutual reciprocal relinquishments of the self." "Without a reserve of privacy," he writes, "we would have nothing to share and, hence, nothing to build upon in our human relationships" (quoted in Silver, " 'Two Different Sorts of Commerce', " p. 43).

3. Sennett, *The Fall of Public Man,* pp. 9–10 and passim. The liberal view of the self as constituted first in privacy, I suggest, is problematized by antebellum romantic writers, first because the act of staking private territory is shown to already involve the shunning of an intimacy that precedes it, mostly intimacy with women, and second because, as I hope to show, the bounded, private self is nonetheless imagined to include within it a space for merger and intimacy with the other.

4. For a discussion of "true womanhood" and intimacy see, for example, Cott, *The Bonds of Womanhood,* Smith-Rosenberg, *Disorderly Conduct,* and, more recently, Hansen, "Rediscovering the Social." Hansen complicates the equation of womanhood with privacy by describing the intricate social networks in which antebellum women were active.

5. Hawthorne, *Marble Faun,* p. 1089. Studies of the construction of unaffective manhood in antebellum American include Leverenz, *Manhood in the American Renaissance,* Herbert, *Dearest Beloved,* and Kimmel, *American Manhood.* Lystra describes heterosexual rituals of courtship as the only space for masculine expressivity in *Searching the Heart.*

6. Rotundo, *American Manhood,* pp. 75–91 and passim. Kimmel, "Masculinity as Homophobia."

7. Newfield, *The Emerson Effect,* pp. 91–109.

8. See, for example, Hedrick, *Harriet Beecher Stowe: A Life,* pp. viii, 76. Hedrick coined the term "parlor literature."

9. Emerson's quotes appear and are discussed in Paul, *The Shores of America,* p. 94 and in Cavell, "Being Odd, Getting Even: Threats to Individuality," p. 304, respectively.

10. Hawthorne, "The Custom House," p. 121. The previous three paragraphs are drawn from a longer discussion on the relationship between literary style and domestic space in antebellum fiction in Shamir, "Divided Plots."

11. See Baym, "Melodramas of Beset Manhood." American romanticism includes, of course, not only melodramas of boundedness but also romances of male bonding, typically between a white man and his racial other. As Wiegman proposes in "Fiedler and Sons," the romances of male bonding serve a specific purpose in American culture, that of casting both the racial other and the homosexual in the presymbolic, imaginary realm, thus serving the power structure of heterosexual white supremacy. I am here concerned with intimacy between white men of the same class, and hence of male bonding within, and despite, the laws of the symbolic.

12. Both the "feminized" and the "queer" Thoreau were born in the last decade or so, the first, for example, in Anderson, *The House Undivided,* p. 79; the second most successfully in Abelove, "From Thoreau to Queer Politics," from whom the phrase is borrowed; and Kaplan, *Democratic Citizenship and the Politics of Desire,* pp. 177–205. Both readings are, in my opinion, somewhat overdetermined, eager to place Thoreau either fully within or fully without heterosexual domesticity and antebellum bourgeois culture. Kaplan's otherwise fascinating reading of Thoreau, for instance, continuously insists on his "adversary stance toward prevalent systems of belief and personal position outside dominant social institutions" (195). My problem with such a reading is that it fails to acknowledge the degree to which Thoreau still remains squarely within the normative gender regime (most clearly in his homophobia) even as he revises it in radical ways. In that sense, Warner's reading in "*Walden*'s Erotic Economy" is more satisfying (and more consistent with queering as a critical act) in that it refuses to "normalize [Thoreau's position] in order to validate it as 'critique,' still less as redemption" (169).

13. Vogler, "Sex and Talk," p. 329. I borrow Vogler's term although what she means by it—an intimacy based on self-forgetfulness and erasure of boundaries—is in many ways different from the logic of intimacy I trace in American romanticism. In both cases, though, "depersonalizing intimacy" is imagined in opposition to confessional intimacy normative in middle-class, heterosexual culture.

14. Thoreau, *Walden,* pp. 456–57. Subsequent references are given parenthetically.

15. Quoted in Bercovitch, *The Rites of Assent,* p. 311.

16. Thoreau, "The Landlord" (1843), p. 187. Subsequent references are given parenthetically.

17. Benhabib, "The Generalized and the Concrete Other," pp. 83–86, and Hawthorne, "The Old Manse," p. 1147.

18. Benhabib, p. 89.

19. Definition of "intimate" is taken from the OED. On the connection between intimacy and an economy of signs see Berlant, "Intimacy: A Special Issue," p. 281.

20. Thoreau, *Journal,* 4:176–77. Subsequent references are given in parentheses.

21. Yacovone, "Abolitionists and the 'Language of Fraternal Love'," pp. 87–88.

22. Warner, 171–72. Interestingly, while this passage sheds light on Thoreau's horror of being consumed by the intimate male other, his imagery soon reverses itself: instead of being swallowed by the reformer, he imagines the latter as intending to "dive into Henry's inmost depths." This reciprocity, where the reformer both swallows and penetrates "Henry," is the monstrous double of the idea of equal commerce in male intimacy that Thoreau constructs elsewhere.

23. Harding, *The Days of Thoreau,* pp. 77–79.

24. Silver points out that older meanings of "commerce" include conversation, communication, and association as well as trade.

25. Nelson, *National Manhood,* pp. ix–x.

26. On that point I depart from the work of Newfield, Ellison, and Nelson, whose keen analyses of intimacy between men in antebellum romanticism has been immensely useful. All three insist on the rigidly and profoundly hierarchical nature of white male bonding, a hierarchy that hides behind the facade of democratic rhetoric of equality. I find that for Thoreau equality, far from a facade, is a necessary precondition for male intimacy. As Kaplan too proposes, for Thoreau "the self is not only expressive; it seeks to meet others on a higher ground than the daily grind of politics, to find them as neighbors and as friends, in ideals of mutuality and reciprocity. Thoreau calls for the founding of a new order in which equals meet and interact without sacrificing the integrity of their personal quests" (194).

27. Ellison, "The Gender of Transparency," p. 585.

28. Quoted in Hixon, *Privacy in a Public Society,* p. 59.

29. Cavell, *The Senses of Walden,* pp. 49–50, 54.

30. On reification and deessentialization in and by the capitalist marketplace in *Walden* see Gilmore, *American Romanticism and the Marketplace,* pp. 35–51.

31. Johnson, *A World of Difference,* pp. 49–56. More recently, Louis Renza made a similar point in relation to Poe, persuasively showing that much of what makes Poe's writing durable is its aesthetics of "radical privacy." See his "Edgar Allan Poe, Henry James, and Jack London: A Private Correspondence."

32. Melville, "Hawthorne and his Mosses," p. 1156. Subsequent references are given parenthetically.

4

Manly Tears

Men's Elegies for Children in Nineteenth-Century American Culture

ERIC HARALSON

> *Malcolm*: Give sorrow words. The grief that does not speak
> Whispers the o'erfraught heart, and bids it break.
> *Macduff*: My children too? . . . All my pretty ones? . . .
> *Malcolm*: Dispute it like a man.
> *Macduff*: I shall do so;
> But I must also feel it as a man.
>
> —William Shakespeare, *Macbeth*

Emmeline Grangerford's "Ode to Stephen Dowling Bots, Dec[ease]d"—
Mark Twain's sendup of women's versifying in *The Adventures of Huckleberry
Finn* (1886)—is commonly viewed as a marker of the derogatory (if notion-
ally "funny") gender stereotyping that attached to the sentimental elegy in a
postbellum culture on the verge of a more ironic and guarded modernism:
"O . . . list with tearful eye, // They got him out [of the well] and emptied
him; / Alas it was too late."[1] Beneath the surface humor, Twain forecast a
kind of masculine anxiety—a "barely camouflaged paranoia about being
feminine," in Frances Kerr's words—that would flourish in the works of Ezra
Pound, Ernest Hemingway, and even the more sympathetic F. Scott Fitzgerald.[2] Citing the young Henry James's distinction between "lachrymose sentimentalism" and "intelligent sadness" as an early battle cry, June Howard
summarizes the "intensif[ying] . . . animus" against wearing one's feelings
too much on one's literary sleeves: "Prestigious writing gradually . . . became

less openly emotional and more ambitiously intellectual, less directly didactic and more conspicuously masculine."3

In belittling Emmeline Grangerford's efforts, Twain indirectly anticipated as well what Jahan Ramazani calls "the economic problem of mourning" that underlies the modern elegy, the "guilty thought that [elegists] reap aesthetic profit from loss."4 No such guilt will ever visit the hopelessly antebellum Emmeline, it is implied, because her gender predisposes her to write verse that has no prospect of aesthetic profit. As Twain elaborates elsewhere, Emmeline's species of writing captures the "nursed and petted melancholy" of women who are conceived of as being perpetually adolescent and as spending themselves indiscriminately in a "wasteful and opulent gush of 'fine language' "—the spontaneous overflow of vapid feelings.5 Moreover, such feelings purportedly come at the expense of cognition or reflection, of any form of mental labor: "She didn't ever have to stop to think."6 Speaking for his moment of transition in American literature, Twain polishes off the caricature of the "saccharine, pious and maudlin . . . grieving poetess" in which, as Allison Giffen writes, "the expression of female grief [is] codified, conventionalized, and ultimately trivialized."7

Owing to the effectiveness of such stigmatizing and its tendency to obscure our view of prior values in American literary culture, what might be called domestic elegy—as distinguished from high elegy in the manner of Milton, Shelley, Tennyson, or Whitman—comes down to us as principally feminine (or at least feminized) in its thematic features and its affective bearings. Juliana Schiesari plausibly observes that male poets have historically enjoyed the "most privileged access to the display of loss," but the generic conventions of high elegy point away from the homelier accents of grief in favor of emotional grandeur, enacting what Celeste Schenk terms "a rite of separation that culminates in ascension to stature" and resulting, ideally, in the transvaluation of the "merely" personal event into universal meanings.8 At the more modest level of the domestic elegy, where female poets have been charged with sentimental and verbal profligacy, men have acquired a reputation for being comparatively austere or unsuited, as suggested by Huckleberry Finn's own abortive attempt to "sweat out a verse or two" for Emmeline Grangerford upon *her* demise.9

Surely nineteenth-century American literature provides some warrant for this stock generalization about gender and self-expression. In fact, self-control under the pressure of strong feeling serves as something of a hallmark of manliness. At the end of James Fenimore Cooper's *The Pioneers* (1823), we recall, the young Oliver Effingham certifies both his masculinity and his aristocratic lineage by demonstrating emotional restraint, "conceal[ing] his face" until "the pride of manhood" has successfully "suppressed the feelings of nature" (his sadness at Natty Bumppo's departure).[10] Although Longfellow celebrates a certain sentimental flexibility in his famous village blacksmith (1842), who mourns a lost wife, the figure is hardly copious in his crying and is literally speech-less as he manfully contains the evidence of his inner agitation: "with his hard, rough hand he wipes / A tear out of his eyes."[11] As for the hero of the popular poem "The Old Lobsterman" (1881), by John Townsend Trowbridge, he is not even able to stay in his home community, much less to speak or to grieve, after the death of his loved ones:

> . . . *The same sad day*
> *Saw wife and babe to the churchyard borne;*
> *And he sailed away, he sailed away,—*
> *For that is the sailor's way to mourn.*

Not unlike Huckleberry, who lights out for the Territory in order to escape a world of social and psychological complexity, the old lobsterman simply sails away with his emotion bottled up inside. If his incapacity for sentimental effusion becomes a cause for sentimentalizing with the audience ("ah! how can he bear to live?"), the poem nonetheless sanctions his "way to mourn" as the right way, the manly way, in its solitary, inexpressive stoicism.[12]

Nor did male poets alone recommend this reserved style of self-carriage to men, as we see from Helen Hunt Jackson's "The Prince Is Dead," written in the late 1880s:

> . . . *the eyes of the king will swim*
> *With tears which must not be shed,*
> *But will make all the air float dark and dim,*
> *As he looks at each gold and silver toy.*

The burden of the poem is to establish that every boy claimed by death had once been prized as a "royal boy," a prince, whether his parents reside in a palace or in the meanest of huts. Yet by the same measure, the sympathetic figure of the king modeled an ideal of behavior for all fathers in distress, irrespective of social class. Tears may blur his vision of objects left behind in the child's playroom, but they "must not be shed," even as he "dumbly writhes" in pain.[13] As in the case of the old lobsterman, this father's suffering may ultimately seem all the more intense for being constrained by masculine decorum, but it cannot signify very richly for the audience (or for the subject's social world) without the mediation of an interpreter such as the poem's speaker.

These examples from Cooper, Longfellow, Trowbridge, and Jackson, which span the century, all point to the challenge that men faced when circumstances of life required them to "give sorrow words" or other means of expression. Although they could listen "with tearful eye" to the testimony of their tragic losses, disputing sadness like a man evidently came more naturally than feeling it, and articulating it, as a man. And even when grown men *were* occasionally moved to "shed tears like girls" in a public setting (the orator Daniel Webster was praised for securing this effect), the phrasing itself served to indicate the aberration: unrestrained waterworks were the specialty of adolescent femininity.[14] In some respects American masculinity was also complying with a new set of prescriptions that appeared in the abundant consolatory and advice literature of the 1830s and after, as Karen Halttunen has shown: "Americans were encouraged to weep . . . [as] a fitting response to death"—a method of reinforcing family unity, benevolence, and piety—but they were also admonished that in manifesting this "most genteel of all sentiments," only "solitary mourning was sincere mourning."[15] Public noising of private grief could seem not only unmanly, then, but also ungentlemanly and theatrical.

Against this backdrop it may come as a surprise to learn that nineteenth-century elegies for children—a particularly sensitive subgenre of domestic elegy—were not the exclusive property of such poetesses as Lydia Sigourney (e.g., "Death of an Infant") or Alice Cary (e.g, "Pictures of Memory"). Indeed, both early and late, and in all regions of the country, the period witnessed the production of a vast body of male-authored elegies for children, or poems that more generally expatiated on the subject of child death. Besides Ralph Waldo Emerson's famous "Threnody," for his son Waldo, one finds John Quincy Adams's "The Death of Children," Daniel Webster's "On the Death of My Son Charles," John Pierpont's "My Child," Bronson Alcott's "Love's Morrow" (for his daughter May), Nathaniel Parker Willis's "Thoughts While Making the Grave of a New Born Child," and James Russell Lowell's sequence—"She Came and Went," "The Changeling," "The First Snowfall," and "After the Burial"—which will be especially useful to this essay. In the

South, Thomas Holley Chivers organized an entire poetic career around the death of his children, beginning with "The Lost Pleiad: An Elegy on the Death of My First-Born" (a favorite of Edgar Allan Poe's), while Henry Timrod, the so-called laureate of the South, offered the affecting "Our Willie." After the Civil War one encounters the examples of Richard Henry Stoddard's "In Memoriam" and John Williamson Palmer's durable "For Charlie's Sake," as well as William Dean Howells's "Change," which movingly records the shattering loss of his grown daughter Winifred: "nothing can be what it used to be / . . . in the deathless days before she died."[16]

Yet this roster of elegiac poems, to which many others might be added, would not have surprised contemporary readers at all. In the case of Stephen Dowling Bots, "no whooping cough did rack his frame / Nor measles drear, with spots," but these diseases, along with scarlet fever, tuberculosis, and typhoid, conspired to claim the life of one out of every six children at midcentury. As Lowell wrote to another father, after losing two daughters, "it seems as if the air were full of deadly, invisible bullets flying in every direction, so that not a step can be taken in safety."[17] Even at the turn of the century, after significant medical advances, communities still remained prey to grim visitations such as the diphtheria epidemic that is captured in *Wisconsin Death Trip*.[18] The sheer volume of these losses (as late as the 1920s, diphtheria still killed thirteen thousand American children annually) meant that few families went unscathed, and all steeled themselves against the dire eventuality of child death, as suggested by Emily Dickinson's sardonic query: "On such a night, or such a night, / Would anybody care / If such a little figure / Slipped quiet from its chair[?]."[19] High child mortality rates put a premium on parental "caring," and yet by the same token, as Karen Sánchez-Eppler writes, the symbolic "[child's] grave locked within the home . . . produce[d] and focus[ed] the family tableau" and simultaneously "constitut[ed] the ideal sentimental reader" of American prose and poetry. Notably, the rhetorical strategy of the monumental *Uncle Tom's Cabin* "had its root," as Stowe said, in the death of her eighteen-month-old son, Charley, in 1849, as she tried to extrapolate from that tragedy to the feelings of the "poor slave mother" forcibly separated from her children.[20] Yet Stowe's novel shrewdly appeals to the political sympathies of white, middle-class fathers as well, instructing them that the mourning of slaves is not only equal in gravity to their own but indistinguishable in nature: the slave sheds "just such tears, sir, as you dropped into the coffin where lay your first-born son."[21]

Stowe's gesture, moreover, indexes large-scale changes in antebellum conceptions of the paternal role, the character of childhood, and the bond between fathers and their offspring. In *Fatherhood in America,* Robert L. Griswold traces a gradual liberalization of child-rearing practices throughout the period: whereas Puritan fathers stressed the inherent "venality" of children and the consequent need to "crush their will," the modern father recognized the "essential goodness and tractability" of his child ("no trace of any evil tendency," as Lowell reported of his daughter Blanche) and cultivated his or her individuality.[22] Buttressing this newly generous scheme of paternal performance was the cult of childhood imported with British romanticism, which posited child nature to be both supremely innocent ("A simple child, // . . . [That] feels its life in every limb, / What should it know of death?") and supremely potent, the child's "exterior semblance" belying the "Soul's immensity" within.[23] Romantic poetry compounded this enhanced estimate of childhood by celebrating new modalities of manhood—by "endowing the male artist" and his male audience (as Rita Felski observes) with "qualities of sensitivity, intuition, and emotional empathy characteristically seen as the province of women."[24] Many American men, especially those from the professional and entrepreneurial classes, would have known Samuel Taylor Coleridge's "Frost at Midnight" (1798), which speculates, with "tender gladness," about the future awaiting the "Dear Babe, that sleepest cradled by [his] side."[25] Similarly, Wordsworth's famous pastoral "Michael" (1800) extolled a venerable sheep farmer for rocking his son's cradle "as with a woman's gentle hand" and for generally providing the child with "female service, not alone / For pastime and delight, as is the use / Of fathers, but with a patient mind enforced / To acts of tenderness."[26]

The moral was not lost on American fathers. Following Wordsworth, Lowell also deprecated men who looked upon their children as merely "an additional digestive" after the evening meal, and he refused to let his wife, Maria White Lowell, fall subject to "diaper despotism," sharing part of the burden of so-called female service. This solicitude owed something to Maria's physical delicacy—she died at thirty-two from tuberculosis and the strain of childbearing—but Lowell's willingness to simulate what he called the "personification of the maternal principle" also reflected a larger Anglo-American cultural trend that held the complete man to be one who spoke to the world in "a truly masculine English" (when he spoke at all), while exhibiting at home the "tender feminine virtues" as well.[27]

Yet if nineteenth-century paternal elegies—or male-authored poems that dramatize or meditate upon the theme of child death—were sentimentally "tender," like kindred verses by women, the different social conditioning and political position of masculinity abridged and modified such emotionalism. For one thing, the gendered spheres of patriarchy ensured that most men (even the forward-thinking Lowell) would miss out on the more routine contact with young children that accrued to women's experience along with their domestic duties and drudgeries. So, for example, when William James's son Herman—"the flower of our little flock"—died of whooping cough and pneumonia in 1885 before reaching his second birthday, the father lamented how, "overwhelmed with business," he had practically lost sight of the child's entire existence: "It seems to me as if I had hardly known him. . . . I left him so to his mother, thinking he would *keep*."[28]

Furthermore, although male authors fully registered the impact of child death, they tended to intellectualize and distance it more than female writers —the note, again, of stoical self-mastery. Emerson acknowledged the psychic pressure of this behavior in his often quoted regret after Waldo died in 1842— "I grieve that grief [cannot] . . . carry me one step into real nature"—but "Threnody" proved how entrenched such behavior could be, showing what Lawrence Buell calls Emerson's "impulse to depersonalize relationships of all sorts."[29] If anything, "Threnody" makes all the more painful reading for moving *away* from the deeply personal note of the beginning, with its heartbreaking image of a "hyancinthine boy" laid low by the "birdlike heavings" of scarlet fever. From there, Waldo's death is rationalized for purposes of public consumption, as the "deep Heart," a variant of the Oversoul, lays a strict injunction upon the bereaved father: "I taught thy heart beyond the reach / Of ritual, bible, or of speech; // And past the blasphemy of grief."[30]

One may doubt how far Emerson has really moved beyond the rituals and speeches of religious convention, which routinely warned (in the words of *Hamlet*) against displays of "impious . . . unmanly grief" that betrayed "a will most incorrect to heaven."[31] As hinted by his extravagant term "blasphemy," the problem with the coping strategy of "Threnody" may be more one of degree than one of kind: *any* substantial showing of sadness activates self-policing against unmasculine impiety. And before we regard the posture as peculiar to Emerson, we should note that the same lesson, minus the philosophical trappings, can be drawn from a much humbler poem such as John W. Palmer's "For Charlie's Sake," a favorite of the Gilded Age. According to Palmer, even a "very poor" farmer could be counted upon to understand the need to avoid effeminate despair at the loss of a son: "wherefore should I fast and weep, / And sullen moods of mourning keep[?]" On the contrary, "for

Charlie's sake [he] will arise" each day and till his "narrow field."[32] Palmer writes for a bourgeois audience, of course, instructing American fathers simply to "deal with it," so to speak, and if possible to convert the dead child into a stimulus to further manly exertion. Unfortunately, men were only too susceptible to this new cultural dispensation that, even as it encouraged Americans to weep, also conceived of mourning as "an occasion for discipline in emotional self-expression."[33]

It is no coincidence that my examples thus far have concentrated on the fate of what Helen Hunt Jackson denominated "royal boys," from Hartley Coleridge and the son Luke in Wordsworth's "Michael" to Stowe's Charley, Emerson's Waldo, and Palmer's fictional Charlie. In the Anglo-American tradition, the gender divide in child elegies might conveniently be traced back to the pairing "On My First Daughter" and "On My First Son" (1603), by Ben Jonson—"firm-footed Ben," in the judgment of Lowell and his literate New England circle. Whereas Jonson's infant daughter departs "with safety of her innocence"—"heaven's gifts" being "heaven's due" to reclaim—the son, another Benjamin, is more acutely missed as the "child of my right hand" ("write" hand), instrumental to the poet's very identity as a maker: "here doth lie / Ben Jonson his best piece of poetry."[34] According to the American version of primogeniture, the "first-born son" invoked in *Uncle Tom's Cabin* would have been the foremost candidate to carry on his father's legacy—his trade, business, or profession, or at any rate, the honor of the family name and the mantle of manly authority and responsibility. Like Stowe and Jackson, even the protofeminist Alice Cary posited that mothers bound to their spinning wheels labored mainly on behalf of the male child who represented the so-called family hope: "many a lad / Born to rough work and ways / Strips off his ragged coat, and makes / Men clothe him with their praise."[35] By a widespread consensus, that is, and not just in the eyes of poet-fathers, the premature extinction of a first-born son (of sons in general) came as a particularly cruel blow to a family's fortunes—indeed, to the communal project of American culture during a period of strenuous nation-building. Sánchez-Eppler brilliantly treats the case of Waldo Emerson and the modes of commercial "replication and commodification" that insinuate themselves into his father's writings about his death.[36] Yet because she focuses on the prose, perhaps we miss a special sore spot for Emerson, who had expected Waldo to sustain *precisely his own role* in the forging of the American democracy. The "budding man" whom "Threnody" memorializes was in effect a Waldo Junior (Emerson preferred to go by "Waldo" himself), and the poem envisions no other career for him than the path already marked out by his father. Had Waldo lived, he would naturally have assumed the same mission of combatting the "ills of ages" with the "wondrous tongue, and guided pen" of the poet, essayist, and public lecturer. To that extent, not merely a family hope but "a *general* hope / Was quenched" when the boy died.[37]

To make a further broad distinction, the men who wrote verses about child death tended to question, or at times even to reproach, the workings of divine providence, whereas women writers more often sought refuge in a mixture of resignation and idealization, the goal of mourning being "passion subdued, / . . . souls serene and christian fortitude."[38] As Jonathan Hall observes, Alice Cary's popular "Pictures of Memory" reimagines a dying boy (a young brother) as "fading seamlessly" into both the natural order and the life everlasting: "He fell, in his saint-like beauty, / Asleep at the gates of light."[39] Likewise, Lydia Sigourney invited readers to see "the signet-ring of Heaven" inscribed upon the brow of all departed children (her dead infants are often generic and genderless).[40] Even Maria Lowell, whose poem "The Morning-Glory" records all the horror of losing her first child before the age of two ("she lay stretched before our sight, withered, and cold, and dead"), moves quickly to transplant the girl to the afterlife: "But in the groves of Paradise, full surely we shall see / Our morning-glory beautiful twine round our dear Lord's knee."[41] This vision of the afterworld is one that male modernism, in the voice of E. E. Cummings, would put down as "a pansy heaven . . . / a fragile heaven of lilies-of-the-valley."[42]

To be sure, the trope of heavenly reunion occurred in men's verse of the nineteenth century as well, but even the most devout of male poets could enter a caveat against divine regulation of the universe, especially when it produced a traumatic rupture in generational succession and the transfer of patriarchal authority. This subtext is audible in "On the Death of My Son Charles," by another powerful antebellum figure, Daniel Webster, Emerson's "completest man."[43] Whereas young Charles should have planted a "filial stone" upon *his* grave, and Webster, as "teacher," should have demonstrated the earthly virtues that lead heavenward, the intervention of death has reversed their roles and perverted the natural sequence: "My son! My father! guide me there."[44] The same note of anguish, along with the same undertone of anger, resounds in the lyric "My Child" by John Pierpont, the combative antislavery and temperance minister, a father to six children and grandfather to financier John Pierpont Morgan. Widely reprinted during the 1840s and later admired by Dickinson, the poem notably does *not* furnish the dead boy with a "smile, / . . . fix'd and holy [upon his] marble brow" (as in Sigourney's "Death of an Infant"); rather, it emphasizes how death has robbed the paternal caress of a reciprocal warmth: "cold is his forehead; / My hand that marble felt." Indeed, Pierpont's most potent line speaks to the inadequacy of standard formulas of solace as the small body, lying in its coffin, meanly counterfeits the child's living form: "Yet my heart whispers that, he is not there!"[45] As Lowell would complain of the "changeling" that death had substituted for his infant daughter: "I cannot lift it up fatherly / And bliss it upon my breast" (the imagery of nursing again blurs the gender line, evoking the intimacy of motherly care).[46]

A similar confrontation with divine will, as well as a similar testing of religious consolation, appears in the work of the mystical Southern poet Thomas Holley Chivers. Before the birth of his daughter Allegra, Chivers had had a dreamlike prevision of her as an angel "play[ing] most ravishingly" upon a golden harp—an intimation that she would come trailing clouds of glory, but perhaps also a harbinger of her early death. And in fact, on Chivers's own birthday in October 1842, the three-year-old Allegra succumbed to typhoid, inspiring *The Lost Pleiad* (1845).[47] When typhoid then claimed three more children in a single year (1848), the poet raised a Job-like wail at the workings of "Death's iron rod," wondering, in "Avalon" (1851), why it had pleased God to see "four little Angels killed by one cold Death" and doubting whether anything besides "bringing back the early dead" could ever repair his sundered psyche: "Can any thing that Christ has ever said, / Make my heart whole?" Again, gender dynamics influenced poetic utterance. Although his first daughter's death clearly was wrenching—"this dark heart of mine . . . / . . . though broken, is still breaking"—Chivers took a page from women's verse, such as "The Morning-Glory," and idealized the girl's angelic femininity as something far too pure to consort with the dross of life in a fallen world: Allegra died "because she was for earth too fair." By contrast, Chivers could find no such convenient ground for acquiescence in the death of his firstborn son, who was lavishly mourned as "my more than Precious One," "my son of Melody," "[my] *Lark*-like Child."[48]

If male authors generally remained more agitated and defiant than their female counterparts—more masculinist, in a word—it may have been partly because they had less recourse to the networks of support and nurture that women elaborated to share and absorb their losses. Hawthorne provides a suitable gender distinction. Whereas in *The Scarlet Letter* young Pearl undergoes a communal "scene of grief" that "develop[s] all her sympathies"—her abundant tears "pledg[ing]" that she will "be a woman" active and commiserative in society—the sculptor Kenyon of *The Marble Faun* discovers that an "insuperable gulf" stands between men, eliminating the chance of their sharing "heart sustenance."[49] Put broadly, women authors trusted more than men in the capacity of writing to forge confidential bonds among fellow sufferers —to capture common feelings of sadness and form a basis for therapeutic exchange. Stowe, for instance, asks another grieving mother: "How is it with you in your heart of hearts[?] . . . I often wonder how your feelings correspond with mine."[50] Yet such an inquiry assumes that one's innermost emotions *can* be communicated and that thereby two separate subjects, with different histories, can achieve a sufficient "correspondence" of feelings to succor one another. This premise seems to hold even when a woman's grief equals that which besets the archetypal male figure (Cooper's pioneer, Longfellow's smithy, Jackson's king) whose gendered response to fate is curtailed expressivity. In her elegy " 'One morn I left him in his bed,' " Elizabeth Stoddard pronounces herself as bereft and isolated as Trowbridge's old sailor—"floating from the world . . . / Apart from sympathy"—yet her inability to express grief paradoxically makes a powerful connection with other women whose bitter experience guarantees their sympathetic intelligence: "Mothers, who mourn with me today," will "understand me, when I say, / I cannot weep, I cannot pray."[51] Stoddard "cannot pray," the reader senses, not because she harbors resentment against God (as with some male poets) but because the momentousness of her son's death has driven all feeling so deep inside—into that "heart of hearts" that only other aggrieved mothers can empathize with. If "best Grief is Tongueless," as Dickinson maintained in 1863, that is partly a condition of bourgeois mourning manners, but partly a factor of the tacit *group* knowledge, among women, that "grief is a mouse" that gnaws away at the "Wainscot in the Breast," however invisible to the world.[52]

By contrast, James Russell Lowell (anticipating Hawthorne) flatly declared that for men, and thus between men, "there is no such thing as consolation": "Death and sorrow . . . are not subjects which I think it profitable or wise to talk about, think about, or write about often. Death is a private tutor. We have no fellow-scholars, and must lay our lessons to heart alone."[53] The scholastic metaphors came naturally enough to a man who "smoked the student's pipe over a thousand volumes," in Henry James's phrase, and who would succeed Longfellow as professor of modern languages at Harvard.[54] But as with Emerson, one senses that Lowell leans rather heavily on his professional self-construction to manage the sorrow of death, asking the familiar discourse of the academy to help him keep a stiff upper lip in the presence of domestic catastrophe. Lowell's critical writings also recommended the strong, silent type of manhood, deploring the "intrusive self-consciousness" of the Victorian sentimentalist and blaming the "degenerate modern tendency" of emotionalism (dating all the way from Petrarch) for enervating the "masculine mood . . . of body and mind" celebrated in the cultures of antiquity.[55] Evidently this reservation carried over into his estimate of overly demonstrative fathers, since he himself claimed to lack "that natural fondness for children" found in people who also "like puppies in the same indiscriminate way."[56] As Robert Lowell noted, he was "the hardest of the Boston-Cambridge group" of fireside poets and transcendentalists, his talent running to wicked satires that were "once the rage of . . . *The Atlantic Monthly.*"[57]

Yet James Russell Lowell was more interesting than this summary might indicate—more ambivalent about sentimentalism, more positive about paternity, and thus, too, more representative of contemporary manhood. If he anticipated the modernist grimness of Robert Frost's " 'Out, Out—,' " for example—when a child dies, Lowell noted, "the mad world . . . dances heedless on / . . . and gives no sign"—he also wrote "On the Death of a Friend's Child" (1844) expressly to give a sign of fellow feeling to the "friend" in question, the editor Charles Briggs. Indeed, Lowell's poem went so far as to agree with the female elegiac tradition that Briggs's son, by virtue of his truncated life, had performed the valuable social "mission" of broadening the base of human sympathy, "open[ing] a new fountain in my heart / For thee . . . and all."[58]

Nor can there be any doubt that in the loss of his own children, Lowell took the hard lessons to heart. First came Blanche, who weighed in at a robust ten pounds on New Year's Eve, 1845, and whom Lowell happily envisioned as a tomboy—a "strong, vulgar, . . . tree-climbing, little wench"—and as a creature "independent . . . of all *man*kind" (emphasis in original).[59] Yet at fifteen months she died from "a malady consequent upon too rapid teething," reducing him—in the words of "The Changeling"—to a "weak" and "poor little violet" thrown upon the mercy of nature for his sustenance.[60] Although Lowell published this suggestively demasculinized self-image to the world, it probably cannot be read as a particular overture to other fathers (or mothers) in the circuitry of grief; he merely added the poem, along with Maria's "The Morning-Glory," to round out a volume of verse that otherwise looked "too skimpy for a favorable impression on the public."[61]

A more profound poem with a more telling history of circulation, "After the Burial," came into being when a second daughter, Rose, died in infancy in 1850 ("she had never spoken, only smiled"). Lowell could not bring himself to arrange a public funeral for her (a "hateful" ceremony), but poured his feelings into verse in the privacy of his commonplace book. Although not averse to copying out the poem in a letter to yet another male friend in mourning, Lowell did not publish it until 1868, possibly owing to his skepticism about the general efficacy (or "profit") of such self-exposure. In fact, "After the Burial" thematizes the inconsolability of the grieving subject and the inutility of traditional sources of collective support. What good is the "goodly anchor" of religious faith, the poet asks, when a child's death has in effect sunk the vessel of consciousness, sending it down into the depths of depression?

> . . . *after the shipwreck, tell me*
> *What help in its iron thews,*
> *Still true to the broken hawser,*
> *Deep down among sea-weed and ooze?*

Like Pierpont and Chivers, Lowell refuses to be comforted by the cliché that his daughter dwells in eternity, for the overwhelming fact at the moment is the certainty of her eternal *absence:* "Immortal? . . . // But that is the pang's very secret,— / [she is] immortal away from me." In other words, he now turns a deaf ear to the same brand of moralizing that he had dispensed only a few years before, in "On the Death of a Friend's Child," replying to his would-be sympathizer:

> *Your logic, my friend, is perfect,*
> *Your moral most drearily true;*
> *But since the earth clashed on her coffin,*
> *I keep hearing that, and not you.*
>
> *Communion in spirit! Forgive me,*
> *But I, who am earthly and weak,*
> *Would give all my incomes from dreamland*
> *For a touch of her hand on my cheek.*

Lowell recognizes that in rejecting the cultural "logic" of recuperation and remaining in the grip of his sorrow, he risks showing both impiety—a will "incorrect to heaven"—and deficient bourgeois civility. And yet by the paradoxical nature of male elegizing, that very resistance could form a basis for solidarity with other fathers in crisis, as the verses evolved from a private meditation to a popular poem, surprising Lowell by "rous[ing] strange echoes in men who assured me they were generally insensible to poetry." If his poem spoke to these other fathers, this is because it also spoke for them, articulating the intense, hopeless pathos of their own losses in a way that blended the sentimental with the stoical. These other men, whom life had sadly provided with the key to "unlock the whole meaning" of Lowell's lines, found spiritual communion in the thought that such communion was impossible, and a measure of consolation in being told that there is no such thing as consolation. "After all," Lowell concluded, "the only stuff a solitary man has to spin is himself" (yet another distaff metaphor for a "truly masculine" spirit).[62]

After reading Lowell's tributes to his daughters, one might expect that the death of his son, Walter, would have inspired an even more tormented expression in his verse, but this does not seem to have been the case. This blue-eyed "fairest boy that ever was seen," who physically resembled Lowell, seemed to be "thriv[ing] finely" but died suddenly during a family sojourn in Rome in the early 1850s.[63] At least one critic has claimed that Lowell "made poetry" out of Walter's passing, but the poem cited as evidence, "Threnodia," dates from a decade earlier.[64] Yet does this finding necessarily invalidate the generalization that male children—the royal boys, the Waldo Emersons and Charles Websters—were believed to count more than girls to the project of American culture, so to speak, and that the early loss of a son hit the American father hardest? If indeed Lowell the poet fell silent after Walter's death, the reason may well be supplied in a late letter to Charles Eliot Norton: "If you only knew how much I wish *I* had a son, and how fresh . . . the life of our little Walter is to me." The *wound* remained fresh, that is, along with the memory of his son's brief life, and the trauma associated with that loss very possibly ended in thoughts too deep for tears or for treatment in verse.

In the last analysis, reading Lowell's elegies establishes a linkage, as well as a transition, between sentimental masculinity of the nineteenth century—sentimental for all its growing constraints—and the modernist sensibility heralded by, say, Robert Frost's "Home Burial" or John Crowe Ransom's "Dead Boy" ("The little cousin is dead, by foul subtraction, // And none of the country kin like the transaction").[65] The phantom caress of a small hand on a father's cheek, the empty little shoe left behind in a corner—these touches would seem more and more to belong to the likes of Sigourney and Cary and perhaps never to have characterized male-authored verse at all. The hard edge of religious skepticism, the case for solitary self-fabrication and self-recourse—these features point ahead to male writers like Lowell's great-grand-nephew Robert Lowell, who would summarize in a bleak elegy for the one-year-old son of fellow poet Allen Tate: "Things no longer possible to our faith / go on routinely usable in nature; / the worst is the child's death."[66] If in the twentieth century nature's uses definitively exceeded the resources of faith (and Lowell clearly means some existential damage beyond the decline of organized religion), they also tested anew the range of men's expressive powers and often found it wanting. Frost's "Home Burial" (1914) can serve as a sort of watershed dramatization of the modern father's predicament and thus also as a terminus of this essay.

Notably, the poem involves the aftermath of yet another little boy's death—a firstborn son, no less—and Frost himself had lost both a young son and an infant daughter, which may explain why he could never bring himself to offer the work in a public reading. As a sign of broad changes in the American gender system, it is the mother in "Home Burial," Amy, who occupies the site of inconsolability and resistance to social reconciliation, to that turning "back to life / And living people" that seems to betray the memory of her child: "I won't have grief so / If I can change it." To her view, the father has proved himself the epitome of such disloyalty from the moment of the boy's death, digging "with your own hand—how could you?—his little grave" and then proceeding to "talk about your everyday concerns": "What had how long it takes a birch [fence] to rot / To do with what was in the darkened parlor?" But Amy's reproach fails to notice how her husband's "everyday" talk is precisely about his grief and his sense of futility. Being a man, he "think[s] the talk is all" and yet he has limited faculties of expression, talking *around* his feelings or displacing them to an idiom of masculine labor in which he is more at ease. Lamenting the destruction of the best fence "a man can build," which "rot[s]" just like a small body in the grave, the father registers at once his failure to protect his progeny by keeping away harm and his resulting hopelessness about building a family and raising a son to take over the land.

Despite the rural Victorian setting, Frost's couple emblematizes an essentially modernist impasse between women who don't "know rightly whether any man" can *speak* rightly about child death—men being "blind creature[s]" in affairs of the heart—and men who think that women morbidly "overdo" grieving and who doubt their own ability to learn a greater emotional fluency: "I might be taught / . . . [but] I can't say I see how." On the argument of this pessimistic poem, the twentieth-century American man had skirted the danger of becoming Twain's Emmeline Grangerford, overcoming as well the perceived sentimental excesses of a James Russell Lowell, but in the process he had buried something vital, fenced out something needful, and compromised even further his capacity to give sorrow words. In a sense that the forlorn father himself neither intends nor fully understands, "it's come down to this, / A man can't speak of his own child that's dead."[67]

Acknowledgment

My gratitude to Allison Giffen of New Mexico State University for her generous help with this essay.

Notes

1. Twain, "Ode to Steven Dowling Bots, Dec'd." in *American Poetry: The Nineteenth Century,* 2:338.

2. Kerr, "Feeling 'Half Feminine': Modernism and the Politics of Emotion in *The Great Gatsby,*" p. 405.

3. Howard, "What Is Sentimentality?" p. 70.

4. Ramazani, *Poetry of Mourning: The Modern Elegy from Hardy to Heaney,* p. 6.

5. Twain, *The Adventures of Tom Sawyer,* p. 527.

6. Twain, *The Adventures of Huckleberry Finn,* p. 820.

7. Giffen, "Resisting Consolation: Early American Women Poets and the Elegiac Tradition," p. 118.

8. Schiesari, *The Gendering of Melancholia: Feminism, Psychoanalysis, and the Symbolics of Loss in Renaissance Literature,* quoted in Steele, "Margaret Fuller," in *Encyclopedia of American Poetry: The Nineteenth Century,* 165; Schenk cited in Giffen, "Resisting Consolation: Early American Women Poets and the Elegiac Tradition," p. 119.

9. Twain, *The Adventures of Huckleberry Finn,* p. 821.

10. Cooper, *The Pioneers, or The Sources of the Susquehanna,* p. 435.

11. Longfellow, "The Village Blacksmith," in *American Poetry: The Nineteenth Century,* 1:376.

12. Trowbridge, "The Old Lobsterman," in *American Poetry: The Nineteenth Century,* 2:197–200.

13. Jackson, "The Prince Is Dead," in *American Women Poets of the Nineteenth Century: An Anthology,* pp. 280–81.

14. Ferguson, *Law and Letters in American Culture,* p. 225.

15. Halttunen, *Confidence Men and Painted Women: A Study of Middle-Class Culture in America, 1830–1870,* pp. 129, 124, 132.

16. Howells, "Change," quoted in Julie Bates Dock, "William Dean Howells," in *Encyclopedia of American Poetry: The Nineteenth Century,* p. 227.

17. *Letters of James Russell Lowell,* 1:177–78.

18. Michael Lesy, *Wisconsin Death Trip* (New York: Pantheon, 1973; reprint, Albu-querque: University of New Mexico Press, 2000.) Film version directed by James Marsh.

19. Dickinson, "On Such a Night, or Such a Night" (#146), *The Complete Poems of Emily Dickinson,* p. 69.

20. Sánchez-Eppler, " 'Then When We Clutch Hardest': On the Death of a Child and the Replication of an Image," in Chapman and Hendler, eds., *Sentimental Men: Mas-culinity and the Politics of Affect in American Culture,* pp. 66–67. Sánchez-Eppler is my source for Stowe's quotations here, as well as for the midcentury mortality rate among American children.

21. Stowe, *Uncle Tom's Cabin,* p. 35.

22. Griswold, *Fatherhood in America: A History,* p. 10; James Russell Lowell quoted in Horace Elisha Scudder, *James Russell Lowell: A Biography,* 1:273.

23. Wordsworth and Coleridge, "We Are Seven," in *The Norton Anthology of English Literature,* 2:71; Wordsworth, "Ode: Intimations of Immortality," in *The Norton Anthology of English Literature,* 2:117–22.

24. Felski, *The Gender of Modernity,* p. 94.

25. Coleridge, "Frost at Midnight," in *The Norton Anthology of English Literature,* 2:215.

26. Wordsworth, "Michael," in *The Norton Anthology of English Literature* 2:98–108.

27. James Russell Lowell quoted in Martin Duberman, *James Russell Lowell,* pp. 89–90; and in Angus Fletcher, "James Russell Lowell," in *Encyclopedia of American Poetry: The Nineteenth Century,* p. 275. Lowell's exemplar of "a truly masculine English" was Lin-coln's Gettysburg Address.

28. *Correspondence of William James,* 3:21.

29. Emerson, "Experience," in *The Norton Anthology of American Literature,* 1:1090; Buell, *New England Literary Culture: From Revolution Through Renaissance,* p. 112.

30. Emerson, "Threnody," in *American Poetry: The Nineteenth Century,* 1:311–18.

31. Shakespeare, *Hamlet,* I.ii.94–95, 185.

32. Palmer, "For Charlie's Sake," in *A Library of American Literature,* 8:261–62.

33. Halttunen, *Confidence Men and Painted Women,* p. 134.

34. Jonson, *The Complete Poems,* pp. 41, 48.

35. Cary, "The West Country," in *American Women Poets of the Nineteenth Century: An Anthology,* pp. 182–83.

36. Sánchez-Eppler, " 'Then When We Clutch Hardest,' " pp. 80–81.

37. Emerson, "Threnody," p. 314 (emphasis added).

38. Bleecker quoted in Allison Giffen, " 'Till *Grief* Melodious Grow': The Poems and Letters of Ann Eliza Bleecker," in *Early American Literature,* p. 228.

39. Hall, "Alice and Phoebe Cary," in *Encyclopedia of American Poetry: The Nineteenth Century,* p. 66; Cary, "Pictures of Memory," in *American Women Poets of the Nine-teenth Century: An Anthology,* p. 178.

40. Sigourney, "Death of an Infant," in *She Wields a Pen: American Women Poets of the Nineteenth Century,* p. 15.

41. Maria White Lowell, "The Morning-Glory," in *American Women Poets of the Nine-teenth Century: An Anthology,* pp. 187–88.

42. Cummings, "if there are heavens my mother will (all by herself) have," in *The Norton Anthology of American Literature*, 2:1484.

43. Emerson quoted in Ferguson, *Law and Letters in American Culture*, p. 207.

44. Webster, "On the Death of My Son Charles," in *The Le Gallienne Book of American Verse*, p. 12.

45. Pierpont's poem "My Child" is quoted and discussed in Farr, *The Passion of Emily Dickinson*, p. 14.

46. *The Complete Poetical Works of James Russell Lowell*, pp. 89–90.

47. Damon, *Thomas Holley Chivers, Friend of Poe*, ch. 7, "Poe and the Lost Pleiad," pp. 128–52.

48. Chivers, "Avalon," in *American Poetry: The Nineteenth Century*, 1:574–81; "To Allegra Florence in Heaven," quoted in Damon, *Thomas Holley Chivers, Friend of Poe*, ch. 7.

49. Hawthorne, *The Scarlet Letter*, p. 181; *The Marble Faun*, in *The Centenary Edition of the Works of Nathaniel Hawthorne*, 4:285.

50. Stowe quoted in Sánchez-Eppler, " 'Then When We Clutch Hardest,' " p. 67.

51. Stoddard, " 'One Morn I Left Him in His Bed,' " in *She Wields a Pen: American Women Poets of the Nineteenth Century*, p. 101.

52. Dickinson, "Grief is a Mouse–" (#793), in *The Complete Poems of Emily Dickinson*, p. 387.

53. *Letters of James Russell Lowell*, 1:175–77.

54. James, "James Russell Lowell," in *Literary Criticism: Essays on Literature, American Writers, English Writers*, p. 517.

55. James Russell Lowell, "Sentimentalism," in *Literary Criticism of James Russell Lowell*, pp. 57–59.

56. Robert Lowell quoted in Wagenknecht, *James Russell Lowell: Portrait of a Many-Sided Man*, p. 144.

57. Robert Lowell, "J. R. Lowell," in *Collected Prose*, p. 194.

58. "On the Death of a Friend's Child," *The Complete Poetical Works of James Russell Lowell*, p. 88; Frost's " 'Out, Out–' " suggests that death is truly arresting only to those most immediately concerned; as for all others, "they, since they / Were not the one dead, turned to their affairs"; *The Norton Anthology of American Literature*, 2:1156.

59. James Russell Lowell quoted in Duberman, *James Russell Lowell*, pp. 89–90.

60. "The Changeling," in *The Complete Poetical Works of James Russell Lowell*, p. 90.

61. Leon Howard, *Victorian Knight-Errant: A Study of the Early Literary Career of James Russell Lowell*, p. 228.

62. *The Complete Poetical Works of James Russell Lowell*, p. 292, 308–9.

63. James Russell Lowell quoted in Scudder, *James Russell Lowell: A Biography*, p. 337.

64. Wagenknecht, *James Russell Lowell: Portrait of a Many-Sided Man*, p. 145.

65. See Cushman, "Home Burial" (pp. 231–32), and Claridge, "John Crowe Ransom" (pp. 589–91), in *Encyclopedia of American Poetry: The Twentieth Century*.

66. Robert Lowell, "For Michael Tate: August 1967–July 1968," quoted in Mariani, *Lost Puritan: A Life of Robert Lowell*, p. 365.

67. Frost, "Home Burial," in *The Norton Anthology of American Literature*, 2:1124–1126.

5

How To Be a (Sentimental) Race Man

Mourning and Passing in W. E. B. Du Bois's The Souls of Black Folk

RYAN SCHNEIDER

W. E. B. Du Bois and his wife, Nina Gomer Du Bois, were living in the slums of Philadelphia when their first child, a son they named Burghardt, was born in October 1897.[1] Du Bois was then in the midst of completing a massive sociological study of African American life commissioned by the University of Pennsylvania—a project that eventually led to the 1899 publication of *The Philadelphia Negro* and helped launch his career as an intellectual and a leading speaker on issues of race relations.[2]

Married in 1896, the same year the Supreme Court ruled on *Plessy v. Ferguson,* the couple had been together a scant three months when Du Bois received his research grant from the University of Pennsylvania. The task of surveying and assessing the poverty-stricken conditions of Philadelphia's African American community kept him extremely busy—he interviewed over twenty-five hundred households in three month's time—and he rarely had more than a few minutes a day to spend with his wife and son. As the appointment at Penn drew to a close, Du Bois began searching for a new position. An opportunity finally arose in January 1898 at Atlanta University, and so the Du Bois family—father, mother, and infant son—moved south.

They arrived in a city where the pervasive and debilitating separation of blacks and whites defined almost every sphere of existence. Stores, restaurants, libraries, transportation, housing—virtually every aspect of life in post-Reconstruction Atlanta—was coded by race. Historian and Du Bois biographer David Levering Lewis notes that the capital of the New South had rebuilt itself into two very separate cities: "a place in which black and white people possessed angry and embarrassed memories of a fast-receding epoch of more informal and comparatively flexible racial separation."³ Although Du Bois's position as a professor at the university afforded some measure of economic security for the family, he and Nina were still subject to the full range of social indignities and restrictions that white Atlantans imposed on all African American residents.

Neither husband nor wife was equipped to battle the comprehensive segregation and unremitting racial hostility that determined life for blacks under Atlanta's segregationist policies. Learning to negotiate the world of Jim Crow was especially difficult for Nina; having spent her early years in Iowa and Ohio, she had been exposed to racial prejudice but had little experience with pervasive segregation and racial violence. Having taken his undergraduate degree at Fisk University in Nashville, Du Bois was perhaps more familiar with overt racism than his wife; even so, he had relatively little experience with the forms of white-on-black aggression that characterized life in the part of the country he described with no little irony in his first autobiography as the "re-born south."⁴

Thus, it would have been all the more difficult to bear the anguish when, in the spring of 1899, husband and wife could not find adequate medical attention after Burghardt became suddenly and seriously ill. Atlanta's white doctors, as a matter of course, refused to treat black patients. And black physicians were all but nonexistent. So when Burghardt's diphtheria worsened, and he grew more and more feverish, there was very little his parents could do but watch. The child struggled for ten days and then died at sundown on May 24. He was two years old.

Less than four years later, with the April 1903 publication of *The Souls of Black Folk*, Du Bois would commemorate his son's brief life and tragic death in an essay entitled "Of the Passing of the First-Born." For Du Bois, writing publicly about his son was an opportunity to give substance to his notion of what an intellectual and race leader—a "race man"—should be and do; it was a chance to put theory into practice by using the tragic circumstances of the boy's death as compelling evidence of the need for radical social change—to ground his public protest against racial inequality in the material facts of his own personal loss.⁵

The boy's death—his passing from this world to the next—becomes interlinked, in the course of the essay, with other notions of passing, specifically the idea that, had Burghardt lived, his pale skin and fair hair would have allowed him to pass as white. Recognizing his son's powerful capacity to generate sympathy from a white audience, Du Bois performs his own kind of passing: he assumes the mantle of a sentimental elegist, employing the commonplace of the sacred or ideal child to characterize his son as an icon of virtue for blacks and whites alike—a child so virtuous and good that his death must serve as a call to disassemble the system of segregation and inequality that hastened it. As an elegy, "First-Born" is remarkable for the intensity, diversity, and sheer volume of its individual feelings and emotions. These expressions of feeling—from fatherly joy and pride to parental grief and rage—have sometimes caused it to be characterized as out-of-place in the overall context of *Souls,* as though Du Bois's expressions of personal emotion in the wake of his son's death are somehow at odds with the larger, more public and political goals of the text. While the other essays reflect the rationality and intellectual weight of Du Bois's representations of African American history and culture, "First-Born" (so this particular critical narrative goes), represents an awkward instance in which the rational and the intellectual are nudged aside or supplanted by the emotional and the personal.[6] Publicizing Burghardt's death and his own emotional response serves as a way for Du Bois to reach out to a potentially hostile white audience; offering his son's loss and his own grief as foundational elements for common sympathy across racial lines, he constructs an affective bond with the potential to enable further identification between blacks and whites.

In memorializing Burghardt, Du Bois joins the ranks of numerous nineteenth- and early twentieth-century (white) fathers who authored elegies for their children. His attempts to satisfy the public and personal demands made manifest by the sudden and painful loss of his son lead him to draw heavily upon the conventions of the father's sentimental elegy—a body of literature that, as Eric Haralson argues elsewhere in this volume, partakes of and diverges from both women's domestic poetry and high elegy and serves as a crucial site for the representation and construction of sentimental masculinity.[7] Like Emerson's "Threnody," Daniel Webster's "On the Death of My Son Charles," and R. H. Stoddard's "In Memoriam," Du Bois's "Of the Passing of the First-Born" is meant to evoke sympathy for the passing of a life, to lament the interruption of the natural progression in which children survive their parents, and to mourn the loss of a father's legacy and namesake.[8]

Moreover, such elegies are meant to circulate the image of the child beyond the realm of the domestic and, in so doing, to secure space for the expression of emotion in an increasingly competitive, commercialized, and socially fragmented public sphere. Reading Emerson's writings about the death of his son Waldo within the context of a rapidly expanding commercial and consumer culture, Karen Sánchez-Eppler points out that images of dead children were often reproduced and circulated to the point of commodification: "As the figure of the dead child becomes itself a commodity of sorts, and as the market tools of replication and circulation are harnessed to the act of mourning—that is, as a figure innocent, intimate, static, and unique becomes an object of mass production—the dead child carries intimacy and affect into the commercial, industrial world where such feelings appear most threatened."[9] And while Du Bois is more concerned with the threats posed by racial segregation and violence than by commercialization and industrialization, his elegy, like those authored by white fathers, creates a space for emotional intimacy in which the warmth and affection of the father-son bond can be represented even as the anguish over its loss can be fully expressed. Just as Emerson, who invokes the sentimental commonplace of the sacred child in his elegy "Threnody," characterizes his son as an intellectual heir and prophet who, by embodying and propagating his father's ideals, could have uplifted his fellow men, so too does Du Bois draw upon sentimental ideology for terms and images by which he could memorialize Burghardt as a child-prophet—one who, had he lived, would have realized *his* father's dreams of establishing racial unity. Like Emerson, Du Bois includes soaring and majestic tributes to his son's virtue, talent, and potential as a leader, counting his death as a loss not just to himself but to a larger world whose inhabitants are suffering more and more from the effects of social fragmentation.

But as deeply as Du Bois immerses himself in the tropes and language of the father's sentimental elegy, his participation—his "passing"—is neither easy nor complete. While Burghardt is portrayed as a powerful icon of sentimental virtue, an angelic child who can pass as white and whose death is held up as common cause for cross-racial sympathy, he is also portrayed, less optimistically, as "a Negro and a Negro's son"—a child who may not look black but who will be interpreted and treated as such by whites (507). Indeed, in one of the essay's most poignant scenes, Du Bois describes white passersby at Burghardt's funeral procession as offering not sympathy but racial epithets: "The busy city dinned about us; they did not say much, those pale-faced hurrying men and women; they did not say much—they only glanced and said 'Niggers!' " (509). So while the essay's embrace of sentiment provides a means of representing emotional intimacy between grieving father and absent son—and, at the same time, holds open the opportunity for blacks and whites together to sympathize with the universal pain of a lost child—that same reliance on sentiment also holds the potential to further alienate the races from each other. If the invitation to sympathize is rejected, and Du Bois strongly suggests that possibility, then sentiment itself becomes suspect, even dangerous, as a means for launching a radical restructuring of race relations.[10] Thus, as I will show, the essay is structured around a complex advance-and-retreat from the sentimental elegy, a strategy based on Du Bois's recognition of both its potential as a form for the expression of masculine feeling and its costs in relation to his project of critiquing the status of race relations. Seen in this light, "First-Born" records Du Bois's own dual status as a sentimental writer and a race man just as it records his son's status as both an easily recognizable version of sentimental culture's sacred or ideal child and an inheritor of his father's role as a race leader.

A Child of Sentiment, A Child of Black Fathers

Before looking more closely at "First-Born's" representation of the dual status of father and son, I must clarify what I mean when I say that Du Bois employs the sentimental commonplace of the sacred or ideal child in his memorialization of Burghardt. Viviana Zelizer, in her study of the changing social value of children in the United States, argues that in the nineteenth century a radical shift began to take place whereby the idea of the child as economic asset was displaced by the concept of the child as sacred object. Withdrawn from the world of labor and production, children were assigned to the domestic sphere and their worth understood in religious or sentimental rather than commercial terms. In Zelizer's words, there emerged a "new normative ideal of the child as an exclusively emotional and affective asset [which] precluded instrumental or fiscal consideration."[11] The reasons for the transition from economic child to sacred child are not easily categorized, but, as scholars of Victorian-era domesticity have shown, they can best be understood as part of a growing interest in the importance of family life in both Europe and the United States that was itself the result of the structural changes brought on by industrial capitalism.[12] As the site of production shifted from farms to factories, the home and hence the family structure, became idealized as sources of virtue and comfort—as safe havens from the potentially corrupting incursions of industrialization and commercialization.

In actuality, of course, the transformation of children from laborers to sentimental icons in the nineteenth century was neither clear-cut nor complete, and it would be difficult to do more than generalize about the different roles a particular child might occupy in his or her family or community. Even after the turn of the century, children in rural communities were still required to labor for the overall good of the family while also devoting time to school or play. In urban areas the children of newly immigrated families were asked not only to perform domestic chores but also to earn money through part- or even full-time jobs. And children in African American families often were expected to perform wage labor and household tasks.[13]

Despite the reality that many children were worth far more to their families as financial rather than emotional assets, the *ideal* child in the American cultural imagination was noncommercial or, to use Zelizer's term, "sacralized." Formerly viewed as sources of labor, children became sentimental icons, their noncommercial status reflecting the increasing importance of domesticity to the identity of both the individual family as well as the nation. The sentimental child—doted on in life and memorialized in death—represented a source of innocence and virtue uncorrupted by the marketplace. As children became more and more precious in the cultural imagination, their deaths, of course, became less and less acceptable. This is not to say that parents of earlier generations were any less affected by the loss of their offspring than parents in the mid to late nineteenth century but rather that the death of children began to seem more threatening or deleterious not only at the personal but also the cultural level.[14]

Throughout "First-Born," Du Bois idealizes Burghardt as a source of pure virtue—a boy whose magnetic appeal drew others close to him and whose goodness had a transforming effect on their lives:

> A perfect life was his, all joy and love, with tears to make it brighter,— sweet as a summer's day beside the Housatonic. The world loved him; the women kissed his curls, the men looked gravely into his wonderful eyes, and the children hovered and fluttered about him. I can see him now, changing like the sky from sparkling laughter to darkening frowns, and then to wondering thoughtfulness as he watched the world. (506)

Even as an infant, contends his father, the boy showed great potential as both a leader and a cultural observer. His early thoughtfulness, implies Du Bois, strongly suggests the possibility for greater and more powerful observations later in life. He is, in essence, not only a perfect example of the sentimental, sacred child but also the precocious embodiment of the ideal public intellectual:

he has the ability to watch the world and learn from it, and he has the capacity to capture and hold the attention of others.

Moreover, Du Bois portrays Burghardt's goodness as explicitly transracial. He is not only an ideal public intellectual in the general sense but, more specifically, he is an ideal race leader since his transforming effect encompasses both blacks and whites: "He loved the white matron, he loved his black nurse; and in his little world walked souls alone, uncolored and unclothed. I—yea, all men—are larger and purer by the infinite breadth of that one little life" (509). Du Bois makes use of the notion of the ideal or sacred child from the outset in "First-Born," drawing upon its potency as a cultural icon to portray Burghardt as an innocent and virtuous angel, his death a tragic loss not only for the family but for all of society—black and white. The essay's reliance on sentimental language and tropes is evident as early as the opening passage, which bears quoting in full because it lays the foundation for the epic-heroic qualities ascribed to the son in later descriptions; moreover, it exemplifies a constellation of issues—fatherhood, male-female relations, physical appearance—which take on crucial significance as the essay progresses:

> "Unto you a child is born," sang the bit of yellow paper that fluttered into my room one brown October morning. Then the fear of fatherhood mingled wildly with the joy of creation; I wondered how it looked and how it felt,—what were its eyes, and how its hair curled and crumpled itself. And I thought in awe of her,—she who had slept with Death to tear a man-child from underneath her heart, while I was unconsciously wandering. I fled to my wife and child, repeating the while to myself half wonderingly, "Wife and child? Wife and child?" . . . Up the stairs I ran to the wan mother and whimpering babe, to the sanctuary on whose altar a life at my bidding had offered itself to win a life, and won. What is this tiny formless thing, this new-born wail from an unknown world,—all head and voice? (507)

In this and other passages, Du Bois is simultaneously joyful over the prospect of having a son and tellingly anxious about the boy's physical appearance. He is at once captivated by the boy's individual charms and haunted by the material actualities of race that he knows will affect the boy's life once he leaves the relative protection of the domestic sphere. He thus moves back and forth between expressing his fatherly pride and lamenting the fact that the son has inherited his father's racial burden: "Within the Veil was he born, said I; and there within shall he live,—a Negro and a Negro's son. Holding in that little head—ah, bitterly! the unbowed pride of a hunted race" (507–8).

Beneath these shifting tides of pride and lament, however, is an abiding desire to locate the father-son relationship within a larger historical and cultural context of black male leadership. The Du Bois men, father and son, take their places in a long line of black male leaders moving steadily toward a vision of racial equality:

> I . . . saw the strength of my own arm stretched onward through the ages through the newer strength of his; saw the dream of my black fathers stagger a step onward in the wild phantasm of the world; heard in his baby voice the voice of the Prophet that was to rise within the Veil. (507)

Not only is Burghardt designated to carry on his father's vision for race relations, he is assigned to do so under the imagined guiding hand of a brotherhood of former black leaders. He is cast as a future prophet of the race, one whose presence will ensure the continued cultural significance of black manhood and whose voice will carry on the "dream" of Du Bois's "black fathers." Declaring his son a descendant of the fathers of the black race not only establishes Burghardt's birthright as future prophet, it also serves as means for Du Bois himself to secure a role in the pantheon of black leaders. Throughout "First-Born," Du Bois seems most at ease describing his relationship to Burghardt when he discusses it as one of current-leader to future-leader, almost as though the boy's standing as an intellectual heir mattered more than his identity as an actual son. The father-son bond appears tightest in those moments, such as I quote in the excerpt above, when both are allowed to dwell in the intellectual fraternity of black father figures.

But when Du Bois views his son in a more domestic context, the distance between them—and Du Bois's unwillingness to bridge it—is strikingly apparent. In moments when the material actuality of Burghardt's existence as an infant supplants his imagined role as a child-prophet, it is Du Bois's wife who performs the work of linking father and son. Throughout the essay she not only controls the caretaking of the boy, she also determines how Du Bois interacts with him at both the physical and emotional levels:

> No hands but hers must touch and garnish those little limbs; no dress or frill must touch them that had not wearied her fingers; no voice but hers

could coax him off to Dreamland, and she and he together spoke some soft and unknown tongue and in it held communion. (507)

It is significant that Du Bois sees his wife and son as speaking their own language—even more so that Du Bois recuses himself from their dialogue, preferring to maintain his status as a detached observer rather than take part in the family communion. He can imagine an intellectual intimacy with Burghardt, but he does not allow himself physical closeness. He acknowledges at the outset of the essay that he required his wife's presence and instruction in order to establish a bond with his infant son, stating in the opening lines: "Through her I came to love the wee thing." In effect he temporarily gives over his stake in his son's physical and emotional life to his wife while maintaining control over Burghardt's potential as a prophet and leader of the race.

Du Bois's attention to the mother-son bond grants his wife a substantial if somewhat idealized presence early in the essay and suggests that he is not entirely comfortable associating himself with the domestic sphere in which she and the boy dwell. His subsequent appropriation of his son's body—the mother disappears from the final pages of the essay—and his establishment of an intimacy based on their shared membership in the fraternity of race men, serves to diminish the presence of the domestic. After the boy's death, when her job as a caretaker and nurturer no longer needs to be filled, Du Bois eliminates her from the text and reasserts his own influence on the boy, ending the essay with a monologue that wavers between anguished lament over the loss of Burghardt's potential as a prophet and bitter hope that he is somehow better off for not having lived to experience the evils of life in a segregated America.

For Du Bois, the urgency of race as a continuing problem in post-Reconstruction America virtually demanded that he use Burghardt's death to his public, political advantage. And the potential of the sentimental elegy to convey racial issues to white audiences without alienating their sympathies compelled Du Bois to make use of its commonplaces almost without reservation as a means of erecting the boy's memorial. I must emphasize that I use the word "almost" as a placeholder, a way of marking that which, finally, cannot responsibly or accurately categorize as either an affirmation or rejection of sentiment on Du Bois's part. To choose between the two would be inaccurate because it would suggest that Du Bois either successfully maintained the potential of his son's black-white body to consolidate the sympathies of members of both races, hence opening the way for political and social change, or that he gave up on sentiment entirely.

To continue explicating Du Bois's carefully choreographed expression of emotional intimacy with his son—and the "advance-and-retreat" strategy he employs with respect to sentimental elegy—I turn to an issue that is central to "First-Born" but that I have touched upon only briefly in my reading thus far: Du Bois's exposure of and anxiety over his son's physical appearance. The boy's status as both black and white or, more accurately, as a black child who can pass as white, serves to flesh out, in both the literal and figurative senses, his father's theories of race and doubleness. To understand how these theories are imbricated in *The Souls of Black Folk* and how they inflect the representation of Burghardt in "First-Born," I will refer to earlier writings by Du Bois, specifically the 1897 essay "The Conservation of Races," which manifest the varied and, at times, contradictory concepts of race he would employ throughout his career.

Using Burghardt as both a metaphor for his famous concept of double consciousness and as an embodiment of his vision of the possibilities and problems of interracial unity, Du Bois raises the political stakes of the boy's memorialization beyond that which would normally be associated with the depiction of a sacred or ideal child. Indeed, Du Bois's memorial of Burghardt raises the stakes of such idealization by recasting the sentimental sacred child in explicitly interracial terms—terms that are still grounded in ideas of virtue and sacrifice, of loss and overcoming, but that are, ultimately, too complicated (and potentially explosive) to be accounted for or contained by these ideas alone.

Race and Doubleness

The first chapter of *Souls* recalls the sense of psychic imprisonment Du Bois experienced as a black child growing up in the largely white community of Great Barrington, Massachusetts:

> The shades of the prison house closed round about us all: walls strait and stubborn to the whitest, but relentlessly narrow, tall, and unscalable to sons of night who must plod darkly on in resignation, or beat unavailing palms against the stone, or steadily, half hopelessly, watch the streak of blue above. (364)

Although neither blatantly hostile nor explicitly hateful, the brand of racism Du Bois grew up with was no less destructive than that he would encounter later in life. The particular torture of being able to view the possibilities for growth and advancement but unable to access them was as galling for Du Bois as outright violence. But it is important to recognize that his depiction of the emotional burdens and restrictions of racism serves to partially obscure a tension between a notion of race that depends on the shared experience of oppression and a concept that assumes a biological basis for racial differences. All blacks in Great Barrington face a similar set of racial barriers—which, Du Bois implies, serves to define them, as a race, in relation to whites—yet, he takes care to note that even the "whitest" of blacks in the town are limited in their opportunities to advance–implying that biology might serve as a defining factor for race as well. Although, in the end, everyone's common experience under segregation places them in the same subjugated position, Du Bois leaves open—indeed, calls attention to—the physiological differences among them.

Anthony Appiah argues that Du Bois's definition of race, particularly in early writings such as "The Conservation of Races," demonstrates a belief in a biological notion of race that is always in tension with the idea of sociohistorical ties that define the concept less in terms of shared blood than of shared experience—in this case, the common experience of oppression. Appiah then proceeds to take Du Bois to task for assuming that his own experience with racism as an African American would hold true for all blacks—no matter what their country of origin or nationality.[15] Modifying Appiah's assessment somewhat, Anita Haya Patterson sees Du Bois's contradictory claims as an intentional and potentially productive strategy rather than an accidental and debilitating misstep: "a deliberate gesture of critique and not a conceptual limitation."[16]

The tension between the biological and the sociohistorical meanings of race is readily apparent in Du Bois's emotional reaction to his son's physical features:

> How beautiful he was, with his olive-tinted flesh and dark gold ringlets, his eyes of mingled blue and brown, his perfect little limbs, and the soft voluptuous roll which the blood of Africa had moulded into his features! I held him in my arms, after we had sped far away to our Southern home—held him, and glanced at the hot red soil of Georgia and the breathless city of a hundred hills, and felt a vague unrest. (507)

The description starts off sounding very much like an idealized portrait—the typical sacred child of nineteenth-century sentimental elegy. But the physical signs of racial difference manifested by the body of his son require a revision of the commonplace. Descriptions of his beauty—"olive-tinted" flesh and the "soft voluptuous roll which the blood of Africa had moulded into his features"—give way to uneasy speculations about signifiers of whiteness since the child's golden hair and blue eyes make him look more "white" than "black." The boy's body serves as a way for Du Bois to draw a parallel between the potential for passing in the racial sense and the certainty of passing in the mortal sense. In making such a connection, Du Bois suggests that his son's death was due less to his illness than to his racial heritage—his history and his fate were readable in his features because the marks that would have allowed him to pass were also the marks that necessitated his death. Here the loving descriptions of the son's physical appearance, so typical of the sentimental elegy, give way to concern over markers of racial identity such as the color of his son's eyes and hair; for Du Bois, Burghardt's capacity to simultaneously embody whiteness and blackness serves as a vexingly concrete manifestation of both the possibilities for racial harmony and the potential for racial obliteration.

In "The Conservation of Races" Du Bois lays the conceptual groundwork for his characterization of Burghardt; as in *Souls,* Du Bois begins by claiming that the development of individual identity must always be understood within the framework of "race"—whether it be biological or sociohistorical (817). Du Bois's first concern is to show that race is critical to a linear understanding of history. In other words, he pushes beyond the model of the individual representative figure as a historical agent—the "great man" theory of history—to establish the importance of racial groups in the study of human development. In effect he is establishing the conceptual basis for understanding the relationship of human action to social change as one in which a collective group, linked together by racial similarities, determines the course of history. This concept is a precursor to the idea of the pantheon of black forefathers in "First-Born" whose dream was to be carried "a step onward in the wild phantasm of the world" by Du Bois and his son.

In a step that seems damaging, at least in theory, to Burghardt's claim to this birthright of collective, black male leadership, Du Bois asserts that racial differences necessarily rely on the appearance of physical differences (817). Even while he seems more concerned with establishing the presence of an abstract set of differences—characteristics more apparent to the humanist than the scientist—he cannot entirely divest himself of the notion that physical differences are markers of distinctions among races and the implication that, if one does not appear black or white, one may not be categorized—either for better or for worse—as such. We can read the slippage between Du Bois's apparent rejection of empirical observation and his return again and again to the importance of biology and blood as an attempt to formulate a way of talking about differences that minimizes the limiting effects of static, physical racial boundaries (a task with which he continues in later writings such as the 1915 work *The Negro*). Recognizing that physical definitions of race are inherently unstable due to the fact that no race is able to maintain any sort of physical "purity," he argues that definitions of race must be dynamic and flexible enough to permit the discussion of differences without always resorting to physical categorization.

Yet, when he describes Burghardt's body in *Souls*, physical categories are precisely what he seems most anxious about. The problem of physical purity is strikingly manifested when Du Bois demonstrates his anger over the fact that his son's "white" blood seemed to have had more of an effect on his appearance than his "black" genetic background:

> Why was his hair tinted with gold? An evil omen was golden hair in my life. Why had not the brown of his eyes crushed out and killed the blue?—for brown were his father's eyes, and his father's father's. And thus in the Land of the Color-line I saw, as it fell across my baby, the shadow of the Veil. (507)

Du Bois's frustration over his son's appearance operates on two levels: he seems offended that the boy's body reinscribes a pattern of racial dominance and oppression whereby whiteness obliterates or limits the possibilities for black expression. Du Bois even goes so far as to imply that his son's appearance is somehow a harbinger of evil: by embodying whiteness through his golden hair and blue eyes, Burghardt perpetuates the taint of the Veil. Even beyond the problem of serving as a signifier of white oppression, however, Burghardt's physical appearance provokes his father's anguish because it may prove to disrupt the generational progression of black male leaders; the material realities of his whiteness may render him unable to carry out the intellectual work of fulfilling the vision of his black forefathers, As such, Burghardt may alter or interrupt not only the history of black male leadership but also the proper progress of race reform.

The confusion over what constitutes race and why it is important is articulated by Du Bois himself in "The Conservation of Races" when, after moving from the sociohistorical to the biological and back again, he poses the question once more:

> What, then, is a race? It is a vast family of human beings, generally of common blood and language, always of common history, traditions and impulses, who are both voluntarily and involuntarily striving together for the accomplishment of certain more or less vividly conceived ideals of life. (820)

His answer conceptualizes race as an ambiguous mix of commonalities—shared cultural practices and vague desires—in which all members are invested to a certain degree but which not all members find equally compelling. It would seem that Du Bois's ambiguity is designed to allow an inclusive understanding of race—one that accepts boundaries insofar as they help hold groups together but rejects them when they become exclusionary or reductive. This definition can be read as an attempt to recognize and retain the utility of racial categorization without falling victim to the possibly negative, racist consequences that such categorization might imply or allow. The ideals are meant to be fixed only insofar as they remain responsible representations of that which the members of the race find valuable (and, one might also add, insofar as it remains possible to maintain distinctions among races based on physical difference). Should the notions of what is valuable as a common goal—or what is recognizable as a common appearance—change, Du Bois leaves open the possibility for such to be acknowledged and made apparent. He thus understands race—here in a conceptual sense and in *The Souls of Black Folk* in a material sense—as a double bind: a necessary marker of difference that may become dangerous if deployed exclusively rather than inclusively.

In *The Souls of Black Folk,* Du Bois refers again and again to the notion of doubleness as a figure for African American subjectivity, the most famous example appearing in the opening chapter:

> It is a peculiar sensation, this double-consciousness, this sense of always looking at one's self through the eyes of others, of measuring one's soul by the tape of a world that looks on in amused contempt and pity. One ever feels his two-ness,—An American, a Negro; two souls, two thoughts, two

unreconciled strivings; two warring ideals in one dark body, whose dogged strength alone keeps it from being torn asunder. (365)

Here Du Bois makes more explicit the tension that he touches upon in "The Conservation of Races": doubleness serves as the focal point of his attempts to conceptualize race in the twentieth century as he identifies the problem of a Negro self that comes to understand itself through the perceptions of the American other. Despite his claims for separateness, Du Bois does not favor the rejection of the double because he knows that, in doing so, a part of the self would be lost: "The history of the American Negro is the history of this strife,—this longing to attain self-conscious manhood, to merge his double self into a better and truer self. In this merging he wishes neither of the older selves to be lost" (365). The double, for Du Bois, must be retained as a way of conceptualizing the Negro self in America not only because it acknowledges the problematic of maintaining and negotiating an unreconcilable racial "two-ness" but also because it recognizes the importance of difference as a necessary element in the process of (re)thinking the relationship of the self and the other. Doubleness, in this sense, is predicated upon a kind of self-reflection that recognizes the role of the other in the formation of the self (and, thus, the interdependence of the two concepts)—but, at the same time, such self-reflection refuses to subordinate the self to the other.

But while the most famous examples of Du Bois's concepts of race and doubleness are articulated in the opening chapter of *Souls,* the problems of self-reflection and the need to find a way of communicating theories of race and doubleness are made concrete in "Of the Passing of the First-Born." Reinscribing his son's biracial appearance as part of his memorial to the boy's memory—and in order to further the project of race reform—renders race and doubleness more than intellectual problems, more than theoretical exercises in reconciling racial "two-ness" or recognizing the role of the white other in the formation of the black self: Burghardt's body becomes a valuable and volatile resource, the cultural and political meanings of which Du Bois must generate and control in order to amplify his message. In exposing Burghardt's body to the public gaze, however, Du Bois must actually confront the racial other it represents. In other words, he must actually put into practice the ideals of self-reflection he theorizes in "The Conservation of Races" and intellectualizes still further in the opening chapter of *Souls.* It is the powerfully disruptive and intellectually unnerving force of this public confrontation with his son's body—a confrontation that cannot, finally, be categorized as either rescue or betrayal, resistance or complicity—that lies at the heart of Du Bois's elegy and that, ultimately, stands as a metaphor for his own dual status as a sentimental writer and a race man in the public sphere. Coming to terms with the material realities of race and duality as they are manifested by his son's body requires Du Bois to bring his story and his son's together, accepting the racial other that he believes, as an intellectual, is a necessary component of African American identity, even as he violently rejects the "golden curls" and "blue eyes" that he also believes, as a keeper of the dream of his black fathers, are evil omens of the obliteration of the race. Burghardt's sentimentalized, sacred body—which also happens to be racially coded as both white and black—serves as a figure for African American identity, a concrete and tragic example of what it means to be identified as American but denied equal status on the basis of race. Literally embodying the actuality and impossibility of black and white coexistence, Burghardt offers the opportunity for imagining the unity of the two races even as his death forecloses the chance that such union might be perpetuated.

As I argued at the outset of this essay, Burghardt Du Bois's death was both a tragedy and an opportunity for his father: taking on the role of the sentimental elegist—even if he did not take it on completely—gave Du Bois the means to represent an emotional intimacy with his son even as his elegy served as a site for developing broader affective bonds between blacks and whites. Casting his son's death not so much as a personal obstacle to be overcome but as an inevitable and tragic result of systematic racial inequality, Du Bois calls upon his white audience to share in the sorrow of the boy's passing—to recognize, in the best and most idealistic tradition of sentimentalism, the value and power of affect to function across, even repair, social divisions. And while it is clear that sentiment is never entirely adequate for Du Bois—it cannot reach those callous whites who muttered racist insults at the boy's funeral procession—it does provide him, in the form of the father's elegy, a space in which to begin the work of memorializing his son and expressing the complex mix of emotions that resulted from his death. Writing as both a sentimental man and a race man in "First-Born," Du Bois pays a personal, emotional tribute to his son's brief life even as he universalizes his loss, characterizing it as emblematic of the larger sense of social fragmentation that *The Souls of Black Folk,* as a whole, is meant to reflect as well as remediate.

Notes

1. According to David Levering Lewis, the couple was living in a one-room apartment on Lombard Street in Philadelphia's Seventh Ward when Burghardt was conceived in February 1897. Nina traveled to Du Bois's home of Great Barrington, Massachusetts, to give birth and recover. When she returned, Du Bois moved the family into a two-story brick home on St. Alban's Place. See Lewis, *W. E. B. Du Bois,* pp. 193–201.

2. Du Bois had already gained a measure of national prominence with the 1896 publication of his doctoral thesis, *The Suppression of the African Slave-Trade to the United States of America, 1638–1870,* as the first volume of the Harvard Historical Monograph Series.

3. Lewis, *W. E. B. Du Bois,* p. 344.

4. W. E. B. Du Bois, *Writings,* p. 419. All subsequent references to Du Bois's writings are to this edition unless otherwise noted and will be cited parenthetically in the text.

5. For an early discussion of the origins of the "race man" concept, see Drake and Cayton, *Black Metropolis;* for a more recent analysis see Carby's *Race Men.* Carby's book, of which Du Bois is a key subject, offers a powerful critique of the gendered assumptions upon which the notion of the race man has been constructed. It reveals the limits and exclusions, especially as they pertain to black women, that have resulted from the privileging of a particular type of black male intellectual as a proper and adequate representative for the African American race as a whole.

6. While the essays that surround Du Bois's treatment of the death of his son employ autobiographical moments to exemplify the problems of black-white relations or to present a universal concept of African American experience, "First-Born," we are meant to understand, is *too* autobiographical, *too* melodramatic, to be approached as a key or exemplary component of Du Bois's treatment of race and race relations in *Souls.* Zamir, for example, suggests that the essay's personal content and tone are somehow at odds with the text's focus on issues of race: "Suddenly, a personal loss that has little to do with the history or politics of racism occupies center stage, and stoic reticence gives way to melodramatic public mourning" (*Dark Voices* 190). Other critics—those interested in the essay's relationship to the high or classic elegy tradition—view "First-Born" with a more sympathetic eye; studying its relationship to the Christian elegy in Europe and America, they see "First-Born" as an intriguing extension of classic conventions that serves, in part, to highlight the need for new forms of elegiac discourse capable of more fully representing the experiences of African Americans. For them, the essay is interesting not so much for what Du Bois says about the loss of Burghardt but because of the traditional forms he appears to be referencing and revising. Rampersad's *The Art and Imagination of W. E. B. Du Bois* and Byerman's *Seizing the Word* both address the essay's status as an elegy. Rampersad argues that the subject matter and tone of "First-Born" are best understood as manifestations of its rootedness in the conventions of the classic elegy. He contends that the essay's form and language result from Du Bois's classical training in rhetoric and oration at Fisk and Harvard and that it exemplifies the articulation of paradox that he sees as one of Du Bois's main goals in *The Souls of Black Folk.* By formalizing the personal, Du Bois seeks, in Rampersad's words, "to reduce apparent chaos or flux to duality, dilemma, or paradox" (73). Building on Rampersad's assessment, Byerman ascribes the essay's formal quality to Du Bois's attempt at revising classic elegiac conventions in order to construct a critique of white-on-black racism,

arguing that "First-Born" achieves its effect by systematically reconfiguring standard features of literary mourning texts (31). For Byerman, "First-Born" is both an example of classic elegiac form and a comment on the inability of that form adequately to account for the particulars of African American experience. In his view, Du Bois's deformation of Eurocentric conventions serves as evidence of the impossibility that such conventions might sufficiently convey the meaning of a racially coded loss.

7. See Haralson's chapter in this volume.

8. In this regard Du Bois seems very much like those white men for whom intimacy, as Nelson suggests in her study of the ideology of manhood and civic identity in American culture, is most easily achieved with dead or absent others. See Nelson, *National Manhood*, pp. x–xi.

9. Sánchez-Eppler, "Then When We Clutch Hardest," pp. 81–82.

10. My argument here builds on that of Mizruchi who points to the funeral scene in "First-Born" as evidence of Du Bois's "consistent declarations of distrust in the sentiments" and "his awareness that appeals to the emotions (of the kind on display in nationalist celebrations like parades and fireworks demonstrations, as well as in universal practices like mourning) have so often been vehicles of intolerance" (*Science of Sacrifice* 269–71). Of course, one could also argue, less polemically, that Du Bois's decision to include the insults in his description of the funeral procession is itself an attempt to consolidate the sympathies of other whites who would have found such callous behavior unthinkable.

11. Zelizer, *Pricing the Priceless Child*, p. 11.

12. For a representative sample see: Cott, *The Bonds of Womanhood;* Halttunen, *Confidence Men and Painted Women;* Lears, *No Place of Grace;* Matthaei, *An Economic History of Women in America.*

13. For descriptions of immigrant family life, see Lasch, *Haven in a Heartless World.* For an analysis of the various kinds of relationships between work and family in African American culture, see Jones, *Labor of Love, Labor of Sorrow.* As Zelizer acknowledges throughout her book, the sacred child was a luxury usually affordable only to those in the middle or upper classes. Children of poorer families or those supported by the state were treated unsentimentally.

14. Zelizer, *Pricing the Priceless Child*, pp. 10–11.

15. Appiah, *In My Father's House*, pp. 30–46.

16. Patterson, *From Emerson to King*, pp. 161–62.

6

The Law of the Heart

Emotional Injury and Its Fictions

JENNIFER TRAVIS

> In its new attitude self-consciousness regards itself as the necessary element. It knows
> that it has the universal, the law, immediately within itself, a law which because of this
> characteristic of being immediately within consciousness as it is for itself, is called the
> Law of the *Heart*
>
> —Hegel, *Phenomenology of Mind*

> Nebraska is particularly blessed with laws calculated to regulate the personal life of her
> citizens. They are not laws that trample you underfoot and crush you but laws that just
> sort of cramp one. Laws that put the state on a plane between despotism and personal
> liberty.
>
> —Willa Cather, *Lincoln Evening State Journal*, 31 October, 1921[1]

In Willa Cather's *A Lost Lady* (1923) the bridge onto the Forrester's property floods and is nearly destroyed the same night Mrs. Forrester reads in a Denver paper that her lover, Frank Ellinger, has married Constance Ogden. The right of way that invites visitors to the property throughout the novel is washing away, and Mrs. Forrester must trudge through mud and rain "up to a horse's belly" to leave Sweet Water for town.[2] Marian Forrester makes her way to the law office of Niel Herbert in order to have one last "conversation" with her lover, a conversation that Niel cuts off by snapping the phone lines before their intercourse becomes too heated.

The lovers' last "conversation" is hardly the "trespass" it once was according to the civil law action of criminal conversation,[3] if only because Niel is able to interrupt the stormy evidence of their affair before it is exhibited over the phone lines for public hearing. Niel takes it upon himself to disrupt the "conversation" between Marian Forrester and Frank Ellinger literally and figuratively in his law office ("It was time to stop her, but how?") by taking the "big shears left by the tinner and cut[ing] the insulated wire behind the desk" (114). He does this at the moment the lovers' indiscretion is in danger of discovery, as they begin to argue, ironically, their need to "play *it* safe" (114, emphasis added).

Niel conceals the evidence of the "crime" while he is managing the law office during the absence of his uncle, Judge Pommeroy; he is reluctantly participating in the profession that thrived on "criminal conversation" proceedings.[4] Yet when Niel should be studying his law books, he instead reads novels; when he should be mastering legal reasoning, he instead is busy constructing fictional "double-lives" (67). Thus Niel Herbert both "knows" (because he takes the protection of Marian Forrester's indiscretion upon himself) and does not "know" (because he does not understand, nor has he mastered, the terms of law enforcement) the dimensions of the so-called "crime" he is witnessing. When earlier in the narrative he overhears Marian's "soft laughter" and Frank's "fat and lazy" laugh drifting through a bedroom window, it is neither his moral nor his legal authority but rather his aesthetic judgment that is offended, for he is not yet learned in the law (71). In fact, it is after the moment of the discovery of the affair (he plays the spurned lover, tossing the bouquet of flowers he has picked for Mrs. Forrester in a ditch) that Niel cements his decision to ditch his legal career and pursue architecture in Boston.

The "criminal conversation" that Niel perhaps unwittingly interrupts is an action understood by civil law as the equivalent of adultery; it enabled a husband (and later a wife)[5] to bring damages against a third party, "the seducer," for the husband's "loss of consortium" (or unique right to sexual relations with his wife). "Criminal conversation," which is not within the domain of criminal law (it is a tort), allows a heavy financial burden to be placed upon a third party not only as punishment for the "trespass" on the property of the wife and on the marriage contract more generally; it also, it is important to recognize, permits compensation for the injured feelings that may result. Moreover, crim. con. (its legal abbreviation) is "conversation" inasmuch as the boundaries that define the act of adultery are often constructed upon circumstantial evidence, "reasonable" speculations, hearsay, and the like, while its damages are assessed by virtue of successful accounts of pain and suffering.[6] Criminal conversation was meant, in other words, to redress the apparent loss of reputation that came with the "conversation" of neighbors, fellow workers, and others who may learn of and gossip about a spouse's "crime." With the growing punitive damages awarded by juries, large sums of cash were meant to abate the "injured honor" of the husband, appease his "mental anguish," and compensate for his "damaged" goods.[7] Although the label of "conversation" would seem to presuppose two participants, the law did not, for many years, recognize the participation of women in the conversation (women do not initiate it nor are they subject to it, they are the objects of "conversation" by law).

Wives in the early criminal conversation cases were neither victims nor actors; they were nonsubjects, the law making no discriminations as to the status of the woman in the "offense." The rendering of the husband as victim, however, had tremendous consequences for the shape of injury law and for later legal definitions of female subjecthood. The claims of emotional injuries suffered by *men*, claims that the action of criminal conversation were meant to redress, indicate the extent of the law's participation in what might be called the historical gendering of injury. This gendering is especially instructive today, given that many feminist legal scholars, from Catharine MacKinnon to Robin West, have developed a narrative of female "victimization," arguing, and often rightly so, for the need for the law to recognize *women* as the injured party in instances of rape, domestic violence, sexual harassment, sexual discrimination, job discrimination, and so on.[8] Since harms done to women, until quite recently, have remained apart from the domain of the protected or the compensable, feminist legal theorists have argued that women's sufferings need to be articulated through the vocabulary of "injury," since this vocabulary has had a "long and legitimated" history within legal discourse.[9] Such an articulation, they argue, would widen the scope of legally recognized injuries, so that harms experienced by women, harms that are often considered outside the law, would be made actionable. Against such expansion, however, lies the "deep structure" of injury law itself; it is a legal arena notable for its suspicion of narratives considered "emotive." Indeed, injury law, argues legal scholar Martha Chamallas, is a field that privileges the physical over the emotive, the material over the heart and mind, and, consequently, men over women. Moreover, the law's distrust of emotion is so pervasive that only recently has a collection of essays, *The Passion of Law* (1999), sought to narrate what its editor, Susan Bandes, calls the "unruly, complex, and emotional story about the place of emotions in the law." The law's own account of itself as emotionless is due, in part, to the perception that emotion "by its very nature . . . threatens much of what the law hopes to be."[10] The law, aspiring to be neutral and seemingly genderless, faces the added threat then that emotional narratives, narratives that might help to extend the domain of cognizable harms suffered by many underrepresented groups, will remain unheard.

It is in light of these complex renderings of emotion in the law that the history of culturally defined and legally actionable emotional injuries—injuries recognized chiefly in men—becomes especially interesting, perhaps surprising even, given the law's self-proclaimed suspicion of "emotive" narratives, narratives that were (and, in many respects, still are) associated with women. That the law in these cases often became a space in which *men* were supposed to have feelings offers crucial evidence against the readings of law as a domain of impartial reason and objectivity, a field unequivocally closed to emotive voices. Indeed, early tort actions such as criminal conversation expose the false juridical dichotomy of passion versus reason, since they demonstrate that men who suffered "emotional distress" could reach out to the law for redress and compensation. This suffering and these early victims are particularly worth our attention in light of the oft expressed presumptions about men's emotional lives, presumptions too often fueled by the misguided premise that sees masculinity (the genderless gender) as either emotionless or essentially repressed with regard to emotions. It is important to note that masculine emotions have not been the subject of widespread cultural disregard so much as men's use of and access to emotional territory has remained largely undertheorized or ignored (as many essays in this collection demonstrate). This essay reads among fictional and factual narratives in the nineteenth and early twentieth centuries, finding that the exemplary early victims of emotional injury, white middle-class men, emerge, in many respects, against the grain of literary and cultural history, against the tendency to view women and marginalized groups as the sole bankers of emotions, and against the culturally effective naturalization of victimization. I want to suggest that what scholars have described as the unacknowledged and uncompensated injuries to masculine status in a modern industrial economy found voice in a compensatory domain—that of domestic relations—in which emotional distress was given legal substance and, in turn, heard. For a novelist such as Willa Cather, the social landscape in post-Civil War America provides an acute occasion to explore the emotional authority of men; for the purposes of this essay, Cather's novel and its cultural framework offer a sustained example of how such authority invokes and shapes the injured psyche, casting it as a valid subject for protection, recognition, and, quite often, recompense. This non-unilateral and often fraught emergence of emotional wounds is particularly important given women's routine condemnation as original investors in the emotions; less regularly do we see, and thus it is more important that we assess, men's historical access to emotional territory, the very territory in which their power often rests.

Returning to Willa Cather's novel, for example, Niel Herbert's authority to unplug Marian Forrester's voice as it wavers dangerously over the telephone lines is not only matched but also exceeded by the power accorded Captain Forrester's (Marian's husband's) unspoken reservoir of related emotional wounds, as I shall go on to discuss. Marian Forrester's criminal and quickly interrupted conversation is but a fictive instance of the factual case (and numerous "heart-balm" actions might offer a similar analytic terrain) in which men like Captain Forrester were constructed as "victims" and, furthermore, compensated for their suffering. I want to take the occasion of the parallel resonances of fact and fiction to revisit and perhaps even resituate these early emotional injury claims, from their primary status as examples of patriarchal property rights wielded against women to their residual status as emotional, relational, and pecuniary melodramas of male affect.[11]

In this "emotion work," to recast Arlie Hochschild's phrase, I join the theorization and the expansion of the emotions that have become the interpretive work of several critical schools, from feminists and "emotionologists," to critical race theorists and some branches of the law and literature movement.[12] Influential legal scholars such as James Boyd White and Robin West often have invoked literary subjects to provide the law with a model of empathetic narrative, for example.[13] The law, these scholars argue, can "soften" its touch by listening to emotionally complex narratives, by regarding literature's subtle and sometimes ambiguous rendering of facts, and by providing the law with multiple voices of feeling. In her influential book, *Residues of Justice* (1996), Wai Chee Dimock has added her own voice to this intepretive school, arguing that literature should be considered a textualization of legal concepts, one that transposes, in her words, the "clean abstractions" of the law into the "messiness of representation."[14] While I agree that literature can amplify the texture and scope of legal concepts in interesting and sometimes surprising ways, I also hope to supplement these interpretive approaches by proposing that literature should be read not solely as a means to "humanize" law but also as a forum from which to analyze the kinds of fictions that the law employs in order to present itself as fully rational, fully neutral, fully unmediated, and, largely, emotionless in its representations. Literature, in other words, is not merely a messy or emotive voice that shakes up legal reason; legal narratives often occasion, if not require, both fictional and, at times, emotive vocabularies. The development of marital emotional distress claims within the legal history of injury law, their modes of evidence, and their perceptions of injuries illustrate how literary invention may be closely aligned with legal narratives, structuring its methods of remedy as well as of reward.

Literary and Legal Fictions

The legal history of criminal conversation is fraught with slips between the literary and the legal. According to Laurence Stone, as legal compensation in English criminal conversation cases was increasingly sought from a lover (rather than seeking his life), crim. con. trials began to attract more attention from a public seeking sensationalism and vicarious sexual stimulation.[15] Newspapers and law reports presented numerous detailed accounts of adulteries, and by the eighteenth century a genre of legal narratives had emerged that rivaled the novel for readers' attention.[16] Although crim. con. never achieved the expansive literary notoriety in the United States that it did in England, where the storybook construction of such cases became a kind of popular entertainment, there was a steady increase and influx of such cases reported in the daily papers. And whereas the pervasiveness of the action led to its abolition in the courts of England, the less numerous, though comparatively sensational cases in the United States[17] meant that although many of the "moral" grounds for such cases have lost their validity, criminal conversation has remained prosecutable, until recently, in a number of states.[18] Despite public exposure and lengthy trials, actions for criminal conversation were growing in popularity in the United States at the turn of the century, and by the 1920s these cases were commanding huge settlements.[19] Yet more than merely salacious reporting or storybook constructions, the law's constitutive dependency on fictionality would become especially striking in the tort of criminal conversation, in which the designation of the "crime" of sexual trespass was itself inspired by the techniques of the literary in that it asked its litigants continually to imagine and to act upon offenses that were sometimes matters of allusion and representation.[20] In many criminal conversation cases in England (where actions were soon deemed inadmissible on the above grounds) and in the United States, there were often no eyewitnesses who had seen the "crime" being committed first-hand, and testimony took the form of a narrative that reconstructed certain events, bits of conversation, and other forms of circumstantial evidence that were finally constructed by a skillful attorney, journalist, and perhaps even later, novelist, to appear "convincing."[21]

Witness the scene of "transgression" between Marian Forrester and Frank Ellinger in Willa Cather's novel, *A Lost Lady*. Marian and Frank make off for the river and surrounding forest in order to "cut cedar boughs for Christmas" (50). They stop and make their way into the thicket where they apparently "converse"; however, the novel does not describe for its readers the details of the action within the forest path. Cather continues, "When the blue shadows of approaching dusk were beginning to fall over the snow, one of the Blum boys slipped into the timber" where he presently heard voices moving near. Frank Ellinger and Marian Forrester emerge from the woods arm in arm, carrying the robes from the coach on which they lay, but no cedar boughs. (The narrator's conscious omission of the cedar boughs is, of course, only of relevance to the reader, as Adolph Blum would not have known the "excuse" for their foray.) After Frank lifts Marian into the coach, not without a long, perhaps amorous embrace, he asks, " 'What about those damned cedar boughs?' "(55); Marian responds, "it doesn't matter," but Frank, ever thoughtful about the appearance of such things, goes back to fetch the evergreens. The Blum boy, who followed their tracks toward the coach, hides behind it where "Mrs. Forrester had been waiting . . . with her eyes closed, feeling so safe, he could almost have touched her with his hand" (55). He hears her breathing, her eyes fluttering, her "soft shivers" as she sits waiting for Frank's return. The Blum boy overhears, but does not fully see the intercourse between the two. From his vantage point, which is both partial (he is hidden from view) and dependent upon circumstances about which he has no knowledge (the evergreens), whatever crimes may have been committed in the "eye of the law," crimes that have not been seen but may be suspected, the narrator tells us, are "safe" with Adolf Blum (56). Indeed, the evidentiary ambiguities that may be enough to warrant proof of conduct in the case law are here felt by Blum as little more than shivers of reminiscence.

Cather's use of the word "safe" with reference to Adolf Blum, like the safety referred to in Marian Forrester's conversation with Frank Ellinger with which this essay began, is meant to invoke precisely its opposite: the potential dangers of misused and misplaced narrative authority. Unlike Blum's "safe" witness, in case after case of criminal conversation, the courts found, as they did in *Wheeler v. Abbott* (1911) that "the conduct of these parties might lead thinking right-minded people to but one conclusion, that is, as expressed by some of the witnesses, 'there was something wrong' "; such *feelings,* according to the courts, were actionable regardless of whether the charges of adultery were vehemently denied, or whether there was any direct proof available. Adolf Blum's lack of ocular evidence, in other words, could still be interpreted in a law court to mean that injurious activity had taken place in the eye of the law. In such cases, the legal panopticon envisions the suspect as the substantive, the ethereal as the physical, and possible fiction as certain fact. In the legal panopticon, moreover, injuries suffered by men may be disassociated from the emotive by a juridical sleight of hand; such injuries, tied as they were to the loss of women's services, might render her relationship with her husband the equivalent of wage labor (without ever allowing this acknowledgement of homemaking as wage labor to see its logical conclusion), his feelings the equivalent of an employer's lost earnings. Hence, emotional injuries suffered by men could be interpreted as scarcely emotional at all.[22] And while the eye of the law could be used to grant authority, to render male suffering visible (while masking the emotive) and viable, it also withdrew authority to render women invisible. According to arguments against wives as plaintiffs in criminal conversation cases the courts found that: "In the eye of the law, the female could not even give her consent to the adulterous acts, and as a result, it was no defense in this form of action that the defendant had been enticed into criminal conversation through the acts and practices of the woman."[23] Because a woman was not seen in "the eye of the law" as having sexual subjecthood, nor could she conceivably express at once either desire or injury, she could not bear witness on her own behalf. Evidentiary rules of law likewise forbade or deemed unworthy the testimony of women within the courts.[24] And yet it was at precisely this juncture that emotional pains suffered by men would increasingly become cognizable by the law through such civil actions as criminal conversation and, quite often, through expanding divorce laws. Thus not only must critics read the law as a space in which emotionality is differentiated—and assigned differential evidentiary weight—along gender lines, readers must also reevaluate the rhetorical renderings of pain and injury, examining the entry of emotion into legal and lay cultures as well as the discourse of traumatic personhood that ensues. Given the view that the law maintained as to its workings, a view that perceived itself as impartial and gender blind—although literary fictions such as Willa Cather's make visible just how dependent the law may be upon the partial glimpses of human eyes for its details—such readings are crucial. Not only do they have the potential to expose how a version of emotional apartheid is an operating fiction of culture, they also may illuminate, as the early criminal conversation cases do, that the extension of emotional reparations may reconsolidate rather than radically challenge—as so many contemporary critics may hope—hegemonic power. In other words, male affective dramas may revive a man's diminished status more readily than they offer models for remedying or reconceptualizing the pain of others.[25]

Tort Trouble

In the account of the emergence of injury law narrated by legal scholars such as Morton Horwitz and Lawrence Friedman, tort law expanded in the middle of the nineteenth century to cope with the growing negligence claims for industrial accidents, especially the escalating damages caused by the railroad. With the rapid pace of industrialization by the middle of the nineteenth century in the United States, injury became a common cost of economic production. The paradox of this expansion in tort law, however, was that as quickly as it sprang up it was consequently curtailed, as Nan Goodman describes in her book, *Shifting the Blame: Literature, Law, and the Theory of Accidents in Nineteenth-Century America* (1998). According to scholars from Horwitz to Goodman, the introduction of legal doctrines such as the fellow-servant rule, the assumption of risk, and negligence meant that the new principles of tort and contract laws often made the recognition and compensation of injury unavailable to those who most suffered, namely industrial workers.[26] Willa Cather, for example, imagines this economy of injury in terms of two classes of citizens who emerged from the railroad's westward expansion: "there were two then distinct social strata in the prairie States; the homesteaders and hand-workers who were there to make a living and the bankers and gentlemen ranchers who came from the Atlantic seaboard to invest money and to 'develop our great West' "(3). Needless to say, Captain Forrester was associated with the latter group of men. "In those days it was enough to say of a man that he was "connected with the Burlington"; he was part of the "railroad aristocracy" (3). Indeed, Captain Forrester, gentleman rancher, who, perhaps ironically, would become the injured party in Cather's novel, made his fortune on this railroad. For the Captain this meant that he would be well acquainted with the dimensions of injury law (developing alongside crim. con. actions) that were making their mark in and through the physical injuries that accompanied expansion. Captain Forrester, a contractor who built "hundreds of miles of roads" for the railroad, would be knowledgeable about the industrial accidents suffered by those "hand-workers" whom he employed (4). The growing branch of injury law, or tort law, which met the growing demand made by these cases, could not be far from Captain Forrester's consciousness, or the consciousness of Judge Pommeroy, whom the Captain keeps as his lawyer on call.[27]

Within the public sphere of commercial law—a sphere overwhelmingly favorable to business interests—the scope of damages and the domain of injury became exceedingly narrow, as Horwitz, Friedman, Goodman, and others have argued. Moreover, law courts, beginning to measure the scope of pain in injury cases in the middle of the nineteenth century, pronounced themselves particularly wary of claims for nonphysical damages, claims, Horwitz has argued, that might damage a prosperous economy. The 1861 English case, *Lynch v. Knight* set the Anglo-American precedent in this matter: "mental pain or anxiety the law cannot value, and does not pretend to redress, when the unlawful act complained of causes that alone."[28] It is all the more notable given such pronouncements, that this other domain of injury— injury psychic in character—was now being addressed and redressed by a sexual and juridical economy, an economy that did permit the category of "male pain" to exact compensation. The work-related injuries identified by Horwitz and others, injuries that were *uncompensated* in commercial tort law, were not the only injuries that were now receiving a new legal definition, as we have begun to see. Yet little attention has been paid by these critics to the private sphere, to the home that the railroad passes on its way into and out of town, and to the boundaries of marital sexual relations where such notions about "injury" often maintained a broader interpretive scope. Indeed, the corporate economic structure that developed in the United States in the middle of the nineteenth century, one of physical injuries and material reparations, coincided with a psychic structure also manifest in and through the law, in which men, regardless of their economic status, could capitalize on their feelings and pains. "Pain" was no longer solely a subjective cry of bodily harm; it was becoming a problem of both compensation and evidentiary representation in the United States. As work relations were adjusting to the needs of a new national economy, and as marriage was increasingly seen as consensual and affectionate, it was a wife's body and her lover's property that helped to constitute and to absorb male pain as an emerging legal category with increasing evidentiary weight. If the laboring man could not beat the corporation at court, he might legally beat his wife—or better, her lover—out of his property (perhaps the gentleman was always already entitled to such a claim).[29]

In Cather's novel it is not only the emergence of the westward railroad "aristocracy" but also the emergence of a corresponding economy, including an emotional economy between the sexes in Sweet Water, that marks the very primacy of injury in Captain Forrester's life. The first episode of injury comes after the Captain learns that he is in financial trouble, that a bank (whose depositors were "wage-earners; railroad employés, mechanics, and day laborers" [sic]) in which he too had invested his savings has failed; upon Judge Pommeroy's retelling of that event, the Captain suffers a stroke (74). Although Niel reassures the reader that "a stroke could not finish a man like Daniel Forrester" (78), the loss of the Captain's name, a name that would soon be the subject of gossips, very well could. For when Niel, the novel's embodiment of what he himself calls "affection and guardianship" (69), later tries to protect the ailing Captain from finding evidence of Marian's affair (by trying unsuccessfully to hide from him a letter addressed from Marian to Frank), Niel comes to understand that the wounded Captain, whom he describes as a "wounded elephant," "knew everything; more than anyone else" already (78, 99). It is two years later, however, soon after the night that Marian has her last word with her former lover—the night that is the subject of gossip between Mrs. Beasley, the telephone operator, and Molly Tucker, the seamstress—that Captain Forrester suffers the stroke that will soon end his life. "Soon afterward, when Captain Forrester had another stroke, Mrs. Beasley and Molly Tucker and their friends were perfectly agreed that it was a judgment upon his wife" (117). Whereas Niel attempts to protect Marian in his law office from disclosing what could be the costly evidence of her affair, he is unsuccessful in managing the gossip coming over the telephone lines, the same lines that will shortly bring "telegraphic news" of Captain Forrester's death (123). Quite apart from Mrs. Beasley's and Molly Tucker's judgment of Captain Forrester's condition, a judgment based on circumstantial and inferential evidence heard over telephone lines, it might be said that the Forresters represent for Cather two different methods of managing their injuries. If Marian Forrester is able to find uneasy protection from Niel Herbert during her angry words with Frank Ellinger, the Captain, perhaps the most congenial, certainly the least conversational figure in the novel, can only internalize his losses. In Cather's novel he finds no compensation for these injuries; indeed, subsequently, he dies.

It is important to note that the Captain's injuries and final death issue directly from his *emotional* losses rather than, as readers might expect, his financial distresses. This, we learn, is the judgment of the townspeople, although none, according to Niel, "could have been crueler" (117). And even when Niel protects Marian, it is the Captain to whom he repeatedly extends his narrative sympathies. Indeed, while Niel admires Marian Forrester, he acknowledges that "her comprehension of a man like the railroad-builder, her loyalty to him, stamped her more than anything else" (65). While Niel conveys the Captain's dramatic demise in the face of Marian's *disloyalty* (when she immediately becomes "lost"), Niel also offers the Captain up as a startling example of the increasing scope of emotional damages that were beginning to gain acceptance in the latter half of the nineteenth century. In some such cases, men such as Niel or the Captain might author narratives that spoke not of bodily, physical harms but of interior, emotional injuries. For a man bringing forward a criminal conversation case, for instance, the catalog of injury included "the deprived comfort, fellowship, society, and assistance of his wife in domestic affairs, and the . . . dishonor and disgrace"[30] for that husband, who "has suffered great mental anguish and injured feelings." Here the tort's focus is on the "intangible or dignitary interests" rather than the economic or physical.[31] Even as tort law elsewhere was defining itself as measures of compensation for injuries largely economic in kind, criminal conversation suits allowed men to act as protagonists in narratives issuing in a broader range of "crimes" known as *emotional injuries*.[32]

By the late nineteenth and early twentieth centuries, literature, along with medicine, psychology, and the law were all describing the development of a new species of emotional wounds and substantially broadening the complexity of their scope. In an expanding corporate economy, what appeared to be the narrowing definition of injury then excluding laborers from just compensation in the law courts, as Horwitz and Friedman have argued, did not discourage these same legal bodies from making awards for emotional injuries to plaintiffs in cases where, for example, sexual relations or "private" marital relations (what Carol Pateman has called the "original" if unacknowledged contract) were at stake.[33] Despite women's presumed status as the very embodiment of emotion, as purveyors of the private sphere, as subjects of and audience for the "sentimental" in nineteenth-century America, in the early emergence of injury law women often found themselves given a limited voice, as men were asserting their more capacious rights in just this regard (including calling emotional expressions economic imperatives). Such early examples of emotional wounds might prompt critics to once again question current cultural definitions of injury, to refine what is perhaps today too easily labeled "hystericism," to ask how the law creates new legally protected interests, why emotions became compensable, who is offered recompense. Although the legal action of criminal conversation is but one small piece in a complex history of legally actionable injuries, it is one, arguably, that begins to shape the grounds and dynamics with which all gender theorists, legal, and cultural critics will have to contend.

Talk Is not Cheap

By 1915 women too had acquired rights in a number of states to bring their "criminal conversation" cases forward.[34] When female subjecthood became a category of legal reasoning, however, the ensuing legal action quickly became devalued (as demonstrated by the speedy motions to repeal this tort action in many states).[35] These "heart-balm actions" (as criminal conversation and alienation of affection suits came to be called) were eventually brought to an end in many jurisdictions in the 1930s on the ground that these were "unfounded actions, coercive settlements, and excessive verdicts."[36] With such legal titles as the 1935 Indiana statute, "An Act to Promote Public Morals," women's conscious agency and evidentiary authority were once again dismissed as self-profiting, misguided, and unconscionable.[37] Such women were, in Niel Herbert's words, "lost." Yet, by reading these "lost" women as the sole source of emotional, irrational, and thus "unfounded" narratives (maintaining men's narratives as economic), by relegating these narratives to the domain of the unactionable, the law claimed for itself an allegedly transparent narrativity, a narrativity seemingly devoid of emotion. Indeed, the banishment of female evidentiary authority from the legal domain became a means for the law to create, once again, the image of itself as neutral and objective, to dangerously disavow its constitutive dependency on gendered notions of injury. Perhaps it is to the literary domain that critics must return, then, in order to see the residual spaces in which the emotional, the sexual, the injurious, and their accompanying evidentiary ambiguities are something other than self-evident. This is not to suggest that literature provides a truer site for their expression but perhaps a richer site, one from which legal reasoning itself might be reexamined, so that its rendering of injuries might finally be recognized for what they often are: not objective self-evidence but discursive representation.

Notes

1. See Bohlke, *Willa Cather in Person: Interviews, Speeches, and Letters*, p. 147. Cather's own historical awareness of contemporary problems in legal reasoning, as evidenced in this epigraph, frames a methodology in which I attribute to Cather's novel a sophisticated consciousness of legal fictions that is unavailable from an investigation of the archives of criminal conversation cases. Yet, as my study has shown, certain practices developed and began to affect the direction of tort law regardless of whether or not Cather, or indeed other novelists, in fact recognized the full dimensions of the issues they had posed for themselves. It is the autonomy as well as the parallel development of law and literature that most interests me.

2. Cather, *A Lost Lady*, p. 129. All references to this work are from this edition and will be cited in the text of the chapter.

3. "In 3 Blackstone's Commentaries, 139, it is said: 'Adultery or criminal conversation with a man's wife [is] a civil injury (and surely there can be no greater), the law gives a satisfaction to the husband for it by action of trespass vi et armis against the adulterer wherein the damages recovered are usually very large and exemplary,' " quoted in Annotation, *Turner v. Heavrin* 182 Ky. 65, 206 S.W. 23 (1918) 4 ALR 562 (1919). Its more current definition (after women were permitted by law to act as plaintiffs) is as follows: "Defilement of marriage bed . . . considered in an aspect of civil injury to the husband or wife entitling him or her to damages; the tort of debauching or seducing a wife or husband." *Black's Law Dictionary*, p. 336 (5th ed. 1979).

4. The growing popularity of criminal conversation cases seems to correspond with the repeal of statutes regulating lawyers' acceptance of contingency fees and attorney-client contracts for fees. Although New York was the first to enact the Field Code of 1848, repealing fee regulation, the American Bar Association did not approve contingency fees until 1908. For a discussion of retainer agreements see Brickman, "Contingent Fees Without Contingencies," p. 29; and Leubsdorf, "Toward a History of the American Rule on Attorney Fee Recovery," pp. 1–2.

5. Women were not permitted to bring this action until the early twentieth century; see: *Nolin v. Pearson* (1906) 191 Mass. 283; *Rott v. Goehring* (1916) 33 N.D. 413; *Frederick v. Morse* (1912) 88 Vt. 126. For states that held that a woman could not bring forward a criminal conversation action see: *Hodge v. Wetzler* (1903) 69 N.J.L. 490, 55 Atl. 49; *Kroessin v. Keller* (1895) 60 Minn. 372, 27 L.R.A. 685, quoted in Annotation, *Wife's Right of Action for Criminal Conversation*, 4 ALR 569 (1919).

6. Literally, criminal conversation was defined as " 'criminal' because it was an ecclesiastical crime; 'conversation' in the sense of intercourse." Prosser, *Handbook of the Law of Torts*, p. 875, n. 75. The circumstantial nature of the evidence involved with the tort was a primary factor leading to its repeal in England. See Stone, *The Road To Divorce*, pp. 232–33. That criminal conversation, which is a tort and not a crime, continues to be named "criminal," announces its relation to the crimes of adultery, fornication, sodomy,

and rape, in which the standard of proof (beyond a reasonable doubt) is much stricter than the civil standard (mere preponderance of the evidence).

7. These words were frequently used to describe the suffering of the husband in a variety of crim. con. and alienation of affections cases. Juries often sympathized with plaintiffs in such cases, deciding for huge settlements that would often bankrupt the third party.

8. See Chamallas, "Writing about Sexual Harassment: A Guide to the Literature"; MacKinnon, *Feminism Unmodified.*

9. See Howe, "The Problem of Privatized Injuries: Feminist Strategies for Litigation," pp. 148–67. See also Chamallas, "Women, Mothers, and the Law of Fright: A History," for a discussion of the gendered aspect of early tort claims.

10. See Bandes, *The Passions of Law,* pp. 2, 7.

11. "When a loss is experienced by a man, the law highlights its tangible and objective aspects and downplays its intangible and relational features," argues Chamallas; yet, when loss is experienced by a woman it is discredited as intangible and relational. I want to suggest that part of revising this evaluation is to acknowledge and revisit the seemingly tangible and objective for its contextual and relational vocabularies. See Chamallas, "The Architecture of Bias: Deep Structures in Tort Law," p. 520.

12. Hochschild refers to emotion work as the "act of evoking or shaping, as well as suppressing, feeling in oneself," in "Emotion Work, Feeling Rules, and Social Structure," p. 563. I am interested in the cultural work such emotions perform.

13. See White, *When Words Lose Their Meaning;* and West, *Narrative, Authority, and Law.*

14. Dimock, *Residues of Justice,* p. 10.

15. L. Simond, a Franco-American tourist writes in 1810–11: "I have heard of 10,000 Sterling awarded in some cases, which is certainly rather dear for a *conversation!* The husband pockets this money without shame, because he has the laugh on his side. . . . The publicity which such prosecutions necessarily occasion, and all the details and proofs of the intrigue, are highly indelicate and scandalous." Quoted in Stone, *The Road To Divorce,* p. 232.

16. Stone, in the above cited work, discusses how the action found its narrative place in the proliferation of pamphlets and sensationalized accounts of the trials. The intrigue surrounding the proliferation of criminal conversation cases (as well as the courts' increasing inability to discern fictitious cases) led to its repeal in England with the 1857 Matrimonial Causes Act.

17. The Beecher-Tilton Affair is among the most notorious of these cases in the United States. See Fox, "The Beecher-Tilton Affair." Fox has also just published a new book on this scandal: *Trials of Intimacy: Love and Loss in the Beecher Tilton Scandal.* See also Korobkin, *Criminal Conversations.* Korobkin writes about the forensic use of sentimentality that characterized not only Tilton v. Beecher, but also other criminal conversation cases and, by extension, the larger field of nineteenth-century legal discourse. While her study argues against readings of the law as a site of super-rationalism set against the outside world of emotion and experience, it does not go far enough toward explaining how sentimental narratives may become a site of unlikely power for those men who wield it deftly.

18. Ironically, actions for criminal conversation have only been barred by statue in Nebraska as recently as 1986 (Laws 1986, LB 877, 1). This came after *Vacek v. Ames,* a 1985 de-

cision that awarded a husband $100,000 in damages for "lost comfort, society, love and protection, pain, suffering, injury to health, degradation and humiliation" to be paid by his wife's lover. See *Proprietary to the United Press International* (December 6, 1985).

19. The settlements in cases were growing larger toward the beginning of the twentieth century, a fact that became a cause of its repeal in many jurisdictions. See *Mohn v. Tingley* 191 Cal. 470., 217 P. 733 (1923) ($75,000 compensatory and $25,000 punitive); *Overton v. Overton* 121 Okla. 1, 246 P. 1095 (1926) ($150,000 reduced to $60,000); *Woodhouse v. Woodhouse* 99 Vt. 91, 130 A. 758 (1925) ($465,000 reduced to $125,000). For a longer list of cases, including cases calling for the repeal of crim. con. see Weinstein, "Adultery, Law, and the State."

20. The *OED* traces the definition for *conversation* as "sexual intercourse or intimacy" back to Shakespeare's *Richard III:* "his Conversation with Shores Wife." *Oxford English Dictionary,* 2d ed., "Conversation." I do not want to suggest that what was considered adultery did not happen but, rather, that quite often what counted as sex was never an objective given.

21. For a discussion of circumstantial evidence in law and literature see Welsh, *Strong Representations: Narrative and Circumstantial Evidence in England.* I would argue that criminal conversation cases are a valuable archive proving that the literary and the legal concepts concerning the evidentiary are very much gendered issues and that the scorn for direct testimony that Welsh finds prevalent in the eighteenth and nineteenth centuries was directly linked to gendered and racial assumptions concerning who could be a reliable narrator.

22. Arguably, foregrounding its economy eased the entrance of emotional injury in the law. See Chamallas, "The Architecture of Bias," p. 493.

23. *Turner v. Heavrin* (1918) 182 Ky. 65, 206 S.W. 23. See also the aforementioned *Wheeler v. Abbott*, 131 N.W. 942 (Neb. 1911). This is an important overview of women's legal subjecthood with regard to criminal conversation.

24. African Americans were also barred from bearing witness on their own behalf. Certainly, the anxiety accompanying the changing status of African Americans in the late nineteenth century played a role in women's rearticulation as valuable property as well as the law's recreation of itself as a space in which white men are "supposed" to have feelings. For a discussion of Cather's novel in relation to questions of racial identity, see Walter Benn Michaels, "Race into Culture: A Critical Genealogy of Cultural Identity," pp. 655–85. For a discussion of "female subjects in the spectacular public discourses of law and testimony," see Wicke, "Postmodern Identities and the Politics of the Legal Subject," pp. 11–33.

25. See Wendy Brown, *States of Injury,* chap. 3, and Berlant, "The Subject of True Feeling," in *Cultural Pluralism, Identity Politics, and the Law,* pp. 49–85. Both critique what Berlant calls the "true subject as the feeling subject," and Berlant argues that "psychic pain experienced by subordinated populations must be treated as ideology, not as prelapsarian knowledge or a condensed comprehensive social theory" (72, 77).

26. "As soon as the universal duty of taking ordinary care was introduced in America, it was curtailed by four important legal doctrines. The first and most important of these was the doctrine of negligence under which the courts defined fault and assigned liability only in the absence of ordinary care which was, generally speaking, construed quite loosely in favor of the risk-taking entrepreneur." See Goodman, *Shifting the Blame,* p. 7.

27. Cather names Captain Forrester's lawyer "Judge"; he is called "Uncle Judge" by Niel, his nephew, while he is referred to as "the Judge" by other characters in the novel. His naming may provide an ironic comment upon the status of judges in the mid-nineteenth century, whose judicial power helped to encourage business interests. In Cather's novel, however, Judge makes poor fiscal judgments, resulting in Captain Forrester's bankruptcy. See Horwitz, p. 205. Judge Pommeroy, expressing his delight that his nephew has decided upon a career as an architect, says, "I can't see any honourable career for a lawyer, in this new business world that's coming up. Leave the law to boys like Ivy Peters, and get into some clean profession," p. 77.

28. *Lynch v. Knight* 9 House of Lords, Case 577, 1861. 11 *English Reporter* 854. Regardless of the increasing popularity of heart-balm actions in the United States, from the earliest days of injury law claims of emotional pain were suspect for a variety of reasons, from the fear of fraudulent claims to the supposed difficulty in measuring damages.

29. Unlike in England, criminal conversation plaintiffs in the United States were not primarily limited to the upper classes, and the principal plaintiffs seem to be drawn from a wide array of social circumstances. For a discussion of the class dynamics in English crim. con. cases, see Staves, "Money for Honor: Damages for Criminal Conversation."

30. *Smith v. Meyers,* 52 Neb. 70, 71 N.W. 1006 (1897). For a discussion of similar rulings and an analysis of alienation of affection and criminal conversation cases and their histories see Davidson, "The Thief Goes Free," p. 629.

31. 41 C.J.S. Crim. Con. 249.

32. This is not an argument for whether tort law should protect emotional or relational interests. For such a discussion see Finley, "A Break in the Silence: Including Women's Issues in a Torts Course," p. 41; and Bender, "A Lawyer's Primer on Feminist Theory and Tort," p. 3; Delgado, "Words that Wound: A Tort Action for Racial Insults," in *Words that Wound: Critical Race Theory, Assaultive Speech, and the First Amendment.* See also Brown, *States of Injury.*

33. See Pateman, "Contracting In," pp. 1–18. Of course, those "unrecognized within the civil realm of sufferers" comprises many, including but not limited to those excluded by virtue of sexuality, nationality, ethnicity, religion, disability, class, gender, and race.

34. See for instance, *Ash v. Prunier* 44 C.C.A. 675, 105 Fed 722 (1901); *Parker v. Newman* 75 So. 479 (1917); *Nolin v. Pearson* 191 Mass. 283, 4 L.R.A. (N.S.) 643 (1906); *Rott v. Goehring* 33 N.D. 413, 157 N.W. 294 (1916).

35. See "Annotation," "Constitutionality, Construction, and Application of Statutes abolishing civil actions for alienation of affections, criminal conversation, seduction, and breach of promise to marry," 158 ALR 235 (1945) and "Annotation," "Constitutionality, Construction, and Application of Statutes abolishing civil actions for alienation of affections, criminal conversation, seduction, and breach of promise to marry," 158 ALR 617 (1947) for a discussion of the motions to end criminal conversation in many states across the United States in the 1930s.

36. See Feinsinger, "Legislation Affecting Breach of Promise Etc." p. 417, for a detailed discussion of the movements to end "heart balm" actions.

37. Feinsinger, "Legislation," p. 420.

7

"The Sort of Thing You Should Not Admit"

Ernest Hemingway's Aesthetic of Emotional Restraint

THOMAS STRYCHACZ

Ernest Hemingway is famously responsible for a narrative aesthetic of emotional restraint. His younger self was searching, Hemingway claims in *Death in the Afternoon* (1932), to "put down what really happened in action; what the actual things were which produced the emotion that you experienced"; he was working to get the "real thing, the sequence of motion and fact which made the emotion and which would be as valid in a year or in ten years or, with luck and if you stated it purely enough, always."[1] Emotion was not to be erased from narrative, it seemed, but expressed in a strategy of metonymic displacement that would allow writers to avoid overtly emotional displays. Hemingway's iceberg theory of writing, which also receives articulation in *Death in the Afternoon,* comes readily to mind. The "dignity of movement of an iceberg is due to only one-eighth of it being above water" (192), Hemingway states. His context is the ability of the true writer to "omit things that he knows." But emotion might be thought of as being similarly submerged beneath the surface of the text, invisible, potent, leaving on display only those actions that are, in Ezra Pound's assessment of the modernist response to Victorian poetics, "austere, direct, free from emotional slither" ("A Retrospect" 12). The expression of these ideas in terms of character would have to be (in Philip Young's term) the Code Hero, that tough, taciturn exemplar of autonomous manhood whose devotion to a private Code of action demonstrates and authenticates the manly "real thing" (*Ernest Hemingway* 36).

As Pound's comments make clear, Hemingway's thoughts on writing accord with other modernists, who worked, in Imagist poems, manifestos, and in concepts such as T. S. Eliot's "objective correlative," to curtail Victorian sentimentalism and to trim the rhetorical excess they saw as its aesthetic sign.[2] Concepts of emotional restraint played a major role in structuring and undergirding what was supposed to be innovative about modernist aesthetics. Modernism was to be not only hard-boiled and tough-minded; it was specifically designed to contravene the outmoded tendencies of an earlier time, when emotional display and rhetorical overflow were thought appropriate. Emotionalism was aesthetically weak because it was not modern; it represented what would have to be made new if cultural productions were ever to become commensurate with a new age. A modernist aesthetics might even amount to a coming-of-age, as Hemingway implies when he equates the "real thing" with the writerly pursuits of his mature years. To the later New Critics, canon-makers extraordinaire, arguments such as these were persuasive. "Poetry," wrote Cleanth Brooks and Robert Penn Warren in the influential teaching anthology *Understanding Poetry* (1938), is "incorrigibly particular and concrete—not general and abstract." This being the case, modernist writers could be seen only as restoring poetry to an ontologically pure state. Indeed, for "people living in an urbanized modern society," poetry becomes a means for "restoring our originally unprejudiced life of the senses." Victorian "prolixity," characterized by "worn conventions, and empty rhetoric," presumably conveys the deadened senses imputed to modern urban society.[3]

The aesthetic realm, however, as Terry Eagleton argues in *The Ideology of the Aesthetic* (1990), cannot be separated from political, economic, legal, and other cultural formations.[4] The force of his argument is nowhere more evident than in recent reinterpretations of modernist aesthetics as being exemplary of a "masculinist 'Modernism.' "[5] In Bonnie Kime Scott's *The Gender of Modernism* (1990), for instance, Scott argues that the "experimental, audience-challenging, and language-focused" writing that used to be regarded as modernism has become "for some of our editors a gendered subcategory" such as early male modernism or masculinist modernism. She continues:

> None of the editors is particularly interested in fitting neglected figures into what is now seen as a limited definition, though there are discussions of the ways in which Djuna Barnes, Mina Loy, and Marianne Moore were admitted to the "male" category to the neglect of important feminine or feminist elements in their work.[6]

Sandra Gilbert and Susan Gubar, in their influential *No Man's Land* (1988, 1989) trilogy, likewise suggest that modernism must be read as "differently inflected for male and female writers." They trace a "link between male discontent and masculinist backlash" against female writers and argue that "modernist men of letters sought to define appropriately virile reactions" in response to the perceived infringements of female writers.[7] Hemingway, not surprisingly, is one of their key examples.

Scott, her editors, and Gilbert and Gubar all argue for the historical contingency of modernist aesthetics, which, far from representing the spirit of the modern age, must instead be seen as the production of gender relations within specific cultural contexts. Language-focused experimentalism was used to promote male hegemony and exclude female writers from the emerging modernist canon; such writing, in its hard-boiled evasion of direct expressions of emotion, might even be considered a substitute for the virility male writers now felt lacking as (according to Gilbert and Gubar) they entered an "ongoing battle of the sexes that was set in motion by the late nineteenth-century rise of feminism and the fall of Victorian concepts of femininity."[8] It would appear that aesthetic strategies for avoiding "emotional slither" stood in for and disguised a deeply rooted misogyny.

Hemingway's aesthetic of emotional restraint has thus been called on to represent at least three separate cultural trajectories. It has been employed to denote an ontologically pure and transcendent aesthetic (a "real thing," which, if stated purely, will "always" be true); to denote an aesthetic that intimately describes the specific social and cultural features of modernity; and to denote an aesthetic that describes a specifically *gendered* response to the conditions of modernity. Though in general agreement with the latter approach, this study puts forward a quite different interpretation of Hemingway's work and of modernism in general by arguing that his evocation of emotion in *Death in the Afternoon,* his apologia for bullfighting, is much more complex than his aesthetic statements and critical perceptions of them would lead us to believe. My analysis of the section following Hemingway's statement of his aesthetic principles, which critiques ostensibly sentimental responses to the plight of horses in the arena, suggests in fact that Hemingway's style is marked by powerful rhetorical transformations and emotional swings. The rhetorical excess that characterizes this scene—which I argue is typical of *Death in the Afternoon*—amounts to a counteraesthetic based not so much on emotional constraint as emotional disarray. We cannot, in other words, describe the book as promulgating the kind of aestheticized emotional restraint that is so often read into Hemingway's work under the rubric of a stylized narrative concision and of character traits such as self-control, quiet endurance, living by a code, and fear of emotional commitment. Though Hemingway certainly pays lip service to aesthetic and emotional constraint in *Death in the Afternoon,* the book more frequently concerns what he refers to in the section on horses as the "sort of thing you should not admit"—a statement that rhetorically invokes a stance of tight-lipped emotional restraint while setting up a lengthy inquiry into precisely what Hemingway says he should not admit, but does.[9]

My analysis leads to several important questions about modernist aesthetics and about the cultural constructions of masculinity that underlie them—as well as about Hemingway's work in general. In what sense can we critique Hemingway's work as an example of masculinist modernism—or critique modernism by way of Hemingway's exemplary masculinism—if *Death in the Afternoon,* which summarizes those famous principles of emotional self-control and rhetorical restraint, actively calls them into question? Conversely, if we view *Afternoon* as exemplary, does not an ethos of emotional disarray imply the need for a new articulation of modernism? And if it does, whence does this cult of emotional restraint emerge? I contend that it is crucial to theorize the ways in which performances of Hemingway's work within the United States academy have themselves been subject to the dissemination of hegemonic masculinities and thus to move toward an understanding of the interpretive horizon within which his work has been situated. In particular, I argue that the history of Hemingway criticism illuminates the often abrasive accommodation of older ideals of masculinity within a new ethos of professionalism, which developed in part to manage the intense strains on constructions of manhood during a time of dramatic economic and cultural change. Middle-class men working in newly professionalized fields of study within the developing university system were forced to struggle with the loss of older, hegemonic forms of masculinity and to restore a sense of masculine virility to a profession that seemed to them feminized and "weightless." Codes of emotional restraint, developed in response to a writer such as Hemingway, helped men express and control ambivalent feelings about the reshaping of individualistic masculine behavior within the new conditions of emerging professional communities.

A closer look at *Death in the Afternoon* reveals an account of manhood-fashioning that puts in question the idea of emotional restraint and thus the very code of manhood for which Hemingway has stood for so long. For several reasons, the long disquisition on the death of horses in the ring in chapter 1 provides a fine starting point. The passage, yoked to that famous discussion of the "real thing," seems to condemn a sentimental—thus exaggeratedly emotional—response to the bullfight. And it promises to exemplify just what is so significant about bullfighting: of the "three acts in the tragedy of the bullfight," Hemingway remarks, it is the "first one, the horse part, which indicates what the others will be, and in fact, makes the rest possible" (98). The horse part that makes everything possible, however, is problematic for both its emotional and its rhetorical dilemmas. Hemingway writes:

> The question of why the death of the horse in the bull ring is not moving, not moving to some people that is, is complicated; but the fundamental reason may be that the death of the horse tends to be comic while that of the bull is tragic. In the tragedy of the bullfight the horse is the comic character. This may be shocking, but it is true. (6)

This short passage begins with a statement that turns out to be a more complicated question than it appears, for the assertion that the death of the horse is not moving demands a quick supplement in favor of greater precision ("not moving to some people that is"). But the supplement itself hides the need for a further question: who are "some people"? Hemingway himself has just undercut any assumptions we might have about who responds to bullfights: "there was no difference, or line of difference, so that these people [those he introduced to the bullfight] could be divided by any standard of civilization or experience into those that were affected and those that were not affected" (4–5). The passage next attempts to establish a "fundamental reason," which is suddenly disestablished in the hesitant "may be" and further undermined by the vague statement that the death of the horse "tends to be" comic. The following sentence returns to secure positions (the bullfight is a tragedy; the horse is comic), preparing the way for the declaration in the next sentence that "it is true." But what is true quickly unravels with the subsequent revelations that, first, the nature of the comedy varies ("the worse the horses are . . . the more they are a comic element"); second, when horses are gored "they are not comic; but I swear they are not tragic"; third, the comic is actually the "burlesque visceral accidents which occur"; fourth, that there is "nothing comic by our standards in seeing an animal emptied of its visceral content"; fifth, the horse is "as comic when what it is trailing is real as when the

Fratellinis give a burlesque of it in which the viscera are represented by rolls of bandages, sausages and other things"; and sixth, disembowelings are sometimes "due to their timing . . . very funny" (6–7).

What, then, are we to make of a comedy in which at times the horses embody a truly comic principle that at others turns out to be merely a consequence of certain accidents of "timing" and at others not funny at all? The convolutions of Hemingway's argument are more than simply appropriate to a complicated question that has perhaps no final answer; they signify the author's own perfectly timed comic play with the rhetorical possibilities of language. In one sense the entire passage is a burlesque—a kind of disemboweling—of Hemingway's own aesthetic principles. The "simplest things" are here conveyed in outrageously long-winded and contradictory fashion. Moreover, the "actual things" themselves seem to vanish before our eyes. The horses' viscera, trailed around the ring, are described nonviscerally as "the opposite of clouds of glory." The Fratellinis are said to burlesque the horses' disembowelings by representing the viscera with "rolls of bandages" (of all things!), but Hemingway's horses are already only representations of horses: they are "parodies of horses," which are even held to look "like birds, any of the awkward birds such as the adjutants or the wide-billed storks" or "a little as a dead pelican does" (6–7). The last thing that can be done with these parodic bird-horses, it seems, is to see them as they really are; alternatively, if this is how they really are, Hemingway seems unable to present them without the most highly (and skillfully) managed contrivances of the rhetorician. One of the "simplest things of all and the most fundamental," violent death, turns out to be puzzlingly complex, for the example of the horses, which follows hard upon this statement, suggests that this book about bullfighting demands a rhetorical extravaganza rather than criteria such as the "real thing" or "simplest things."

As a corollary, diverse responses to the passage would seem possible: shock or distress at Hemingway's levity; disgust at his lack of concern for the horses; appreciation of his serious attempt to bracket off sentimental reactions; puzzlement at the muddled track he takes toward his goal; a combination of these, and more. The narrative, mimicking horses trailing pieces of themselves around the ring, provokes a tense emotional disarray.[10] What would seem most compromised in this carnival of perspectives and tone changes is our ability to develop a holistic emotional and intellectual attitude toward the horses' deaths. The passage on the horses, which Hemingway himself views as crucial to what follows, puts in doubt the possibility that this book reaches for a "real thing"—some elemental force, some principle of emotional constraint inscribed into action—embodied in yet beyond the reach of writing itself. Indeed, rather than presenting the "sequence of motion and fact" that made the emotion, *Afternoon* provokes an emotional disarray that variably constitutes the "real thing" under scrutiny. We cannot posit a sequence of facts in the deaths of the picador horses that captures and disguises an emotional experience as long as unpredictable rhetorical transformations keep forcing us to deploy varying emotional responses. While any interpretation of *Death in the Afternoon* must come to terms with Hemingway's rhetoric of truth, purity, completion, and transcendence, this discussion suggests that the book, by insisting precisely on its rhetorical status, emphasizes a discourse of incompletion, free play, and emotional variance.

The kind of debate Hemingway opens with his account of the horses is everywhere implicit in the seriocomic rhetorical performances, as well as in the failures, self-dramatizations, self-doubts, and metaphoric gorings that characterize this narrative. Hemingway returns to the subject at the end of the first chapter, for instance, where he attempts to portray the work of the bullfighter Cagancho, who:

> sometimes standing absolutely straight with his feet still, planted as though he were a tree, with the arrogance and grace that gypsies have and of which all other arrogance and grace seems an imitation, moves the cape spread full as the pulling jib of a yacht before the bull's muzzle so slowly that the art of bullfighting, which is only kept from being one of the major arts because it is impermanent, in the arrogant slowness of his veronicas becomes, for the seeming minutes they endure, permanent. That is the worst of flowery writing, but it is necessary to try to give the feeling, and to someone who has never seen it a simple statement of the method does not convey the feeling. Anyone who has seen bullfights can skip such flowerishness and read the facts which are much more difficult to isolate and state. (13–14)

The passage turns, in part, on the issue of imitations. Cagancho, possessing the kind of authentic arrogance and grace that gypsies have, would therefore seem to be the real thing against which any other bullfighter's grace must appear an "imitation." Flowery writing, similarly, is held to be only imitative of "the facts" and the experience of watching a bullfight. In fact, the passage is a good deal more complex. If Cagancho only "sometimes" performs truly, it could hardly be said that he absolutely embodies qualities that turn out to be contingent on the moment of performance; moreover, if all arrogance and grace only "seems" an imitation of that possessed by gypsies, how can we be sure that gypsies actually possess the original and authentic expression of these qualities? Can we be sure that the truth about arrogance and grace has not succumbed to hyperbole or, in Hemingway's terms, "flowerishness"? It is as if Hemingway, far from knowing truly and writing purely about arrogance and grace, has merely sought to defer the moment when absolute knowledge of it could be gained.

But we also have to ask what is wrong with "the worst of flowery writing" if it does "try to give the feeling" of watching a bullfight and if technical explanations, which have no room for flowerishness, are "like the simple directions which accompany any mechanical toy and which are incomprehensible" (179). Hemingway's self-conscious criticism is puzzling, for beautifully sculpted phrases such as "the cape spread full as the pulling jib of a yacht," placed delicately in a sentence that strives to mimic, in its rising crescendo of dovetailed clauses, Cagancho's slow and statuesque suertes, appear to fulfill Hemingway's own criterion for writing that endures always: capturing the "sequence of motion and fact which made the emotion." One might argue that metaphors such as "planted as though he were a tree" and "cape spread full as the pulling jib of a yacht" are contrived imitations of the original "sequence of motion and fact," the presentation of which still evades Hemingway's best efforts. If he fails, however, it would seem less a function of the author's skill than a property of the act of writing itself. After all, a "simple statement of the method does not convey the feeling," and the difficult "facts" are to be read, oddly enough, only by those who need not rely on reading because they have been personally present at the corrida. In the latter case no writing could ever suffice to make the bullfight truly present, while in the former case it would appear that the bullfight can only be truly represented by "flowerishness." The writer is forced against his own principles, which were to have begun with the "simplest things" and the "real thing," into an unconscionable exercise of rhetoric. In either case Hemingway faces a predicament. Language is either inadequate to convey real things or always standing in the way of the real thing, transmuting all that is into representations that liberate a linguistic free play: capes become jibs, bullfighters become planted trees, description becomes flowerishness. We attend the arena only to find, as it were, the scene of writing.

At this juncture, three points are worth emphasizing about *Death in the Afternoon*. First, Hemingway's allegedly tough-minded pursuit of the "real thing" constantly yields to a plangent sense of linguistic freeplay. Second, as a corollary, elements of doubt and undecidability intrude into what appear to be the most fundamental rules governing the aesthetic, moral, and psychological experience of bullfighting. Third, Hemingway's strategies attune us to the vagaries of possible emotional responses, which overwhelm the strategic displacement of emotion into an aesthetic of action and fact. The problem is that these formulations stand as a direct affront to the array of connections between style and masculinity that readers created from the early moments of Hemingway's career and that are still typical of scholarly and popular responses. Covertly or otherwise, scholars have assumed that the properties of Hemingway's style signify a peculiarly "masculine" mode of perception. Sometimes this relationship is conveyed metonymically in a language associating style with the phallic properties of a "masculine" writing, as does Paul Rosenfeld when he speaks of Hemingway's "stubby verbal forms," the "brute, rapid, joyous jab of blunt period upon period," and his "rigidity of effect."[11] Other writers are more overt, as when Virginia Woolf criticizes Hemingway's "self-consciously virile" style in *Men Without Women* (1927).[12] Later scholars extended observations like these into important accounts of Hemingway's artistic development. Philip Young's provides a classic example: "Hemingway's style is the perfect voice of his content. That style, moreover, is the end, or aim, of the man. It is the means of being the man. An old commonplace takes on new force: the style *is* the man." Young has in mind the wounded Hemingway hero whose only recourse is the "rigid restraint which the man feels he must practice if he is to survive," which is evoked by "laconic and carefully controlled" conversation, a "hard and clean prose style," and the "intense simplicity of the prose." Heroic action and an emotionally disciplined prose style are thus interchangeable for Young; style is deeply masculine because it embodies the responses to the travails suffered by Hemingway's sense of threatened manhood.[13]

But scholars have found this flawless match of style and masculinity in surprisingly few of Hemingway's works. After *In Our Time* (1925) and *The Sun Also Rises* (1926), which are usually (but not always) thus acclaimed, scholars and reviewers began to treat the principle of a restrained masculine style as an ideal from which Hemingway had fallen or which he could never recoup unselfconsciously. Because accounts of these iterated failures depended on securing an original ground of authentic masculine style, however, they had the effect of stabilizing the very principle so often put in question by Hemingway's work. *Death in the Afternoon* is exemplary in this respect, for its rhetorical strategies have consistently been read as destroying his normally "virile" style. Critics have, for instance, tended to read Hemingway's style in this book as an exaggeration or overintensification of masculine characteristics, which is to say that by and large critics have refused to see the author's performance as "manly" at all. They have seen Hemingway's claims for the "real thing" as a pose and his manly restraint as being compromised by an overwrought rhetoric. For Lawrence Broer, Hemingway's fascination with the torero in *Afternoon* encourages in subsequent work an "unnerving impulse toward confessionism and exhibitionism—toward the melodramatic display of costume and ritual and toward sensationalistic shows of bravado."[14] Many other critics traduce the shift of manly characteristics into fake "exhibitionism." Max Eastman's infamously disparaging review of Hemingway's book (entitled "Bull in the Afternoon") provides a classic example. Though Hemingway favors "straight talk" and despises the "sentimental poppycock most regularly dished out by those Art nannies and pale-eyed professors of poetry," the author himself, according to Eastman, falls into the same trap. The book on bullfighting Eastman considers "juvenile romantic gushing and sentimentalizing of simple facts," which ironically arises out of Hemingway's obsession with killing and bloodshed. The "commonplace that Hemingway lacks the serene confidence that he *is* a full-sized man" leads the writer to romanticize the bullfight in what Eastman terms, brilliantly, a "literary style . . . of wearing false hair on the chest."[15] Eastman, then, joins Broer and others in reading *Afternoon* in terms of an obsession with manhood gone awry, which so far distinguishes Hemingway from the experience of authentic manhood—and from his own once authentic style—that, for Eastman, the author simply produces the kind of sentimental (and by association feminine) gush that the "full-sized man" had eschewed.

Critics such as Eastman are in a sense correct. Rhetorical and emotional disarray challenges the most salient features of a putative masculine style—that simple, straightforward ("straight talk"), unsentimental pursuit of the "real thing"—deeply problematizing the gendered concept of emotional restraint and the modernist principles built on it. Early critics, beginning with the premise that authentic masculinity signified tight-lipped self-control, could hardly avoid reading *Afternoon's* rhetorical strategies pejoratively as exhibitionistic and overwrought. Their evaluation of the book was governed by preexisting definitions of (masculine) modernism; and their confidence in an authentic masculine modernism was underscored by the exemplary failures of *Afternoon.* Exposing this reciprocal relationship, however, has several important consequences. It suggests that the "masculine" (or exaggeratedly masculine) style of *Death in the Afternoon* is not a formal or immanent attribute of the text but must be "engendered" through acts of interpretation. And it suggests that what was at stake in this "engendering" was nothing less than the preservation of powerful forms of authentic masculinity in the face of a work that, puzzlingly, seemed to trope the very notions of masculinity and modernism. Style is not the man, in this sense, but a social practice linking interpretation and evaluation to hegemonic ideals of manhood.

The questions we must now pose, therefore, do not concern Hemingway's concepts of masculinity but the scholarly audience whose response has been to construct the author's texts as unproblematically bespeaking their gender—or problematic only insofar as their textuality bespeaks an overwrought masculinity or contemptuous misogyny. How might an understanding of the cultural pressures on late nineteenth- and early twentieth-century constructions of manhood in the United States help us to grasp the critical reception of Hemingway's work? How might it inform the determination of critics to resurrect concepts of masculine emotional restraint from a work that, by their own admission, seems ironically at odds with the normative aesthetic principles and masculine textuality Hemingway at times espouses? What are the problematics of gender to which Hemingway's work might have seemed response and antidote—and perhaps, ultimately, inadequate? More specifically, to what extent might we owe conventional assessments of Hemingway's modernism to the cultural work produced by scholars—typically male scholars in the formative years of Hemingway studies—who were themselves invested in an ethos of emotional restraint? The account of the cultural underpinnings of professional work in this chapter has the value of challenging common interpretations of *Death in the Afternoon,* the masculine textual economy to which it is held to subscribe, and the advent of a masculinist modernism of which Hemingway's work has seemed such an obvious example.

As many historians have pointed out, dramatic economic and cultural changes in the last thirty years of the nineteenth century fostered a crisis of cultural authority among the hegemonic groups of the United States. The traditional relations of European-American, middle-class men to work, leisure, the city, and cultural pursuits began to warp under the rapid development of consumerism, corporate capitalism, vast bureaucracies, and the rationalization of American economic and social life. Under intense scrutiny was the concept of the "self-made man," which Michael S. Kimmel suggests can be read as an interlocking system of values defining "Marketplace Man." Marketplace Masculinity, according to Kimmel, "describes the normative definition of American masculinity. It describes his characteristics—aggression, competition, anxiety—and the arena in which those characteristics are deployed—the public sphere, the marketplace."[16] At the turn of the nineteenth century, those entrepreneurial values, which powerfully associated the fact of economic might with ideals of male agency and dominance, were beginning to seem particularly vulnerable as increasing numbers of middle-class men found their lives caught up in new corporate economies. Corporate modes of social and business life limited men's opportunities for individualistic enterprise, executive power, and autonomous action. In the new marketplace, values of competition and independent effort that once pertained to individuals began to seem largely symbolic.

These transformations were felt with particular intensity by men within emerging professional groups, which, according to some cultural historians, developed in part to manage and control that profound shift of American society toward corporate capitalism. Richard Fox and T. J. Jackson Lears, for instance, note the "emergence of a new stratum of professionals and managers, rooted in a web of complex new organizations (corporations, government, universities, professional associations, media, foundations)," whose function was to manage new social and psychological strains, provide expert guidance to increasingly complex social relations, promote new forms of economic power and social status, and, not incidentally, construct workable definitions of American manhood.[17] But the authority achieved by professionals was curtailed by their complicity with the structures of corporate capitalism they sought to control. Among men for whom entrepreneurial competition could be understood as a hegemonic ideal but rarely experienced in the corporate, "outer-directed" professional world, the anxiety of competition was replaced by the anxiety of losing touch with authentic masculine identities. Middle-class professionals, though supposedly expert guides to new and disorienting social structures, began to experience their selfhood as "fragmented, diffuse, and somehow 'weightless' or 'unreal.' "[18]

As corporate modes of existence made the myth of the "self-made man" increasingly suspect, hegemonic constructions of manhood responded by reconfiguring and imaginatively consolidating the power of individual men. E. Anthony Rotundo, for instance, argues that the late nineteenth century saw the invention of a cult of *"passionate manhood"*:

The most dramatic change was in the positive value put on male passions. In the closing years of the century, ambition and combativeness became virtues for men; competitiveness and aggression were exalted as ends in themselves. Toughness was now admired, while tenderness was a cause for scorn.[19]

Masculinity, as Victor J. Seidler writes, began to be "learnt through defining itself against emotionality and connectedness"; more particularly, Seidler argues, men began to "suppress feelings that [did] not fit into a model of instrumental action."[20] Ideals of a tough-minded, strenuous life for men thus went hand in hand with a rigorous encoding of many types of emotional expression as "feminine." By the end of the century, a series of mechanisms had arisen to urge men toward a determined pursuit of ideals that were no longer simply the prerogative of men; they were constitutive of manhood itself, which now had to be seen as a distinctive attribute that could and should be defined, articulated, and indeed demonstrated by way of an energetic display of "manly" qualities.

Such mechanisms compensated for a profound sense of anxiety about the objective realities of a rationalized and corporate existence. T. J. Jackson Lears, for instance, calls attention to a "therapeutic ethos": a "new gospel of therapeutic release preached by a host of writers, publishers, ministers, social scientists, doctors, and . . . advertisers."[21] Anxious to restore a powerful and coherent sense of masculine identity, male professionals advocated therapy in many different ways: the creation of a "muscular" culture of male strength and martial valor, a return to traditional ideals of craftsmanship, and a "recovery of the primal, irrational forces in the human psyche."[22] We might argue an evolving modernist aesthetics played a similar role for many male intellectuals: pursuing "what really happened in action," dismissing "emotional slither," attempting to discover the (masculine) "real thing," modernist writers and the scholars who legitimated them were, like other middle-class men, imaginatively constructing a masculine realm of tough-minded action curiously articulated through deeply aestheticized forms of expression.

Scholars in the burgeoning systems of higher education in the United States were positioned in such a way as to experience and respond to new constructions of economic power and gender with especial intensity. In part this was because of the very nature of professional work. Professionalization, according to Eliot Freidson, involves defining a body of "formal knowledge" and legitimating it by virtue of its association with institutions of higher education.[23] All discourses formalized within the university move toward creating an organized, coherent body of knowledge, sets of laws, special techniques of analysis, and (as Foucault reminds us) an organizing sense of what kinds of knowledge, information, and questions must be excluded from consideration. The esoteric nature of this higher knowledge presupposes the formation of a "community of competence"—a group of experts distinguished by their shared competence in a particular body of knowledge. And formal knowledge grants these communities special kinds of social authority. As Magali Sarfatti Larson argues: "Characteristic of the occupations that apply esoteric knowledge . . . is, by definition, their struggle for a privileged or exclusive right to speak in and about their domain. The 'intellectuals' in any field of activity . . . are those who act with the conviction—or, at least, as if they were convinced—that the right to speak is a form of power." Professional authority is created by possessing "symbolic capital"[24] or (in Pierre Bourdieu's terminology) "cultural capital." The possession of "symbolic capital" offers professionals the opportunity to practice outside the exigency of market forces by floating expert insight, information, and special languages as pseudocommodities. Instead of deriving value from market operations, symbolic capital counts on the prestige investing the specialized and esoteric knowledge that experts possess.

Economic and social relations based on the possession of expert knowledge accorded professionals new forms of power. But they also enacted a series of structural changes that were in many ways inconsistent with hegemonic constructions of masculinity. Professionalism not only replaced capital with cultural capital; it displaced the ideologies that comprised what might be called the masculine capital of American middle-class men. Aggression and competition are certainly present in professionalized occupations. Nevertheless, professionalism encouraged new cooperative modes of behavior: bodies of formal knowledge had to be structured; discursive boundaries policed; professional organizations founded; and credentials awarded. The ideology of the "self-made man" had to be parlayed into other forms as membership in small communities of competence became a norm and men struggled to ground a masculine economy in the possession of symbolic capital.

That struggle was particularly profound among men whose vocations involved them in cultural and purely intellectual work. In the academy, masculinity was becoming a subject of discourse in fields such as literature, sociology, and anthropology. According to Abigail Solomon-Godeau, the "recent visibility of masculinity itself as, variously, a disciplinary object of knowledge, a subject of artistic or literary investigation, and a political, ethical, and sexual problematic . . . attests . . . to a destabilization of the notion of masculinity such that it forfeits its previous transparency, its taken-for-grantedness, its normalcy."[25] This destabilization would seem to be a feature, however covertly expressed, of early twentieth-century academic discourse. Despite a common insistence on universal masculine values and despite the more subtle annexing of all human value and meaning to a masculine hegemony, male scholars, as the developing field of Hemingway studies suggests, were aware of masculinity as an emerging field of inquiry to which their various acts of writing and teaching would contribute, and which had already begun to make suspect supposedly natural and universal constructions of masculinity. In this sense alone, masculinity had to be seen as displaced from its moorings as the ontological essence of male behavior; it had to be seen as profoundly rhetorical.

Moreover, as Ann Douglas points out in *The Feminization of American Culture* (1977), by the late nineteenth century cultural pursuits in the United States were already viewed as deeply feminized, a perception that emerged from and was instrumental in consolidating the doctrine of separate spheres, whereby women attended to cultural matters and men to the virile, competitive world of business. For intellectuals, men of letters, and professionals within the newly emerging academies, the feminization of culture contributed to their sense of pursuing a "weightless" vocation, as the poet George Cabot Lodge suggested when he wrote: "I don't do anything here, nothing tangible. I work five hours a day or six, and what on—a miserable little poetaster. I want to get home and get some place on a newspaper or anything of that kind, and really do something."[26] Men's unease with the "effeminate" aspects of cultural endeavors might inspire, as it does for Lodge, an interest in becoming a journalist, who by the end of the century had come to be seen, Christopher Wilson argues, as the "high priest of 'experience,' the expert on 'real life,' " and the writer who could delve into the "muck of American life."[27]

Scholarly work was thus from the beginning of the twentieth century forced to negotiate the cultural significances of masculinity and to construe accounts of masculine privilege or failure in the light of several powerful and often contradictory psychosocial forces. Attuned to symbolic social structures, male professionals within emerging systems of higher education were well placed to benefit from and consolidate new forms of authority associated with expert knowledge and communities of competence. The men whose task was to conceptualize and disseminate epistemologies of masculinity constantly experienced their authority as contingent on symbolic capital; indeed, their role, which was in part to manage complex psychosocial accommodations to a society founded on corporate authority and consumerism, depended on elaborating and legitimating the discourse on weightless forms of existence. Yet newly shaping masculine roles in the early twentieth century could not abandon constructions of masculinity that still possessed great imaginative power, as Lodge's fantasy of becoming a journalist suggests. The merely symbolic nature of masculinity could not be easily admitted amid the logic of "Marketplace Man," whose authority was that of a powerful, autonomous, and distinctly nonsymbolic manhood.

Something of the complexity of these accommodations of new definitions of manhood within a countervailing and compensatory yearning for tough, manly roles can be gained from an analysis of Van Wyck Brooks's *Sketches in Criticism* (1932), a compendium of bellwether essays on the contemporary cultural horizon. Brooks, like many other intellectuals of this period, demonstrates a vexed relationship to the dominant condition of American society, which he characterizes as possessed of a vast energy that is stifled or even pathologically misused. Dedicated to the "world of trade," Americans, according to Brooks, have turned their:

> society into a machine, which produces only one standardized product. . . . The machinery of business speeds forward faster and faster, and, as it speeds, human nature becomes, beneath the surface, more and more recalcitrant. The most cynical . . . of men begin to ask themselves whither they are going and for what purpose.[28]

In a society whose "industrial process has devitalized man" (141), a neurotic lack of energy and purpose is the understandable consequence; Americans, in fact, have created a "nation of neurotics" (166).[29] But a paradox quickly emerges, for it seems as though it is really the "nerves of sensitive men"—intellectuals and writers—that are really at risk from being overstrained by the "mechanistic life" (45).[30] By way of contrast, Brooks betrays a fascination with the average male American, who is (here he is quoting Lowes Dickinson) "masterful," "aggressive," "brutal," "ruthless," "ambitious, self-reliant, active for the sake of activity . . . valuing nothing but success, recognizing nothing but the actual"; he is a "European stripped bare, and shown for what he is, a predatory, unreflecting, naive, precociously accomplished brute" (34). Intellectually unredeemed and ominously predatory he might be, but the average "masterful" male in this perspective seems far from the devitalized being Brooks elsewhere portrays.

Brooks moves toward resolving this paradox by articulating a relationship between the devitalization consequent upon misdirected industrial energies and a turn-of-the-century cult of the strenuous life. In essays on Theodore Roosevelt, William James, and Jack London, Brooks reads the strenuous life as masking a deep underlying malaise, variously understood as "fatigue," a "fleeting dream," and a sense of the "unreal" (36). As Brooks's attack on London suggests, the Red-Blood, the type of the self-reliant, masterful man:

> is not quite what he seems, the strong man rejoicing in his strength
> and spreading himself like the green bay-tree: he protests too much for
> that. . . . The Red-Blood . . . is, oddly enough, the most neurotic of
> men. Whatever his physical equipment may be, he is always the victim of
> an exaggerated sense of inferiority that drives him to assert himself. . . .
> Jack London's note was from the first the note of an abnormal self-
> assertiveness. (248–49)

Aggression and self-assertion are thus rooted in and display the real neurosis —an argument that duplicates assessments of *Death in the Afternoon* in 1932 and after, where the neurosis of the "strong man" is interpreted as the transposition of masculine autonomy into rhetorical excess (in Brooks's terms, "he protests too much"; "an exaggerated sense of inferiority . . . drives him to assert himself"). An abnormal self-assertiveness, like the frequent attacks on Hemingway's self-consciousness, associates the failure of masculinity with the self betrayed into self-display and emotionalism.

Brooks's answer to cultural devitalization is literature and the life of the mind; essay after essay touts the importance of literature, arguing that where "everything tends towards a regimentation of character," novelists can "test and explore the possibilities of life" (94). But here Brooks encounters a conundrum: though he claims that a regimented, neurotic society might well value creative impulses (93), the simple fact, as he insists on many occasions, is that the intellectual life is alienated, isolated, and passive. His response is to appropriate the hegemonic metaphors of a powerful masculinity that he elsewhere tries to dismiss. A "great literature is a reservoir of spiritual energy" (35), proclaims Brooks, and the American novelist has the "power of . . .

directing the floods of energy that refuse to flow in the old channels" (98). A neurotic nation awaits a "few men who are able to look our conventional life in the face and reject it . . . not through any neurotic need to escape, but at the command of a profound personal vision" (45). And while discarding the lure of a Rooseveltian strenuous life in the backwoods, Brooks calls for a "concerted plan for the reforestation of our spiritual territory" (36). Steering his conception of masculinity away from strenuous (and neurotic) self-display on the one hand and predatory commerce on the other, Brooks's real goal is nothing less than calling into being culturally sensitive men who are strenuous, active, entrepreneurial, directive, powerful, and autonomous.

Brooks does not ultimately deny the strenuous life of the mind; he tries to restore to it hegemonic concepts of powerful masculinity. It is at this point that Brooks's analyses of the neurasthenic displays of London and other thinkers, who discover only an empty self-assertiveness in attempting to reconcile themselves to a "busy, practical, 'tough-minded' world" (42), become fully meaningful. His strategy is brilliant. Their red-blooded displays ring false because Brooks has worked so assiduously to situate the tough-minded world of industrial processes as the cause of blocked, misdirected, neurotic energies: Marketplace Man is the devitalized victim, cut off from restorative, healthy masculine values and thus forced simply to put them on display. But in a wonderful sleight of hand, Brooks recoups those values for sensitive men. Brooks's powerful, autonomous thinker, tough-minded entrepreneur of ideas, therapeutically releasing the blocked energies of society, has become Marketplace Man outside the marketplace. He embodies the forcefulness associated originally with the masterful entrepreneur while directing merely symbolic traffic. In the terms of professionalism I have laid out above—the expert investing symbolic capital—Brooks's thinker is the consummately powerful professional.[31]

Sketches in Criticism suggests something of the tensions and accommodations unfolding in the life of an intellectual such as Van Wyck Brooks in the first decades of the twentieth century. In his work a powerful materialism is the agent that crushes and marginalizes sensitive men, whose "weightlessness" is variously mourned as America's imaginative loss, derided as the failure of weak-minded thinkers, and reimagined as the key to understanding a "nation of neurotics." Just as clearly, Brooks seeks to evade the weightlessness of the symbolic world of literature and knowledge by recourse to hegemonic ideals of passionate manhood. The downfall as well as the power of Brooks's strategy is that it represents a wholly symbolic transaction. It works by freeing symbolic masculine values from their historical genesis in the nineteenth century, "floating" them, and reattaching them to "finer types" whose actual psycho-social experience, as Brooks admits on many occasions, seems more weight-less than powerful. One way of putting this is to say that his claim for the powerful thinker is so much rhetoric: eloquent, persuasive, and completely unreal. Yet in another sense the very "hollowness" of Brooks's claims testify to their power. For they are truly hollow only if we posit the existence of real men who really embody those masculine values and whose self-possessed authority thus disproves Brooks's rhetorical claims. In fact, the opposite would seem the case: at a historical juncture when the terrific strains of a burgeoning corporate and consumer economy were making notions of autonomy and self-possession seem phantasmic, men could no longer experience those values except as rhetoric or fiction. Brooks then might be held to grasp accurately the symbolic nature of manhood. And Brooks, it might be said, also successfully invests masculinity—being symbolic—into precisely the form it had to take under consumer capitalism: he parlays it into symbolic capital.

As scholars, reviewers, and critics struggled to rearticulate definitions of American manhood, Hemingway's work, with its overt emphasis on masculine experience, inspired an important series of perspectives on the construction of twentieth-century masculinities. In this respect the pronounced contours of the critical discourse on Hemingway tell us more about the development of professionalism in the first half of the twentieth century and about attempts by men to derive new constructions of masculinity than about his work itself. Particularly important to that developing discourse were the concepts of Code and Code Hero, which, though staples of Hemingway scholarship from the early days, were named and made most visible in the work of Philip Young:[32]

> This is the Hemingway "code"—a "grace under pressure." It is made of the controls of honor and courage which in a life of tension and pain make a man a man and distinguish him from the people who follow random impulses . . . and are generally messy, perhaps cowardly, and without inviolable rules for how to live holding tight.[33]

The Code, with its "inviolable" rules and built-in "controls," imparted a veneer of universality and coherence to concepts that, as they became more and more obviously part of a discursive regime, seemed fragile and in constant need of discursive supplement. The Code encoded precisely what was becoming *un*obvious, unnatural, and local rather than universal; it parlayed men's yearnings to have the concepts that shaped their lives be more than merely symbolic; it invested their symbolic capital into a form that seemed the antithesis of all that was symbolic; it suggested a yearning to preserve and protect a vanishing sense of authentic manhood. As we saw with Lodge and Brooks, professionals' fears of the weightlessness of symbolic capital could be allayed, or at least displaced, by exercising their right to speak about forms of masculinity that seemed tough, real, and active. The taciturnity and restraint of the Code Hero, moreover, played a major role in allowing academics to adjust to the project of symbolic capital. Speaking about men who "held tight" to their speech and emotional responses and who seemed to owe their manhood to a model of instrumental action eased the complex accommodations made necessary by a contemplative life. Academics could at least imaginatively project (and protect) figures unconstrained by emotional vicissitudes (the problem with Young's "random," "messy," "cowardly" characters) and the putatively feminine trouble of speaking too much; they could identify with characters whose speaking seemed pure, straightforward, unornamented, unexaggerated, and thus nonrhetorical.

But working with symbolic capital did not only connote a feminized life of contemplation for male academics; it was the very root of their social authority. The ability to create symbolic capital by wielding esoteric discourses, as we have seen, demarcates a group possessing very real power even as it implies the weightlessness of discourse itself. The professional authority enjoyed by academics is deeply rhetorical in the sense that it enjoins the proliferation of esoteric languages and the dissemination of bodies of formal knowledge on no other grounds than the consolidation of symbolic discourse. However psychologically and culturally powerful the notion of tough, virile men delving into the muck of American life, then, professionals within the academy nevertheless sought to articulate and justify the new social status pertaining to professional work. Shielded from the overt competition of "marketplace man" and from the "real world" experiences of journalists, and disconnected in all but imagination from the virile roles projected in popular fiction, professionals had also to shape masculinities in ways that made them conformable to new historical and cultural realities. The linked concepts of the Code and Code Hero thus had to be more than an abrupt refusal to countenance the widening gap between the objective reality of men's real lives and culturally sanctioned ideals. Uncomplicated characterizations of silent men in action could not adequately represent and manage the dilemma that for intellectuals language—their symbolic capital—was the very source and expression of their cultural authority.

The formulation that allowed the concepts of Code and Code Hero to express yearnings for autonomous manhood while signifying new forms of cultural authority was an *aesthetic* of emotional restraint. Hemingway's promise to "put down what really happened in action" and to control emotional outbursts by conveying the "actual things . . . which produced the emotion" made style into a form of symbolic capital that simultaneously masked and consolidated its own symbolic nature. On the one hand, Hemingway's style could be admired as a virile act because (and as long as) it seemed to hide the rhetorical operations that characterized the fashioning of manly principles such as taciturnity and heroic action. As Philip Young's comment that the "style *is* the man" suggests, at its most purely laconic Hemingway's style could be seen to erase itself and allow manhood, unadulterated by its contingency on merely rhetorical strategies, to shine forth. The Code, similarly, could be imagined not as an abstract formulation but as a series of actualizations of the experience and longings of men in the real world. From these perspectives, the dramatic rhetorical shifts and emotional transformations of *Death in the Afternoon* could only be attacked for promoting and indeed exhibiting an unmanly dependence on style. A fetish of style, that is, overburdens the attainment of manhood if manhood must be read as the erasure of rhetoricity.

Yet the formulation of the "style *is* the man" also opens up the possibility of articulating manhood in terms of a property for which one must, as a critic, constantly argue. The unfolding debate about the stylistic improprieties of *Afternoon* affirms the fact that a manly style can be assumed as a given but can never function as a given; if manhood truly were the uncompromised essence scholars saw in an aesthetic of emotional restraint, it would need no articulation. In fact, the debate tacitly acknowledges the metaphoricity of manhood, which, clearly, can no longer be trusted to evidence itself. In order to secure its validity, scholars were forced to evoke repeatedly principles of masculine conduct. Manhood was argued for (or against). It was enacted repeatedly in scholarly reviews, articles, books, and learned arguments, as well as in the classroom. Those repeated enactments are consistent with—indeed, contingent upon—the rules of professional discourse, for symbolic capital demands constant investments of unattached, ungrounded, ever negotiable cultural currency. Intellectuals must replenish and thus grant authority to a "weightless" discourse. Accusations that Hemingway's posturing compromised his virile style in *Afternoon* were then simply the occasion for performing over and over again fantasies of the "real" manly thing. In the process, scholars exposed precisely what they were intent on hiding: the moment when manhood itself would begin to seem, incredibly, alienated from its own self-evident being amid the deeply rhetorical practices of their profession.

I have argued that the aesthetic principles of emotional and stylistic restraint Hemingway puts forward in *Death in the Afternoon* have been powerfully wedded to theories of a masculinist modernism; that the book itself dramatically overturns its own stated principles; that scholars in noting this have nonetheless erected upon those principles stable concepts of modernism and (less overtly) masculinity, from which much of Hemingway's work has subsequently been excluded; and that the correlation of modernist aesthetic theories with a code of masculine emotional restraint should be seen primarily as a construction of the early twentieth-century academy as male scholars struggled to accommodate hegemonic ideals of masculinity within new systems of symbolic capital. This account of professionalism is thus more than another approach to Hemingway; it urges us to reconceptualize genealogies of literary, cultural, and gender history.

This argument implies, for instance, that attempts to establish new gendered histories of modernism might tell us more about definitions of masculinity currently deployed in the academy than about modernism itself. I would argue that recent feminist critiques of masculinist modernisms have reversed the evaluations of earlier male scholars by employing precisely the same interpretive strategies. They have, that is, extrapolated from the aesthetic theories of male writers such as Hemingway *as if* those theories possessed a representative significance about a masculine textual economy at work in modernist writing. It is what consigns Hemingway to Scott's "gendered subcategory" and motivates the "appropriately virile reactions" perceived by Gilbert and Gubar in the work of male modernists; and it is what allows Scott's "important feminine or feminist elements" to appear at the heart of a newly expanded or differently inflected modernism. These scholars do uncover many of the ways in which early definitions of modernism, so transparent-seeming, in fact incorporated formations of power and gender. But they also assume that masculinist interpretations of writers such as Hemingway, far from being produced in response to historically and culturally specific crises of masculinity, simply grasped the truth about these textual masculine yearnings. And they assume that the definitions of masculinity they deploy are not problematically structured by the contemporary discursive possibilities of debates about gender.

The rich rhetorical production in a work such as *Death in the Afternoon* suggests that aesthetic theories of putting down what really happened in action were themselves deeply rhetorical and can be elaborated into a complete account neither of modernism nor of masculinity, whether we are speaking of early male or late-feminist scholars. The aesthetic theories promulgated in *Afternoon* work beautifully to ground such discussions—but only when detached from the problematic work in which they appeared. Likewise, we are on firm ground as long as, but only as long as, we take seriously the assumption that Hemingway's works concern, or should concern, the "sort of thing you should not admit" and thus incorporate, and pay tribute to, a specifically masculine textual economy: the management of rhetorical excess and the displacement of emotion into action. My reading of *Afternoon* indicates that concepts of emotional restraint have actually constrained interpretation of a work, of an author, and of an entire literary period. The "sort of thing" that accounts of gender and of modernism need to begin to admit is that the hard work of developing more subtle and flexible theories about literary production—and about the cultural and professional situations of those who respond to it—has scarcely begun.

Notes

1. Hemingway, *Death in the Afternoon,* p. 2. Subsequent references are given in parentheses.

2. "The only way of expressing emotion in art," according to Eliot, is "by finding an 'objective correlative'; in other words, a set of objects, a situation, a chain of events which shall be the formula of that particular emotion; such that when the external facts, which must terminate in sensory experience, are given, the emotion is immediately evoked." ("Hamlet and His Problems" 124–25).

3. Brooks and Warren, *Understanding Poetry,* p. 68.

4. The "construction of the modern notion of the aesthetic artifact," Eagleton writes, is "inseparable from the construction of the dominant ideological forms of modern class-society" (3).

5. Schenck, "Charlotte Mew," p. 317.

6. Scott, *The Gender of Modernism,* p. 4.

7. Gilbert and Gubar, *No Man's Land,* pp. xii, 36, 37.

8. Ibid., p. xii.

9. *Afternoon* is far from unique among Hemingway's works, which, as I have argued elsewhere, are so often characterized by rhetorical performances and theatrical displays of masculinity. For a longer discussion of such matters, see my "Dramatizations of Manhood in

Hemingway's *In Our Time* and *The Sun Also Rises*," "Trophy Hunting as a Trope of Manhood in Hemingway's *Green Hills of Africa*," and my book *Hemingway's Theaters of Manhood*.

10. Some readers have noted rightly that the entire book is a problematically fragmented work. Its "miscellaneous materials" (Benson, *Hemingway* 75) might be collated, as Hays interestingly points out, under the rubric of a "modern omnium-gatherum, like the great Renaissance essay collections using a single topic as a focus by Robert Burton or Sir Thomas Browne"; but, as Hays himself admits, *Afternoon* is "several books masquerading as one" (*Ernest Hemingway* 63).

11. Rosenfeld, "Review," pp. 67–68.

12. Woolf, *Men without Women*, p. 107. The list continues indefinitely. One could cite J. B. Priestley characterizing Hemingway's "bluff, masculine, 'hard-boiled,' apparently insensitive style" (Rosenfeld, "Review" 136–37); or D. H. Lawrence placing Hemingway as the descendant of the "lone trapper and cowboy" whose motto is "[d]on't get connected up" and whose stylistic correlative is the brevity of sketches that are "so short, like striking a match . . . and it's over" (73); or Cyril Connolly noting the "ferocious virility" (111) that characterizes *Men Without Women;* or T. S. Matthews referring to the "masculinity of Hemingway's 'anti-literary' style" (122).

13. Young, *Ernest Hemingway,* pp. 174–80. Young's work is far from exceptional, as Benson's forthright account suggests. Benson argues that: "Hemingway's emphasis on the masculine point of view is easily the most characteristic aspect of his writing, and although it is only one among many elements in his work used to channel emotion into non-sentimental directions, it serves to unify them all. Firmly within the masculine tradition are . . . the lusty and direct encounters with life rather than intellectualizations of experience, the dramatizations of the circumstances leading to emotion rather than the discussion of emotion, the continual satirization of pretense and illusion, and the emphasis on virile and direct language (30). Benson then draws out what seems obvious about Hemingway's aesthetic: "Hemingway was vitally concerned with re-establishing what he felt were the proper roles of man and woman in their relationship to each other," pivotal to which is the writer's attack on a "feminine tradition in literature" (30).

More recently feminist scholars have come to similar conclusions about Hemingway's style with a much more critical eye. Pullin, for instance, develops the political implications of Hemingway's style by arguing that the "exact and detailed reporting of the experience of sensations of an extreme kind, painful physically or emotionally" ("Hemingway and the Secret Language of Hate" 184) is precisely what diminishes his writing. By featuring isolated male protagonists whose true commitment is to the "moment of action" (178), that is, Hemingway ignores character and in particular the humanity of his female characters, and in so doing constructs a "secret language of hate." Style and language for Pullin are thus deeply male—and misogynist.

14. Broer, *Hemingway's Spanish Tragedy,* p. 114.

15. Eastman, "Bull in the Afternoon, pp. 94, 96.

16. Kimmel, *Manhood in America,* pp. 123–24.

17. Fox and Lears, *The Culture of Consumption,* p. xi.

18. Ibid., p. xiii.

19. Rotundo, *American Manhood,* pp. 5–6.

20. Seidler, *Rediscovering Masculinity,* p. 7.

21. Fox and Lears, *The Culture of Consumption,* p. xi.

22. Lears, *No Place of Grace,* p. 57.

23. Freidson, *Professional Powers.*

24. Larson, "The Production of Expertise," pp. 35, 61.

25. Solomon-Godeau, "Male Trouble," p. 70.

26. Quoted in Martin, *Harvests of Change,* p. 15.

27. Wilson, *The Labor of Words,* p. 17.

28. Brooks, *Sketches in Criticism,* pp. 23, 165–66. Subsequent references are cited parenthetically.

29. Others survey the contemporary scene in very similar terms. Canby claims that "we Americans are walking reservoirs of potential enthusiasm, or, if not enthusiasm, energy" (*Harvest* 9). But the "turbid rush toward material prosperity" (60) has created a backlash. The "nervous instability and almost hysterical experimenting" (104) of contemporary literature Canby attributes to the "excessive strain" of a society awash in the "fogs of its nervosities" (11). "Something is weary in the imagination of civilized man which must be invigorated" (68), Canby argues. Herbert Muller speaks of a forceful but "feverish" and "frustrate and sterile" age (*Modern Fiction* xi, 421). Hartwick writes of the "vanishing morale" (*Foreground* 170) of the United States. Loggins refers to the "strenuousness and excitement of our age" (263), but considers World War I as a turning point in American culture insofar as "strenuousness ended in futility, in nothingness" (5).

30. This sense of a weak-minded, overrefined, effeminate cultural role for intellectuals was rife in the early twentieth century. Hemingway for Canby is an example of a "literature of pathology" (*Harvest* 123), the product of a society "sick from too much knowledge and too fevered thinking" (122). And as for the professor: " 'Professor' in the press has become a term to beat a dog with. A Ph.D. is a label on the rear with 'Kick Me' printed on it" (*Definitions* 267). Spingarn notes that "even dilettante criticism is preferable to the dogmatic and intellectualist criticism of the professors" (291), and Boyd weighs in sarcastically with "literary criticism in this country has, at least, the charm of consistent irrelevancy" (*Criticism in America* 309). Lewisohn likens Henry James to a "type of oldish bachelor, not unknown to university campuses" (*Expression* 261). And Connolly critiques the "ivory tower attitude, which arises from a disbelief in action" (*Enemies* 52).

31. Other thinkers also attempt to claim a particularly tough-minded role for scholarly and literary pursuits. Canby sounds very much like Brooks in claiming a "breakdown of values" (*Harvest* 271) consequent upon the failure of a liberal education to be "convertible into what [is] currently regarded as success" (270), and then encouraging intellectuals to fight to create a tough-minded riposte. He writes of a "conflict within the stream of American life itself, two currents of energy, each vital, but one a turbid rush toward material prosperity which began with colonization, and the other a tiny powerful current, fighting the mainstream" (60). Advocating a kind of muscular literary response, Canby argues that the public needs to learn how to do some "hard reading" (173); "[m]ore wrestling with books," he says, is "badly needed." And again: "more men are needed in literature. To throw a bomb at a triumphant materialism is a 'man's job' " (262).

32. Young's ideas were anticipated, sometimes explicitly, by many scholars and reviewers.

In 1938, for instance, Schwartz wrote about a "definite code by which characters are judged and by which they judge each other" ("Ernest Hemingway" 117); even earlier, Kirstein had analyzed Hemingway's "anatomy of a kind of bravery and cowardice" ("The Canon of Death" 65). The question of Hemingway's codes was also broached by Penn Warren and Hicks, Warren writing: "The code and discipline are important because they can give meaning to life which otherwise seems to have no meaning or justification. . . . [M]an can realize an ideal meaning only in so far as he can define and maintain the code" ("Hemingway" 11).

33. Young, *Ernest Hemingway,* p. 36.

8

Road Work

Rereading Kerouac's Midcentury Melodrama of Beset Sonhood

STEPHEN DAVENPORT

Jack Kerouac became a 1950s icon, King of the Beats, with the release of three novels in a thirteen-month period between September 5, 1957, and October 2, 1958. *On the Road* (1957), *The Subterraneans* (1958), and *The Dharma Bums* (1958), which chronicle, respectively, events that took place in 1946–1950, 1953, and 1955–1956, marked Kerouac as a postwar novelist of social critique. With the release of *Doctor Sax* (1959) and *Maggie Cassidy* (1959), which together cover most of the 1930s and chronicle his adolescence as a working-class Canuck in Lowell, Massachusetts, Kerouac novels began to take on the look of a sustained autobiographical project. Three years later in the preface to *Big Sur* (1962), he would give the project a name, "The Duluoz Legend," and explain it as "remembrances . . . written on the run," a series of "chapters" comprising "one enormous comedy, seen through the eyes of poor Ti Jean (me), otherwise known as Jack Duluoz, the world of raging action and folly and also of gentle sweetness seen through the keyhole of his eye."[1] One of the primary remembrances is work, figured as vocational identity or career. Another is mortality. In fact, it would take the death of his father in 1946, twenty years after his only brother's death, to give Kerouac the impetus to write what would become his first published novel, *The Town and the City* (1950).

I present this sketch to make clear from the beginning that the roots of Kerouac's Duluoz Legend, which precede his Beat celebrity and countercultural associations, grow out of very specific pre–World War II biographical circumstances. That is, while the damage that informs his road-going is cultural and aesthetic, tied to his ethnic and modernist inheritance of loss, it is also personal and familial. In *The Town and the City,* which culminates in the father's death, Kerouac recreates his family, tripling the number of Kerouac children along gender lines (two boys and one girl becoming six and three, respectively), only to lose two of the fictional sons, one to childhood disease (a faithful doubling of Kerouac's dead brother, Gerard) and another to World War II. Unlike the novels that follow and come to comprise the Duluoz Legend, *The Town and the City* is a family saga that positions members of the Martin family as collective protagonist and follows their fortunes as they make their way through the 1930s and most of the 1940s. Even so, it is the figure of a single hitchhiker, a surviving son, who closes the novel. His father just buried, Peter Martin, like Jack Duluoz, takes to "the road again, traveling the continent westward, going off to further and further years, alone by the waters of life, alone, . . . looking down along the shore in remembrance of the dearness of his father and of all life." As he goes, he carries with him "a wild hum of voices, the dear voices of everyone he had known."[2] Included in that "hum" are the voices of Peter's family, his brothers and sisters, his mother and father. Because older brother Joe, planning to buy a farm, marry, and raise children, agrees to take responsibility for their mother and youngest brother, Peter Martin has the freedom he needs to be the westering son and, when a merchant marine job opens, go to sea.

It is my goal in this essay to articulate the emotional work of male flight, in particular the ways in which American road narratives by men might be read profitably as expressions, not evasions, of woundedness and grief. Writing about such narratives, Ronald Primeau outlines and elaborates four road subgenres: "protest, the search for a national identity, self-discovery, and experimentation or parody."[3] While Kerouac figures in Primeau's handling of all four, I will argue here for a fifth that might help us read Kerouac's road as a variation born of grief, of masculine anxiety over abandonment by other males, over family loss. The abandoned or grieving male takes to the road, or lives in the fantasy of doing so, not to escape family in Adamic flight but to encounter it in a recuperative space, a zone territorialized purposefully by familial rhetoric and professional goals. It is my contention that the Duluoz Legend's overlapping family narratives—a young man leaving home to find surrogates for his deceased father and older brother, a son staying home to be his father's surrogate as emotional and economic caretaker of his mother, a writer struggling to find his place in a patrilineage of traveler-writers that will someday make him a literary father—constitute a valuable midcentury melodrama of beset sonhood that might help us situate Kerouac's road cure within a network of family practices that will, in turn, improve our reading of other wounded-son road narratives.

In the draft of *On the Road* that Kerouac delivered in 1951 to Robert Giroux at Harcourt Brace, the story opens not with Sal Paradise's divorce but with the death of his father. That this version of *On the Road* picks up where *The Town and the City* leaves off underscores the connection between father absence (or family loss) and the son's road in the Duluoz Legend. The son, a variation on the American orphan-hero, sets the stage in the first chapter of *On the Road* for what he later calls in *Vanity of Duluoz* (1968) his youthful decision to make his "career as an American careener."[4] It is in the yoking of these familiar narratives, careening and careering, that Kerouac grounds his protagonist, who, if he is to reach his goals, must negotiate simultaneously the horizontal movement of careening, or romantic escape, and the vertical movement of careering, or realist return to economic obligations associated with the publishing world's ladder of success and a son's responsibilities to family as surrogate for his dead father. To articulate this double movement, I will read Kerouac's road against those in Arthur Miller's *Death of a Salesman* (1949) and Tennessee Williams's *The Glass Menagerie* (1944), each of which is informed by a similar careening-careering dynamic.

In both plays, as in the Duluoz Legend, the loss of a father or a brother or a son, or some combination of the three, becomes a primary impetus for the abandoned male to seek his cure on the road. Tom Wingfield, for instance, dreams of replicating the behavior of his absent merchant marine father and, in the process, regaining his health and vigor. Decades have passed since Willy Loman was abandoned, yet the road to Alaska, the one his father took and his brother mistook, ending up in Africa instead, remains the answer to Willy's need for emotional connectedness and his dreams of success as a worker. As for Biff, the Loman son beset by unresolved father-son conflicts and similar feelings of incompletion, the road west leads him nowhere but back home over and over again.[5] Regardless of the formal elements that mark them off as plays, these contemporaneous texts are invaluable in helping us understand the Kerouac hero's divergence from the myth of a male repeatedly shedding his past and moving indiscriminately across the American landscape in search of ever newer kicks.[6]

The reality is that the Kerouac hero's flight depends on his willing participation in a delivery-and-retrieval system of interconnecting roads and round-trip shipping patterns. He never leaves without returning on one road or another because, unlike the Adamic hero who "seem[s] to have sprung from nowhere," the Kerouac hero sprang from a very definite somewhere, a working-class French-Canadian family on New England soil between World War I and the Great Depression.[7] However necessary in the 1950s such entrenched myth-making might have been in describing and promoting the Americanness of American literature, the implication that place, or sociohistorical conditions, should in our reading of that literature take a back seat to space, what R. W. B. Lewis called "the unbounded, the area of total possibility," is unfortunate. Such an approach closes off, ironically, the very possibility of fuller and freer critiques of the hero's set of relations to the "actual" or "waiting" or "whole world" these critics separated him from.[8]

Lawrence Buell implies as much when he writes about the "forgetting" we must do when confronted with "such myths of American distinctiveness as Puritan inheritance or Adamic innocence."[9] Either we are socialized, as Buell says, into forgetting the differences or we ignore them. Flight from family and social conditions becomes a ready-made masculine fiction, a national myth, that disables our reading of Kerouac's road and flattens the complexity of any number of midcentury melodramas of beset sonhood that might aid in our critique of emotion in literature written by American men during that period. In Kerouac's case, a key part of those relations involves the loss of his older brother and father, which manifests itself in emotional wound and repeated attempts at recuperation on the road. If Kerouac's meteoric rise depended on a novel, *On the Road,* that reworked Joseph Campbell's monomyth of the hero-quest, Americanizing it with the primary figures of the cross-country bus, the automobile, and long stretches of interstate highway, the elaboration of his project, his melodrama of beset sonhood, depends on the family history the Kerouac hero carries with him everywhere he goes.

Peter Martin, the son who closes *The Town and the City,* may feel "alone" out on the road, even as he carries with him intervening voices and memories, and *On the Road*'s Sal Paradise may have only one aunt and a distant brother tethering him to the ground of material and emotional relations, but neither of them is Henry Nash Smith's "anarchic and self-contained atom."[10] During a summer of fire-spotting atop Desolation Peak, the Kerouac hero may, as a result of solitary confinement, alcohol deprivation (he is an alcoholic), spiritual self-questioning, and the physical fact of Mount Hozomeen bearing down on him, feel a "terrible and sublime isolation."[11] He may even participate in a little Adamic myth-making himself as he does in *Desolation Angels* (1965) when he describes his life as "a vast and insane legend reaching everywhere without beginning or end," but he does so only to ground himself in the next few sentences in events that he carefully dates 1942 and 1953. Even on Desolation Peak, where the Kerouac hero combines careening and careering as he turns his travels into literature, the real world (the hero's real world) intrudes. At the end of a long letter to his mother he adds, "I'll take care of you wherever you need me—just yell. . . . Don't ever think for one minute that you are alone." And then he explains, "She is 3,000 miles away living in bondage to ill kin."[12] He might have said the same thing about himself. Boundedness, not openness, informs Kerouac's road.

While road-going is a familiar activity in the midcentury melodramas under study here and one that marks them as distinctively American, it is memory or the disembodied family voice—the "wild hum," for instance, that follows Peter Martin down to the crossroads or the two-word postcard ("Hello—Goodbye!"[13]) from the Wingfield father—that grounds the road-going space in social relations and personal history. As the subtitle of *Death of a Salesman* (i.e., *Certain Private Conversations in Two Acts and a Requiem*) implies, some of the conversations are so private as to be taking place inside Willy Loman's head. Separated from his older son as well as his father, he feels the father-son separation in both directions. Talking to the ghost of his brother, Willy pleads for company: "Can't you stay a few days? You're just what I need, Ben, because I—I have a fine position here, but I—well, Dad left when I was such a baby and I never had a chance to talk to him and I still feel—kind of temporary about myself."[14] Willy's admission that his father's desertion has had a permanent effect on him—he mentions his mother only once in passing (48)—underscores the seriousness of his father-inflicted psychic wound and the significance of his need for male family members. If Ben would stay for a while, be the big brother and surrogate father Willy needs, perhaps Willy would feel less disconnected. But Ben himself is "temporary," a figment of Willy's imagination. He is also a brother Willy has not heard from for at least twelve or thirteen years.

Deserted by his father, estranged from his older and favored son, and unable to maintain contact with his older brother/surrogate father, Willy is triply wounded. Efforts to make contact with an absent male family figure, to communicate a conflict, to resolve it, to find a surrogate if necessary are, on both Willy's and Biff's parts, attempts at recuperation.[15] For Willy, the stakes are even higher. To these three wounds, we can add his sense of emasculation or loss of self-esteem because of his demotion at work and consequent inability to support himself and his wife, Linda. A business offer made by brother Ben—"I've bought timberland in Alaska and I need a man to look after things for me" (85)—becomes the subject of a key fantasy for Willy, one that might unite him with his brother and his sons. It is a fantasy not only of financial reversal but of masculine community, of familial connectedness. Willy's father is part of the fantasy as well, since Alaska is the frontier for which he abandoned his family. Unlike his brother and father, however, Willy is no frontiersman.

Even if he were so inclined, he is exhausted, his relationships with his sons are strained, his wife and younger son are rooted in the city, years have passed since Ben made the offer, and the frontier, at least in the way Willy thinks of it, is closed. Like most midcentury American men, Willy must give up, as Joe L. Dubbert puts it, his fantasy of *"space"* and "accept living in *place,* in a community, in a social environment, interacting with other men doing the same."[16] On one level, *Death of a Salesman* is a study of his refusal to do just that; on another, it is a study of the interdependency of his failures to use space appropriately as a worker (i.e., he does not make his sales territory pay), as an adventurer (i.e., he stays put when he might have struck it rich elsewhere), and as a family member (i.e., he is eventually incapacitated by his fantasies of open space). In each case, the consequences are predictably tragic.

Willy Loman's attempts at combining careening and careering, made possible by his life as a salesman, finally fail for good. Well past sixty years of age, he can no longer negotiate the road. In fact, the road for Willy, once his source of income, is now the emblem of his imminent death. If he does not asphyxiate himself with the tube he keeps hidden behind the heater, America's proliferation of automobiles will: "The street is lined with cars. There's not a breath of fresh air in the neighborhood" (17). And if he is not killed by his inability to negotiate the road, either horizontally or vertically, because the road as he once knew it is no longer available to him, he will drive his car into something. The play begins with Willy's return home because he cannot make his car work: "I suddenly couldn't drive any more. The car kept going off the shoulder, you know?" (13). It ends with a burial caused by a crashing of his car on a road that no longer allows him movement sufficient to maintaining his career or his dream of familial recuperation.

The voices circulating in the text of *The Glass Menagerie,* as well as on stage during a production, are circulating also in Tom Wingfield's head (or "memory") (7, 23), his version of the "wild hum" becoming, through his poetic reconstruction, Tennessee (or Tom) Williams's play. The disembodied family voice calling the son to the road is the father's two-word postcard: "Hello—Goodbye!" Asked about his responsibility to his family as surrogate breadwinner, Tom Wingfield replies, "I'm like my father. The bastard son of a bastard!" (80) And like the "bastard" who sires him, the "bastard son" sets out to leave his dependents behind: "I descended the steps of this fire escape for a last time and followed, from then on, in my father's footsteps, attempting to find in motion what was lost in space"(114–15). These "footsteps" are both literal and figurative. On the one hand, they organize his father's specific movement away from "place" (i.e., St. Louis) as well as his generalized movement through "space" (i.e., frontier). Although that which has been "lost in space" is registered collectively—the effect on the family's economic well-being concrete and measurable—it is also felt personally by the son as an emotional wound, an emptiness to be filled only by other males. The Wingfield son seeks an opportunity to recuperate family, even if his search for one part entails his desertion of others (i.e., mother and sister).

On the other hand, Wingfield's search is figurative. Even the thought of following in his father's "footsteps" is a curative. His blood "boiling," his health returning, he prescribes adventures for himself that he associates with the masculine world of war, Clark Gable, and by association his father. On the surface, the site of recuperation, whether sea or land, appears to be Judith Fetterley's "all-male world, a world without women, the ideal American territory."[17] Yet the world Wingfield comes to occupy is hardly a woman-free zone, for into it he carries the material for his "memory play," which includes the women in his family: "I would have stopped, but I was pursued by something. It always came upon me unawares, taking me altogether by surprise. . . . Then all at once my sister touches my shoulder. . . . Oh, Laura, Laura, I tried to leave you behind me, but I am more faithful than I intended to be!"(115). The lost something he hopes to recuperate in the process is not his father per se, actual or ideal, but the emotional health that father absence has cost him and his family. Standing in nostalgic and frustrated counterpoint to the father's postcard, the son's is the play itself. The wounding father's "Hello—Goodbye!" becomes the wounded son's "Goodbye—Hello!"

From his earliest days as a writer, Kerouac grounded his road in family matters. Even before his father died, the open road and orphan status, plot devices available to him in any number of adventure tales, had become key focal points in his imagination. At the age of twelve he wrote and printed what was perhaps his first extended fiction, a nickel-notebook tale about an orphan making his way, Huck Finn-like, down the Merrimac River. In imitation of his father, in those days a self-employed printer putting out a weekly theater-and-cinema flier and entertaining his son and others with stories about his advertising days on an RKO circuit around New England, Kerouac turned out a number of his own publications: racing sheets, newspapers, cartoon strips. This emulation of his father's work, which combined travel and careerist publishing goals associated with the arts, had its roots then in familial and homosocial desire. Kerouac fantasized about his position in a world of men similar to the one he imagined his father inhabited, working a circuit and playing poker backstage with vaudeville celebrities. If his father could make a career on the road, he could make a career of it.

At the age of sixteen, Kerouac wrote a football novella about another orphan. Having left one college and its baseball team to see America by foot, Bill Clancy walks into another college town and becomes an important part of its football team. When asked where he comes from, he answers, "Nowheres."[18] When pressed, he reveals that his parents died long ago, his father before he was born and his mother when he was five, and that he eventually left his aunt and sisters to find his own way. Only writing, or the absence of it, disqualifies Bill Clancy as the perfect Kerouac "football-hero-hobo" prototype.[19] Ironically this unfinished story about a hobo-orphan-athlete who walks away from college to see America predates by three years Kerouac's own departure from Columbia University. As he tells the story in *Vanity of Duluoz,* one Saturday evening in September 1941, only weeks into his sophomore year at Columbia, scholarship-athlete and class president Jack Duluoz walks away from his dream of Ivy League success. "Ah shucks," Duluoz tells himself, "go into the American night, the Thomas Wolfe darkness, the hell with these bigshot gangster football coaches, go after being an American writer, tell the truth, don't be pushed around by them or anybody else or any of their goons" (104). Out there, on roads far from Madison Avenue and the politics of amateur sports, Duluoz will swap his penthouse-and-martini dream for a hard-knocks traveler-writer apprenticeship.

Though Duluoz will sail in the merchant marine during World War II and practice his literary craft with friends and fledgling fellow writers, it will take his father's death in 1946 to send him on the series of road adventures that will make him famous. Tom Wingfield, on the other hand, expresses no desire for celebrity or remuneration. Combining careening and careering successfully, or giving every indication of it in the narration of his play, he says nothing about attempts or strategies that might solidify his identity as any particular kind of worker beyond the possibility that he is making his living as a writer. We know for sure only that Wingfield claims to have moved for a time in a kind of Adamic timelessness through a space mediated by family ties. More than anything, it is memory that forces his participation in the rhetoric of escape and return and it is memory that makes him yet another son who comes home if only to tell his story, to talk it out emotionally, to reveal his dependency, often a willing dependency, on his identity as son (and brother).

If Wingfield imagines a space where he might live outside familial obligation, Duluoz, like Willy Loman, cannot because his dream of success is tied to his dream of family. In "The Archaeology of Gender in the Beat Movement," Helen McNeil implicates *On the Road* in its Beat refusal to participate in what she calls a "discourse of responsibility": "freedom for the quest must be absolute; the Beat hero is responsible only to that quest and sometimes to his friends."[20] The Duluoz Legend is stripped of its emotional complexity if this claim is true. In none of the Duluoz novels is the hero's freedom absolute. In fact, the Legend depends on the hero's elaboration of surrogacy and the second-male position in triangulated relationships, at the heart of which is the rhetoric of family systems and family-based responsibilities. As second male (dependent son or younger brother), the Kerouac hero is bound by the presence or absence of the first male (father or older brother). In *The Town and the City*, for instance, patriarch George Martin loses his successful printing business through "neglect" and "gambling" (195) and, after a protracted illness, dies. Because the oldest son, Joe, pledges to play first male (surrogate father) by staying put and providing a home for his mother and youngest sibling, the others are cast in the role of second male. By distributing among the three oldest Martin sons—Joe, Francis, and Peter—the duties to family and self the father found irreconcilable, Kerouac allows the father's conflicting desires to be played out safely in the next generation of males.

In the Legend proper, Duluoz shares Peter Martin's conflicted sense of duty. Although Duluoz agrees to his father's deathbed request that he become emotional and financial caretaker of his mother—"He'd said, 'Take care of your mother whatever you do. Promise me.' " (*Vanity* 299)—his willingness or ability to fulfill it is compromised by his own career goals. By keeping the effects of the conflict open through constant negotiation of vertical and horizontal movement, Duluoz sustains the tension between familial rupture and recuperation; by situating the opportunity for personal as well as familial wholeness in an idealized world of men, he combines, however problematically, his duties to self and family. Steadfast in his refusal to settle fully into the position of family head, a role that would entail a different career path, he maintains his role as second male to his father's first. He will use the road to chase after his own career, to replicate in some fashion his father's work experiences, to heal himself (and, as best he can, his family) through movement and a clear pattern of surrogacy.

It was only when Duluoz and his father became sick at the same time—with thrombophlebitis and cancer, respectively—that he realized their interdependence. Frightened by his own mortality, as well as his father's, the son hoped to make amends for old disagreements about his having walked away from Columbia University. Home from the hospital, he vowed to "write a huge novel explaining everything to everybody, . . . to keep [his] father alive and happy, while Ma worked in the shoe factory, the year 1946 now, and make a 'go' at it" (*Vanity* 299). When Peter Martin, the Duluoz prototype, went home to care for his dying father, he saw him for the first time as "his brother and his mysterious son too" (*Town* 468). Duluoz, upon finding his father dead, felt abandoned: "You have forsaken me, my father. You have left me alone to take care of the 'rest' whatever the rest is" (*Vanity* 299). That he feels "alone" in the absence of his father, despite the presence of his mother and a sister who might take over the role as their mother's primary provider and companion, is central to our understanding of his role as second male and grieving son. On the road he will rebuild his family's male base, careful always to preserve his position as second male since it is that position that affords him the freedom of movement he needs to make his career as a traveler-writer and to do the emotional work he can do only on the road.

At its most basic, his desire to find surrogates for his father and brother is homosocial. From male bonding he hopes to reap emotional benefits unavailable to him through relationships with women.[21] Although many of Duluoz's male friends are potential replacements for Gerard, the lost brother, the two who best represent the hopes and disappointments of his search are Cody Pomeray and Japhy Ryder. If Duluoz mythicizes his older brother's saintliness in *Visions of Gerard* (1963), chronologically the Legend's opening chapter, he does the same to Pomeray and Ryder in later chapters. About Cody Pomeray—or Dean Moriarty, as he is known in *On the Road*—he writes,

Then a complete silence fell over everybody; where once Dean would have talked his way out, he now fell silent himself, but standing in front of everybody, ragged and broken and idiotic, right under the lightbulbs, his bony mad face covered with sweat and throbbing veins, saying, "Yes, yes, yes," as though tremendous revelations were pouring into him all the time now, and I am convinced they were, and the others suspected as

much and were frightened. He was BEAT—the root, the soul of Be-
atific.[22]

Pomeray is also, in Duluoz's (or Paradise's) words, "the Idiot, the Imbecile, the
Saint of the lot" (193) and "the HOLY GOOF" (194).[23] The embodiment of
the breath and muscularity of Duluoz's aesthetic of spontaneous prosody,
Pomeray is described as an originating source.[24] And although Duluoz sees
himself in *The Dharma Bums* as "an oldtime bhikku in modern clothes wan-
dering the world . . . in order to turn the wheel of True Meaning," it is Japhy
Ryder whom Duluoz regards as "the number one Dharma Bum of them
all."[25] As Holy Goof and Bodhisattva respectively, Pomeray and Ryder are
spiritually equipped to replace Gerard in Duluoz's life.

The qualities that first attract Duluoz to Pomeray, the ones that make
Pomeray the Holy Goof (e.g., his eccentricities, his propensity for play, his
enormous appetite for experience, his capacity for sudden movement), are the
same qualities that finally disqualify him as a potential replacement for Gerard. Tim Hunt describes the Pomeray character as simultaneously "prophet
and fool: prophet for the awareness of primal vitality that he evokes in his
most intense gesture, and fool for his refusal to recognize more clearly the way
his allegiance to impulse and energy is gradually damning him."[26] If *On the
Road* celebrates unmediated action, it also indicts it. The second and fourth
of the novel's five parts culminate in Duluoz's disappointment in Pomeray's
behavior. Abandoned by Pomeray in both cases, the latter while suffering
from dysentery in Mexico City, the former when he is dropped off penniless
with Marylou, Pomeray's girlfriend, in San Francisco, Duluoz comes to echo
the words and sentiments of the women who complain about his buddy.
When Marylou asks Duluoz if he understands that Pomeray is a "bastard"
who abandons people "any time it's in his interest," Duluoz responds yes
(170). Regardless of how attractive a potential surrogate brother he remains to
Duluoz, Pomeray proves himself more than once a "rat" (303).

Japhy Ryder's entry into the Legend in *The Dharma Bums* supplies a positive counterpoint to Pomeray's negative male energy. Combining Pomeray's
physicality with Gerard's spirituality, Ryder appears to be the male who might
provide Duluoz with the brotherhood he craves. Although Ryder, like
Pomeray, is far more spontaneous sexually than Duluoz and, in his words,
"distrust[s] any kind of Buddhism or *any* kinda philosophy or social system
that puts down sex" (26), he differs from Pomeray in his treatment of sex
as an opportunity for spiritual and communal growth, not personal gain or

aggrandizement. Even when Ryder encourages Duluoz, again like Pomeray, to engage in group sex, he does so within the context of a Tibetan Buddhist ceremony called "yabyum," thus providing a religious corollary to Gerard (24–27).

As an experienced outdoorsman and Orientalist about to depart for an indefinite stay in a Japanese Buddhist monastery, Ryder serves as a role model for Duluoz and a font of inspiration and information about recuperative spaces. Not only does he present Duluoz with a strong model of survival and adaptation regardless of the space he occupies, but he also tries to strengthen Duluoz's relationship to his work. In addition to teaching him how to pack a rucksack for a long stay in the wilderness and making it possible for him to write in relative solitude the following summer as a fire spotter in the Cascade Range, Ryder lectures him about drinking too much. In fact, they have an argument about it not long before Ryder leaves for Japan: "How do you expect to become a good bhikku or even a Bodhisattva Mahasattva always getting drunk like that?" (149). Later in the day as Duluoz continues to drink, Ryder questions his ability to handle solitude: "I don't see how you're even going to gain enlightenment and manage to stay out in the mountains, you'll always be coming down the hill spending your bean money on wine" (150). As a description of Duluoz's alcoholic decline, this scenario is prophetic. It is Ryder's sincere concern for Duluoz's well-being that separates him from the self-involved Pomeray and nominates him as the preferable surrogate brother.

In addition, Ryder has a father who provides companionship as well as a model of wholeness. At his son's going-away party, the elder Ryder responds to the beat of bongos and his son's nakedness by dancing as energetically and suggestively as anyone there, proving himself "the maddest father [Duluoz] ever saw" and "a pure Dharma Bum father" (153, 154). Unlike Duluoz's father, who lost his business and afterward struggled, often bitterly and in ill health, to make his living as an itinerant printer, the elder Ryder is open-minded and youthful, vigorous and successful (in his case, as a contractor). Separately the Ryders furnish Duluoz with healthy examples of masculinity; together they model a healthy father-son relationship. The likelihood, however, that Duluoz might realize a surrogate brother and father in the Ryders disappears when Japhy sails for Japan.

As positive an influence as Japhy Ryder is before his departure, the possible loss of Pomeray as surrogate brother is even more significant because he comes the closest of Duluoz's acquaintances to taking the place of Gerard. In addition to being Gerard's potential spiritual equivalent, he is born just after Gerard dies, a fact that Duluoz underscores in *Visions of Cody* (1972) as he remembers "the day of his [Gerard's] funeral 1926, year of Cody's birth."[27] In a three-page passage of the "Joan Rawshanks" section, Duluoz refers to Pomeray seven times as "the brother I lost."[28] Abandoned to the streets in his early teens by his vagabond, alcoholic father, Pomeray is an ideal partner for Duluoz. He even has his own "lost brother," a cousin from childhood who, he says, was the "one man in the family who took tender concern for me" (*Road* 215–16). That claim makes all the more powerful a moment earlier in the novel when Pomeray's separation from family was formalized by the same cousin, who tracked him down after seven years to deliver the news: "I came to see you tonight because there's a paper I want you to sign for the family. Your father is no longer mentioned among us and we want absolutely nothing to do with him, and, I'm sorry to say, with you either, any more."[29]

The elder Pomeray has everything to do with the family that Duluoz and Cody are forming. As tangible object of their search, he strengthens their bond as "lost brothers," even if he remains "the father [they] never found" (*Road* 310). In *Big Sur,* one of the last chapters of the Legend, the absent Pomeray father appears in surrogate form and registers the complexity of the abandoned sons' needs and the emotional work they do for each other. As Duluoz explains it, "He really loves me like a brother and more than that, . . . I remind him of his old wino father but the fantastic thing is that HE reminds ME of MY father so that we have this strange eternal father-image relationship that goes on and on" (134). It is only the "image" that lasts, however. Just as Duluoz and Pomeray's relationship expresses the "legend of male love" Catherine R. Stimpson ascribes to the Beats, it also recalls Beat "counter-legends, stories of bonding gone wrong, adhesion gone sticky."[30]

If fatherless, brotherless Pomeray provided Duluoz with his best opportunity to recuperate his family of origin, the triangulated union Duluoz entered into with Pomeray and his wife, Evelyn, soon after his father died offered the greatest potential for reconstructive surrogacy and emotional fulfillment. At the cabin of a friend years after the failed polyandrous experiment, Duluoz looks out to sea with Evelyn and recalls the union as his lost chance:

> She really loves me, used to love me in the old days like a husband, for awhile there she had two husbands Cody and me, we were a perfect family till Cody finally got jealous or maybe I got jealous, it was wild for awhile I'd be coming home from work on the railroad all dirty with my lamp and just as I came in for my Joy bubblebath old Cody was rushing off on a call so Evelyn had her new husband in the second shift then

when Cody come home at dawn all dirty for his Joy bubblebath, ring, the phone's run and the crew clerk's asked me out and I'm rushing off to work, both of us using the same old clunker car in shifts. (*Big Sur* 130)

A little later when alone with Cody, Duluoz is forced to remember why the union never worked in the first place. Describing another potential triangulated relationship, this one with a girlfriend Duluoz has never met, Pomeray says, " 'That's what we'll be old buddy, you and me, double husbands, later on we'll have whole Harreeeem and reams of Hareems boy, and we'll call ourselves or that is' (flutter) 'ourself Duluomeray, see Duluoz and Pomeray, Duluomeray, see, hee hee hee' " (135).

What the double-husband trope offered Duluoz was the opportunity to transcend his status as second male in the role of husband at the same time as he figuratively restored his childhood family to wholeness. It was a "perfect," if temporal, unity in which he operated as Cody's equal as lover, worker, and thus "poppa." Their "Duluomeray" bond strengthened through self-replication (a single "ourself"), they worked at the same job, drove the same car, took the same bath, played with the same kids, and slept with the same woman, their wife.[31] In this, his "perfect family," he and Pomeray enjoyed the same constellation of roles: husband, brother, father, and son. Theirs was to be, in Duluoz's estimation, "some kind of new thing in the world actually where two men can be angelic friends and not be homosexual and fight over girls" (135). The Duluoz-Evelyn-Cody marriage promised to expand the boundaries of traditional marriage and provide the double husbands with the father and brother figures necessary to heal their familial wounds.

If it had all worked as Duluoz had hoped, Evelyn might have enjoyed the complementary roles of wife, sister, daughter, and mother. But because of the differences in the men's intent, theirs became, in Stimpson's words, a "counter-legend," another story of "bonding gone wrong." With it, it seems, went any chance of Duluoz's ever transcending his status as second male. The opportunity to recuperate his family of origin gone, Duluoz returned to the road, once again incomplete, wounded, in search of the family that would remain always out of reach. It is near the end of *Tristessa* (1960), after he fails to get the title character, a heroin-addicted prostitute, to leave her junkie partner, an old friend of his, that Duluoz names the problem. After calling himself "Oedipus Rex" and the "positional son in woman and man relationships," he asks, "King, bing, I'm always in the way for momma and poppa—When am I gonna be poppa?"[32]

The answer is never. As second male, Duluoz remains the "positional son." That the completion of his search for brother and father surrogates is always suspended is not only part of the narrative structure of the Legend (i.e., each novel a chapter leading to another) but a defining element of the melodrama that keeps him moving. Between World War I and World War II, Freud's argument that properly managed grief (i.e., grief completed in a timely fashion) might break the emotional bonds and liberate the grieving person was being challenged by, as Peter N. Stearns puts it, "the new antigrief regime" argument that grief was primarily "an inappropriate or dysfunctional attempt to restore proximity."[33] At the heart of Kerouac's project, or Duluoz's "remembrances," lies exactly that, the dream of proximity, of familial recuperation, the same dream operating in *Death of a Salesman* and *The Glass Menagerie*. Regardless of the differences in the ways the abandoned sons— Willy Loman, Tom Wingfield, and Jack Duluoz—respond to their loss, the road is for them a place where they might express, not escape, emotion and obligation.

If it is obligation that brings Duluoz and Wingfield home, or keeps Loman from leaving in the first place, it is also obligation that makes the road such a central part of these midcentury melodramas. It is on the road after all, in the double movement of careening and careering, that they seek to heal the body of the family, to restore it if only symbolically to its prior wholeness, to take on emotional and, with the exception of Wingfield, financial responsibility. Writing about the American Adam, Pamela Boker makes the standard connection between "the paralyzing effects of adolescent idealism and the repression of grief in American thought and fiction."[34] Where the "antigrief regime" policed excess emotion in American culture at mid-twentieth century, so our Adamic inheritance has kept us looking for male figures whose exhibition of grief seems insufficient or blocked in some way. Not surprisingly, we locate in these road narratives what we are looking for: males who appear always to be running away from, rather than toward, emotional engagement, sons who are either overinvested in their families of origin or underinvested, perpetually narcissistic, adolescent, and irresponsible. We need, I argue, to rethink what we too easily dismiss as male flight, to reconsider the importance of family and the reality of family systems in mid-twentieth-century melodramas like the Duluoz Legend, *The Glass Menagerie,* and *Death of a Salesman.*

In 1949, as actor Lee J. Cobb was pitching Willy Loman's Alaskan timberland dream to Mildred Dunnock's Linda in New York's Morosco Theatre,

Kerouac was watching his Colorado ranch fantasy collapse all around him. On an exploratory trip financed by the one thousand dollar advance he had received for *The Town and the City*, Kerouac's love of the West failed to rub off on his family. His mother decided she preferred an urban or milltown existence back East and arranged to return to her old job in the shoe factory. His brother-in-law, a Southerner, longed to return to rural North Carolina and soon took Kerouac's sister and infant nephew with him. Like Willy Loman, Kerouac had hoped to make what Kay Stanton calls "the Green World" his family's home.[35] There, in Kerouac's words, on "some kind of 'homestead,'" a ranch or a farm, he would combine family romance and frontier, or pastoral, myth.[36] There he would make good on the deathbed promise he had made to his father. He would make a home for his mother, perhaps even his sister's family, and fulfill his role as the good son.

In a series of letters written the year before to Neal Cassady, Kerouac elaborated on his ranch fantasy. It began as a two-guy affair, Kerouac and a childhood buddy with farming experience leasing and working a small two-house ranch in "partnership," his buddy's family occupying one house and Kerouac the other with a future wife and six children. In a subsequent letter those two houses become one: "a big home with about twenty people in it, whole families at the same time, something going on all the time, . . . one big tumultuous house." When Neal and his wife, Carolyn, question the practicability of a sprawling multifamily home at the same time America's housing patterns are turning to Leavittowns and the production of small one-family units, Kerouac suggests "various friendly encampments on the same land," his sister's family and his mother in one, the Cassadys living nearby in "perfect compatibility" with Kerouac and a wife.[37] Eventually a building would be converted into a Beat dormitory for all their traveling friends, who might or might not stay long enough to help work the ranch but who would certainly enjoy "big jazz-record parties" in the basement of the Cassady-Kerouac house.

It is in this Colorado ranch fantasy that we might locate the constituent parts of the mid-twentieth-century melodrama of beset sonhood that Kerouac will play out imaginatively in his writings, the chapters or books that will make up his Duluoz Legend. "Already started my super book," Kerouac writes in a 1952 letter to John Clellon Holmes, "not only about the hip generation but another fictional arrangement of my family life."[38] Whether located in "one big tumultuous house" or "various friendly encampments," these arrangements become the stuff Kerouac novels are made of. And at the heart of those arrangements are the holes left by the deaths of his older brother in 1926 and his father in 1946, holes he will fill with the product of his careening and careering, his "super book," which is also his "family" book.

Notes

1. Kerouac, *Big Sur,* p. v. Subsequent references are cited in the text.

2. Kerouac, *The Town and the City,* pp. 498–99. Subsequent references are cited in the text.

3. Primeau, *Romance of the Road,* p. 15.

4. Kerouac, *Vanity of Duluoz,* p. 105. Subsequent references are cited in the text.

5. For a discussion of family-systems theory and how it might be applied to the reading of a post–World War II male-escape narrative, see Hurt, "Family and History in *Death of a Salesman,*" pp. 134–41. As Hurt explains, the Lomans' actions are understood as "well-intended, if sometimes misguided, attempts to preserve the family and survive within it" (137).

6. One of the most widely read and most often quoted treatments of the Beat phenomenon appeared in the November 30, 1959, issue of *Life*. In "The Only Rebellion Around," O'Neil warned readers that collectively the Beat rebels "have raised their voices against virtually every aspect of current American society" (232). The long list that follows begins with "Mom, Dad."

7. Lewis, *The American Adam,* p. 91.

8. Ibid., pp. 91, 198.

9. Buell, "American Literary Emergence," p. 413.

10. Smith, *Virgin Land,* p. 89.

11. Ibid.

12. Kerouac, *Desolation Angels,* pp. 11, 10.

13. Williams, *The Glass Menagerie,* p. 23. Subsequent references are cited in the text.

14. Miller, *Death of a Salesman,* p. 51. Subsequent references are cited in the text.

15. In *Communists, Cowboys, and Queers,* Savran writes, "Their fantasies are deeply enmeshed in the production of gender, fashioning two closely related masculine ideals. For Willy, Ben embodies a rugged and heroic vitality. . . . For Biff, meanwhile, the dream of being a cowboy represents an attempt to recover the power that deserted him when he discovered his father's adulterous liaison in Boston" (34–35). These fantasies of recuperation arise out of their woundedness, or their feelings of "temporariness."

16. Dubbert, *Man's Place,* p. 10.

17. Fetterley, *Resisting Reader,* p. 6.

18. Kerouac, *Atop an Underwood,* p. 10.

19. Ibid., p. 9.

20. McNeil, "Archaeology," p. 187.

21. In a letter drafted in 1943 but never sent to hometown friend Cornelius Murphy, Kerouac described conversations with a Navy psychiatrist: "He wanted to know of my emotional experiences and I told him of my affairs with mistresses and various promiscuous wenches, adding to that the crowning glory of being more closely attached to my male

friends, spiritually and emotionally, than to these women. This not only smacked of dementia praecox, it smacked of ambisexuality." See Charters, *Jack Kerouac,* p. 62.

22. Kerouac, *On the Road,* p. 195. Subsequent references are cited in the text.

23. See Hunt, *Kerouac's Crooked Road,* pp. 238–49, for a comparison of Dean Moriarty and Cody Pomeray.

24. Both of Kerouac's statements about his compositional method, "Belief and Technique for Modern Prose" and "Essentials of Spontaneous Prose," reprinted in Charters, *The Portable Beat Reader,* pp. 57–59, promote this idea of the masculine artist. Kerouac uses jazz and motion pictures to explain his double aesthetic of spontaneity and vigorous movement and the role it plays in the production of his texts. Ideally this aesthetic produces a text coursing with, in Eric Mottram's words, "breath and muscularity." See Mottram, "A Preface to *Visions of Cody,*" p. 50.

25. Kerouac, *The Dharma Bums,* pp. 6, 10. Subsequent references are cited in the text.

26. Hunt, *Kerouac's Crooked Road,* p. 70.

27. Kerouac, *Visions of Cody,* p. 97. Earlier in *Visions of Cody,* written in 1951–1952 and published posthumously, 1927 is given as the year of Pomeray's birth (50). In either case, 1926 or 1927, the suggestion is that Pomeray is Gerard reincarnated.

28. Ibid., pp. 318–20.

29. Ibid., p. 179. For another version of this incident, see Kerouac, *Visions of Cody,* p. 366.

30. Stimpson, "Beat Generation," p. 378.

31. In Duluoz's closed model, Evelyn's value increases as she becomes a key participant, is given a voice, achieves insider status; in Cody's open sexual economy, she is devalued at the rate female capital is accumulated. Duluoz's replication of men becomes Pomeray's replication of women. For an elaboration of the double-husband trope and Evelyn's relationship to it, see Davenport, "Complicating 'A Very Masculine Aesthetic,' " pp. 211–68, especially pp. 240–54.

32. Kerouac, *Tristessa,* p. 93. For the most sustained Oedipal reading of the Duluoz Legend, see Jones, *Jack Kerouac's Duluoz Legend.*

33. Stearns, *American Cool,* p. 159.

34. Boker, *The Grief Taboo,* p. 2.

35. Stanton, "Women and the American Dream," p. 67.

36. Charters, *Jack Kerouac,* p. 201.

37. Ibid., pp. 155, 149, 158–59.

38. Ibid., p. 382.

9

Men's Tears and the Roles of Melodrama

TOM LUTZ

While collecting anecdotes for a cultural history of tears, I performed an informal survey of actors, asking how they made themselves cry on stage and in front of the camera.[1] They answered in one of two ways. A minority thought of crying as a purely physical process and took the idea of sense memory (per Stanislavski, Strasberg, and other proponents of "method acting") to mean purely sensual memories—they remembered the actual physical sensations of weeping in order to open the valves again.[2] The majority used something more akin to the stereotypical acting coach's suggestion to remember one's dying dog, or some other bit of narrative that could trigger tears. One actor from the sense memory group demonstrated for me by breathing heavily, in violent, jerky gasps, and within seconds tears were running down her face. An actor who used the narrative method, who also demonstrated for me, explained that she quite literally thinks of Old Yaller.

As this last suggests, the narrative source of the actor's tears often was not memory per se but a story that had been read or seen, and in some cases imagined or fantasized. I began to notice in the trigger stories and scenes these actors described to me a prevalence of melodramatic miniplots, stories that were either lifted from a melodramatic film or recognizably structured like one. One actor, for instance, who regularly replaces his tear-producing scenarios as they get "used up," developed a new trigger scene soon after the birth of his son: he is on the *Titanic* as it is sinking (this was just before the James Cameron film), and he is handing his wife and baby son into a lifeboat. This vision could make him break down into sobs almost immediately. In response to my questions he told me that his crying had something to do with the fact that others—the captain of the ship, the first mate, the other men taking charge of the situation, the women and children—were watching and approving. He cried imagining himself heroically doing his duty, weeping, in effect, at how perfectly he was fulfilling traditional male roles: keeping his family safe, maintaining his emotional equilibrium, calmly and valiantly administering in the face of disaster. And he was doing it all in the eyes of witnesses, including the local authorities and other heroic men. Since it was the *Titanic,* in fact, it seemed the eyes of history itself were on his courageous self-sacrifice, his manly act. This daydream, this minimelodrama, made him weep at the sublimity of so consummately fulfilling an iconographic social role. His way prepared by previous melodramas of male heroism, he weeps in a kind of ecstasy at his own fantasy of role fulfillment. And in case after case, I found, what turned on actors' faucets was an image of perfect role fulfillment.

I am interested in this implicit conjunction of social fantasy and physical sensation. What is it that connects our role images and our sense memories, our sociological and physiological selves? And since, as I am going to argue, the flashpoint for tears in melodramatic films is always an image of role fulfillment, what can this conjunction tell us about our gendered response to melodrama? Classic Hollywood melodramas, often called "women's films" or "weepies" by both those in the industry and critics, have been analyzed by film scholars in terms of their ideological force, since they so obviously engage fundamental cultural debates about gender roles. In this chapter I propose to use some of the findings of experimental psychologists and neurologists to help resolve what has been an ongoing debate in film studies about whether (and how) film melodrama reinforces or resists gender ideology, through specific attention to classic family melodramas, especially the small subset known as "male weepies." Like "women's films," "male weepies" were constructed in order to induce tears, and they did so, I will argue, by staging crises and fantasy resolutions of role performance.[3] Men's tears at male melodramas, I will suggest, are overdetermined by pressures to strive to fulfill and at the same time reject the dominant male roles of the time.

Not coincidentally, studies of the physiology and social meanings of tears have often been conducted by exposing subjects to melodramatic film, making a ready-made bank of data that has not heretofore been utilized by film scholars.[4] Many such experiments by social psychologists have shown what common sense would suggest, that socialization is the central fact in people's understanding of their own tears and that crying is both learned and situation specific.[5] These studies combine to make several other things clear as well—among them that men and women cry at different rates, in relation to different filmic stimuli, in ways determined by their own gender and that of their immediate neighbors in the audience, and that in general women are more likely to cry than men. One physiological theory developed in the 1980s attempted to explain the varying rates of male and female tears by pointing to the role of prolactin, a female hormone (i.e., produced in greater quantities by women), in the production of tears; this has, in the last few years, been counteracted by new studies showing that testosterone is also important to tear production.[6] The basic physiology I am interested in here is shared by both male and female bodies, largely unaffected by race, class, sexuality, or other social positions: the fact that there are two branches of the autonomic nervous system, the sympathetic and the parasympathetic nervous systems, and that they play different roles in the arc of an emotional experience. The sympathetic system readies the body for exceptional action, as in the case of the adrenaline-laden "fight or flight" response to fear; the parasympathetic system returns the body to homeostasis, to its "steady state." I am hoping that my attention to the relation between the physiology of tears and the ideological work of melodrama may suggest further research into the relation of physiology and cultural history, since my argument is that our physiological responses, however mechanically universal, are overdetermined by our relation to specific, historically evolving social roles, that our emotional responses to fictions involve our imaginative involvement in characters' social dilemmas, and that fictions about role crises thereby help manage the revamping of such roles.[7]

And at the same time I am hoping to resolve, through analyzing the gender ideologies of films that induce tears, an argument that still exists in physiology, about when tears appear in the arc of an emotional experience, whether they are part of the arousal process, and therefore induced by the sympathetic nervous system, or the recovery process, and therefore induced by the parasympathetic nervous system. At stake in such discussions is the question of whether crying itself is a sign of arousal or recovery and thus whether it signals distress, for instance, or the cessation of distress. As long ago as 1930 F. H. Lund argued, in the very first issue of the *Journal of Social Psychology*, that tears were regulated by the parasympathetic nervous system, that they accompanied physiological recovery rather than arousal, his prime evidence the fact that the lacrimal gland is primarily innervated by a parasympathetic nerve. Paralysis of the parasympathetic pathway to the lachrymal gland makes crying impossible, and thus it is clear that without the parasympathetic system kicking in, and therefore without some sense of relaxation or recovery, crying could not happen. Robert Sadoff, Nico Frijda, and Jay Efran and Timothy Spangler, among others, all argue for this perspective: after a period of intense sympathetic arousal, a burst of parasympathetic activity occurs, which in turn induces tears.[8] There is, however, evidence on the other side as well: Deborah Kraemer and Janice Hastrup found heart rate increases during crying at a film, suggesting sympathetic activity, and James Gross, B. L. Fredrickson, and Robert Levenson, using a wide range of measures, found a complex mixture of nervous activity: monitoring heart rate, pulse, skin temperature, skin conductance, and several other indicators of autonomic activity at the same time indicated that both the sympathetic and parasympathetic systems were at work.[9]

The main problem with the design of experiments on all sides of this issue is that crying has many different social as well as physiological functions. The communicative function of tears, as Silvan Tomkins wrote in the 1960s, can be to "negatively motivate" others to help meliorate the crier's distress, and would thus be a form of affective action.[10] Even crying that begins as a parasympathetic process can be used in a motivated, aroused attempt at communication—a perfect example is the scene in George Cukor's *Adam's Rib* (1949) in which Spencer Tracy begins to cry in resignation, sees the effect it has on his wife, and cries some more. Since the crying subjects in psychological experiments are intrusively observed, sometimes holding lachrymaries to their cheeks to collect tears, sitting next to other weepers, sometimes with many electronic measuring instruments attached, sometimes with researchers hovering, almost always with strangers present, distress levels may be very different than in a "natural" setting. Steven Holston found that the attempt to control crying while watching a film increased sympathetic nervous activity, and so some of the sympathetic activity found by researchers may be the result of attempts to stop crying that has already begun.[11] And since the awareness of one's own tears can itself, in turn, cause emotional reactions such as fear, anxiety, shame, or anger, the physiology of even the simplest crying episode is very complex. If melodrama was simply an ideological buttress, one would expect to see purely parasympathetic response—after a period of sympathetic excitation in which social roles are tested, the audience sees those roles reinforced and relaxes. If melodrama were a revolutionary genre, as some have claimed, one would expect sympathetic, excitatory responses taking precedence. What we find, however, is that there is a mix of both forms of nervous activity, indicating, I therefore want to argue, pressures toward both social conformity and social change. The flashpoint for tears in these films is the character's recovery of his or her proper social role after an exciting foray into social disruption, but that return is always a notably compromised or transformed version of the role, a return that arouses a different set of emotions. An analysis of male melodramas, primarily from the 1950s, will demonstrate the basic conservatism of the genre, then, but a conservatism that is complicated by the fact that male roles sometimes demand contradictory behaviors and are always in flux, and further complicated by the way in which this basic narrative arc, in which social disruption is consistently rearticulated as recovery, normalizes social disruption even as it encourages social discipline. In other words, the conservatism of the genre is exactly that which can help make it a tool of social critique and social change even as it makes us weep for traditional roles.

The debate over the political torque of melodrama in cultural studies is downright venerable and traditional in its own right by now, and there are any number of voices at the poles of the discussion. Roger Bromley, to take a random example, argues that "representations of individuals and their personal/social relationships in popular fictions are recognized as natural and obvious; they exclude any other mode of representing or seeing man/woman and their relationships."[12] In other words, popular fictions not only reinforce ideologically determined social relations, they make it impossible for audiences to imagine change. Christine Gledhill, Charlotte Brundson, and Pam Cook make similar arguments—for Cook, melodrama relegates "women's desires in the imaginary, where they have traditionally been placed."[13] Simon Shepherd—again to take a paradigmatic example from among many— suggests the opposite, by showing that the popularity of early melodrama is absolutely compatible with its ability to "unsettle" its audience.[14] He writes about melodrama's (French) revolutionary origins and revolutionary potential. Other critics have attempted to make sense of both these forces. Thomas Elsaesser made a distinction between the ideologically laden morals propounded by melodramas and the use, in the most "sophisticated" examples, of music, lighting, and structure to subvert or undercut that moral.[15] Laura Mulvey suggested that although female transgression is punished in melodrama, female protagonists' subjectivity produces an excess that the narrative cannot contain.[16] Karen Chandler leaves such formalist arguments and looks instead at the audience reception of melodrama and how its conventions "function in the lives of audience-members." She points out, in her challenge to reductionist appraisals of pop culture's effects, that "convention does not determine interpretation."[17] Chandler argues against a "simple model of social containment in which disparate texts condition a similar, passive response in audiences," favoring the acknowledgment of "audience members' ability to shape narrative to their particular needs" (28).

In his influential *The Melodramatic Imagination*, Peter Brooks argued that melodrama arose in the nineteenth century as a secularized search for morality in a world losing its traditional moorings, in particular its belief in religion and in the naturalness of social conventions.[18] Characters in melodrama tend to fulfill the "primary psychic roles" of "father, mother, child," according to Brooks, in order to make stark the Manichaeism, the clear division into good and evil, that the nineteenth century wanted to continue to believe in after the supposed death of God. But of course for most people God never died, and melodrama lives on for reasons that have nothing to do with nineteenth-century secularization and everything to do with contemporary desires. The continued lure of melodrama, its continuing power to make us cry, lies in the fact that the fathers, mothers, and children are not just "psychic roles," as Brooks would have it, but social roles that actual people can fail or succeed in fulfilling. The demands felt by actual fathers, mothers, children, siblings, husbands, and wives are precisely the social pressures to which melodrama responds.

One criticism of Brooks's work is its supposed ahistoricity—Michael Hays and Anastasia Nikolopoulou, for instance, explain that their collection of essays on melodrama is meant as a corrective to Brooks's representation of melodrama as having a "dehistoricized, or 'transhistorical' " core.[19] Hays and Nikolopoulou put quotes around "transhistorical" to announce how ridiculous they think such an idea is. On the other hand, they say that "the genre's structural malleability" allows for simultaneous incorporation of "the discourses of imperialism, nationalism, and class and gender conflict" (x), which takes as wide a swath of history as Brooks. Brooks's argument *is* historical, after all—it is an argument about melodrama in the nineteenth century arising out of other historical trends. I am trying to make a more or less structural, and therefore transhistorical, argument at the level of generic conventions and a more or less historical one at the same time—that melodrama stages crises of role fulfillment and fantasy resolutions to the often insoluble contradictions of gender roles; as the roles change, so do the melodramas. As Robert Lang has written, melodrama "makes ideological contradiction its subject matter," and part of that ideological contradiction is created by the historical changes roles undergo, even as those contradictions become, especially when thematized in a culture's narrative and other discourses, a force for further change.[20] The successful resolutions of melodrama may represent what *Los Angeles Times* film critic Kenneth Turan has called the "triumph of the ordinary," but to the extent that the "ordinary" is itself fluid rather than fixed, multiple rather than singular, so are the melodramatic plots that stage the problems inherent in filling them and the hermeneutic horizons they make available.[21]

Robert Lang's *American Film Melodrama* is one of the strongest arguments for reading melodrama as "a struggle against, or within, the patriarchy," in which "a repressed identity" seeks release.[22] Lang assumes that in patriarchal culture, femininity is a failure of masculinity (8) and that, following Lacan, femininity is structured as a lack, particularly a lack of economic or social power. Jackie Byars argues that melodramas "mystify existing domination, inequality, and injustice," but sometimes "allow residual and emergent—potentially progressive—elements into the ideological process."[23] Stanley Cavell, in his *Contesting Tears: The Hollywood Melodrama of the Unknown Woman,* argues that for the subgenre he has identified, the genre's "designs upon our tears" are related to "the woman's assignment . . . to prove the man's existence" through "taking on his subjectivity, overcoming his skepticism by accepting that subjectivity as undeniable."[24] For both Lang and Cavell, as in much of the criticism, the essential roles are female and patriarchy determines those roles and their insufficiency. There is room for different responses—as Cavell writes, one "has a choice of reactions," whether to weep along with the heroine's "tears of 'sacrifice,' or (more recently) scorn for the society that requires it" (182). In each of these cases, attention is given to the multiplicity of ideological forces at work, but in each case it is some form of patriarchy that is reinforced or critiqued.

But all of this misses an essential feature of melodrama. In films from the 1925 and 1937 versions of *Stella Dallas* (King Vidor) through the 1983 *Terms of Endearment* (James L. Brooks) and beyond there is unquestionably a strong criticism of male prerogative. The most severe criticisms in these films, however, are leveled not against accepted male roles but against men who do not live up to their traditional responsibilities.[25] In *Terms of Endearment* this means that the cheating husband (the role played by Jeff Daniels as a college professor) is at fault, not the role of husband. The grandmother's boyfriend (Jack Nicholson) is flawed not because he is a patriarch but because he refuses to fully become one. Nicholson's character is held up to ridicule at first because he has basked too long in his youthful glory as an astronaut while continuing to squire around a string of women far too young for him. The problem with the playboy role here, just as it is in a long string of melodramas and comedies, is not patriarchy: it is that the man is avoiding patriarchy by refusing to take on the one thing every patriarch needs, a wife and family. When he finally plays the patriarch by acting like a father figure to the young boys who have lost their mother, the audience is again primed for tears, as if in appreciation of his reversion to patriarchal presence.

The famous "women's films" produced by Hollywood studios in the 1930s and 1940s specifically for female audiences quickly collected disparaging nicknames—weepie, weeper, tearjerker, sob story, soaper, four-hankie job—because of their ability to make women cry by staging crises of female role performance. In *Stella Dallas* the climactic moment comes when a poor woman (Barbara Stanwyck in King Vidor's 1937 version) gives her beloved daughter up to her rich and powerful ex-husband. She lets her maternal sense of responsibility—the child will have more opportunities and privileges with her father—take precedence over her own desire to be with her child. The desires are mutually exclusive, but the responsibility of the role triumphs and the audience of women for whom the film was made, the makers hoped, will collapse in tears.

"Male weepies" were designed to get the same response from men. The earliest of them—*The Champ* (1931), also directed by Vidor—inverts the plot of *Stella Dallas:* it is the story of a man (Wallace Beery) who gives his son (Jackie Cooper) up to the care of his newly wealthy ex-wife. His sense of parental responsibility demands that he relinquish his claims on his child, and he does so. At the end of the film, Beery, a semi-washed-up boxer, is dying of injuries sustained in the ring and sustained in part because he wouldn't stay down when he should have, knowing his son was watching; he was trying to be a good father in his son's eyes rather than the failure he knows he is. Beery won an Oscar for the role, and critics still comment on both the melodramatic kitschiness of the film and its power. *The Champ* is unreadable through theories of melodrama in which male economic power reigns—Beery is the one who is cut out of the realms of power and money his ex-wife inhabits, and it is his desires that remain always in the imaginary realm. The ex-wife's desires are realized in the end, as is her role—as Beery dies, Cooper, who had been until then a bit standoffish, turns toward her and says, as the last line of the film, "Mother!"

As social roles change over time, and the expectations for role fulfillment change, so melodramatic representation can lose its power to elicit tears. The scorn with which melodrama is often met can be at least partially explained by this: the self-sacrificing woman, for instance, has lost some of the appeal it once had as a form of heroic role performance. And the pathetically inadequate father such as Beery finds little sympathy among contemporary audiences. When *The Champ* was remade in 1979 with Jon Voight as the boxer and Ricky Schroder as the son, directed by Franco Zeffirelli, the plot remained almost exactly the same. But Voight is more successful in his postboxing life and there is a new discourse of female independence added to the themes. Whereas Beery played a likable but hopeless alcoholic, Voight plays a not-too-bright, sometimes drunk, but viable man, whose wife left him not because, as in the earlier film, he was a bum, but because she wanted more than he could offer. The 1931 version undoubtedly drew some of its force from the sexual liberation of the flapper, the revision of divorce law in the 1920s, and ongoing concern about what these and other changes meant for men's roles, as well as concern about men's wage-earning ability after the crash of 1929. The 1979 version clearly asked its audience to consider what it meant to be a man under the new regime brought about by feminism. Beery knew why his wife left him—he was a drunk and a loser—while Voight needs to know, and he suspects that her desires are fundamentally greedy. Beery is happy for his ex and her new money, Voight rejects the idea that money and position are the stuff of true happiness and pines for the past. Still, in both cases, as in *Stella Dallas,* the films argue that the kid should live with the money. The 1920s and the 1970s both saw major changes in the gender system, with concomitant discussions about men's and women's freedoms and responsibilities, and the differences are significant—men in the 1920s had relatively clear financial and social goals and they could share their success in meeting them with women, while men in the late 1970s competed with their ex-wives not just over the kids but over occupations and the means to self-determination as well. Men needed to live up to their responsibilities to be good fathers in either case, but in the late 1970s men were given an added imprecation to hold onto male dignity despite the threat of female independence.

Halfway between these eras, the 1950s was the heyday of the male weepie. Male roles were in serious revision in the United States, as World War II veterans, men in gray flannel suits, Hollywood cowboys, rebels, beatniks, swingers, and upright suburban husbands and fathers all shared the cultural stage. David Lusted has discussed the 1950s Western as a form of male melo-drama that "deals with problems of homosocial identity" and explores "chang-ing expectations and notions of masculine identity," particularly crises of male identity created by class mobility; clearly, as in the case of such central 1950s male melodramas as the post-Western *Giant* and non-Western *Rebel Without a Cause* (to be discussed below), class mobility is an issue.[26] But many other aspects of male role fulfillment are important as well. Barbara Ehrenreich has identified the 1950s as the beginning of a "male revolt—though hardly organized and seldom conscious of its goals—against the breadwinner ethic," one that "stemmed from dissatisfactions every bit as deep, if not as idealistically expressed, as those that motivated our founding 'second wave' feminists."[27] This revolt was at least in part due, according to Joe Dubbert, to the "erosion of individualism" caused by the "absorption of many individuals into very large organizations, businesses, industries, and colleges."[28] Dubbert is siding here with the social critics of the 1950s, who agreed that men could not, in contemporary society, be the self-determining, self-fulfilling individuals earlier ideologies would have them be; instead they were becoming what William Whyte called organization men, Vance Packard status seekers, and David Reisman anomic individuals.[29] Throughout the 1950s popular magazines ran articles on men's plight that identified con-formity as a problem, and these were written not just by men—as in the case of George Leonard's "The American Male: Why is He Afraid to Be Different?"—but by women as well, such as Dorothy Kilgallen's "The Trou-ble With Men," Lauren Bacall's "I Hate Men," and Romona Barth's "What's Wrong with American Men?" Robert Lowry, writing in *American Mercury* in 1953, claimed that American men, incapable of significant agency in a corpo-ratized world, simply felt out of control of their own lives.[30] The Beat Gen-eration of writers, the bebop subculture, rock 'n' rollers, and pop philosophers such as Hugh Hefner, whose *Playboy* began publication in 1953, all took up where these essayistic and sociological critiques ended, offering alternatives to the emptiness of male experience in the new order, alternatives to being what Robert Lindner called "robotized" and Cameron Shipp the "suckers."[31] As Norman Mailer would write in "The White Negro" in 1957, "to be cool is to be equipped," to be in control in some new way, and Hefner also preached self-determination as the key to escaping conformity and exercising some control over one's own life—the place to start, he suggested, was to reclaim living space from the domination of women, by living in bachelor apartments rather than suburban family homes.[32] This is obviously too complex a history to delve into in any detail—I cite these few texts and developments simply to suggest that the male melodramas of the 1950s were responding not to the long history of patriarchy but to contemporary developments. The male weepies tried to evaluate this refashioning of male roles in complex ways, ways that can be called neither revolutionary resistance to nor reactionary reinforcement of patriarchy as such, but instead provided new symbolic role models that attempted to respond to both traditional and contemporary pressures.

Douglas Sirk documented the confusions about and battles over male role performance in several of what he called his "impossible stories," particularly in *Magnificent Obsession* (1954) and *Written on the Wind* (1956), both of which open with millionaire bachelor protagonists who are wasting their lives in dissipation, avoiding the cultural imperatives to get married, have children, work, or take responsibility for their actions. In *Magnificent Obsession* the rich playboy (Rock Hudson) indirectly causes the death of a doctor and, in part through empathizing with the doctor's widow (Jane Wyman), has a conversion to responsibility as he attempts to comfort her. She, running from him in horror, is struck by a car and blinded in the accident. Hudson quits drinking and carousing and, in remarkably little time, becomes a brilliant surgeon with the express purpose of curing her blindness. He keeps his identity—his part in the death of her husband—a secret from her while he cures her and she, responding to his growing love for her, falls in love with him. When she is cured of her blindness, she has to decide whether to be true to her original anger or her new love and after some tension and confusion goes with the latter. Hudson's character then becomes a settled family man. At first the other characters wonder if he can be properly forgiven and trusted. When it becomes clear that his conversion is sincere and permanent, and the community accepts it as such, the woman he loves bursts into tears and the audience is meant to reach its emotional peak. He is fulfilling his role (as husband, professional, neighbor, man) and being recognized for it. The narrative nonetheless has what Geoffrey Nowell-Smith has called a "shameless contradictoriness,"[33] since it is his freewheeling lifestyle that allows him both his early obsession with bachelor pleasures and his more magnificent obsession with Wyman's eyesight; in his attempts to cure her he follows her to Switzerland, to Santa Fe, both playgrounds of the rich, and his medicine is as much seduction as career.

Written on the Wind doesn't even pretend to be upbeat, making *Magnificent Obsession* by comparison seem out of date in its class dynamics and its optimism. The carefree playboy of *Magnificent Obsession* may exercise the recklessness of the rich, but he is a far cry from the thorough debauchery of the Texas oil millionaires in *Written on the Wind*. Robert Stack plays an oil baron who is ruthless and rapacious, both sexually and economically, and the nymphomania of his sister (Dorothy Malone), along with Stack's sterility, complete the picture of dissolute depravity created by the refusal to enact socially responsible roles. Stack's role as a robber baron is out of date, represented as an economic role that has no place in the modern world. When he decides to seduce his best friend's girlfriend (Lauren Bacall), she resists, and in so doing forces him to adopt more appropriate male behavior. He conforms just enough to win her hand. His conversion is not entirely trustworthy, however, if for no other reason than that it happens too early in the film. The best friend, played again by Rock Hudson, is a more modern man than Stack—a professional (a geologist) rather than a business buccaneer, a man who respects women rather than abuses them, and a man who respects the boundaries other people's roles dictate. He does not, like Stack, poach other men's women and accepts the marriage of Stack and Bacall. When Bacall becomes pregnant, however, Stack, who had been told he was sterile, is convinced that Hudson is the father and all hell breaks loose. Stack dies accidentally but Hudson is charged with his murder. Malone's character—as a nymphomaniac an obviously paradigmatic case of role failure in the 1950s—demands sex from Hudson in exchange for her testimony at his trial. The millionaires are too depraved to be saved, and the story ends in tragedy, the audience's tears caused by the protagonists' utter failure, despite the desire, primarily on the part of Hudson and Bacall but also on the part of the aristocrats, to find happiness in acceptable roles. The film argues that only such role acceptance can save them.

Nonetheless, in both of these films marriage and family are not enough. The dislocations in the culture caused by economic and sexual inequality are too large for the simple reversion to traditional roles. Each film argues that a more detailed and ethically nuanced notion of the role—whether husbandly, professional, or patriarchal—is required of men. One can't just be a successful businessman, one must also be a respectful lover; one can't simply be a scientist, one also needs compassion; one can't just enjoy male privilege, one must earn it. The answer to these people's problems is not readily available from stock cultural models—the solutions seem, in fact, to be written on the wind. In Sirk's *All That Heaven Allows* (1955), more of a woman's film than a male weepie, the male protagonist, again played by Hudson, is an unconventional man—a kind of Thoreauvian Hollywood beatnik who has an oddball collection of friends (poets and artists of mixed generations who we recognize as Bohemian because they drink Chianti) and who, like a *Playboy* philosopher, decorates his own living space. The happy ending here, the plot-delayed marriage, is directed at integrating the female protagonist's desires for both freedom and traditional role-fulfillment. In such a film, male countercultural attitudes are constructed as foils rather than social problems; in the male weepies male countercultural attitudes are more vexed, with countercultural females used as foils.

Vincent Minnelli's *Home from the Hill* (1959) is the most heterogeneous of these tales, telling the story of a Texas rancher with two sons, one legitimate and one illegitimate. The father tries to make his somewhat effeminate legitimate son into a hunter and he-man like himself but fails. His illegitimate son acts as his ranch foreman and is the one who carries him home when he gets drunk. The bastard son does all the work of being the good son and gets no parental respect or even recognition. In fact, he is such a good son that he marries a young woman left impregnated and abandoned by the legitimate heir. Not only that, he keeps constant vigil over his father's wife—who had also rejected him all along—when she becomes ill. In the final scene, when the father is dead and his wife is revived, she invites the illegitimate son to gaze at his father's headstone, which she has had inscribed with his name right alongside that of his prodigal half-brother. Thus the bastard son, the good son, is finally recognized for what he is, both by his "step" mother and by his own father from beyond the grave, as it were. Finally acknowledged by the family, he wells up, and so does the music, and again it is the recognition of role fulfillment that serves as the flashpoint for the audience's tears. Left unanswered are the sociostructural issues such a resolution implies—who inherits the ranch?

George Stevens's *Giant* (1956) based on Edna Ferber's bestselling novel, is an epic melodrama that stages these changes in role identity in terms of class, the generation gap, and regional differences. Elizabeth Taylor, the spoiled daughter of a wealthy Virginia family, marries a Texas ranch owner (Hudson) full of courtly manners and ideas, and is also loved by the dirt-poor, crass ranch hand (James Dean). The rest of the film, which covers a period of over twenty years, charts the battles between Taylor and Hudson over issues of noblesse oblige (she thinks the Mexican workers should receive medical care, he thinks they "have their own ways"), between Hudson and Dean (who strikes oil on his tiny claim and becomes fabulously wealthy), and between Hudson and his son (Dennis Hopper), who doesn't want to take over the ranch but instead wants to become a doctor. Taylor plays an accidental feminist, who thinks it absurd that ladies are excluded from political discussions and that men make all the decisions. This is part conviction, part eastern liberalism, and part brattiness—she just doesn't see why she can't do whatever she wants whenever she wants. Her willfulness is contrasted with that of another strong woman—a stereotypical spinster tyrant who is Hudson's sister and helps run the ranch—but Taylor represents something new, a compassionate conservative, one might say, and one whose job is not to reinforce the patriarchal role of her husband but to modify it to respond to contemporary conditions. The battle between Hudson and his son is also a battle over proper roles for men in the changing world. Hudson's bullying, macho braggadocio, and his sense of generational continuity are shown to be relics halfway through the film, while the professional medical man, once again, is represented as the way of the future. The son and mother also challenge older notions of male privilege by fighting racism—Hopper marries a Mestizo woman and Taylor gets the Chicano workers proper medical care. But later in the film Hopper tries to fight to protect his wife's honor and is roundly beaten; Hudson, having seen the light, at the end of the film, does the same and wins. The "epic" struggle to define men's roles continues. The battle between Hudson and Dean also works both ways, since Hudson's elitism starts as a target of satire, only to be recuperated by Dean's drunken, craven nouveau-riche dissipation. Dean uses the leverage of his oil wealth in a classic alpha male struggle with Hudson, including an attempt to seduce his daughter. He becomes more and more rich, famous, alcoholic, and crude. Hudson, meanwhile, finally comes around, accepts his son's decisions, fights (literally) against racism himself, and accepts the changed nature of his family and society and thus the changed nature of a man's role within them.

Nicholas Ray's *Rebel Without a Cause* (1955), starring James Dean a year before his appearance in *Giant,* argues that the problem of male roles, in a cultural logic made familiar by feminist scholars, transcends and trumps class roles. The filmmakers consciously chose to focus on middle-class youth having the kind of problems—delinquency, aimlessness, knife fights—associated with lower-class youth. And Dean's upper-middle-class father (Jim Backus) is as guilty as the middle-class father of Dean's girlfriend (Natalie Wood) and the entirely absent upper-class parents of Dean's friend (Sal Mineo) in not adapting to the changed environment. Dean's parents dote on him and fight with each other, Sal Mineo's parents are divorced and his father absent, and

Natalie Wood's parents are no-nonsense, conventional, and distant. There is an obvious incestuous subtext to Wood's relation to her father, and that kind of patriarchy is condemned as the source of her delinquency. Dean's father is henpecked, often seen wearing an apron, and unable to take a moral stance on any issue, and that kind of nonpatriarchal stance is shown to be if anything worse. And finally, if Dean's father's doting is a mistake, Mineo's father's absence is no answer, since it means that his mother is never home either, and this combines, we are to assume, to make Mineo effeminate (or gay) and neurotic (or gay), perhaps psychotic. In *Home From the Hill* Robert Mitchum says to his son's girlfriend's father, "All our children deserve better parents," and this is one of the messages of *Rebel*. When his parents fight, Dean screams "You're tearing me apart!" and when his father is too much of a coward to give Dean the advice he asks for, Dean jumps on him and starts to beat him in a final overturning of patriarchal rights.

Dean, Wood, and Mineo retire to an abandoned house, where as critics have noted they play at being a happy family, Dean and Wood reclining in each other's arms while Mineo sits on the floor, gazing up at them fondly. Much has been said about the homosexuality represented in the film, but I am more interested in the dream the film offers at this point of a new kind of family, one that would make all aberrations acceptable. Part of the film's power clearly comes from Dean's charisma, but this is not simply a case of what Richard Dyer calls the "masking effect of the ideology of character": by feeling we are identifying with a unique person, Dyer argues, we ignore the fact that we are identifying with a normative figure.[34] Dean is not a normative figure in *Rebel*. Most of the heroes of male melodrama, as I hope has become clear, are not normative but exceptional figures, individuals who invent or at least suggest new norms when the old ones fail. Mineo attaches himself to Dean because Dean is a strong male figure but also because he is gentle and caring. Dean is not just antipatriarchal and he doesn't simply recoup patriarchy—he is a new man, one who may or may not be a solution to the contradictions embedded in the role; audience tears are cued, however, whenever he comes closest to embodying a new way. As Raymond Massey, playing Dean's father in yet another male melodrama, *East of Eden* (Elia Kazan, dir. 1955) says, "Well, times have changed."[35]

Writing about the ending of Nicholas Ray's melodrama *Bigger Than Life* (1956), which shows a family torn to pieces by the father's megalomania but tearfully reunited in his hospital room, critic Thomas Schatz calls such resolutions "narrative sleight-of-hand," and the melodramatic wish-fulfillment fantasies these films purvey do constitute a form of chicanery, I suppose.[36] But the melodramatic arguments these films make about social roles all take place within a social arena permeated with conflicting ideas about those roles. The status quo that they seem to endorse is always more of an argument about what that status quo should be than a neutral representation of existing mores. The weeping of audiences at melodramas is overdetermined in part because of these competing cultural values. It is only when the role is badly inhabited and then reclaimed that melodrama works its tearful magic. Audiences are meant to cry tears of relief when protagonists return from their outlaw or depressive or alcoholic days to their redeeming social performances (as when James Stewart comes back from his suicidal drunken binge and apologizes to his family in Frank Capra's 1946 *It's a Wonderful Life*), and the tears shed in such cases may be in direct proportion to the fantasy of role abandonment that precedes them. In the male weepies of the 1950s this means that the vacuum created by the evacuation of social proprieties is quickly filled with more important social values, and the perfect melodramatic conclusion to the outlaw tale is when the rebel's search for authenticity itself ends, coincidentally, in some other form of role fulfillment. The "bad" legitimate son in *Home From the Hill* rejects patriarchy and thereby fulfills his social responsibility to determine his own future; the "good" illegitimate son rejects his social ostracism and fights for recognition, making the world safe for patriarchy's bastards.

And even in less obvious cases, the fantasies of role fulfillment can be arguments for the reevaluation of social roles. *Magnificent Obsession* argues that bachelor freedom is acceptable when accompanied by professional commitment, *Giant* and *Written on the Wind* that patriarchal economic power needs to be directed by professional and social values of justice and equality. *Rebel Without a Cause* collapses in its title a critique and recouping of rebellion—what is needed is not conformity but a cause. In each of these cases the arguments for role fulfillment are in the service of an argument about social or cultural change. In each case, in other words, the narrative—and the audience's emotional involvement in that narrative—comes to rest, eliciting a flood of parasympathetic tears, in a resolution that also includes a call to action, eliciting the sympathetic tears of an aroused sense of social possibility.

The most significant essay in film studies addressing tears and melodrama is an article by Steven Neale published in 1986.[37] Neale argues, following literary critic Franco Moretti, that melodrama's effect is conditioned by the powerlessness of the viewer, that the resolution of melodrama is always in important ways "too late" for the characters. This mourning response is accompanied, he speculates, by an eternalization of the wish, as if our mourning for lost possibility and our demand for continued possibility combine to elicit tears. The powerlessness Neale and many other critics claim is central to melodrama is that which leads Torben Grodal to his conclusion that passive autonomic response rather than action determines our emotional response to these films, but those critics who find in melodrama (or its reception) a powerful social critique need the other half of Neale's theory. In her article on *Stella Dallas* Linda Williams argues that melodrama works to the extent that we identify with "all the conflicting points of view" represented and therefore find ourselves both "within and against" the social mores of the represented world.[38] The 1950s male melodramas represent their men as "within and against" their own worlds, as rebels without fully articulated causes. Joy Van Fuqua, in an offhand comment in her critique of the male melodramas of the 1990s writes that "1950s male melodramas denied the male subject a possibility of transformation . . . without a simultaneous transformation of social relations,"[39] a statement that seems finally insupportable given the transformations noted above, but her point is nonetheless well taken: the men represent at best transitional compromises in relation to their own desire for change. The parasympathetic tears, the recuperative tears of letting go, of the recognition and acceptance of loss, are compounded by tears of demand, however infantile they may be as a form of social action: demand for a kind of resolution even more dramatic than those the films employ. Williams begins her essay by quoting a character from a Marilyn French novel who is remembering her own tearful reaction to *Stella Dallas* and describing her "shock of recognition—you know, when you see what you sense is your own destiny up there on the screen or the stage. You might say I've spent my whole life trying to arrange a different destiny."[40] The recognition of social destiny and the desire to alter it account for the data collected by social psychologists and physiologists, for the doubleness of critics' accounts of film melodrama, and for our tears.

Notes

1. This essay follows up on and in some places amends suggestions I made in Lutz, *Crying*, pp. 97–98, 264–67.

2. Cf. Cole, *Acting* and Moore, *Stanislavski Revealed*. Most actors, in fact, use the full gamut of possibilities in ways that they are not fully consciously aware of, all of which work because each allows access to the same system at different points along the complicated

feedback loops of the various brain and body systems involved. Remembering sad thoughts can kick off a crying jag as well as recreating the physical accompaniments or, for that matter, imagining oneself to be very sad. Even recreating the facial contractions of crying or the heavy staccato breathing that accompanies it can cause a person to feel like crying. Paul Ekman, who had developed a system of facial expressions that illustrate specific emotional states, performed experiments in which he asked subjects to contract certain facial muscles, without telling them why. By assessing their moods before and after the experiment, Ekman showed that contracting the muscles of the face that a person makes when anguished is enough to increase people's feelings of anguish. Cf. Ekman et al., *Emotion in the Human Face* and Ekman, *Darwin and Facial Expression*. And the webs of interrelation among the various systems and subsystems of the body involved in emotion may be even more complex. If the neurophysiologist Antonio Damasio is right, in *Descartes' Error*, we can even have an emotional response without any rational thought whatsoever and we can have one without any physical sensation, too.

3. Until recently the most sophisticated theory of film response from a physiological perspective employed a somewhat vague notion of excitation that, as narrative tension builds and then resolves it, engages our autonomic nervous system and thereby gives us feelings. See Tan, *Emotion and the Structure of Narrative Film*. Grodal, in *Moving Pictures*, has linked physiology to film genres by focusing on a distinction made by some physiological psychologists between autonomic responses and actions. If a situation impels us toward action and we cannot act—as when watching a film—we will have an autonomic response, such as hyperventilation or weeping. See Grodal, pp. 39–61, 253–74,

4. Frey and Langseth, *Crying*; Gross, Frederickson, and Levenson. "Psychophysiology of Crying"; Kraemer and Hastrup, "Crying In Adults"; Martin, Guthrie, and Pitts, "Emotional Crying"; Martin and Labott, "Mood following Emotional Crying"; Efran and Spangler, "Why Grown-Ups Cry."

5. John and Sandra Condry, for instance, showed that both men and women, told that the crying infant in a film was a girl, described it as afraid; told that it was a boy they identified the same crying infant as angry ("Sex Differences"). Experiments such as those of Choti, et al., demonstrated that men and women show more stereotypical crying behavior—the men cried less and the women more—when they watched a film in opposite-sex pairs ("Gender and Personality").

6. The argument about prolactin was developed by Frey and Langseth, *Crying*, and Vingerhoets, Assies, and Poppelaars, "Prolactin and Weeping"; about testosterone by Azzarolo et al., "Androgen Support."

7. Grodal suggests that sympathetic responses are "active-aversive-controlling" (they can result in the "fight or flight" response, for instance) while parasympathetic responses are "passive-accepting." Since we can never control what we see unfolding on a movie screen, we are necessarily passive and thus necessarily limited to palpitations, blushes, shivers, and tears rather than more active responses. Film melodrama, in particular, Grodal argues, "achieves its emotional effects" in two ways: "by representations of passive experiences, situations which make voluntary response impossible and evoke autonomic response," that is by making agency and action impossible, and "by abstraction—by

representations of prototypes," the prototypical sons, mothers, fathers, daughters, good guys, and bad guys of melodrama. Melodrama suggests at every turn that individuals are unable to determine their own fates, both in naturalistic and social terms, and combined with a high level of passion—which Grodal links to the passive—this leads to inactive, emotional responses. The understanding audiences gain from melodrama is a kind of "mental software" for "experiencing the passive aspects of life" (*Moving Pictures* 195, 264, 254). I take this to be a misreading of the literature on weeping and the autonomic nervous system.

8. Sadoff, "On the Nature of Crying and Weeping"; Frijda, *Emotions;* Efran and Spangler, "Why Grown-Ups Cry."

9. Kraemer and Hastrup, "Crying in Adults"; Gross, Frederickson, and Levenson, "Psychophysiology of Crying."

10. Tomkins, *Affect, Imagery, Consciousness,* 2:15.

11. Holston, *Film-Induced Sadness.*

12. Bromley, "Natural Boundaries," p. 36.

13. Gledhill, *Home Is Where the Heart Is;* Brundson, "A Subject for the Seventies"; Cook, "Melodrama and the Women's Pictures."

14. Shepherd, "Melodrama as Avant-Garde," p. 520.

15. Elsaesser, "Tales of Sound and Fury," pp. 2–15.

16. Mulvey, "Notes on Sirk."

17. Chandler, "Agency and *Stella Dallas,*" pp. 28, 41.

18. Brooks, *Melodramatic Imagination.*

19. Hays and Nikolopoulou, *Melodrama,* p. x.

20. Lang, *American Film Melodrama,* p. 18.

21. Turan, "Triumph," p. 1.

22. Lang, *American Film Melodrama,* p. 4.

23. Byars, *All That Hollywood Allows,* p. 131.

24. Cavell, *Contesting Tears,* p. 151.

25. King, dir., *Stella Dallas* (1925); Vidor, dir., *Stella Dallas* (1937); Brooks, dir., *Terms* (1983).

26. Lusted, "Social Class," pp. 66, 74.

27. Ehrenreich, *Hearts of Men,* pp. 13, 12.

28. Dubbert, *Man's Place;* see also Stearns, *Be a Man!;* Mosse, *The Image of Man;* Kimmel, *Manhood in America.*

29. Whyte, *Organization Man;* Packard, *Status Seekers;* Reisman, *Individualism Reconsidered;* Reisman, Denny, and Glazer, *Lonely Crowd;* see also Bell, *Work and Its Discontents;* Handlin, "Searching for Security"; Hacker, "New Burdens."

30. Lowry, "Is This the Beat Generation?"

31. Lindner, *Must You Conform?,* p. 23; Shipp, "Men," pp. 32–33.

32. Mailer, "The White Negro," p. 357.

33. Nowell-Smith, "Minelli and Melodrama," p. 72.

34. Dyer, *Heavenly Bodies: Film Stars and Society,* p.16.

35. Kazan, dir., *East of Eden* (1955).

36. Schatz, *Hollywood Genres,* p. 86.
37. Neale, "Tears and Melodrama," pp. 6–22.
38. Williams, " 'Something Else Besides a Mother,' " pp. 18, 23.
39. Van Fuqua, " 'Can You Feel It Joe?' " pp. 29, 35n.
40. French, *Women's Room,* p. 227, quoted in Williams, "Something Else," p. 2.

10

Men's Liberation, Men's Wounds

Emotion, Sexuality, and the Reconstruction of Masculinity in the 1970s

SALLY ROBINSON

We are headed for a crisis of substantial proportion. We will be forced to consider our own self-identities long before we are liberated from them.

Why, then, has an inquiry about the liberation of straight white males now seen the light of day? Because these persons are in trouble!

—Glenn Bucher, "The Enemy: He Is Us"[1]

In his 1972 novel, *The Water-Method Man,* John Irving creates a protagonist who literally embodies the emotional and social crisis afflicting straight, white, middle-class men in post-women's liberation America. Fred "Bogus" Trumper cannot "commit" to a long-term relationship; he is emotionally stunted, repressed, unable to express his desires and emotions honestly, and, consequently, tends to engage in self-destructive behavior. He can't finish his Ph.D. dissertation, can't commit to his new girlfriend (having virtually begged his first wife to leave him with their young son), and can't quite settle into his new career. He is stuck, blocked, and paralyzed. But it is not only his psychology that militates against the flow of emotion, life, and affiliation; Irving creates a somatic equivalent of Trumper's emotional state by giving him a penis that doesn't work properly. It, too, is blocked, making urination painful and sex, "typically, unmentionable."[2] After years of balking at having an operation to unblock what his urologist refers to as his "narrow and winding road" (12), Trumper has the operation and, miraculously, finishes his dissertation, agrees to marry his girlfriend (who has just had his child), settles into a job, and makes peace with his first wife and his son. Having gotten his plumbing unblocked, his emotional passages follow suit.

Irving's somatization of Trumper's emotional blockage is based on a construction of masculinity that remains dominant in American culture, a construction that is epitomized in the apparently unimpeachable truth that men aren't permitted to express their emotions. This truth, rarely contested, is linked by a complex and fascinating logic to the equally uncontested truth that male sexual energies must be released lest men implode from the force of their suppression. Such truths received somewhat surprising support in the mid to late 1970s as a barrage of books on "male liberation" emerged to detail the predicament of straight white, professional men whose lives were imagined to have been thrown into crisis by the various liberation movements of the 1960s and early 1970s. Popular studies of, and novels about, men trying to come to terms with a masculinity recently attacked as dangerous rely on a set of rhetorical figures to negotiate between the privileges of patriarchal power and the guilt induced by the feminist critique of that power.[3] These rhetorical figures all have to do with *blockage,* and the prevailing diagnosis of what's wrong with masculinity is that men have been forced to repress, suppress, and even oppress; and, as a result, male bodies and male minds are on the verge of shutting down.

The construction of masculinity as dangerously blocked competes with an increasingly visible, post-women's liberation understanding of masculinity as dangerously expressive of violent emotions and sexuality. "Every man is a potential rapist," writes Marilyn French in *The Women's Room* (1977), a diagnosis that ratifies the construction of masculinity as always on the verge of explosion, even as it argues *for* the blockage of male emotional and sexual energies. Contemporaneous with the radical feminist critique is a "masculinist" critique offered in books such as Herb Goldberg's *The Hazards of Being Male: Surviving the Myth of Masculine Privilege* (1976), Warren Farrell's *The Liberated Man: Beyond Masculinity: Freeing Men and Their Relationships with Women* (1974), and Marc Feigen Fasteau's *The Male Machine* (1974). In part based on a limited understanding of women's liberation as a program for personal growth rather than a movement for social justice, men's liberation discourse focused on the psychological and bodily harms suffered by men whose health was endangered by the blockage of emotional expression.[4] The male liberationists represent white, middle-class heterosexual men as both literally and metaphorically wounded; but *not,* as we might expect, by women, feminism or even the radically shifting social terrain of gender. Instead, these texts give us men who are wounded by their power, their responsibilities, and indeed, by patriarchy itself.[5]

My interest in the discourse on men's liberation stems from its embryonic analysis of a socially constructed masculinity that, from the late sixties on, was "marked" as the much maligned dominant in American culture. The rhetorical strategies that characterize elaborations of male blockage and the wounds of patriarchy, moreover, are part of a larger cultural move to reimagine white masculinity within the parameters of an identity politics that requires wrongs in order to claim rights. But, as Leonard Michaels suggests in his 1978 fictional satire of men's liberation groups, *The Men's Club,* men lacked what made "liberation" necessary: oppression. "I thought about women again," the narrator says, "Anger, identity, politics, rights, wrongs. I envied them. It seemed attractive to be deprived in our society. Deprivation gives you something to fight for, it makes you morally superior, it makes you serious."[6] Lacking the social grounding for a collectivized and politicized call for rights, white men in post-1968 American culture enthusiastically begin to elaborate wrongs, constructing narratives about individualized psychological and bodily wounds. While women, people of color, lesbians, and gay men were able to argue convincingly that they had been disenfranchised socially by their marginalized position in U.S. society and culture, the middle-class white men most likely to join men's lib did not attempt to claim a social disenfranchisement; instead, they increasingly began to argue that they were personally and individually wounded by a vaguely sketched "society" that, while awarding them power and privileges, produced psychological and bodily symptoms of powerlessness. Trumping women's blocked opportunities with men's blocked emotional expression, the men's liberationists substituted the personal for the political instead of forging a link between them.

After analyzing the entanglement of the emotional with the sexual in men's liberationists' laments over male inexpressivity, I will return to the Irving and Michaels novels in order to foreground the paradoxes of blockage and release animating these popular psychologies. These novels suggest that male power is expressed through cycles of blockage and release and so foreground, somewhat ironically, the impossibility of translating the individualistic, personal, and bodily vision of male wounding and health to the social and political realms. I will also read in the novels an incipient critique of the therapeutic value of male release for resolving crises in masculinity. My goal is not to question whether men are emotionally repressed or not, but rather to ask: What cultural work is done by announcing that men are emotionally blocked and physically wounded by such blockage? What constructions of masculinity, and of emotion, are produced through a discourse on male inexpressivity?

The Hazards of Being Male

In *The Liberated Man,* Warren Farrell argues that men are "emotionally constipated" and that "real emotions are stuck in [man's] system" (71). Using a bodily metaphor to describe an emotional blockage, Farrell here travels a rhetorical path characteristic of texts interested in critiquing the "straitjacket" or "harness" or "machine" of traditional masculinity. Blurring the boundaries between the emotional and the physical, and between the metaphorical and the literal, Farrell suggests that men's emotional constipation actually *produces* ulcers and other somatic symptoms:

> In [the standard workplace] atmosphere, men cannot help but be either emotionally incompetent (unable to handle emotions expressed by others) or emotionally constipated (unable to express their own emotions) or both. His emotional constipation leaves no outlet for his stomach but ulcers. One wonders if there is such a thing as a liberated top executive, or does the trip through the bureaucracy maim them all? (71)

Farrell means "liberation" literally, as well as figuratively, and the dominant trope of his and other studies of "constipated" masculinity is *flow*: if masculinity and men are to be liberated from the "harness" of the male role, emotional energies must be released, the tears must flow. Men are "maimed" by their own power and by the "male role" that requires blockage of emotional energies: expression is the cure for what ails men.

Bodily wounds have a persuasive power that does not depend on the social; and images of male bodies at risk work to legitimize a discourse that often veers into the apolitical and asocial. It is a function of the psychologized representation of the costs and benefits of male privilege that Farrell's account, antisexist and women's liberationist in intent, ends up appearing like an opportunistic appropriation of the "victim" position for successful white, heterosexual men.[7] Banking on the appeals of male pain, Farrell invites his groups to focus on how patriarchy wounds them; "consistently," he says, "*the technique of asking 'How is this also hurting us?' enabled us to discover how our own self-interest was being threatened by the same phenomenon that threatened women*" (239, emphasis in original).[8] The assumption here is that men suffer identical, or at least identically traumatic, hurts from the patriarchal system that channels women and men into narrow forms of personal expression. If all that is threatened by patriarchy is "self-interest," or fulfillment of individual goals, then a therapeutic solution is adequate and social revolution becomes unnecessary.[9]

The men's liberationists take from contemporary feminism a validation of emotional release, a sanction for airing pain and grievances, and, most important, a permission to express rage. According to Goldberg's *The Hazards of Being Male: Surviving the Myth of Male Privilege,* men should take women's lead, open the floodgates, and express a heretofore "heavily repressed male rage" (17). Goldberg, like Farrell, begins from the premise that feminism has the potential to liberate men because, having given women the license to be "strong" and independent, men can abandon the many onerous tasks and ways of being that patriarchal culture has forced on them. The key term in Goldberg's diagnosis of the crisis in masculinity is "blockage," a trope he uses repeatedly to describe man's general and specific "inability to respond to his inner promptings both emotionally and physiologically" (16). Men "block" their "conquering" impulses (56); they "block the flow of tears" (60); "emotional upsets and disturbances" are "blocked out of awareness," endangering man's mental health (69); men's genuine fears of marriage and economic "slavery" are "blocked out" (73); the contradictions between the male's different roles are "blocked out and repressed for self-protection" (106); and, finally, men "block out the symptoms of malaise until the illness is so overwhelming that it disables them completely" (112). Men emerge as both psychically and physically wounded and must be taught "how to survive the myth of male privilege"; for Goldberg, that myth covers over the reality of white male bodies at risk. Self-control and control of others is not the route toward social power; it is, instead, a certain path toward ulcers, cancer, mental breakdown, and pain. The literal and figurative merge here, as the bodily and emotional work entirely in tandem: if men continue to control themselves, Goldberg warns, "emotional starvation" will eventually produce "drinking binges, wild driving, a blatantly destructive affair, or a violent outburst, among other [problems]. All are spoutings of the inner, hidden volcano" (69). This language, typical of men's liberationists' description of the evils of male blockage, carries a barely veiled threat: placing limits on the expression of male impulses will lead men not only into the self-destruction of ulcers and cancer but also into the very modes of male destructiveness and power against which women's liberation had so recently and powerfully taken a stand.

Repressed emotions are here understood as material, physical entities, and the language of flow and release, blockage and outlet invokes what anthropologists Lila Abu-Lughod and Catherine A. Lutz argue is the dominant construction of emotion across disciplines: "Emotions are psychobiological processes that respond to cross-cultural environmental differences but retain a robust essence untouched by the social and cultural."[10] Constructions of masculinity as dangerously blocked imply that the release of emotion is *inevitable:* in a construction of emotion as "psychophysical" product, rather than socially situated process, the men's liberationists insist that blocked emotions *will* come pouring out in one way or another. The prevalence of liquid metaphors buttresses this construction: emotions are blocked, pent-up, bottled up, and must flow, be channeled, find an outlet. The truism that men aren't "allowed" to cry and thus to release pent-up emotions is central to the men's liberationists' construction of blocked masculinity.[11] Tears are represented as liquid emotions that, when released, facilitate the "softening" of a rigid masculinity. Most work on gender and emotion has stressed how a gendered rhetoric of emotional control reinforces women's subordination within societies that privilege rationality, self-control, and the stable boundaries between interiority and exteriority that emotions appear to breach.[12] But the men's liberationists' emphasis on emotional expression, not control, as the sign of healthy masculinity prompts us to ask *not* how emotional *control* serves patriarchal ideology but how a rhetoric of *expression* and letting go does. Prescriptions for emotional "release," like rules about emotional control, require that emotion be conceptualized as a psychophysical essence; whether a society requires control or liberation of emotion, emotions are figured as material, even liquid substances that flow or not—rather than, for example, a state of mind.

Why are emotions conceptualized in this way? This question is related to the question of why it is that "blockage" is always unhealthy, particularly for men. The answers must be sought in the slippage between "emotion" and "sexuality." For, isn't it the case that the ideology of emotional thrift and spending, blockage and release, runs parallel to an ideology of sexual thrift and spending, blockage and release?[13] If affective energies are constructed as psychobiological material—released through the shedding of tears or the outbursts of physical aggression—sexual energies are construed as even more literally fluid. Indeed, as Lutz has argued, in contemporary American culture "a popular discourse on the control of emotions runs functionally parallel to a discourse on the control of sexuality; a rhetoric of control requires a psychophysical essence that is manipulated and wrestled with and directs attention away from the socially constructed nature of emotion."[14] The functional parallel Lutz identifies between popular discourse on emotion and on sexuality is no coincidence; a popular conceptualization of emotion as a *bodily* material that always seeks its outlet (despite personal or social attempts to block its flow) takes its meaning and force from an analogy with sexuality. And, conversely, a construction of sexuality as a *material* force that always seeks its outlet (despite personal or social attempts to block its flow) finds support in the less obviously interested masculinist construction of emotion as psychophysical essence. The idea that men are emotionally blocked owes its sense and its dominance to a particular construction of male heterosexuality and the male body: male sexual energies are constantly flowing, sexual arousal "automatic" and uncontrollable, and any blockage of these energies, and the substance through which those energies are expressed, leads either to psychological and physical damage or to violent explosions. "Emotional discharge," in Goldberg's terms, is meaningful only in analogy to sexual discharge, and the blockage of male sexual and emotional energies become identically dangerous. Neither emotion nor sexuality need to be thought of in these terms and the dominance of the model of emotional and sexual blockage and release works to naturalize a particular construction of blocked masculinity that is violently at odds with the spirit behind women's demands that men "open up," express themselves honestly, and release their repressed emotions.

It is important to note that the emotions most often identified as dangerously blocked are anger and resentment rather than, say, love and fear. Because the men's liberationists take their cue from women's liberationists, it perhaps makes sense that anger and resentment would be the dominant emotions. Yet, what are men angry at, or resentful of? Where women are angry at blocked opportunities, the men who seek Goldberg's or Farrell's help appear to be resentful about the mere fact of blockage. Because American masculinity has always been about the freedom to move forward (into the frontier or up the career ladder), blockage is, by definition, a threat. For those who have been nurtured on inalienable rights and "natural" entitlements, blockage must appear particularly threatening.[15] But, further, in focusing on the blockage of anger, for instance, the male liberationists "masculinize" emotion, making release look violent, like "hurricanes" gathering force and "volcanoes" threatening to erupt. Sexuality, too, is framed as always potentially violent and explosive, a "natural" force that, according to Goldberg, is endangered by the feminist tinkering with elemental impulses. Claiming that "men invariably try to accommodate female [sexual] needs rather than fulfill their own [!]" (40), Goldberg urges men to "forget all the old imperatives regarding male obligations to satisfy the female" (51). Men are counseled to reject the new "super-gentle and super-sensitive" feminized sexuality, diluted by "the defense against anger [that] will spell the death of spontaneous sexuality" (62). In framing sensitivity *as* repression, Goldberg's analysis subtly constructs true, unrepressed masculinity as the antithesis of the sensitive male—invitations to cry notwithstanding. In doing so, he cements the analogy between violence, sexuality, and male "liberation"; sexual energies and violent impulses are psychophysical essences that naturally seek an outlet.

The seemingly unimpeachable assumption that emotional and sexual forces *must* be set flowing constructs a blocked masculinity in order to legitimize various forms of release and, thus, to recuperate a masculinity that has suffered from the feminist critique of male power and privilege. In this construction, evidence of men's emotions comes only in the "release" of those emotions. Thus what ails the emotionally repressed man is not his failure to experience or understand a range of emotion; rather, the failure can be attributed to a vaguely apprehended social order that "requires" men to block the *expression* of emotion. It's important to stress here that for Goldberg, whose notion of "repression" is decidedly un-Freudian, direct expression is the only healthy thing that can be done with emotions. No theory of sublimation puts the reins on Goldberg's desire to allow men the uninhibited expression of impulses; no theory of the part repression plays in the formation of the subject is evident here either. Men become conscious of their emotions and impulses *only through expression,* and thus release is the only way that men are to be "liberated" from their bonds. While Goldberg's emphasis on release can be read as simply part of the antirepression orientation of popular seventies therapies, what distinguishes a men's liberation approach to healthy masculinity from, say, a Human Potential approach, is that it is piggy-backed onto a *political* movement for equal rights. A program for personal growth and freedom from restraint thus cashes in the moral currency attached to political movements—*and* at a moment when Goldberg's clients (successful white men) belonged to precisely the category that was being "marked" as the *enemy* of liberation. Rather than confronting the gap between the personal and the political, the men's liberationists instead draw on a rhetoric of personal injury and pain and thus enter the field of "liberation" both acknowledging and disavowing the political.

The discourse on men's liberation operates within a therapeutic model that, as many cultural analysts have pointed out, works to evacuate the social, "translat[ing] the political into the psychological."[16] This is perhaps most clearly demonstrated in Warren Farrell's *The Liberated Man*. Farrell anatomizes the hurts caused by adherence to a rigid patriarchal script and even offers a blueprint for male liberation: radically, Farrell calls for flexible work schedules, payment for housework, better affirmative action programs, and better childcare to bring men into childrearing and to free women for work. But, strangely, this part of the book exists entirely in isolation from the second half, in which Farrell describes his work with men's consciousness-raising groups and offers aid and advice to those men who wish to participate in such groups. Farrell councils the men to *feel,* rather than "intellectualize," and to stress the personal over the political. For Farrell "liberation" means "psychological freedom" (4), and the revolutionary social programs he describes seem merely tacked onto the program for personal liberation. In comparison to the rather dramatic narratives of consciousness-raising at the center of Farrell's project and his interest, the feminist analysis appears positively tepid, vague, and unsatisfying—including the hopeful if not altogether convincing "twenty-one specific areas in which men can benefit from women's liberation" (175).

Nowhere does the slippage between the personal and the political become clearer than in the arena of consciousness-raising, a process for which Farrell evinces an almost religious devotion. The consciousness-raising sessions Farrell details in *The Liberated Man* bear little resemblance to Goldberg's vision of men's consciousness-raising groups as just another agent of male blockage, devoted, as he imagines them to be, to rehearsals of guilt and self-flagellating analysis of male privilege and power.[17] But neither do Farrell's groups resemble women's consciousness-raising groups, which, as Alice Echols argues, were devoted to discussion of social, not self-transformation. While some mocked feminist consciousness-raising as therapy, Echols notes that "proponents of consciousness-raising made every effort to distinguish it from therapy. They argued that the purpose of consciousness-raising was to analyze male supremacy in order to dismantle it, while the purpose of therapy was to carve out personal solutions to women's oppression."[18] The rise of more psychological and personal, less theoretical and political, types of consciousness-raising would coincide with the rise of cultural over radical feminism in the mid-seventies; but the initial impetus for consciousness-raising was quite distinct from the therapeutic impulse evident in the men's groups Farrell describes. That therapeutic impulse is made visible by an opposition between liberating "feelings" and the "intellectualization" that stanches the flow of feelings. "Intellectualization" means overanalysis, but in the context of the liberation movements from which these discourses spring, it also means *politicization*. Goldberg even goes so far as to claim that the "three basic processes that contribute to the physical deterioration of the male body . . . are intellectualization, macho rigidity, and guilt" (107). Guilt and intellectualization are both legacies of the women's movement: guilt for the exercise of male power and privilege, and intellectualization as the political analysis that produces that guilt. True to the spirit of the therapeutic, Farrell sees consciousness-raising groups as focused on self- and not social transformation: the goal is to "develop each other's awareness of alternative ways of overcoming the limitations on our lives that have evolved from our view of ourselves as masculine or feminine" (217). Rather than focus on guilt or theorize the social construction of gender, these men are encouraged to express their pain.

Farrell's emphasis is on male introspection as a positive good, no matter what kind of knowledge that introspection produces, what kinds of outbursts it authorizes, or what kinds of emotions it liberates. Introspection, however, is always tied to *expression;* while Farrell suggests a difference between having and showing emotions, he does so only to say it doesn't matter. Thus two kinds of blockage are collapsed together, and *expression* becomes an a priori good, the route toward masculine health, far more important than self-awareness or consciousness of emotion. The emphasis on the blockage of *expression* over the blockage of awareness works, subtly in Farrell's case, to legitimize various forms of release as the goal of male liberation and to construct the male body as a fragile vessel full of simmering impulses and thwarted desires. While Farrell appears to contest the ideology of male release animating Goldberg's book, he ends up reinforcing a romanticized image of dominant masculinity as hurt by its own power and the necessary blockage of its "natural" impulses. That the title of Farrell's latest book, *The Myth of Male Power* (1993) echoes Goldberg's *The Myth of Male Privilege* is evidence of the once feminist Farrell's seduction into a view of men as entirely powerless, the "disposable sex."[19]

The paradox evident throughout the discourse on men's liberation is that the model of blockage and release authorizes two contradictory takes on men and power: men are wounded, weakened, and "oppressed" by patriarchy, male privilege, and power; and men are naturally prone to expressions of sexual power and sexual violence. Because of the psychologized, therapeutic solution favored by the men's liberationists, both constructions of masculinity ultimately work to reinforce, rather than contest, male dominance. In their analysis of the "straitjacket" of traditional masculinity, the male liberationists substitute a bodily economy of emotional and sexual "energy" for a social system that prohibits and permits certain kinds of emotional expression based on gender. This substitution makes natural a powerful male heterosexual release,[20] in part because emotional and sexual release are both constructed as inevitable outpourings of bodily material that, if blocked, will cause severe damage. The cure for what ails these men is not, as we might have hoped, the abolition of patriarchy; rather, it is the uninhibited release of emotional energies and "natural" impulses.

The Wisdom of the Penis

Like men's liberation discourse, John Irving's *The Water-Method Man* is obsessed with images of blockage and flow. But, unlike the popular psychologies devoted to male liberation, Irving's novel directly confronts the paradoxes involved in prescriptions for male release. While the men's liberationists ultimately offer a therapeutic solution to a political problem, Irving's novel suggests that therapies aimed at "liberating" men from macho rigidity actually work to legitimize the very forms of "release" that feminists were reading as the "expression" of male privilege. Patriarchy and its rigid gender system is not endangered by male expressivity, Irving's novel suggests; male expressivity, on the contrary, can easily promote the circulation of not entirely benign male energies. Further, the novel suggests that emotional blockage can feed male privilege: the blockage imposed by women and familial obligations is not the same thing as blockage chosen by men who, in being "inexpressive," retain power over the women who demand that they "open up." Ironically, a novel that has no clear feminist intent ends up pointing toward the antifeminist effects of the seemingly profeminist male liberationists.

Irving sets up two competing versions of male blockage/release and does so by creating a cast of male characters whose differing responses to the demands of mature manhood complement Bogus Trumper's and together create a map of male liberation. The late Merrill Overturf haunts Trumper and the novel, an adolescent marked mainly by his incontinence—in both literal and metaphorical ways. Trumper romanticizes Merrill as the essence of male liberation, and Merrill's early death in mysterious circumstances functions to martyr him as a free spirit who is simply too much for the middle-class world to which Trumper ultimately swears allegiance. Trumper is clearly hurt by the "blockage" of the energies that Merrill represents. Not able to accept the "harness" of a traditional masculinity, Trumper's blocked energies find more self-destructive, if also self-indulgent, outlets. Ralph Packer speaks for male liberation, too, as he helps Trumper "escape" from his wife, Biggie, and, later, gives him sanctuary in New York. There is the never seen but often remembered Harry Petz, a graduate student in comparative literature who is mythologized as the man who cracks under the stress of what Warren Farrell calls the "strait jacket" of masculinity (9). Petz haunts the narrative as a warning of what will happen to Trumper if he allows himself to be trapped by women and by the familial obligations that can staunch the flow of healthy male energies. Finally, there is Couth who has managed to evade the "professions" that Warren Farrell suggests might "maim" the hapless if successful middleclass man. Couth is a photographer, a handyman, and an entirely free-flowing spirit: he is, in short, the epitome of liberated manhood. Rather than intellectualize, like Trumper, or stress out, also like Trumper, Couth goes with the flow. Where Trumper freezes with anxiety "contemplating the horror of having to look for a real job" (162), Couth just goes about the pleasant business of living on an island off the coast of Maine. Not worried either about owning property or making a mark on the world, Couth is the antithesis of the never solvent but always obsessing Trumper. There is nothing wrong with Couth's penis, either; he's not a member of that "rare fraternity," "the urinarywounded" (165).

But Couth is not the hero of this novel. Bogus Trumper commands our interest because he is the wounded man who nevertheless manages to express a good deal of power. Irving represents Trumper as the epitome of silent and "blocked" masculinity; as his girlfriend Tulpen later accuses, he "doesn't come across": "No one knows you, Trumper!," she says; "You don't *convey* anything" (94). Tulpen's complaint echoes Biggie's; and, since both women want to tie Trumper down to domesticity—and thus to impede his "flow"—the novel suggests that the "release" the women want is irrevocably at odds with the "release" that Trumper yearns for. Being blocked is, thus, a form of self-*preservation* for Trumper, since the women in his life are constantly trying to acculturate him into mature and responsible manhood, a project for which they require his consent. His resistance to giving it remains fierce until the end of the novel, but instead of exalting in his triumph, Trumper revels in his own inadequacy as husband and father and, later, lover. His failures *are* his triumphs, and Irving's representation of Trumper's emotional state suggests that he is pleasurably wounded by his desertion of his family. Rather than healing those wounds, Trumper's "liberation" leaves him wallowing in his painful-pleasurable state, guilt and triumph coming together in the portrait of a happily humiliated and failed man. The therapeutic "cure" that Trumper will eventually choose proves far less satisfying a resolution than his display of wounded masculinity.

The Water-Method Man spends a good deal of narrative energy dwelling on Trumper's physical and psychic wounds, and exploring the pains that accompany his attempts both to be responsible and to evade that responsibility. In Iowa City, for example, Trumper follows his aroused penis into a ridiculously ill-planned encounter with a student, which ends with him naked and abandoned in swampy and rugged terrain. Rather than put on his shoes—or, for that matter, remove the condom from his exposed penis—Trumper tramps barefoot through frozen broken corn stalks and other debris, ending up with "festering foot wounds, chiefly punctures and lacerations" (208). These wounds signal Trumper's martyrdom, offering a corporeal equivalent of the psychic pain he suffers when Biggie throws him out—after he forgets the condom and urinates into it while Biggie watches. Lurching around the house seeking scissors (for some unaccountable reason), Trumper presents a spectacle of humiliated masculinity, "banging along on his knees, cradling the bulbous rubber in one hand" (191). It is important that it is Trumper's anatomy that expresses, and clues him into, his emotional and psychic blockages.

Irving's somatization of Trumper's emotional blockage is based on the acceptance of what Herb Goldberg calls "penis wisdom": a belief in the ability of the heterosexual male body to signify problems of gender identity in ways often "more perceptive than conscious thought" (37). The penis, for example, "knows" when a man is not attracted to a woman and so "decides" not to enable penetration. While Irving does not go so far as to anthropomorphically endow the penis with this degree of intentionality, his novel does suggest that emotional and sexual blockage are intimately related. Irving's representation of Trumper's urological and sexual problems points to a belief in such penis wisdom, as the physiological condition and activity of the penis signifies the (often repressed) emotional condition of the man. Forgetting the condom is a way for Trumper to force Biggie's hand, to "act out" his desire to get out of the marriage, since he is unwilling to express his emotions in language and other direct forms of communication. Specifically, the condom blocks the flow of urine and also presents evidence of Trumper's unacknowledged desire to leave Biggie. Goldberg's use of a plumbing metaphor to describe the wise penis is particularly significant in the context of Irving's novel where plumbing allusions flow as freely as the energies male liberationists would release. Goldberg writes: "The penis is not a piece of plumbing that functions capriciously. It is an expression of the total self. In these days of over-intellectualization it is perhaps the only remaining sensitive and revealing barometer of the male's true sexual feelings" (39). The penis *is* a piece of plumbing, according to Goldberg, but one that functions *meaningfully* rather than "capriciously." Paradoxically, a discourse that attempts to contest that construction of male sexuality as entirely focused on the performance of the penis ends up endowing the penis with the "sensitivity" that both women's and men's liberationists would argue more properly belongs in the emotional rather than the bodily realm. Men's emotions are only "expressed," then, by the physical acts of erection and ejaculation.

Representing the penis as the spout of a plumbing system also reinforces the construction of male sexuality as a liquid, material force that flows through the body. In Irving's novel, as in men's liberation discourse, that construction of sexuality parallels the construction of emotion and makes emotional release metaphorically dependent on sexual release. *The Water-Method Man* really runs with these metaphors, as the novel is nearly obsessed with plumbing, blockage and flow and is full of vignettes of painful or problematic urination. The diabetic Merrill Overturf looks with "bewildered pain" (125) at his own uncontrolled acts of bodily "expression," and Trumper experiences excruciating pain when, with an adolescent case of the clap, the "tip of his life" (146)—that is, his penis—is blocked. Irving does not spare the details of this pain, as Trumper remembers how he "straddled the hopper and peed what felt like razor blades, bent bobbypins and ground glass" (145). Metaphorically, too, the novel is full of references to blocked and freely flow-ing plumbing; in an early chapter, entitled "Old Tasks & Plumbing News," for example, we hear that even Trumper's *toilet* is clogged. In each of his let-ters to Couth, Trumper asks his friend to "flush all seventeen of the johns for me" (26, 37) at the Pillsbury mansion in Maine where Couth is caretaker, and to which Biggie eventually moves after the break-up with Trumper. (Couth has neither clogged toilets nor blocked emotions.) Finally, the water-method of the novel's title refers to the urologist's advice that drinking mass quantities of water before and after sex might literally flush out the pain that normally accompanies both sex and urination. All of these literal and metaphorical references to blockage and release converge in the novel's representation of Trumper's physiological and emotional "therapy," the end toward which the novel inexorably tends.

The novel is structured as a therapeutic narrative, but subtly offers a critique of that therapeutic model.[21] Irving's critique is emphatically "apolitical" and is thus quite different from the critique I offered in the first part of this essay. Far from criticizing therapy for offering a personal solution to a political problem, Irving instead criticizes therapy for offering a one-size-fits-all model of psychological and social adjustment—particularly to norms of masculinity. As is true of Irving's entire corpus, *The Water-Method Man* eschews the collective in favor of the individual, the political in favor of the personal.[22] What the novel is interested in is conceptualizing a male liberation that evades both the pitfalls as therapy as a process of adaptation[23] and the pitfalls of a female-sponsored (and possibly feminist) attempt to put the brakes on male "expression." Trumper's physiological therapy, the unblocking of his penis, is accompanied by a psychological therapy, as he reluctantly participates in the making of "Fucking Up," the film about his life that his friend Ralph writes and directs. Together, the film and the operation enable—or, rather, force—Trumper to own up to his responsibilities. As he sardonically tells Dr. Vigneron, his suave French urologist, "I'm a new man. I'm not the old prick I was" (318). But while the ending of the novel signifies the liberation of Trumper's emotional and creative energies, it also signifies his acceptance of the "male role" that men's liberationists warn will produce blockages of all kinds.

After the operation he goes back, to Iowa City and to his "blocked" dissertation, and embarks on a different kind of "therapy" (349). Swearing off the self-destructive habits of his youth, he becomes a kind of monk-scholar and finishes his degree. It is seeing "Fucking Up" that does the trick, a therapy after all, in the viewing if not the making. Returning to Tulpen—and new baby Merrill—he admits that his "straight, honest feelings were a long way down in a bog"—more metaphorical liquidity—"a bog he had been skirting for so long that now it seemed impossible to dive in and grope" (365). But dive in he does, and the last scene in the novel gives us a male liberation into emotional commitment, freely flowing friendship and love, and babies popping out everywhere. We know Trumper has fully taken the therapeutic plunge when we're told that a niggling little snake in this paradise found will be "processed": "He knew that back in New York there'd be a week of trying to understand" the jealousy that Tulpen feels for Biggie (378). The artificiality of this ending points to some ideological confusions that are sutured over in the interests of closure.

While *The Water-Method Man* ends in a conventionally happy way, the novel is nevertheless bathed in a nostalgia for the adolescent male liberation modeled by Merrill Overturf. Because Merrill haunts this novel so fully, the ending is compromised by the suspicion that love-fest aside, it's no fun being "straight"—a term that, in the late sixties and early seventies, equated male heterosexuality with the "establishment." As Charles Gaver puts it in his contribution to the heady *Straight/White/Male*, "the term *straight* refers to a bland, bigoted manner of existing, as in the phrase *straight and narrow*. Part of the problem with un-gay people is just that: they are too inhibited to enjoy and celebrate the gay things in life."[24] "Inhibition" is another word for inexpressivity, and the straight man is a blocked man, not only by individual temperament but by belonging to a normative category. Trumper does, in fact, go "straight" by the end of the novel and, not surprisingly, this is the language in which his penile problems are described: his narrow and winding road gets "straightened out" by the operation and, despite the fact that Trumper is obviously thrilled to be cured of his physiological problem, he is at least a little bit regretful at having become "normal." This is not, after all, a novel in which "normal" is a badge of honor or authenticity, and the happily heterosexual if slightly hippyish spectacle of family life and responsible adulthood with which the novel ends cannot erase an evident nostalgia for Trumper's earlier "blockage."

The Embarrassments of Emotional Incontinence

The women in Irving's novel aim to block the free flow of male sexual energies and to acculturate the men into mature and responsible manhood. But they also require that the men "communicate" openly, experience, express, and share their emotions—as long as those emotions are "soft" and "safe" and *not* an expression of male priority, privilege, or power. What Irving represents as women's contradictory demands are also evident in men's liberation discourse; but there such contradictions are studiously repressed in the interest of emphasizing the importance of flow and the dangers of blockage. These contradictions are even more marked in Leonard Michaels's *The Men's Club*, where the representation of a feminist-inspired men's consciousness-raising group leads subtly but inevitably to a warning against the a priori privileging of male release. The novel suggests that if women, and the "feminized" therapeutic culture to which they want to acculturate men, invite male release, then men cannot be responsible for the consequences. Satirizing the men's liberationists, Michaels's novel foregrounds how calls for the liberation of men are based on a misreading of feminism as a program for personal growth rather than a demand for political change. The novel goes even further, warning that the version of male dominance we have now is positively benign compared to the version that will be unleashed if men actually take up the call to unblock their impulses. What was mostly implicit in men's liberation discourse becomes explicit here: men can only experience and express their emotional impulses by transforming them into physical impulses. Metaphorical desires and feelings get translated into literal, physical needs as this men's consciousness-raising group devolves into a quasi-Darwinist spectacle of animalistic masculinity.

The entire novel takes place in the first session of a "men's club," where a group of emotionally repressed men get together to talk about their lives in an effort to reproduce the dynamics and outcomes of women's groups. Predictably, the talk immediately turns to sexual experiences, and the men in the club take turns narrating tales of bizarre transactions with what quickly turns out to be an alien and incomprehensible "opposite sex." The novel plays on the stereotype of emotionally repressed masculinity, but rather than making fun of men or critiquing masculinity, Michaels ultimately targets the therapeutic culture that requires men to participate in the touchy-feely emotional expressiveness of consciousness-raising. Kramer, the host of the men's club, is a practicing psychotherapist whose language comes under sharp and biting critique by the narrator, the club's members, and, finally, his wife Nancy. The narrator, for example, mocks the ethos of free and open communication touted by popular seventies therapies: "It was time to be supportive, as they say. Go out of oneself feelingly. Leap the psychic fence. Stand in Cavanaugh's space. Let him know I feel what he feels" (60).

Here, as elsewhere, Michaels is simultaneously mocking the men and legitimating their understanding of the "truth" of masculinity. Unlike women's consciousness-raising groups, focused on "anger, identity, politics, rights, wrongs" (13), the men do not attempt to generalize from their experience nor to theorize the route to social (or even personal) change. Instead, they nervously engage in aimless and opaque conversation, warding off any insights that might prompt them to change the way they perform their masculinity. Instead of liberation, the men find themselves "embarrassed by [their] own incontinence" (107). Performance of masculinity is the best way to describe what happens in the men's club, but it is a performance that seems inevitable. While lampooning a therapeutic culture of manly sensitivity, the novel keeps intact a construction of dominant masculinity as emotionally blocked and, further, naturalizes that construction by making men appear constitutionally incapable of expressing "genuine" emotion. At the same time, in the many stories of sexual conquest and/or wounding that the men tell, the novel naturalizes a construction of male sexuality as automatic and unstoppable: men risk bodily and mental health by acceding to women's demands that they curb their sexuality. While individual men might blame women for forcing them to curb their "primitive" manly impulses, the true target of scorn is the soft and feminized therapeutic culture and its futile efforts to tame dominant masculinity.

While the novel pays some lip service to the idea that men and women are hurt by male inexpressivity, it quickly becomes apparent that the energies that women want men to release are not the same ones that men want to release. The narrator ratifies this difference as he admires in his friend Cavanaugh a model of masculinity always on the verge of explosion but even more powerful for his ability to rein in emotional and other energies. A former professional basketball player, Cavanaugh represents a primitive and volatile masculine force kept in check and "blocked" by the civilizing requirements of social and family life. "He descended from heroes. Invincible, murderous, rapacious stock" (60), but is now domesticated by the "symbolic manacle" of family life and white-collar work. Like Trumper in *The Water-Method Man*, Cavanaugh is the figure for an emotionally blocked and sexually explosive masculinity: he doesn't communicate with his wife, and the force of his unexpressed emotional and sexual needs produces bodily trauma, paralyzing him under the force of his unexpressed emotions: "Soon there was nothing in my body but anger. I got into fights with my own teammates. I couldn't shave without slicing my face. I was smoking cigarettes. I had something against my body and wanted to hurt it" (25). Cavanaugh opens the valves of his emotional system inward rather than outward, engages in a form of self-mutilation, and offers his bodily wounds as evidence of his disempowerment. Other participants in the club have ulcers, asthma, migraines, and other bodily problems stemming from the repression of emotional expressivity.

Cavanaugh's blocked rapaciousness will eventually find an outlet in the novel's crescendo, where we learn that the true "release" comes only when the men "express" themselves physically. The narrator's admiration for the dammed masculine force circulating and recirculating in Cavanaugh's powerful body predicts the physical release toward which the narrative inexorably tends. The first step toward this release is a highly mediated attack on women's groups and on feminist attempts to curb male "appetites." The group of men "rape" the refrigerator and devour the food and wine that Kramer's wife, Nancy, has prepared for her women's group meeting the next evening. Michaels explicitly describes this as a violation and invites the reader to see the episode less as a critique of a raping masculinity than evidence of its inevitability. He describes the refrigerator thus: "Standing alone, raped, resonant with humiliation. Our ice mother. We'd seized her food" (50). The men indulge themselves in a ritual of consumption that unites pleasure and pain, innocence and guilt. The "rape" of the refrigerator is both a violation of women's groups and an attempt to appropriate and literally incorporate women's claims of victimization. But it is also a dark celebration of male privilege, and it is in the context of this episode that Michaels articulates most clearly what drives these privileged men to believe in their natural entitlement. Comparing the seizure of the food to the pillaging of jungles from monkeys, the narrator implies that it's fine for animals to be made homeless, for refrigerators to be raped, for women's food to be stolen, and for forests to be devastated—all for men's pleasure. Acknowledging that they are "lucky to be men," the narrator revels in the privileges afforded to men and notes that "number one has more fun. The preparations for the women's group would feed our club. The idea of delicious food, taken this way, was thrilling" (43).

The rape of the refrigerator is only the first act in the physical display of male expressivity; the second is an episode in which the men throw knifes at the beautiful table ("stolen" from jungles), quickly followed by the howling that turns this consciousness-raising group into a spectacle of animalistic masculinity, predicting the Robert Bly-inspired return of the "wild man" in the late eighties. As with the rape of the refrigerator, the house is wounded as the men project their hostilities toward women and feminist demands that they "communicate" onto the domestic space that signifies femininity. Michaels presents this devolution into violence as inevitable and exhilarating, a welcome release of repressed energies that outstrips the tame and feminized remedies of psychotherapies, and one that is worth quoting in its entirety:

The howling was liquid, long, and thick in the red room, heart of Kramer's house. His cherished table lay on its side like a dead beast, stiff-legged and eviscerated, streaming crockery, silver, wine, meat, bones, and broken glass. We sounded lost, but thought we'd found ourselves. I mean nothing psychological. No psycho-logic of the soul, only the mind, and this was mindless. The table's treasure lay spilled and glittering at our feet and we howled, getting better at it as the minutes passed, entering deeply into our sound, and I felt more and more separated from myself, closer to the others, until it seemed we were one in the rising howls, rising again and again, taking us up even as we sank toward primal dissolution, as-senting to it with this music of common animality, like a churchly cho-rus, singing of life and death. (161)

This epiphany, a moment of communion between men that has the power to lift them out of themselves, suggests that the men have expressed themselves in the only way that men can—and it's sheer poetry, a moment to be enjoyed and reveled in and not analyzed, a moment that recalls Warren Farrell's in-junction just to "feel" rather than intellectualize. Do the men appear ridicu-lous here, or sublime? The novel does not allow us to dwell on this question for very long because Michaels chooses this intense moment of male bonding to reintroduce a feminine presence, and it's hard to imagine a choice more geared to frame the woman as an alien, invasive presence, and men as the misunderstood objects of feminist scorn.

Nancy errs in (mis)reading this masculine experience as an adolescent and ridiculous exercise in male dominance. Michaels deflects attention away from the mindless destruction and acting out of male entitlement that this scene signifies by shifting focus away from the behavior to Kramer's ridiculous therapeutic response to Nancy's anger. What looks silly is not the men nor the mindless masculinity they perform but Kramer's attempt to water the spectacle down with psychobabble, to which Nancy responds with a vicious mockery that escapes no one but the hapless Kramer. In a dialogue almost painful in its mockery of the clueless "analyst" Kramer, Nancy parodies her husband's language. Appearing to buy Kramer's line that the devastated house is a form of "creative expression," and thus sacrosanct, Nancy disappears into the kitchen to return with a cast-iron skillet, and whales on Kramer's head. Meanwhile, the narrator is fantasizing about having sex with Nancy, and the other men are busily noting her appearance, clothes, haircut, intent on either ignoring or trivializing her anger. When she hits Kramer, he is stunned for only a minute and then returns to therapy-speak: "I feel you're feeling anger" (172), he says, as the blood runs down his face. Nancy retreats, and her behavior wonderfully metaphorizes the novel's satire of recipes for male expressivity: she flushes the toilet repeatedly, in what the narrator describes as "violent annihilations" (175).

The Men's Club suggests that if men are forced to participate in a feminized therapeutic culture that invites them to "express themselves," then it is inevitable that such expression will result in the release of those male energies that simmer below the surface of a "civilized" facade. Although articulated in slightly different terms, Michaels's representation of the inevitably physical expression of male needs and desires echoes the male liberationists' focus on the *bodily* effects of emotional repression and of patriarchal power. Both *The Men's Club* and *The Water-Method Man* point to the fact that the masculinity described by men's liberation discourse is so fully dependent on a naturalized construction of dangerous male energies that it is impossible to believe that the endpoint of male liberation would be the expression of "softer" emotions such as compassion, sympathy, and so on. Because the blockage-release model defines the male body as a cauldron of warring impulses and emotions, masculinity gets naturalized as powerful but vulnerably so, its power dependent precisely on the regulation of "natural" male energies. If men are to be "liberated," they must be liberated from nature; and such liberation almost always produces a new cycle of blockage. Male liberation, as it is theorized in these texts, is an impossible goal; *not* because actual men cannot change but because the model of blockage and release naturalizes a powerful-powerless masculinity that is, by definition, resistant to change.

The discourse of men's liberation sketches out the contours of a new masculinity: a masculinity defined by the pain of emotional blockage but one defined, as well, by the painful necessity of restraining the "primitive" impulses that always threaten to emerge. This image of a simmering male body whose psychophysical energies are always circulating and recirculating in an effort to avoid both destruction and self-destruction constructs a masculinity that embraces pain as a manly credential even as it threatens to release those natural male energies that cause pain to others. Men *must* restrain their dangerous impulses, but men *cannot* restrain them; men *must* release their blocked emotions, but men *cannot* release them. It is in the space between the "must" and the "cannot" that the physically and psychically wounded man emerges, *not* as a pathological, or even "failed" man, but as the norm of a masculinity that can only attempt to be "healthy."

Notes

1. Bucher, *Straight/White/Male*, pp. 6–7.

2. Irving, *The Water-Method Man*, p. 12. Further citations will be included in the text.

3. Ellison's intriguing analysis of liberal guilt in the nineties is relevant to my analysis here, although I would say that Farrell is motivated by liberal guilt, while Goldberg emphatically is not. According to Ellison, liberal guilt is always about race, and it is most often represented as an emotion that afflicts men or, as Ellison puts it, "it names a form of discomfort that matters politically when men suffer from it" ("A Short History of Liberal Guilt" 348). Liberal guilt evinces "ongoing crises of masculinity" (348) that have dramatized "anxieties" about liberalism since the Enlightenment. Liberal guilt "designates a position of wishful insufficiency relative to the genuinely radical" (345)—and, I would add, to the genuinely disenfranchised. While Ellison does not go in this direction, her analysis suggests that liberal guilt, an embarrassing position, becomes the sign of a wounded white masculinity. So, while liberal guilt might spring from an uncomfortable recognition of one's privilege in relation to racial others, it ends up signifying a kind of fantasized (and depoliticized) disempowerment in the face of others' "genuine" disenfranchisement. In the men's liberation discourse that is my subject here, guilt is one emotion that must be disavowed because it works to "block" the flow of positive male energies. Rather than see this as a sign of the conservative politics of this discourse, as Ellison might, I will suggest that the impulse behind "freeing" men from guilt over their privileges is central to the project of personalizing, psychologizing, and depoliticizing the very concept of "liberation."

4. Or, one might say, modeled on a particular strain of women's liberation. While it is certainly true that a major impetus behind, and effect of, feminism in the 1970s was what Bardwick calls the "new hedonism" that comes with an emphasis on personal growth and the other code words of the human potential movement, the personal and psychological is always moored to the political and social in feminist discourse and activism. See Bardwick, *Women in Transition: How Feminism, Sexual Liberation, and the Search for Self-Fulfillment Have Altered Our Lives*. Ehrenreich and English have suggested that, in certain key respects, the "Me!" decade was a male phenomenon, leaving women outside the personal revolutions announced by and enacted in popular seventies therapies. See their discussion of the singles culture and popular psychology, *For Her Own Good: 150 Years of the Experts' Advice to Women*, pp. 297–311. Echols argues that early radical feminism, too, was eventually overwhelmed by the rise of a cultural feminism that, like other sixties movements, shifted from the political to the personal in the late sixties and early seventies. See Echols, *Daring to Be Bad: Radical Feminism in America, 1967–1975*, particularly chap. 2.

5. The crisis in masculinity mapped by men's liberation discourse is specifically a crisis in heterosexual masculinity, encapsulated by the shifting meanings of the term "straight." By the early seventies "straight" had mutated from a general term used by the hip to describe the "establishment" to a more specific term used to describe heterosexuality. This shift in the meanings of a popular term points to an ambivalence about male sexuality and

sexual identity in men's liberationist discourse. These books are generally aimed toward the more hip of America's heterosexual, white, middle-class men; but those hip credentials are endangered by an increasingly visible gay population not only labeling all heterosexuals as "straight" but necessarily implicating even the most hip among them in perpetuating the status quo. "Damn it all," one of Warren Farrell's consciousness-raisers cries in the middle of an excited conversation about same-sex desire, "when I hear you guys talk about bisexuality I feel like my heterosexuality is abnormal' " (Farrell, *The Liberated Man* 246). While being "abnormal" is no cause for shame with this group, being unliberated is; thus bisexuality becomes the safest route toward the release of a liberated but still hetero sexuality. Further references to Farrell will be cited in the text.

6. Michaels, *The Men's Club*, p. 13. Further references will be cited in the text.

7. White, middle-class men—so unimpeachably the norm that neither Farrell nor Herb Goldberg have index entries under "race," "black," "white," "class," "working class," "civil rights," or "ethnicity"—are damaged by the very system that supposedly works to their benefit. Economic concerns are strikingly absent from these texts, except insofar as the man in need of liberation is one suffering from the stresses of a professional or managerial position.

8. Even while lamenting the fact that men aren't "allowed" to be passive, the male liberationists construct men as the passive targets or recipients of a gender ideology in which they "are directly denied the freedom to experience and express emotion in all but the most narrow channels" (Fasteau, *The Male Machine* 31). Passive verbs abound in men's liberation discourse: men are "forced," "not permitted," "not allowed," "excluded." Goldberg lists nineteen "impossible binds" in which men find themselves (again, passive construction), and each of these binds leads to an "Either way he loses" conclusion (*The Hazards of Being Male* 96–106). Nowhere in Goldberg's analysis are the hazards of being male offset by the benefits of being male: from the shockingly high rate of male fetal death (179) to the repressed man who suffers for having erupted in violence and beat his son (72), Goldberg portrays even violent men as wounded and endangered. And, while never identifying the *causes* of male repression (except to point to a vague notion of socialization), Goldberg does not shy away from prescribing a cure: what men need is the therapy he offers, a long and slow process. "The male would be well advised to give himself the gift of a thorough and total experience, allowing it the time it requires and that he deserves. After all he has spent a lifetime denying his feelings. Undoing this process requires a full commitment and a constant awareness of how important this is to his survival" (70). Further references to Goldberg's *The Hazards of Being Male* will be included in the text.

9. See Ehrenreich, *The Hearts of Men: American Dreams and the Flight from Commitment,* chap. 9, for an analysis of how the men's liberationists used the language of the Human Potential movement and of feminism to justify the evasion of responsibility and the breadwinner's role. She notes that "male self-interest could now be presented as healthy and uplifting; the break from the breadwinner role could be seen as a program of liberal middle-class reform" (119). See also Kimmel, *Manhood in America: A Cultural History,* chap. 8, for a discussion of men's liberation.

10. Abu-Lughod and Lutz, "Introduction: Emotion, Discourse, and the Politics of Everyday Life," p. 2.

11. Of course, the spectacle of male tears has become something quite different in post-Clinton American culture, where the public display of emotion has become evidence of a sincerity that often substitutes for real political commitment, backed by real social policy. We are inhabiting a moment that evinces the further development of the trends I am analyzing here, what Fred Pfeil has referred to as the "therapization" of the social. See Pfeil, *White Guys: Studies in Postmodern Domination and Difference,* pp. 150–53. On tears and gendered conceptualizations of emotion, see Pinch, *Strange Fits of Passion: Epistemologies of Emotion, Hume to Austin,* pp. 128–34. On the public display of sentiment in the nineties, see Ellison, "A Short History of Liberal Guilt."

12. Recent feminist work on men and emotion has begun to challenge the assumption that emotion is "feminized" in historically constant ways, as this volume will attest. See also Pinch, *Strange Fits of Passion* and Ellison, "Cato's Tears," pp. 571–601.

13. Interestingly, understandings of impotence have long been based on models of blockage and release that shift in response to changes in medical and social constructions of male heterosexuality. In the American 1920s, for instance, as Mumford argues, a Victorian construction of impotence as caused by excessive sexual expression gives way to a construction that targets excessive continence or repression as the cause of impotence. This shift accompanies a larger shift in the understanding of the economy of male sexual desire and energy from a finite and closed system to an unlimited and self-replenishing one. In both cases male sexual energy is imagined as *substantial,* a fluid that can be saved or released; what changes is the meaning of that release. Mumford concludes that "the scientific consensus on what caused impotence and how to treat it was shifting gradually away from a Beardian model of scarcity, depletion, and saving toward a psychological model of abundance, repression, and spending" (" 'Lost Manhood' Found" 49). By the 1920s physicians were "more likely to prescribe therapies of sexual release, rather than restraint, while some psychologists went so far as to argue that restraint itself caused impotence" (50). Men's sexual problems stemmed more from the "psychological guilt" induced by sexual release than from the release itself. Not surprisingly, when physicians began to prescribe sexual release as a cure for impotence, medical attention turned to women as the erotic objects who did, or did not, arouse sufficient desire for that release to be accomplished (53)—a version of Goldberg's "penis wisdom." See also White, *The First Sexual Revolution,* chap. 4, for an analysis of shifting evaluations of sexual thrift and release.

14. Lutz, "Engendered Emotion," p. 72.

15. In this light, as I argue in chapter 2 of *Marked Men: White Masculinity in Crisis,* we might read the conservative academic attack on "political correctness" and its wider public circulation in the mid-eighties and early nineties as a narrative of protest against the blockage of white and male verbal expression.

16. Peck, "The Mediated Talking Cure," p. 152. See also Bordo, " 'Material Girl': The Effacements of Postmodern Culture."

17. "Many men join them," Goldberg writes, "because they want to please their women or to learn how not be male oppressors. Consequently there is a subtle group climate of self-hate and guilt induction. The target is oneself and each male is cautious about using words or relating in ways that are 'typically male chauvinist' " (142). Such self-censorship, Goldberg implies, is yet another form of blockage, and he advises his clients

and readers to see feminism as an opportunity for male liberation rather than the occasion for guilt.

18. Echols, *Daring to be Bad*, p. 87.

19. I am referring to the title of Farrell's *The Myth of Male Power: Why Men are the Disposable Sex* (1993), a disturbingly antifeminist tract characterized by a hysterical tone and almost surreal interpretation of endangered men. In Farrell's consciousness-raising groups, for instance, members are encouraged to say what they feel rather than what they think.

20. Sattel, in "The Inexpressive Male: Tragedy or Sexual Politics," pp. 469–77, was alone in arguing for what can be called the "sexual politics" explanation of male expressivity. For Sattel, male inexpressivity "empirically emerges as an intentional manipulation of a situation when threats to the male position occur" (469). Ten years later, Jack Balswick, in a book that takes Sattel's title, argued that the desire to retain power cannot explain the motivations for male inexpressivity, given the pain that it produces, both psychically and physically. See his *The Inexpressive Male*.

21. The novel's simultaneous use and critique of therapeutic narrative recalls what Andrew Gordon analyzes in Barth's *The End of the Road* (1958). According to Gordon, that novel is less interested in critiquing a therapeutic model per se (in this case, Freudian psychoanalysis) than it is in exposing what Gordon calls (echoing Philip Reiff) the "triumph of the therapeutic." See "The Triumph of the Therapeutic in *The End of the Road*," pp. 41, 22. I have argued elsewhere that these oppositions are at the heart of Irving's repudiation of feminism in *The World According to Garp*. See chapter 3 of my *Marked Men*.

23. See Peck, "The Mediated Talking Cure," pp. 135–36, for a discussion of therapy as a mode of individualized adaptation to social changes.

24. Gaver, "Gay Liberation and Straight White Males," p. 62.

11

The Politics of Feeling

Men, Masculinity, and Mourning on the Capital Mall

JUDITH NEWTON

What matters is what ordinary men do with their feelings of grief, of outrage, of affection for each other, and of longing for lives richer in meaning. My hope is that men will channel these feelings toward riskier social action and farther-reaching change.

—Michael Schwalbe, *Unlocking the Iron Cage*.[1]

Days of Tears and Atonement

The latter days of the twentieth century have witnessed two remarkable mass meetings of men on the Washington Mall, the Million Man March on October 16, 1995, with an estimated 400,000 to 700,000 participants, and the Promise Keepers Stand in the Gap Assembly on October 6, 1997, with an estimated 500,000 to 800,000. Both of these epic gatherings embodied elements of a "male romance narrative" about which second wave feminists, black and white, were to express considerable skepticism and concern. Both assemblies, for example, involved men going off with other men and leaving women, to all intents and purposes, behind—an element of male romance that Spike Lee was to celebrate in "Get on the Bus," his 1996 road film about black men journeying to the Million Man March. Both prompted men to share feelings and to bond emotionally with each other through holding hands, embracing, praying together, and, at the end of the Million Man March, repeating the words "I love you. I'm sorry" to the men nearby. Speakers at both assemblies exhorted men to be reborn symbolically within a community of brothers and to take their place as transfigured citizens of the nation. Finally, both employed a man-as-citizen rhetoric at times that verged on excluding women from the public sphere.[2]

Organized expressions of male romance narratives are not hard to come by in U.S. history. Elements of them have informed nineteenth-century men's clubs and religious movements, the formation of boy's organizations, such as the Boy Scouts, and, in our own day, the rituals of fraternities, street gangs, and weekends or evenings with the guys.[3] The sheer repetition of such narratives, indeed, with their frequent affirmations of male power, has sometimes provoked feminists to pronounce that men in men's groups are "men in bad company." But feminist ruefulness and wittiness aside, what men "do" with such narratives is historically variable.[4] Organized expressions of male romance narratives may resist, even as they are complicitous with, patriarchal and other structural inequalities.

Despite their man-as-citizen rhetoric, for example, and despite pointed differences in their constituencies and agendas as well, both Promise Keepers and the Million Man March enacted utopian dramas of tears and atonement with regard to men's neglect, abandonment, and abuse of women and children. The Million Man March, defined as a "day of atonement, reconciliation, and responsibility," featured a long line of speakers, from a variety of political perspectives, urging black men throughout the day to "straighten their backs," stop making excuses, atone for misusing women and girls, assume responsibility as husbands and fathers, and engage in the "love" work of practicing "courtesy in the bedroom, gentleness in the kitchen, and care in the nursery." A few speakers exhorted black men to practice "more egalitarian" familial relations and to "atone" for sexism as well.

Two years later speakers at the Promise Keepers' Stand in the Gap Assembly called upon their participants to take out pictures of a family member whom they had wronged and to "admit mistakes"—to confess, to atone, and to ask forgiveness for abuse, selfishness, spiritual and psychological absence, pushing children away, letting wives take responsibility for children, and for sacrificing family on the "altar of machismo," greed, and pleasure. A final speaker urged participants to practice specific modes of masculine reform by assuming "a second job" of washing dishes, putting children to bed, and working on the (marriage) relationship.

While I could only watch the Million Man March, I was able to attend the Stand in the Gap Assembly, and as I stood on the mall in the pleasant October sun, watching a sea of men kneeling or lying prostrate, family pictures before them, many weeping with remorse, I could not help but think *both* of the changes that feminists had once hoped for from men and of the fact that no feminist I know of had ever imagined a gathering such as this! Perhaps a million men, the majority of them white and middle-class, admitting to faults at the nation's capital? Truly contrite men asking women's forgiveness, a short walk from the White House? Men, in the shadow of the Houses of Congress, dedicating themselves to a "second job" of child care, dishes, and working on relationships? It seemed an almost hallucinatory end to a decade marked by an historical outpouring of dialogue on "new" masculinity, manhood, and men.[5]

These mass gatherings at the nation's capital, moreover, brought to mind other assemblies that I had listened to or attended—most particularly the 1963 March on Washington (during which Martin Luther's King's "I have a dream" speech prompted *me* to tears and a life of involvement in progressive politics). Media accounts, indeed, and speakers at both gatherings directly invoked King's memory and the memory of the 1960s as a whole. "I have a *new* dream," Promise Keepers' African American Vice President for Reconciliation proclaimed. That this historic demonstration, staged in the name of far-reaching social change, appeared to haunt both latter-day gatherings on masculinity and men only contributed to the giddy experience of feeling that changing men had been raised, however momentarily, to the level of an important national priority.

These epic gatherings, moreover, while they implicitly evoked traditional associations between citizen, nation, and masculinity, with all the gender inequality that these associations have historically implied, also gave male citizenry a forward-looking cast. Both assemblies, for example, presented male citizens as "affective" beings, as men who feel; but, more important, they presented male citizens as men who feel regret about their mistreatment of women, children, and each other and who pledge themselves to act more tenderly, more responsibly, and, at times, more justly in the future. For two days at the nation's capital men's personal behavior toward women and children was linked in a foundational way with their public, political identities and the gap between personal and political was momentarily narrowed.

For the same two days, finally, male citizens were imagined as something more than white and middle-class. The Million Man March, as might be expected, affirmed the identification of black men with a black "nation" while also laying claim to black men's having first-class citizenship within the U.S. nation as a whole: "this capital belongs to each of you." But the overwhelmingly white Promise Keepers' gathering, with its mixed race speakers, its sessions on antiracism, and its 14 percent African American attendance, challenged the historical association of citizen with the white and the middle class as well. Thus, if neither the Million Man March nor the Stand in the Gap Assembly could be said to have delivered what bell hooks has referred to as "the longed-for feminist manhood,"[6] each did at least enact a male romance that challenged as well as supported the status quo. Similar contradictions informed the male romance narratives of the late 1960s and 1970s past, narratives that the Million Man March and the Promise Keepers' movement clearly inherited, reworked, and, I will argue, carried forward.

Feminist Encounters with Male Romance

Elements of male romance narrative, for example, informed at least two modes of late sixties and seventies politics that were organized by (largely) straight men in the context of early feminisms and of the decline of the New Left and of the early Civil Rights Movement. These were the mainly white and multistranded "men's movements" of the 1970s and 1980s and various forms of black nationalism in the same period.[7] One of the most immediate organized responses to white second wave feminism, for example, and to the decline of white, male-led political movements, was the development of white male consciousness-raising groups in which men went off together, shared their feelings, engaged in homosocial bonding, supported each other in changing attitudes, feelings, and behavior, and pledged themselves as a community of brothers and reborn citizens to fight male domination of women. For some men the link between consciousness-raising and larger structural change lay in the future: "We feel strongly that as men we need to see our problems as products of the larger society, and that ultimately our solutions can only come with a collective unity of men, women, minorities, gays, and working people."[8] For others it was important to spread awareness of the fact that male consciousness-raising could change the way politics were carried on: there is a "new way to do things that isn't tied up in competitiveness and feeling better than others."[9] Still other men held fast to the belief that consciousness-raising *was* a form of social change, that "values" mattered and that "a change in any society is not first apparent in its overarching framework. It occurs much nearer the center—in the aspirations and attitudes of those who have created its framework."[10] Men's consciousness-raising groups, in some respects, reconstituted male romance narrative as a form of self-criticism and as a friendly response to, and extension of, feminist political strategies.[11]

Consciousness-raising groups, moreover, did evolve over time into profeminist political organizations. The National Organization for Men Against Sexism (NOMAS), for example, the largest antisexist group for men, has passed resolutions against sexism and in its various incarnations has participated in the struggle for the Equal Rights Amendment, conducted a "Campaign to End Homophobia," and supported the annual "Brother Peace: An International Day of Men Taking Action to End Men's Violence."[12] NOMAS has also instituted task forces on such issues as eliminating racism, ending men's violence, sexual harassment, pornography, gay and reproductive rights.

Profeminist organizations, however, remained small and as men's groups proliferated in the 1970s and 1980s "men's movement" politics diversified to include less feminist-friendly agendas. What ultimately united white men's organized responses to feminism, indeed, and what informed much writing by and about white men in the 1970s and 1980s, was not, in the end, solidarity in rejecting male domination. Rather, it was a shared investment in escaping the wounding nature of what was referred to as "the male role"—the economic, social, cultural forces that identified dominant masculinity with economic competition, successful breadwinning, and stultifying efforts to ignore or suppress feelings of vulnerability, anxiety, fear, grief, hurt, remorse, love, tenderness, and nurturing.

White feminist response to these efforts to throw off the emotional limitations of dominant masculine codes was predictably ambivalent. While often acknowledging the political usefulness of such "emotion work" for men, white female feminists also expressed the (not unfounded) fear that even profeminist men might be focusing more on their own emotional expressivity or on intimacy with children or other men than on the problems they had in intimate relations with women. White feminists also expressed concern that men's "emotion work" might take the place of larger structural forms of fighting male domination and thereby end in securing men "the best of both worlds"—a more humane masculinity and continued privilege and power. That was hardly the romantic conclusion that female feminists had hoped for.[13]

While some politicized white men in the 1970s focused on wounds inflicted by "the male role," or by fathers playing that role and wounding their sons in turn, most politicized black men in the late 1960s and early 1970s were focusing on the crippling injuries imposed by "the man" and by white racist institutions. It was not "the male role" itself, moreover, but being denied elements of "the role" (in the form of racist roadblocks to equal competition and successful breadwinning) that was often identified as a source of wounding for black men.[14]

Since black nationalisms in the 1970s strongly identified race liberation with the empowerment of black males, men's writing on black power raised issues of masculinity all along.[15] More than one black feminist, moreover, saw elements of male romance in black power organizations that featured male leadership, idealized brotherhoods, and uneven expressions of the desire that sisters "step back" so that brothers could move forward.[16] In the Black Panther Party, however, patriarchal desire was in tension with the organization's uneven efforts to correct some forms of male domination, and overall the masculine ideals espoused by cultural nationalists and the Black Panther Party both were mixed. One set of ideals, for example, emphasized defiance, armed self-defense, courage, discipline, the mastery of theory, revolutionary agendas, coolness, and virility, as expressed, for example, in the Panther uniform of black leather, powder blue shirts, sunglasses, and guns. Another and related set emphasized not only "dying for" but serving "the people." These ideals were expressed in such nurturing activities as the Panther breakfast programs for children, food and clothing giveaways, shoe factories, and alternative schools. Similar ideals were also expressed in the Kawaida doctrines of Ron Maulana Karenga's (male dominant) cultural nationalist US. These doctrines promoted unity, spirituality, family, and community and gave rise to the invention of Kwanza and to the institutionalization of mentoring programs for young boys.[17]

It was the more familial and communal ideals of Black Power masculinity that would live on in the black nationalist writing of the 1980s and 1990s, following the destruction of the Black Power movement. These more communal ideals developed in the context of black feminist criticism of the more patriarchal and more violent elements of black nationalist masculinities, the public "gender wars" over black women's literary portrayal of black men, the dismantling of affirmative action programs, the deleterious effects of economic restructuring, and the transformation of the cool street masculinity of the 1970s into something "colder," more self-destructive, and more misogynist.[18]

Black nationalisms of the 1980s and 1990s, as black feminists have pointed out, continued to enact regressive elements of male romance narratives from the past—by, for example, promoting a notion of men and women's (unequal) complementarity and by remaining staunchly antigay. Nonetheless, the masculine ideals that many black nationalist writers embraced in the 1980s and early nineties were more nurturing, more tender, and more critical of the emotional suppression called for by dominant white, but also black, masculine norms than those that characterized the 1970s nationalist past.[19] Jawanza Kunjufu, for example, in his 1982 book *Countering The Conspiracy to Destroy Black Boys,* defines "male seasoning" as a "conspiracy designed to make you a skeleton with no feelings and compassion for your children, women or brothers." "I believe being a man," he continues, "may be best expressed by telling your wife 'I appreciate you,' by bringing your son to your chest, and by telling your fellow brothers when you are hurting and need their help."[20] Molefi Asante, in his 1988 edition of *Afrocentricity,* urged black men to adopt the values of *nija,* which included "feeling before belief," cooperation, gentleness, and equal respect for men and women; while in 1990 Haki Madhubuti in *Black Men: Obsolete, Single, Dangerous?* defined loving family ties and, in particular, men's display of love and caring to wives and children, as the foundation of a black nationalist politics. It is the expressive and more nurturant masculinities of white men's liberation and black nationalisms, masculinities somewhat loosely tied to a larger politics of structural change, which Promise Keepers and the Million Man March rework. Both raise, in the process, some familiar questions about the use and political value of "emotion work" for men.

Some Wounded Sons Move On

The emotionally expressive, more nurturant masculine ideals that the white men's movements and the black nationalisms of the last two decades came to extol were ideals produced by men "getting on the bus" with other men—while also thinking about the women, and the feminist discourses, which they could never really leave behind. These were ideals that men, to some degree, "chose," or at least partially fashioned, for themselves, and, almost by definition, they were not precisely the ideals that feminist women would have chosen for them. This historical stubbornness on the part of men (wanting to set terms for their own change!) is surely one source of the vague but persistent feminist conviction that men "can never get it right." The idea that it might be necessary, let alone, politically respectable, to negotiate what counts as antisexist change remains somewhat foreign even now to some feminist imaginations.[21]

That heterosexual men, individually and collectively, *have* set terms for developing more expressive, more tender, and more nurturant masculine ideals has much to with the fact that loving relations with children, rather than, say, intimacy with women or other men, appear to have been the area of greatest interest and emotional growth. Certainly the deluge of media writing on new, absent, returning, responsible, and loving dads, along with the burgeoning scholarly work on the history of fatherhood and especially on the emergence of the "nurturant" or "generative" father, suggest the prophetic nature of Jack Sawyer's observation, in the profeminist *Men and Masculinity* in 1974, that "of all the areas in which men are beginning to examine themselves and go beyond the limits of the traditional masculine role perhaps the one to bear the most sweet fruit will be our relations with children."[22]

There are good reasons, moreover, that men seeking ways of being more emotionally expressive, the movements they join, and media coverage and production of both have made love for children, rather than love for women or for other men, the privileged site for exploring, celebrating, and encouraging greater feeling on the part of men. Intimacy with children does not so easily evoke the anxiety over homosexuality that often haunts men's intimacy with each other. Loving relations with children may also permit men to become more feeling human beings without having to struggle with whatever anger and resentment they may feel about feminist challenges to traditional gender arrangements and, let it be said, about feminist blind spots and rigidities as well.

Intimacy with children, moreover, does not so readily evoke the anxiety that many scholars of masculinity now argue is characteristically present in men's attempts to be intimate with adult members of the gender that cannot help but represent the overwhelming power of pre-oedipal moms. Anger and anxiety both inhibit men's very interest in, not to mention their performance of, the love work involved in being open and intimate with women. Fathering, moreover, especially fathering a son, involves a large degree of self-nurturing as well. Men invested in becoming more open to feelings of vulnerability and love express these feelings to their sons, teach their sons to be different men, and in the process become different men themselves. Nurturant fathering is a means by which wounded sons may become the longed-for fathers of themselves.[23]

Nurturant fathering, particularly of the hands-on-the-dirty-diaper form, also speaks to long-standing feminist demands. It is an arena in which men's self-interest *has* undeniably intersected with feminist politics. For men sincerely eager to restore masculinity as a "moral identity" in U.S. culture or for men simply eager to find a masculine identity to "feel good about" once more, some positive response to feminist demand is now liable to seem desirable, or at least wise.[24] Generative fatherhood, moreover, despite feminist fears that fathering is the site par excellence of men's securing the best of both—a fuller humanity *and* what Bob Connell calls the patriarchal dividend—*has* had benefits for both women and children.[25] It has alleviated some of the burden upon women who work a double shift; it may have impact in the future on public policy regarding child care leaves, day care, and the rest; it does, in a culture of working parents, provide more loving care for children; and it can generate a capacity for intimacy and caring in men that is potentially transferable to women and, as I will suggest, to social relations at large.[26]

The age, at any rate, in which men's movements focused on wounded sons appears to have ended. The mythopoetic movement of the late 1980s and early 1990s may have dwelt upon distant fathers and injured offspring, but the Afrocentric nationalisms of the 1990s, the Million Man March, and Promise Keepers all seem bent on urging wounded sons to grow up and move on as nurturant fathers or father figures. Thus the black nationalist Na'im Akbar in his 1990 *Visions for Black Men* defines responsible fathering as a crucial step in the passage from emotional "boyhood" to "manhood," while Haki Madhubuti's "What's a Daddy?" names love, quality time, listening, building a child's self-love and self-esteem, being slow to criticize, nonviolence, and not incidentally, taking an equal share of housework as the crucial elements of what fathering should mean.[27] This turn to nurturant fatherhood was also featured at the Million Man March, where it was most poignantly dramatized by the half-dozen children who stepped to the microphone and exhorted the epic crowd of, sometimes tearful, black men to protect them from abuse and to fill their needs for "unconditional love."

Promise Keepers' conferences are also given to exhorting stadiums full of male participants to "grow up and act like men" or to "get off the career track; get on the father track." Promise Keepers, indeed, despite its official embrace of a masculinity seen as divinely ordained and thus eternal, betrays no little investment in the working assumption that masculinity is learned and performed. Thus, in addition to recommending prayer and asking men to join "accountability groups" in local churches after they return home, Promise Keepers specializes in on-site forms of behavior modification, literally walking its conference participants through a series of exercises aimed at changing their speech, behavior, and self-concept.

At the 1995 conference in Oakland, for example, participants were called upon ritually to repeat the words "I was wrong. I am sorry. Please forgive me" for several minutes in preparation for being more open and more loving to their children. And at the 1996 conference in Los Angeles Promise Keepers' sons were brought into the stadium en masse (they had been attending their own break-out groups) and urged to run toward the platform in a great stream while Promise Keepers' men were asked to stand and to repeat the words "We love you. We will always be there for you" over and over again in a loud roar. It was a moment of such intensity that it brought tears to the eyes not just of participants but of mainstream media men.

The turn to nurturant fathering, of course, is not new in U.S. history and is a product of forces much larger than men's movements, media, and individual men's desire to be more emotionally expressive and to control the uses to which that expressiveness is put.[28] The return to nurturant fathering is also a product of profound challenges to dominant definitions of manhood that have attended transnational capitalist development and economic restructuring. The deleterious effects of these processes are most evident in the United States, as elsewhere, in the increasing gap between rich and poor and in the expansion of a vast pool of low-paid workers of color. But the domestic consequences of transnational capitalism are now also experienced as a "crisis" for even white, middle-class men and therefore for dominant definitions of masculinity as well.

Corporate downsizing, a decline in real wages, and the necessity of two incomes to sustain a middle-class life have hit white male members of the middle class for whom they have undermined the identification of dominant masculinity with self-making, primary breadwinning, and authority as head of house. Coupled with the continued entry of white women and mothers into the labor force, consequent challenges to traditional gender arrangements at work and at home, and critiques of white, straight, middle-class masculinity by identity movements on every front, this has deeply challenged and indeed changed dominant forms of masculinity. Being straight, white, middle-class, and male has lost material as well as moral authority, a phenomenon often represented in the early 1990s by the media-hyped "emergence" of the "angry white male."

The precipitous drop in wages and employment for black men of the middle and lower classes, moreover, and the dismantling of affirmative action and worker safety nets, the related rise in black, female-headed households, the continuing racism of U.S. culture, the absence of a viable antiracist movement, black feminist critiques of black masculinity, and the colder, more violent masculinity of the urban streets, have contributed to an even greater loss of material and moral authority for black men. This phenomenon has also been represented and, indeed, partially constructed, in the media's persistent images of the angry and violent black male. The responsible and nurturing fatherhood offered by black nationalisms and Promise Keepers supplies an alternative basis on which middle-class masculinities, black and white, may be born again as moral and as something to feel good about once more.

Celebrations of fatherhood, to be sure, particularly those that focus on the father as the cure for social ills, have individualized social problems that require collective action, have involved scapegoating lower-class black families as the source of national decline, and have promoted a return to traditional forms of male authority. They have deeply contributed to maintaining the invisibility of economic and social structures that stand at the very heart of the crisis over masculinity that Promise Keepers and black nationalisms address.[29] These are realities that we dare not forget. At the same time, however, we should resist the hasty conclusion that all invocations of fatherhood and family values, like all male romance narratives, are merely well rehearsed modes for enforcing patriarchy—a caution all the more meaningful in the context of "gay family values" and the struggle for same-sex marriage. That "traditional family values" at the Million Man March were sometimes defined so as to include the equal partnership of men and women, that nurturant fathering seemed at times to require that fathers join black political organizations, and that Promise Keepers' caring fatherhood meant embracing a labor-sharing "second shift" suggest that family melodrama like male romance is a variable genre, open to continuing reconstruction and a range of political uses.

Reinventing the Husband: Promise Keepers and "Gender Vertigo"

The torrent of media work in the 1990s on new, single, returning, responsible, nurturing fathers has been accompanied by little more than a rivulet of work on new, improved, more nurturing, more emotionally open husbands or male partners. (My search for male profeminist scholarship on issues of intimacy with women, moreover, turned up no more than a trickle.) Despite men's "emotion work" over the last twenty years, working on the (heterosexual) relationship, when it is seen as men's work at all, receives relatively little public expression. This is not a surprising outcome, however, if masculinity, as much current theorizing maintains, involves the compulsive staging and conquest of anxiety—over and against men's persistent, identity-threatening desire to merge with the pre-oedipal mother and the repressed feminine within.[30] Feminist discourses, moreover, especially those that have vigorously called on men to change while insisting that men "can never get it right" or those that have called on men simply to relinquish masculinity altogether have contributed to men's massive performance anxiety in this regard. It is not surprising, for example, that the mythopoetic movement whose participants, by and large, were often involved with, or sympathetic to, feminists, devoted so little time to discussing relations with women and rendered feminism itself "unspeakable."[31]

Early consciousness-raising groups for men did invest effort in emotion work involving female partners, and some elements of reinventing the husband or heterosexual male partner have appeared in men's scholarly and popular work on white and black masculinities, in black nationalist writing, and in recent films such as "Love Jones" and "Good Will Hunting," but Promise Keepers is the first mass men's movement to make men's intimate relations with women a central feature of "emotion work" for men. What I call "love work" in Promise Keepers contexts, along with child care, dishes, and ironing, is an official part of a husband's official second shift, and it includes such (right on) tasks as not being childish, not having temper tantrums, and taking responsibility for one's actions. ("Lots of men are jerks," one Promise Keeper explained to me.) Love work for men also includes spending more time at home, talking about your feelings, showing your vulnerabilities, admitting your faults, saying you're sorry, changing your behaviors, demonstrating that you care, being gentle, being selfless—"like on a hot day giving her the glass of lemonade"—having date nights with your wife, and being willing to go into couples therapy.

It seems clear, moreover, that the semipublic confession, apology, and behavior-modifying rituals that take place at Promise Keepers' stadium events are not meant to function as a substitute for change at home. Promise Keepers participants at these events are strongly encouraged to join or form small "accountability" groups in their local churches and many do. A mixture of

Bible study, consciousness-raising, and group therapy, these groups meet once a week, sometimes over breakfast and often work through one of the dozen or so Promise Keepers guides for men, which offer Bible verses, prayers, questions for discussion, and projects to compete.

The guide to successful marriage, for example, written by E. Glenn Wagner, Promise Keepers' white vice president, calls on men to examine themselves in relation to a list of marriage "breakers": hardness of heart, excess baggage, unresolved conflicts, and unreasonable demands. It also provides a questionnaire aimed at uncovering whether individual men are "workaholic." Sections on communication, explicit action, sacrificial giving, forgiveness, complete acceptance, commitment, praise, and romance and fun explain and list possible forms of each. This group work, moreover, along with stadium events, appears to have good effects. Both in California and in Dallas, the women I interviewed reported that Promise Keepers' conferences, men's groups, and the concept of men's servanthood had made a dramatic change for the better in their marriages and that Promise Keepers' husbands spent more time with the family, were more tender and loving, and less angry than before. It is not for nothing that one media account dubbed Promise Keepers "masculinity anonymous."

Promise Keepers, of course, is vulnerable to the charge that it extracts a high price for this reinvented spouse, and the movement is regularly accused by some female feminists and many male progressives of covertly, or baldly, substituting one form of traditional masculine power for another—servant/leadership in the home making up for a diminished sense of power and control in the economic/public sphere. (The African American speaker Tony Evans is repeatedly cited in this regard.[32]) That Promise Keepers' publications and speakers tout men's "servant/leadership" cannot be denied. Indeed, the evocation of such leadership may play a central role in containing the anxiety or "gender vertigo" that the demand for intimacy with women often entails for men.[33] But it is far from clear that "servant/leadership" operates as simply or as uniformly as many critics assert or too hastily assume.

Promise Keepers' publications and conference talks, for example, have interpreted biblical injunctions about male leadership in both conservative and liberal ways, with most conference interpretations emphasizing leadership as a form of servanthood and responsibility. Wagner's *Strategies for a Successful Marriage*, for example, is one of the more liberal Promise Keepers' publications: "The macho idea that men must make all the decisions, or have the final say, is not what marriage is about. Marriage is about a vibrant partnership."[34] My ethnographic work with Promise Keepers, moreover, suggests that there may be considerable regional variation in how men's servant/leadership is interpreted. Thus, in the Bible Belt the men I interviewed often *did* claim to be the head of house and to make final decisions, although they acknowledged that since becoming Promise Keepers they actually listened to what their wives said! In California, however, where the men I interviewed were characteristically in dual-career families, white and African American men and women regularly reported acting like a "team." The majority of men, indeed, could remember *no* occasion on which they made a decision over their wives' heads.[35] Indeed, for the California men I talked to, patriarchy seemed more mythic than actual, seemed to operate in that "lonely hour of the last instance."

The evocation of male leadership, however, as emblematic as that leadership might be, undoubtedly does function to some degree as a means of limiting the anxiety or "gender vertigo" that attends undoing the protective strategies of maintaining distance or control in domestic relationships with women. It may in fact sustain the willingness, and, indeed, the very ability, of some Promise Keepers' husbands to be more open, more vulnerable, more humble, more giving, and more intimate with their wives. What may be more foundational, however, in this regard is that 90 percent of Promise Keepers are already "born again," have already "given" themselves to Jesus before attending Promise Keepers' functions.[36] Thus they already perform a masculinity that is marginal with respect to dominant cultural norms.

Giving oneself to Jesus, for example, which involves the regrounding of one's identity and manhood in God, seems to alleviate the need, which many men had felt before, to "prove" their manhood through such traditional means as economic or academic success, athletic performance, drinking, and sexual conquest. The alleviation of this need to prove one's manhood, in turn, appears to facilitate the ability of some men to love their neighbor and to forgo the "sad rule of the fist." Many men who earnestly attempt to live out these ideals report feeling some distance from dominant masculine codes.[37] Thus, a black man living in southern California noted that black Christian men are stereotyped as "marshmallows" although, in his opinion, "it takes a real man to stand up and be ethical," or as a young, earnest, and well-built Promise Keeper from Northern California put it, "being macho's easy, but begin born again, well . . ."

Men who already perform a marginalized masculinity and who, in this case, maintain a strict view of homosexuality as out of bounds, may be more open than other men to "undoing masculinity" in some forms. My ethnographic work with progressive academic men, for example, and the work of some male profeminist scholars on different populations suggest that men who inhabit a marginalized masculinity early on may more easily identify with the feminine and with women and may find it less unsettling than other men to further distance themselves from dominant masculine norms.[38] (The same is true for men who come to disassociate themselves from dominant masculinity and to identify with a woman's vulnerability because of encounters with abusive fathers.)

Born again masculinity, moreover, also involves belief in the possibility of miraculous transformation and in the sustaining power of "the Comforter," or "Holy Spirit," beliefs that Promise Keepers' conferences draw upon for the purposes of converting men from the old man of the flesh. Thus belief in the agency of a higher power, the nondominant masculine ideals and habits that Promise Keepers bring with them, as well as the ideological evocation of traditional masculine authority in the home may help explain why Promise Keepers has made real inroads in getting many men to take on the love work of admitting faults, saying they're sorry, and working on intimate relations with women. Certainly, there have been no mass movements amongst secular men of late that have overtly taken on this kind of gender project.

Promise Keepers and The Politics of Feeling: Love Work and Race Reconciliation

It is far from clear, nonetheless, what future directions Promise Keepers' reinvented husbanding will take in local churches since local and national bodies support very different readings of the Promise Keepers' message. The men's ministry leader of a liberal church in Northern California, for example, identifies himself as feminist and the members of his Promise Keepers' men's group, whom I interviewed at length, universally described their marriages as partnerships. The Southern Baptist establishment, in contrast, perhaps in response to the very questions over headship that Promise Keepers' ambiguous rhetoric has raised, recently took the official stance that male headship does indeed mean that women must "submit" and that men are heads of house in the first, rather than the last, instance.[39]

At any rate, Promise Keepers' most original contribution to organized articulations of male romance lies elsewhere. Indeed, it lies precisely in the way that Promise Keepers moves beyond a "focus on the family," a fixation on the role of fathers in salvaging the nation, and its own attempts to reinvent the husband. It lies in the way that Promise Keepers attempts to channel ordinary men's "feelings of grief, of outrage, of affection for each other, and of longing for lives richer in meaning" toward "riskier social action and farther-reaching change."[40] It lies in the way Promise Keepers seeks to channel domestic "love work" into an antiracist project.

In its changing articulation of its racial project—"racial reconciliation" seems to have become eradicating racism in the church by the year 2000— Promise Keepers' mixed-race board has borrowed liberally from African American and black nationalist cultural and political traditions that have grounded manhood in antiracist struggle and that have tried, most recently, to turn a focus on families and communities into the basis for a black, antiracist coalition.[41] In its effort to extend this masculine ideal to white, and 60 percent conservative, middle-class men Promise Keepers draws upon the consciousness-raising and behavior-modifying "emotion work" associated with white men's movements of the 1970s and 1980s, on the self-help movement, and on Evangelical men's ministries as well, deftly combining them with venerable black and white evangelical traditions of belief in the possibility of miraculous healing, transformation, and conversion.[42] The role of black staff and black members of the Promise Keepers' board in this postmodern bricolage should not be underestimated.

The close relation that Promise Keepers initiates between domestic love and antiracist sympathy informs the structure of Promise Keepers' conferences, including the Stand in the Gap Assembly, where emotions raised in sessions on the family are called up and drawn upon by sessions on race. Both visual evidence and interviews with Promise Keepers' men suggest that sessions on the family involve great emotional involvement on the part of most participants while sessions on race involve far less for white participants. The perceived disparity in white participant involvement, of course, is not hard to understand, since many of Promise Keepers conservative white participants have little history of hearing that a "committed" relation with a man of color and a stand against racism are defining elements of what it means to be a man.

Participation levels for men of color, while somewhat different, are also mixed. Most men of color, for example, listen intently to the sessions on race, and many confide that it was race reconciliation that brought them to Promise Keepers in the first place. For black participants, in particular, it is hardly new to hear that "being a man" entails taking a stand against race injustice. But men of color also find it unusual to be asked to atone for their racism toward each other and for bitterness toward whites, and many are deeply wary of coalition. There is good reason, then, that Promise Keepers' participants are taken through a series of sessions involving acknowledgment of fault, expressions of remorse, dedication to, and exercises in the practice of new attitudes and behaviors within familiar, and deeply cathected, domestic contexts, before Promise Keepers' conferences introduce the session on race.

Since Promise Keepers' articulation of their racial project has evolved since 1995 toward a far more structural understanding of what racism means, its appeal to white conservative men has become more tenuous. At the Oakland conference in 1995, for example, Promise Keepers' conferences staged racial difference, by and large, as a matter of skin color and cultural variation and racism was defined as a matter of attitude rather than as structural inequality as well. As attitude, its resolution could be imagined as individual and ritually performed—by, for example, embracing a man of another color and repeating the words "I have failed you. Things will be different."

In 1996, owing in large part I believe to the greater number and influence of staff and board members of color, racism was more structurally defined. At the Los Angeles conference that year speakers called upon white participants to give up privilege and to ask forgiveness for, among other things, participating in politics that hurt brothers of color, standing at a distance from the latter's needs, refusing to acknowledge historical racism and the resulting privileges that they, as white men, have enjoyed, and of having neglected the heart of the city. Speakers also assigned participants the task of entering into a "committed relation" with a man of another race and attending the stand in the Gap assembly together the following year. At the assembly in 1997, finally, participants were assigned the task of eradicating racism in the church by the year 2000.

The hard-hitting rhetoric of 1996, according to some Promise Keepers' staff and leadership, produced a deluge of letters from white participants complaining of being made to feel guilty, of being hit on the head, of not knowing what to do. One spokesman told me that several clergy who attempted to instigate race reconciliation in their churches after having attended a Promise Keepers' Clergy Conference were subsequently fired and that potential corporate sponsors offered to help fund the organization, in its financial difficulties, on the condition that they drop the racial reconciliation effort. To their credit, the Promise Keepers' board was not deterred, although they have instituted a softening of rhetoric. At the 1998 conference in Sacramento Raleigh Washington, the African American Vice President for Reconciliation reminded his audience at several points that he was calling not for "guilt" but for "understanding."

Although sessions on race often produce the most powerful sermonizing at Promise Keepers' conferences—and some of these men can *really* preach—conference sermons, once again, are just a prelude to the emotion work that Promise Keepers are encouraged to engage in at home. Promise Keepers, for example, in its characteristic attention to detail, has produced workbooks on race reconciliation as well as on marriage, books designed in the former case to lead small men's groups through a series of steps for changing racial attitudes and behaviors. The books supply scripture focused on love, service, and sacrifice, readings on racism and ethnic difference, bibliographical suggestions for further reading, exercises for practicing racial sensitivity, and guidelines for entering into a committed relation with a man of another color and for listening to, learning about, and sharing feelings and vulnerabilities with this "other."[43] Books also include suggestions for putting racial reconciliation into further action—through linking up with a differently raced congregation, for example, or through involvement in community projects. Several Promise Keepers' speakers, moreover, including the Vice President for Reconciliation, are involved in community development projects through their local churches and are active in creating community businesses, in offering job training and after school mentoring, and in doing other forms of antipoverty and antiracist work.

Reading Our "Others"

Men "getting on the bus" with other men to forge a "committed relation" with each other and eradicate racism in the church by the year 2000—it's male romance all right and at its grandest. From a distance, at least, this articulation of male romance cannot help but evoke what Robyn Weigman has described as a "central U.S. drama," the bonding of a white man with a man of color and their "romantic flight from civilization into each others arms." As Weigman argues, the complicitous possibilities of this narrative are multiple and they have been enacted many times in U.S. literature and culture.

The man of color, for example, may function largely to assist in the white man's redemption and rebirth. Or the cross-racial pair may bond through gender to reestablish black liberation as a "male quest novel" and to beget the American nation once again as male.[44] These are some of the troubling readings to which such a narrative is open.

In the historically specific case of Promise Keepers, moreover, one could add even more. Promise Keepers' narrative of cross-racial bonding might end, for example, in serving the need of the overtly politicized Christian and secular right by further mobilizing men of color for conservative policies, or it might do little more than facilitate the global Christianizing goals of U.S. evangelical organizations, which also apologized for racism between 1994 and 1995.[45] Promise Keepers, itself, has launched a global initiative.

Since the Promise Keepers organization sees homosexuality as sin and does not embrace gay civil rights, the bond inevitably contributes to a climate in which discrimination and violence against gays are flourishing.[46] Finally, in laying claim to leadership of antiracist struggle, the male bond, despite the nobility of its purpose, could strengthen the exclusion of women from citizenship and render gender inequality even less visible as an issue that should engage male hearts and minds. As one profeminist Promise Keepers pointed out, "Promise Keepers has never taken a stance against, or asked forgiveness for, sexism."

As with most narratives, however, resistant readings are also possible. I have given some and I will offer more. It is ironic, for example, that a movement so vigorously critiqued as patriarchal should take so seriously the insight—which was once a central tenet of feminist politics—that the domestic and public worlds are of a piece and that attention to matters of love, relation, and community are at the heart of life and are an essential part of changing the world. An ethic of love, as bell hooks reminds us, informed civil rights that, while reformist," had the power to move masses of people to act in the interest of racial justice."[47] Black women, indeed, as Belinda Robnett points out, played a major role in creating the mass base for this movement through building relationships of trust and care between the movement and black communities.[48]

The embrace of emotional labor, moreover, as part of a *serious* politics for men remains a longed-for feature of the feminist manhood that women on the left began to call for more than twenty years ago.[49] Certainly, the set of lines that appeared at the bottom of the agenda for the 1997 Million *Woman*

March suggests the continuation of a related sentiment: "We will no longer tolerate disrespect, lack of communication, negative interaction, antisocial and dysfunctional behavior and the denial that problems such as these affect our ability to progressively and productively move forward."[50] In drawing upon domestic love work for the labor of race reconciliation, Promise Keepers speaks to these long-standing political concerns.

The mid-nineties, finally, have seen the formation and expansion of progressive political coalitions that bring together an emphasis on relationship and caring, a serious dedication to (other forms) of progressive structural change, along with a suspension of the feminist nostrum that men "can never get it right." They are represented in groups such as the ecumenical "Politics of Meaning" and the cross-racial Christian "Call to Renewal," which, along with remnants of the Rainbow coalition, have vigorously supported gender, race, and economic justice as well as gay civil rights.[51]

These new politics of feeling insist that any serious strategies for meeting social crises, including those produced by an unregulated global economy, must involve a new ethos of "compassion, community, and civility," which must itself be grounded in personal relationships as well as in relations in the public sphere. At the heart of this politics, as a deeply implied but unnamed project, is the massive reconstruction of dominant masculine ideals—such as economic individualism and success, competition, winning, the suppression of tenderness and nurturing, and the insistence politically that one's line alone is right. It is a final irony that Promise Keepers, which as an organization is far from embracing most of the political agendas of these groups, has nonetheless done more than any other to produce a mass version of the masculinity of caring and compassion that the politics of meaning imply as necessary but do not name.

What politics will speak to the ultimately almost four million men who have participated in the Promise Keepers movement? The politics of the religious right, with its passionate embrace of free market ideology? The politics of newly compassionate conservatives, whose compassion still extends to lowering taxes for the rich? The politics of the Christian Call to Renewal, which opposes corporate welfare, supports economic, race, and gender justice, and embraces gay civil rights and whose numbers already equal those of the organized religious right? And how will secular feminists and progressives relate to these new coalitions that share many of their politics but define themselves as beyond left and right? Perhaps the time *has* come to let go of past rigidities in reading the always suspect narratives of our seeming others. Perhaps the time *has* come to give more justice to, to borrow from, and to refashion them where we can.

Notes

1. Schwalbe, *Unlocking the Iron Cage*, p. 245.

2. This equation of citizenship with masculinity was less pronounced at the Million Man March than at the Stand in the Gap Assembly, since speakers at the latter included several women and since almost all the women and some men—most notably Jessie Jackson and Maulana Karenga—made reference to black women's political leadership and to sexism as well as racism as a form of national disgrace.

3. For an overview of male romance narratives in action see Kimmel, *Manhood in America*, pp. 168–81. See also Carnes, *Secret Ritual and Manhood in Victorian American;* Clawson, *Constructing Brotherhood: Class, Gender, and Fraternalism;* and Lyman, "The Fraternal Bond as a Joking Relationship," pp. 86–96.

4. This popular response to men's consciousness-raising is cited in Segal, *Slow Motion: Changing Masculinities, Changing Men*, p. 281.

5. The University of California reference system, for example, tells us that between 1988 and 1990 the number of books catalogued each year with the title words "masculinity," "masculinities," "manhood," "men and feminism," and "men's movements" had increased four times and that between 1989 and 1995 the number of such titles had multiplied seven times over. During the same six years the production of scholarly essays with these title words tripled and the number of articles in popular magazines had multiplied by a factor of ten.

6. The phrase is from hooks, "Malcolm X: The Longed-for Feminist Manhood," pp. 243–50.

7. For detailed accounts of the many different men's movements in the 1970s and beyond see Clatterbaugh, *Contemporary Perspectives on Masculinity: Men, Women, and Politics in Modern Society* and Messner, *Politics of Masculinities: Men in Movements.* For accounts of black nationalisms see McCartney, *Black Power Ideologies: An Essay in African American Thought* and Gardell, *In the Name of Elijah Muhammad: Louis Farrakhan and the Nation of Islam.* For feminist readings of black nationalisms during this period see Wallace, *Black Macho and the Myth of the Superwoman;* hooks, "Love as the Practice of Freedom" and "Malcolm X: The Longed For Feminist Manhood," pp. 183–96, 243–50; and Harper, *Are We Not Men? Masculine Anxiety and the Problem of African-American Identity*, pp. 3–38, 39–53.

8. Pleck and Sawyer, *Men and Masculinity*, p. 161.

9. Ibid.

10. Nichols, *Men's Liberation: A New Definition of Masculinity*, p. 319.

11. For accounts of early consciousness-raising groups see Pleck and Sawyer, *Men and Masculinity*, pp. 159–61, 173; Segal, *Slow Motion*, pp. 279–84; and Seidler, *Recreating Sexual Politics: Men, Feminism and Politics*, pp. 15–16.

12. Program for Building Bridges for Multicultural Men's Community: 18th National Conference on Men and Masculinity, San Francisco, July 8–11, 1993.

13. See Segal, *Slow Motion*, pp. 284–91; Messner, *Politics*, pp. 38–42.

14. See Cade, "On the Issue of Roles," p. 102.

15. On black power, the Black Arts Movement and the idea that "black identity itself bespeaks a masculine status" see Harper, *Are We Not Men?*, pp. 50, 68.

16. Beale, "Double Jeopardy: To Be Black and Female," in *The Black Woman*, p. 93.

17. Both strands of masculinity, the defiant warrior strand and the familial and communal one, had been embodied in Malcolm X, far and away the most important model for the masculinities of black power.

18. On "cool" turning "cold," see Connor, *What is Cool? Understanding Black Manhood in America*.

19. For a feminist critique of Afrocentric black nationalisms for ahistoricity and gender conservatism, see White, "Africa On My Mind: Gender, Counter-Discourse and African-American Nationalism."

20. Kunjufu, *Countering The Conspiracy*, p. 24.

21. As a profeminist black male scholar so lucidly put it, in a 1993 interview with me, "if the terms of getting it right are simply only determined by (female feminist) constructions of the feminist, then no we can't. But if getting it right means that we can come together and talk about the ways in which possibilities might unfold from those two points then maybe we could do something."

22. Sawyer, "Men and Children," p. 53. On "generative fathering" see Hawkins and Collahite, *Generative Fathering: Beyond Deficit Perspectives;* on nurturant fathering see La Rossa, *The Modernization of Fatherhood: A Social and Political History;* May and Strikwerda, "Fatherhood and Nurturance"; and Griswold, *Fatherhood in America: A History*.

23. On the therapeutic nature of fathering see Hawkins et al., "Rethinking Fathers' Involvement in Child Care: A Developmental Perspective."

24. I take these helpful terms from Schwalbe's discussion of the mythopoetic men's movement in *Unlocking*.

25. Connell, *Masculinities*, p. 29

26. See Hawkins, et al., "Rethinking," which argues that emphasizing the personal growth involved in fathering "casts wives in a nonadversarial position that is more likely to motivate change in fathers than is a conflictual one" (542). Object relations theorists such as Dinnerstein (*The Mermaid and the Minotaur: Sexual Arrangements and Human Malaise*) and Chodorow (*The Reproduction of Mothering: Psychoanalysis and the Sociology of Gender*) have also argued that if men were equally to care for infants and young children, the shift in family dynamics might alleviate our cultural tendency to identify the overwhelming power of the primary caretaker with women as a special group and might lesson our unconscious investments, as women as well as men, in sustaining social relations that contain women's power.

27. Akbar, *Visions for Black Men*, pp. 13–15; Madhubuti, *Black Men*, pp. 189–90.

28. On the turn to nurturant fathering in the early twentieth century, see La Rossa, *The Modernization of Fatherhood* and Griswold, "Generative Fathering: A Historical Perspective," pp. 71–86.

29. For a trenchant analysis of these tendencies, see Stacey, *In the Name of the Family: Rethinking Family Values in the Postmodern Age*.

30. Much of this work builds on the object relations theory of Chodorow and Dinnerstein. See Beneke, *Proving Manhood: Reflections on Men and Sexism;* Chapman, *Entitled to Good Loving: Black Men and Women and the Battle for Love and Power;* Connell incorporates elements of this theorizing in *Masculinities* as does Rogin in *Ronald Reagan.* For studies of masculinity as anxiety that do not draw on object relations theory see Kimmel, *Manhood;* Breitenberg, *Anxious Masculinity in Early Modern England;* Harper, *Are We Not Men?;* and Bhabha, "Are You a Man or a Mouse?"

31. See Schwalbe, *Unlocking,* pp. 110–12. See also Pfeil, *White Guys,* p. 190.

32. The lines in question are from Evans's "Spiritual Purity" in one of the earliest Promise Keepers' publications, *Seven Promises of a Promise Keeper,* pp. 73–82. They urge men not to "ask" but to "take" back their role in leading the family. Evans attempted, without much success, to revise himself at the Stand in the Gap Assembly by insisting that he meant spiritual leadership only and that he didn't mean men should be despots. He was also the speaker who urged men to take on a "second job." Evans's essay was removed from subsequent editions of this collection. Promise Keepers' National Director of Education, Rodney L. Cooper, also African American, gives a more liberal reading of servant/leader by arguing that before the Fall Eve was "ruling with" Adam and that "they were in a partnership." See *Double Bind: Escaping the Contradictory Demands of Manhood,* p. 93.

33. I take this helpful concept from Connell's *Masculinities:* "To undo masculinity is to court a loss of personality structure that may be quite terrifying: a kind of gender vertigo" (137).

34. Wagner, *Strategies for a Successful Marriage,* p. 59.

35. The one exception was a man who decided to buy a blue jacket for his son while on a shopping trip with his wife. He stuck with his decision, over his wife's objection, because he had been heavily persuaded by her to participate in the shopping venture in the first place. "If you want me to go shopping with you," he had told her, "you have to let me make some of the decisions."

36. "Promise Keepers' Poll Results," p. A19.

37. One Promise Keeper speaker who works in men's ministries estimates that this group is perhaps 25 percent of those who identify as born again.

38. See Newton and Stacey, "The Men We Left Behind Us: Narratives Around and About Feminism in the Lives and Works of White, Radical Academic Men," pp. 120–42; Schwalbe, *Unlocking the Iron Cage;* and Awkward's "A Black Man's Place(s)," pp. 15–17.

39. See Stammer, "A Wife's Role Is 'to Submit,' Baptists Declare."

40. Schwalbe, *Unlocking the Iron Cage,* p. 245.

41. See Cade, "On the Issue of Roles" p. 106: "And now we tend to think of a Man in terms of his commitment to the Struggle."

42. "Promise Keepers' Poll Results."

43. Washington and Kehrein, *Break Down the Walls.*

44. For an account of this romance narrative see Weigman, "Fiedler and Sons."

45. See Dart, "Southern Baptists Vote to Issue Apology for Past Racism" and Lee, "Racial Reconciliation Tops NAEs Agenda." Certainly one reading of race reconciliation on the part of evangelical U.S. churches is that it is bent on keeping black men, in particular, within the Christian fold, a fold, which in the United States at least, is still largely

white dominated and white centered in its understanding of race relations and race progress.

46. Some Promise Keepers' participants both see homosexuality as a sin and support gay civil rights. Organizations such as the Christian Call to Renewal also include members who embrace both positions.

47. hooks, "Love as the Practice of Freedom," p. 244.

48. On the role of women in the civil rights movement who built "the emotional intimacy so necessary for persuading the masses to take risks," see Robnett, *How Long? How Long? African-American Women in the Struggle for Civil Rights*, p. 193.

49. See, for example, Rowbotham,"The Women's Movement and Organizing for Socialism": "Sisterhood extends the notion of collectivity which is present in solidarity. It's not merely the public act of being together consciously, it is the personal care and love without which growth and creativity are impossible" (82). Seidler, in *Recreating Sexual Politics,* makes a similar argument about the continuing separation of personal and political on the left and argues that "no systematic critique of the traditions that dominate the Left has emerged"(16). See hooks's criticism of black power for suppressing the love ethic that had governed civil rights, "Love," p. 245.

50. "The Million Woman March Mission Statement."

51. The Politics of Meaning, for example, in seeking to change the "bottom line" in the United States from "selfishness to caring" and to enact concrete forms of economic and social change, adopts an "ethos of love and caring" in its political processes and relations that is based on early feminist political ideals. "The Boundaries of Politics: Values and Spirituality in the Public Sphere," p. 26. On dismantling the assumption that men can never get it right see "Answering the Standard Objections to the Politics of Meaning," p. 40. The Call to Renewal, an ecumenical Christian coalition, which has described itself as a "clear and visible alternative public voice to the Religious Right" also combines an emphasis on face-to-face relations and caring with action plans to combat poverty and white supremacy. See "The Call to Renewal," http://www.ari.net/calltorenewal/ctr970304.html.

Bibliography

A Succinct Narrative of the Life and Character of Abel Clemmens. Morgantown, W. Va., 1806.

Abelove, Henry. "From Thoreau to Queer Politics." *Yale Journal of Criticism* 6, no. 2 (1993): 17–27.

Abu-Lughod, Lila, and Catherine A. Lutz. "Introduction: Emotion, Discourse, and the Politics of Everyday Life." In *Language and the Politics of Emotion,* edited by Lila Abu-Lughod and Catherine A. Lutz, 1–23. Cambridge: Cambridge University Press, 1990.

Akbar, Na'im. *Visions for Black Men.* Tallahassee, Fla.: Mind Productions, 1991.

"An Account of a murder committed by Mr. J— Y—, upon his family, in December, A.D. 1781." *The New-York Weekly Magazine* 2, nos. 55 and 56 (1796).

Anderson, Douglass. *The House Undivided: Domesticity and Community in American Literature.* Cambridge: Cambridge University Press, 1990.

"Answering the Standard Objections to the Politics of Meaning." *tikkun* 11, no. 3 (1996): 35–75.

Appiah, Anthony. *In My Father's House: Africa and the Philosophy of Culture.* New York: Oxford University Press, 1992.

Aronowitz, Stanley. "My Masculinity." In *Constructing Masculinity,* edited by Maurice Berger, Brian Wallis, and Simon Watson, 307–20. New York: Routledge, 1995.

Asante, Molefi Kete. *Afrocentricity.* Trenton, N.J.: Africa World Press, 1988.

Auden, W. H. *About the House.* New York: Random House, 1965.

Awkward, Michael. "A Black Man's Place(s) in Black Feminist Criticism." In *Representing Black Men,* edited by Marcellus Blount and George P. Cunningham, 3–26. New York: Routledge, 1996.

Axelrod, Alan. *Charles Brockden Brown: An American Tale.* Austin: University of Texas Press, 1983.

Azzarolo, Ana Maria, Austin K. Mircheff, R. L. Kaswan, F. Z. Stanczyk, E. Gentschein, L. Becker, B. Nassir, and Dwight W. Warren. "Androgen Support of Lacrimal Gland Function." *Endocrine* 6, no. 1 (1997): 39–45.

Bacall, Lauren. "I Hate Men." *Look,* 3 November 1963, 36–37.

Baker, Carlos. *Hemingway: The Writer as Artist.* London: Oxford University Press, 1952; Reprint: Princeton University Press, 1963.

Balswick, Jack. *The Inexpressive Male.* Lexington, Mass.: Lexington Books, 1988.

Bardwick, Judith M. *Women in Transition: How Feminism, Sexual Liberation, and the Search for Self-Fulfillment Have Altered Our Lives.* Sussex, U.K.: The Harvester Press, 1980.

Barth, Romona. "What's Wrong with American Men?" *Reader's Digest,* no. 55, November 1959, 23–25.

Baym, Nina. "Melodramas of Beset Manhood: How Theories of American Fiction Exclude Women Authors." In *The New Feminist Criticism: Essays on Women, Literature and Theory,* edited by Elaine Showalter, 62–80. New York: Pantheon, 1985.

Beale, Frances. "Double Jeopardy: To Be Black and Female." In *The Black Woman,* edited by Toni Cade, 90–100. New York: Signet, 1970.

Beidler, Philip D. "Franklin's and Crevecoeur's 'Literary' Americans." *Early American Literature* 13, no. 1 (1978): 50–63.

Bell, Daniel. *Work and Its Discontents.* Boston: Beacon Press, 1956.

Bender, Karen. "A Lawyer's Primer on Feminist Theory and Tort." *Journal Of Legal Education* 38 (1988): 3–37.

Beneke, Timothy. *Proving Manhood: Reflections on Men and Sexism.* Berkeley: University of California Press, 1997.

Benhabib, Seyla. "The Generalized and the Concrete Other: The Kohlberg-Gilligan Controversy and Feminist Theory." In *Feminism as Critique,* edited by Seyla Benhabib and Drucilla Cornell, 77–95. Minneapolis: University of Minnesota Press, 1987.

Benson, Jackson J. *Hemingway: The Writer's Art of Self-Defense.* Minneapolis: University of Minnesota Press, 1969.

Bercovitch, Sacvan. *The Rites of Assent.* New York: Routledge, 1993.

Berlant, Lauren. "Intimacy: A Special Issue." *Critical Inquiry* 24, no. 2 (1998): 281–88.

———. "Poor Eliza." *American Literature* 70, no. 3 (1998): 635–68.

———. *The Queen of America goes to Washington City.* Durham, N.C.: Duke University Press, 1997.

———. "The Subject of True Feeling: Pain, Privacy, and Politics." In *Cultural Pluralism, Identity, and the Law.* Amherst Series in Law, Jurisprudence, and Social Thought, edited by Austin Sarat and Thomas R. Kearns, 49–84. Ann Arbor: University of Michigan Press, 1999.

Berthoff, Rowland. "Independence and Attachment, Virtue and Interest: From Republican Citizen to Free Enterpriser, 1787–1837." In *Uprooted Americans: Essay to Honor Oscar Handlin,* edited by Richard L. Bushman, 99–124. Boston: Little, Brown, 1979.

Bhabha, Homi K. "Are You a Man or a Mouse?" In *Constructing Masculinity,* edited by Maurice Berger, Brian Wallis, and Simon Watson, 67–68. New York: Routledge, 1995.

Bly, Robert. *Iron John: A Book About Men.* Reading, Mass.: Addison-Wesley, 1990.

Bohlke, Brent L., ed. *Willa Cather in Person: Interviews, Speeches, and Letters.* Lincoln: University of Nebraska Press, 1986.

Boker, Pamela A. *The Grief Taboo in American Literature: Loss and Prolonged Adolescence in Twain, Melville, and Hemingway.* New York: New York University Press, 1996.

Boone, Joseph A., and Michael Cadden, eds. *Engendering Men: The Question of Male Feminist Criticism.* New York: Routledge, 1990.

Bordo, Susan. " 'Material Girl': The Effacements of Postmodern Culture." In *The Female Body: Figures, Styles, Speculations,* edited by Lawrence Goldstein, 106–30. Ann Arbor: University of Michigan Press, 1991.

"The Boundaries of Politics: Values and Spirituality in the Public Sphere." *tikkun* 9, no. 4 (1994): 24–34.

Bourdieu, Pierre. *Distinction: A Social Critique of the Judgment of Taste.* Translated by Richard Nice. Cambridge: Harvard University Press, 1984.

Boyd, Ernest A. *Criticism in America, Its Functions and Status.* New York: Harcourt, Brace, 1924.

Breitenberg, Mark. *Anxious Masculinity in Early Modern England.* Cambridge: Cambridge University Press, 1996.

Brickman, Lester. "Contingent Fees Without Contingencies." *UCLA Law Review* 37 (1989): 29–39.

Broer, Lawrence. *Hemingway's Spanish Tragedy.* Bermingham: University of Alabama Press, 1973.

Bromley, Roger. "Natural Boundaries: The Social Function of Popular Fiction." *Red Letters* 7 (1978): 34–60.

Brooks, Cleanth, and Robert Penn Warren. *Understanding Poetry.* 1938. Reprint, New York: Holt, Rinehart, and Winston, 1976.

Brooks, James L., dir. *Terms of Endearment.* Paramount, 1983.

Brooks, Peter. *The Melodramatic Imagination: Balzac, Henry James, Melodrama, and the Mode of Excess.* New Haven: Yale University Press, 1976.

Brooks, Van Wyck. *Sketches in Criticism.* New York: E. P. Dutton, 1932.

Brown, Charles Brockden. *Wieland, or The Transformation: An American Tale* and *Memoirs of Carwin* 1798. Reprint, edited by Sydney J. Krause and S. W. Reid. Kent, Ohio: Kent State University Press, 1977.

Brown, Wendy. *States of Injury: Power and Freedom in Late Modernity.* Princeton: Princeton University Press, 1996.

———. "Wounded Attachments: Late Modern Oppositional Political Formations." In *The Identity in Questions,* edited by John Rajchman, 199–227. New York: Routledge, 1995.

Brundson, Charlotte. "A Subject for the Seventies." *Screen* 23, no. 1 (1982): 3–4.

Bucher, Glenn, ed. *Straight/White/Male.* Philadelphia: Fortress Press, 1976.

Buell, Lawrence. "American Literary Emergence as a Postcolonial Phenomenon." *American Literary History* 4, no. 3 (1992): 411–42.

———. *New England Literary Culture: From Revolution Through Renaissance.* Cambridge: Cambridge University Press, 1986.

Burns, Edward, ed. *Staying on Alone: Letters of Alice B. Toklas.* New York: Liveright, 1973.

Burrows, Edwin G., and Michael Wallace. "The American Revolution: The Ideology and

Psychology of National Liberation." In *Perspectives in American History*, vol. 6. Harvard University: Charles Warren Center for Studies in American History, 1972.

Byars, Jackie. *All That Hollywood Allows: Re-Reading Gender in 1950s Melodrama*. Chapel Hill: University of North Carolina Press, 1991.

Byerman, Keith E. *Seizing the Word: History, Art, and Self in the Work of W. E. B. Du Bois*. Athens: University of Georgia Press, 1994.

Cade, Toni. "On the Issue of Roles." In *The Black Woman: An Anthology*, edited by Toni Cade, 101–10. New York: Signet, 1970.

"The Call to Renewal." http://www.ari.net/calltorenewal/ctr970304.html.

Canby, Henry Seidel. *Definitions: Essays in Contemporary Criticism*. New York: Harcourt Brace, 1922.

———. *Seven Years' Harvest*. New York: Farrar and Rinehart, 1936.

Capra, Frank, dir. *It's A Wonderful Life*. RKO, 1946.

Carby, Hazel V. *Race Men*. Cambridge: Harvard University Press, 1998.

Carew-Miller, Anna. "The Language of Domesticity in Crevecoeur's *Letters from an American Farmer*." *Early American Literature* 28, no. 3 (1993): 242–54.

Carnes, Mark C. *Secret Ritual and Manhood in Victorian America*. New Haven: Yale University Press, 1989.

Cary, Alice. "Pictures of Memory." In *American Women Poets of the Nineteenth Century: An Anthology*, edited by Cheryl Walker, 178. New Brunswick, N.J.: Rutgers University Press, 1992.

Cather, Willa. *A Lost Lady*. 1923. Reprint, New York: Vintage, 1990.

Cavell, Stanley. "Being Odd, Getting Even: Threats to Individuality." In *Reconstructing Individualism: Autonomy, Individuality, and the Self in Western Thought*, edited by Thomas C. Heller, Morton Sosna, and David E. Wellbery, 278–312. Stanford: Stanford University Press, 1986.

———. *Contesting Tears: The Hollywood Melodrama of the Unknown Woman*. Chicago: University of Chicago Press, 1996.

———. *The Senses of Walden*. San Francisco: North Point Press, 1981.

Chamallas, Martha. "Consent, Equality, and the Legal Control of Sexual Conduct." *Southern California Law Review* 61 (1988): 777–845.

———. "The Architecture of Bias: Deep Structures in Tort Law." *University of Pennsylvania Law Review* 146 (1998): 463–531.

———. "Women, Mothers, and the Law of Fright: A History." *Michigan Law Review* 88, no. 3 (1990): 814–64.

———. "Writing about Sexual Harassment: A Guide to the Literature." *UCLA Women's Law Journal* 4 (1993): 37–58.

Chandler, Karen. "Agency and *Stella Dallas*: Audience, Melodramatic Directives, and Social Determinism in 1920s America." *Arizona Quarterly* 51, no. 4 (1995): 27–44.

Chapman, Audrey. *Entitled to Good Loving: Black Men and Women and the Battle for Love and Power*. New York: Henry Holt, 1995.

Chapman, Mary, and Glenn Hendler. "Introduction." In *Sentimental Men: Masculinity and the Politics of Affect in American Culture*. Berkeley: University of California Press, 1999.

Charters, Ann, ed. *Jack Kerouac: Selected Letters, 1940–1956*. New York: Viking, 1995.

—, ed. *The Portable Beat Reader.* New York: Viking, 1992.

Chivers, Thomas Holley. "Avalon." In *American Poetry: The Nineteenth Century,* edited by John Hollander, 1: 574–81. New York: Library of America, 1993.

Chodorow, Nancy. *The Reproduction of Mothering: Psychoanalysis and the Sociology of Gender.* Berkeley: University of California Press, 1978.

Choti, Suzanne E., Albert R. Marston, Steven G. Holston, and Joseph T. Hart. "Gender and Personality in Film-induced Sadness and Crying." *Journal of Social and Clinical Psychology* 5, no. 4 (1987): 535–44.

Claridge, Henry. "John Crowe Ransom." In *The Encyclopedia of American Poetry: The Twentieth Century,* edited by Eric L. Haralson, 589–91. Chicago: Fitzroy Dearborn, 2001.

Clatterbaugh, Kenneth. *Contemporary Perspectives on Masculinity: Men, Women, and Politics in Modern Society.* Boulder, Colo.: Westview Press, 1990.

Clawson, Mary Ann. *Constructing Brotherhood: Class, Gender, and Fraternalism.* Princeton: Princeton University Press, 1989.

Cohen, Adam. "The Atlanta Massacre." *Time,* 9 August, 1999, 22–26.

Cohen, Daniel A. "Homicidal Compulsion and the Conditions of Freedom: The Social and Psychological Origins of Familicide in America's Early Republic." *Journal of Social History* 28, no. 4 (1995): 725–64.

Cole, Toby, comp. *Acting: A Handbook of the Stanislavski Method.* New York: Crown, 1995.

Coleridge, Samuel Talor. "Frost at Midnight." In *The Norton Anthology of English Literature,* edited by M. H. Abrams et al., 2:215. New York: Norton, 1962.

Condry, John and Sandra Condry. "Sex Differences: A Study of the Eye of the Beholder." *Child Development* 47, no. 6 (1976): 812–19.

Connell, R. W. *Masculinities.* Berkeley: University of California Press, 1995.

Connolly, Cyril. *Enemies of Promise.* Boston: Little, Brown, 1939.

———. Review of *Men Without Women,* by Ernest Hemingway, *New Statesman,* 26 November, 1927. In *Hemingway: The Critical Heritage,* edited by Jeffrey Meyer, 110–12. Boston and London: Routledge and Kegan Paul, 1982.

Connor, Marlene Kim. *What Is Cool? Understanding Black Manhood in America.* New York: Crown, 1994.

Cook, Pam. "Melodrama and the Women's Picture." In *Imitations of Life: A Reader on Film and Television Melodrama,* edited by Marcia Landry, 248–62. Detroit: Wayne State University Press, 1991.

Cooper, James Fenimore. *The Pioneers, or The Sources of the Susquehanna.* 1823. Reprint, New York: Signet, 1964.

Cooper, Rodney L. *Double Bind: Escaping the Contradictory Demands of Manhood.* Grand Rapids, Mich.: Zondervan, 1996.

Cott, Nancy. "Divorce and the Changing Status of Women in Eighteenth-Century Massachusetts," *William and Mary Quarterly* 33, no.3 (1976): 596–610.

———. *The Bonds Of Womanhood: "Women's Sphere" in New England, 1780–1835.* New Haven: Yale University Press, 1977.

Crane, R. S. *The Idea of the Humanities.* Chicago: University of Chicago Press, 1967.

Crevecoeur, J. Hector St. John. *Letters from an American Farmer.* 1782. Reprint, edited by Susan Manning. Oxford: Oxford University Press, 1997.

Cukor, George, dir. *Adam's Rib*. MGM 1949.

Cummings, E. E. "if there are heavens my mother will(all by herself)have." In *The Norton Anthology of American Literature*, 5th edition, edited by Nina Baym, 2:1484. New York: Norton, 1998.

Cushman, Stephen. "Home Burial." In *The Encyclopedia of American Poetry: The Twentieth Century*, edited by Eric L. Haralson, 231–32. Chicago: Fitzroy Dearborn, 2001.

Cvetkovich, Ann. *Mixed Feelings: Feminism, Mass Culture, and Victorian Sensationalism*. New Brunswick, N.J.: Rutgers University Press, 1992.

"Curing Homophobia and Other Conservative Pathologies." *tikkun* 8, no. 5 (1993): 9–93.

Damasio, Antonio. *Descartes' Error: Emotion, Reason, and the Human Brain*. New York: Putnam, 1994.

Damon, S. Foster. *Thomas Holley Chivers, Friend of Poe*. New York: Harper, 1930.

Dart, John. "Southern Baptists Vote to Issue Apology for Past Racism," *Los Angeles Times*, 21 June, 1995, A28.

Davenport, Stephen. "Complicating 'A Very Masculine Aesthetic': Positional Sons and Double Husbands, Kinship and Careening in Jack Kerouac's Fiction." Ph.D. Diss., University of Illinois at Urbana-Champaign, 1992.

Davidson, Cathy. "Preface." In *No More Separate Spheres! Special Issue of American Literature* 70, no. 3 (1998): 443–63.

Davidson, Marshall. "The Thief Goes Free: Stealing Love in Tennessee." *Tennessee Law Review* 56 (1989): 651–60.

Davis, David Brion. *Homicide in American Fiction, 1798–1860*. Ithaca, N.Y.: Cornell University Press, 1957.

Delbanco, Andrew. *The Death of Satan*. New York: Farrar, Straus, and Giroux, 1995.

Delgado, Richard. "Words that Wound: A Tort Action for Racial Insults, Epithets, and Name Calling." In *Words that Wound: Critical Race Theory, Assaultive Speech, and the First Amendment*, edited by Mari J. Matsuda, Charles R. Lawrence III, Richard Delgado, and Kimberly Williams Crenshaw, 89–110. San Francisco: Westview Press, 1983.

Dickinson, Emily. "On such a night, or such a night" (#146). In *The Complete Poems of Emily Dickinson*, edited by Thomas H. Johnson, 69. Boston: Little, Brown, 1960.

———. "Grief is a Mouse" (#793). In *The Complete Poems*, ed. by Johnson, 387.

Dimock, Wai Chee. *Residues of Justice*. Berkeley: University of California Press, 1996.

Dinnerstein, Dorothy. *The Mermaid and the Minotaur: Sexual Arrangements and Human Malaise*. New York: Harper and Row, 1976.

Ditz, Toby. "Shipwrecked; or, Masculinity Imperiled: Mercantile Representations of Failure and the Gendered Self in Eighteenth-Century Philadelphia." *Journal of American History* 81, no. 1 (1994): 51–80.

Dock, Julie Bates. "William Dean Howells." In *Encyclopedia of American Poetry: The Nineteenth Century*, edited by Eric L. Haralson, 227. Chicago: Fitzroy Dearborn, 1998.

Douglas, Ann. *The Feminization of American Culture*. New York: Avon, 1977.

Drake, St. Clair, and Horace Cayton. *Black Metropolis: A Study of Life in a Northern City*. New York: Harcourt, 1945.

Du Bois, W. E. B. *Writings*. Edited by Nathan Huggins. New York: Library of America, 1986.

Dubbert, Joe L. *A Man's Place: Masculinity in Transition.* Englewood Cliffs, N.J.: Prentice Hall, 1979.

Duberman, Martin. *James Russell Lowell.* Boston: Houghton Mifflin, 1966.

Dyer, Richard. *Heavenly Bodies: Film Stars and Society.* New York: Macmillan, 1986.

Eagleton, Terry. *The Ideology of the Aesthetic.* Oxford: Blackwell, 1990.

Eastman, Max. "Bull in the Afternoon." *New Republic,* 7 June, 1993, 94–97.

Echols, Alice. *Daring to Be Bad: Radical Feminism in America, 1967–1975.* Minneapolis: University of Minnesota Press, 1989.

Edwards, Jonathan. "Sinners in the Hands of an Angry God." In *The Heath Anthology of American Literature,* vol. 1, 3d ed., edited by Paul Lauter. New York: Houghton Mifflin, 1979.

———. *A Jonathan Edwards Reader.* Edited by John E. Smith, Harry S. Stout, and Kenneth P. Minkema. New Haven: Yale University Press, 1995.

Efran, Jay S., and Timothy J. Spangler. "Why Grown-Ups Cry: A Two-Factor Theory and Evidence from *The Miracle Worker.*" *Motivation and Emotion* 3, no. 1 (1979): 63–72.

Ehrenreich, Barbara. *The Hearts of Men: American Dreams and the Flight from Commitment.* Garden City, N.Y.: Anchor/Doubleday, 1983.

Ehrenreich, Barbara, and Deirdre English. *For Her Own Good: 150 Years of the Experts' Advice to Women.* New York: Anchor Books, 1979.

Ekman, Paul, ed. *Darwin and Facial Expression: A Century of Research in Review.* New York: Academic Press, 1973.

Ekman, Paul, Wallace V. Friesen, and Phoebe Ellsworth. *Emotion in the Human Face: Guidelines for Research and an Integration of Findings.* New York: Pergamon Press, 1972.

Eliot, T. S. "Hamlet and his Problems." In *Selected Essays.* New York: Harcourt Brace Jovanovich, 1950.

Ellison, Julie. "A Short History of Liberal Guilt." *Critical Inquiry* 22, no. 2 (1996): 344–71.

———. "Cato's Tears." *ELH* 63, no. 3 (1996): 571–601.

———. "The Gender of Transparency: Masculinity and the Conduct of Life." *American Literary History* 4, no. 4 (1992): 584–606.

Elsaesser, Thomas. "Tales of Sound and Fury: Observations on Family Melodrama." *Monogram* 4 (1972): 2–15.

Emerson, Ralph Waldo. "Threnody." In *American Poetry: The Nineteenth Century,* edited by John Hollander, 1:311–18. New York: Library of America, 1993.

———. "Experience." In *The Norton Anthology of American Literature,* 4th ed., edited by Nina Baym et al., 1:1090. New York: Norton, 1994.

Evans, Tony. "Spiritual Purity." In *Seven Promises of a Promise Keeper.* Colorado Springs, Col.: Focus on the Family, 1994.

Ewing, Charles Patrick. *Fatal Families: The Dynamics of Intrafamilial Homicide.* Thousand Oaks, Cal.: Sage, 1997.

Faludi, Susan. *Stiffed: The Betrayal of the American Man.* New York: William Morrow, 1999.

Farr, Judith. *The Passion of Emily Dickinson.* Cambridge: Harvard University Press, 1992.

Farrell, Warren. *The Liberated Man: Beyond Masculinity: Freeing Men and Their Relationships with Women.* New York: Random House, 1974.

————. *The Myth of Male Power: Why Men Are the Disposable Sex*. New York: Simon and Schuster, 1993.

Fasteau, Marc Feigen. *The Male Machine*. New York: McGraw Hill, 1974.

Feinsinger, N. P. "Legislation Affecting Breach of Promise." *Wisconsin Law Review* 10 (1935): 417–30.

Felski, Rita. *The Gender of Modernity*. Cambridge: Harvard University Press, 1995.

Ferguson, Robert A. *Law and Letters in American Culture*. Cambridge: Harvard University Press, 1984.

Fetterley, Judith. *The Resisting Reader: A Feminist Approach to American Fiction*. Bloomington: Indiana University Press, 1978.

Fiedler, Leslie. *Love and Death in the American Novel*. Rev. ed., New York: Dell, 1966.

Finley, Karen. "A Break in the Silence: Including Women's Issues in a Torts Course." *Yale Journal of Law and Feminism* 1 (1989): 41–73.

Fitzgerald, Neil. "Towards an American Abraham: Multiple Parricide and the Rejection of Revelation in the Early National Period." M.A. thesis, Brown University, 1971.

Fletcher, Angus. "James Russell Lowell." In *Encyclopedia of American Poetry: The Nineteenth Century*, edited by Eric L. Haralson, 275. Chicago: Fitroy Dearborn, 1998.

Fliegelman, Jay. *Declaring Independence: Jefferson, Natural Language, and the Culture of Performance*. Stanford: Stanford University Press, 1993.

————. *Prodigals and Pilgrims: The American Revolution Against Patriarchal Authority, 1750–1800*. Cambridge: Cambridge University Press, 1982.

Fox, Richard Wightman. "Intimacy on Trial: Cultural Meanings of the Beecher-Tilton Affair." In *The Power of Culture*, edited by Richard Wightman Fox and T. J. Jackson Lears, 103–43. Chicago: University of Chicago Press, 1993.

————. *Trials of Intimacy: Love and Loss in the Beecher Tilton Scandal*. Chicago: University of Chicago Press, 1999.

Fox, Richard Wightman, and T. J. Jackson Lears. *The Culture of Consumption: Critical Essays in American History 1880–1980*. New York: Pantheon, 1983.

Fraiman, Susan. *Cool Men and the Second Sex: Reading Left Intellectuals*. Forthcoming.

Franklin, Benjamin. *Benjamin Franklin's Autobiography*. Edited by J. A. Leo Lemay and P. M. Zall. New York: Norton, 1986.

Freidson, Eliot. *Professional Powers: A Study of the Institutionalization of Formal Knowledge*. Chicago: University of Chicago Press, 1986.

French, Marilyn. *The Women's Room*. New York: Summit, 1977.

Frey, II, William H., and Muriel Langseth. *Crying: The Mystery of Tears*. New York: Harper and Row, 1985.

Fried, Charles. "Privacy [A Moral Analysis]." In *Philosophical Dimensions of Privacy: An Anthology*, edited by Ferdinand David Schoeman, 203–22. Cambridge: Cambridge University Press, 1984.

Frijda, Nico. *The Emotions*. New York: Cambridge University Press, 1986.

Frost, Robert. "Out, Out—." In *The Norton Anthology of American Literature*, 5th ed., edited by Nina Baym. 2:1156. New York: Norton, 1998.

Gardell, Mattias. *In the Name of Elijah Muhammad: Louis Farrakhan and the Nation of Islam*. Durham, N.C.: Duke University Press, 1996.

Gaver, Charles. "Gay Liberation and Straight White Males." In *Straight/White/Male*, edited by Glen Bucher, 51–70. Philadelphia: Fortress Press, 1976.

Giffen, Allison. " 'Till Grief Melodious Grow': The Poems and Letters of Ann Eliza Bleecker." *Early American Literature* 28, no. 3 (1993): 222–41.

Gilbert, Sandra, and Susan Gubar. *No Man's Land: The Place of the Woman Writer in the Twentieth Century.* Vol. 1, *The War of the Words.* New Haven: Yale University Press, 1988.

Gilmore, Michael T. *American Romanticism and the Marketplace.* Chicago: University of Chicago Press, 1985.

Gilroy, Paul. *The Black Atlantic: Modernity and Double Consciousness.* Cambridge: Harvard University Press, 1993.

Gledhill, Christine. *Home is Where the Heart Is.* London: British Film Institute, 1987.

Goldberg, Herb. *The Hazards of Being Male: Surviving the Myth of Masculine Privilege.* New York: Nash, 1976.

Goodman, Nan. *Shifting the Blame: Literature, Law, and the Theory of Accidents in Nineteenth-Century America.* Princeton: Princeton University Press, 1998.

Gordon, Andrew. "The Triumph of the Therapeutic in *The End of the Road.*" *Delta* 21 (1985): 31–42.

Grabo, Norman S. *The Coincidental Art of Charles Brockden Brown.* Chapel Hill: University of North Carolina Press, 1981.

Griswold, Robert L. *Fatherhood in America: A History.* New York: Basic Books, 1993.

———. "Generative Fathering: A Historical Perspective." In *Generative Fathering,* edited by Alan J. Hawkins, Shawn L. Christiansen, Kathryn Pond Sargent, and E. Jeffrey Hill, 71–86. Thousand Oaks, Calif.: Sage, 1997.

Grodal, Torben. *Moving Pictures: A New Theory of Film Genres, Feelings, and Cognition.* New York: Oxford University Press, 1997.

Gross, James J., B. L. Frederickson, and Robert W. Levenson. "The Psychophysiology of Crying." *Psychophysiology* 31, no. 5 (1994): 460–68.

Hacker, Helen M. "New Burdens of Masculinity." *Marriage and Family Living* 19 (1957): 227–33.

Hall, Jonathan. "Alice and Phoebe Cary." In *Encyclopedia of American Poetry: The Nineteenth Century,* edited by Eric L. Haralson, 66. Chicago: Fitzroy Dearborn, 1998.

Halttunen, Karen. *Confidence Men and Painted Women: A Study of Middle-Class Culture in America, 1830–1870.* New Haven: Yale University Press, 1982.

———. *Murder Most Foul: The Killer and the American Gothic Imagination.* Cambridge: Harvard University Press, 1998.

Handlin, Oscar. "Searching for Security." *Atlantic Monthly* 187, no. 1 (1951): 25–27.

Hansen, Karen V. "Rediscovering the Social: Visiting Practices in Antebellum New England and the Limits of the Public/Private Dichotomy." In *Public and Private in Thought and Practice,* edited by Jeff Weintraub and Krishan Kumar, 268–302. Chicago: University of Chicago Press, 1997.

Harding, Walter. *The Days of Henry Thoreau: A Biography.* New York: Dover, 1962.

Harper, Phillip Brian. *Are We Not Men? Masculine Anxiety and the Problem of African-American Identity.* New York: Oxford University Press, 1996.

Hartwick, Harry. *The Foreground of American Fiction.* New York: American Book Company, 1934.

Hawkins, Alan J. and David C. Collahite, eds. *Generative Fathering: Beyond Deficit Perspectives.* Thousand Oaks, Calif.: Sage, 1997.

Hawkins, Alan J., Shawn L. Christiansen, Kathryn Pond Sargent, and Jeffrey E. Hill. "Rethinking Fathers' Involvement in Child Care: A Developmental Perspective," *Journal of Family Issues* 14, no. 4 (1993): 531–49.

Hawthorne, Nathaniel. "The Custom House." 1850. Reprinted in *Nathaniel Hawthorne: Novels.* New York: Library of America, 1983.

———. "The Old Manse." 1846. Reprinted in *Nathaniel Hawthorne: Tales and Sketches, etc.* New York: Library of America, 1982.

———. *The Marble Faun.* 1860. Reprinted in *Nathaniel Hawthorne: Novels:* New York: Library of America, 1983. Columbus: Ohio State University Press, 285.

———. *The Scarlet Letter.* 1850. Reprint, edited by Sculley Bradley, New York: Norton, 1962.

Hays, Michael, and Anastasia Nikolopoulou. *Melodrama: The Cultural Emergence of Genre.* New York: St. Martin's Press, 1996.

Hays, Peter. *Ernest Hemingway.* New York: Continuum, 1990.

Hedrick, Joan D. *Harriet Beecher Stowe: A Life.* New York: Oxford University Press, 1995.

Hegel, G. W. F. *Phenomenology of Mind.* Translated by J. B. Baillie. New York: Harper Colophon, 1967.

Hemingway, Ernest. *Death in the Afternoon.* 1932. Reprint, New York: Penguin, 1966.

Herbert, T. Walter. *Dearest Beloved: The Hawthornes and the Making of the Middle-Class Family.* Berkeley: University of California Press, 1993.

Hixon, Richard F. *Privacy in a Public Society: Human Rights in Conflict.* New York: Oxford University Press, 1987.

Hochschild, Arlie Russell. "Emotion Work, Feeling Rules, and Social Structure." *American Journal of Sociology* 85 no. 3 (1979): 551–74.

———. *The Managed Heart: Commercialization of Human Feeling.* Berkeley: University of California Press, 1985.

Holbo, Christine. "Imagination, Commerce, and the Politics of Associationism in Crevecoeur's *Letters from an American Farmer.*" *Early American Literature* 32, no. 1 (1997): 20–65.

Holbrook, Evan. "The Change in the Meaning of Consortium." *Michigan Law Review* 22 (1923): 1–9.

Holston, Steven G. "Film-Induced Sadness and Crying: Instructional Parameters and Autonomic Correlates." Ph.D. Diss., University of Southern California, 1991.

hooks, bell. "Love as the Practice of Freedom." In *Outlaw Culture: Resisting Representations.* New York: Routledge, 1994.

———. "Malcom X: The Longed-for Feminist Manhood." In *Outlaw Culture: Resisting Representations.* New York: Routledge, 1994.

Horrid Massacre! Sketches of the Life of Captain James Purrinton. Augusta, Me.: Peter Edes, 1806.

Horwitz, Morton. *The Transformation of American Law, 1780–1860.* Cambridge: Harvard University Press, 1977.

Howard, Leon. "The Late Eighteenth Century: An Age of Contradictions." In *Transitions in American Literary History*, edited by Harry Hayden Clark, 49–89. New York: Octagon Books, 1967.

———. *Victorian Knight-Errant: A Study of the Early Literary Career of James Russell Lowell*. Berkeley: University of California Press, 1952.

Howard, June. "What Is Sentimentality?" *American Literary History* 11, no. 1 (1999): 63–81.

Howe, Adrian. "The Problem of Privatized Injuries: Feminist Strategies for Litigation." In *At the Boundaries of Law*, edited Martha Albertson Fineman and Nancy Sweet Thomadsen, 148–67. New York: Routledge, 1991.

Hughes, Robert. *The Culture of Complaint: A Passionate Look into the Ailing Heart of America*. New York: Oxford University Press, 1993.

Hunt, Tim. *Kerouac's Crooked Road: Development of a Fiction*. Hamden, Conn.: Archon-Shoe String, 1981.

Hurt, James. "Family and History in *Death of a Salesman*." In *Approaches to Teaching Miller's 'Death of a Salesman'*, edited by Matthew C. Roudané, 134–41. New York: Modern Language Association, 1995.

Irving, John. *The Water-Method Man*. 1972. Reprint, New York: Ballantine Books, 1990.

Jackson, Helen Hunt. "The Prince Is Dead." In *American Women Poets of the Nineteenth Century: An Anthology*, edited by Cheryl Walker, 280. New Brunswick, N.J.: Rutgers University Press, 1992.

Jacobus, Mary. "The Question of Language: Men of Maxims and *The Mill on the Floss*." In *Writing and Sexual Difference*, edited by Elizabeth Abel, 37–52. Chicago: University of Chicago Press, 1982.

James, Henry. "James Russell Lowell." In *Literary Criticism: Essays on Literature, American Writers, English Writers*, edited by Leon Edel, 517. New York: Library of America, 1984.

James, William. *Correspondence of William James*, edited by Ignas K. Skrupskelis and Elizabeth M. Berkeley, 3:21. Charlottesville: University of Virginia Press, 1993.

Jehlen, Myra. "J. Hector St. John Crevecoeur: A Monarcho-Anarchist in Revolutionary America." *American Quarterly* 31, no. 2. (1979): 204–22.

Johnson, Barbara. *A World of Difference*. Baltimore: Johns Hopkins University Press, 1987.

Johnson, Claudia. *Equivocal Beings: Politics, Gender, and Sentimentality in the 1790s: Wollstonecraft, Radcliffe, Burney, Austen*. Chicago: University of Chicago Press, 1995.

Jones, Jacqueline. *Labor of Love, Labor of Sorrow: Black Women, Work, and the Family From Slavery to the Present*. New York: Basic Books, 1985.

Jones, James T. *Jack Kerouac's Duluoz Legend: The Mythic Form of an Autobiographical Fiction*. Carbondale, Ill.: Southern Illinois University Press, 1999.

Jonson, Ben. *The Complete Poems*, edited by George Parfitt. New Haven: Yale University Press, 1975.

Kaplan, Morris B. *Democratic Citizenship and the Politics of Desire*. New York: Routledge, 1997.

Kazan, Elia, dir. *East of Eden*. Warner Brothers, 1955.

Kelley, Robin D. G. "Looking for the Real 'Nigga.' " In *Yo' Mama's Disfunktional: Fighting the Culture Wars in Urban America*. Boston: Beacon Press, 1997.

Kerouac, Jack. *Atop an Underwood: Early Stories and Other Writings.* Edited by Paul Marion. New York: Viking, 1999.

———. *Big Sur.* 1962. Reprint, New York: Penguin, 1992.

———. *Desolation Angels.* 1957. Reprint, New York: Perigee-Putnam, 1980.

———. *The Dharma Bums.* 1958. Reprint, New York: Signet-NAL, 1959.

———. *On the Road.* 1957. Reprint, New York: Penguin, 1991.

———. *The Town and the City.* 1950. Reprint, New York: Harcourt Brace Jovanovich, 1978.

———. *Tristessa.* 1960. Reprint, New York: Penguin, 1992.

———. *Vanity of Duluoz: An Adventurous Education, 1935–1946.* 1968. Reprint, London: Granada, 1982.

———. *Visions of Cody.* 1970. Reprint, New York: Penguin, 1993.

Kerr, Frances. "Feeling 'Half Feminine': Modernism and the Politics of Emotion in *The Great Gatsby.*" *American Literature* 68, no. 2 (1996): 405–31.

Kilgallen, Dorothy. "The Trouble With Men." *Nation's Business* 39, no. 7 (July 1951): 30–32.

Kimmel, Michael S. *Manhood in America: A Cultural History.* New York: Free Press, 1996.

———. "Masculinity as Homophobia: Fear, Shame, and Silence in the Construction of Gender Identity." In *Theorizing Masculinities,* edited by Harry Brod and Michael Kaufman, 119–41. Thousand Oaks, Calif.: Sage, 1994.

Kimmel, Michael S. and Michael Kaufman. "Weekend Warriors: The New Men's Movement." In *Theorizing Masculinities,* edited by Harry Brod and Michael Kaufman, 285–99. Thousand Oaks, Calif.: Sage, 1994.

King, Henry, dir. *Stella Dallas.* Goldwyn/UA, 1925.

Kinz, Linda. *Between Jesus and the Market: The Emotions that Matter in Right-Wing America.* Durham, N.C.: Duke University Press, 1997.

Kirstein, Lincoln. "The Canon of Death." In *Ernest Hemingway: The Man and His Work,* edited by John K. M. McCaffery. Cleveland: World Publishing, 1950. First Published in *Hound & Horn* 6 (January/March 1933): 336–41.

Kolodny, Annette. *The Lay of the Land.* Chapel Hill: University of North Carolina Press, 1975.

Korobkin, Laura Hanft. *Criminal Conversations (The Social Foundation of Aesthetic Forms).* New York: Columbia University Press, 1998.

Kraemer, Deborah L., and Janice L. Hastrup. "Crying in Adults: Self-Control and Autonomic Correlates." *Journal of Social and Clinical Psychology* 6, no. 1 (1988): 53–68.

Kunjufu, Jawanza. *Countering the Conspiracy to Destroy Black Boys.* Chicago: African American Images, 1985.

———. *Countering the Conspiracy to Destroy Black Boys.* Vol. 2. Chicago: African American Images, 1986.

La Rossa, Ralph. *The Modernization of Fatherhood: A Social and Political History.* Chicago: the University of Chicago Press, 1997.

Lang, Robert. *American Film Melodrama: Griffith, Vidor, Minnelli.* Princeton: Princeton University Press, 1989.

Larson, Magali Sarfatti. "The Production of Expertise and the Constitution of Expert Power." In *The Authority of Experts: Studies in History and Theory,* edited by Thomas Haskell, 28–80. Bloomington: Indiana University Press, 1984.

Lasch, Christopher. *Haven in a Heartless World.* New York: Basic Books, 1979.

Lawrence, D. H. *Studies in Classic American Literature.* Garden City, N. Y.: Doubleday, 1953.

———. Review of *In Our Time*, by Ernest Hemingway. In *Hemingway: The Critical Heritage*, edited by Jeffrey Meyer, 72–74. Boston: Routledge and Kegan Paul, 1982. First published in *Calendar of Modern Letters* 4 (April 1927): 72–73.

Lears, T. J. Jackson. *No Place of Grace: Antimodernism and the Transformation of American Culture, 1880–1920.* New York: Pantheon, 1981.

Lee, Helen. "Racial Reconciliation Tops NAE's Agenda." *Christianity Today* 39, no. 4 (April 1995): 97.

Leland, John. *A True Account how Matthew Womble Murdered his Wife, Who Was Pregnant, and his Four Sons.* Stockbridge, Mass., 1793.

Lesy, Michael. *Wisconsin Death Trip.* New York: Pantheon Books, 1973. Reprint, Albuquerque: University of New Mexico Press, 2000. Film version directed by James Marsh (1999).

Leubsdorf, John. "Toward a History of the American Rule on Attorney Fee Recovery." *Law and Contemporary Problems* 47 (1984): 9–35.

Leverenz, David. *Manhood in the American Renaissance.* Ithaca, N.Y.: Cornell University Press, 1989.

Lewis, David Levering. *W. E. B. Du Bois: Biography of a Race.* New York: Henry Holt, 1993.

Lewis, Jan and Peter N. Stearns, eds. "Introduction." In *An Emotional History of the United States.* New York: New York University Press, 1998.

Lewis, R. W. B. *The American Adam: Innocence, Tragedy, and Tradition in the Nineteenth Century.* Chicago: University of Chicago Press, 1955.

Lewisohn, Ludwig. *Expression in America.* New York: Harper, 1932.

The Life and Confession of Isaac Heller, Alias Isaac Young. Liberty, Ind.: C. V. Duggins, 1836.

Lindner, Robert. *Must You Conform?* New York: Rinehart, 1955.

Loggins, Vernon. *I Hear America. . . . Literature in the United States Since 1900.* New York: Thomas Y. Crowell, 1937.

Longfellow, Henry Wadsworth. "The Village Blacksmith." In *American Poetry: The Nineteenth Century,* vol. 1, edited by John Hollander, 197–200. New York: Library of America, 1993.

Lowell, James Russell. *The Complete Poetical Works of James Russell Lowell.* New York: Houghton Mifflin, 1896.

———. *Letters of James Russell Lowell.* Vol. 1. Edited by Charles Eliot Norton. New York: Harper and Brothers, 1894.

———. "Sentimentalism." In *Literary Criticism of James Russell Lowell,* edited by Herbert F. Smith, 57–59. Lincoln: University of Nebraska Press, 1969.

Lowell, Maria White. "The Morning-Glory." In *American Women Poets of the Nineteenth Century: An Anthology,* edited by Cheryl Walker, 187–88. New Brunswick, N.J.: Rutgers University Press, 1992.

Lowry, Robert. "Is This the Beat Generation?" *American Mercury* 76, no. 1 (1953): 16–20.

Luciano, Dana. "A Perverse Nature: Edgar Huntly and the Novel's Reproductive Disorders." *American Literature* 70, no. 1 (1998): 1–27.

Lund, F. H. "Why Do We Weep?" *Journal of Social Psychology* 1, no. 2 (1930): 136–51.

Lusted, David. "Social Class and the Western as Male Melodrama." In *The Book of Westerns,* edited by Ian Cameron and Douglas Pyle, 63–74. New York: Continuum, 1996.

Lutz, Catherine A. "Engendered Emotion: Gender, Power, and the Rhetoric of Emotional Control in American Discourse." In *Language and the Politics of Emotion,* edited by Lila Abu-Lughod and Catherine A. Lutz, 69–91. Cambridge: Cambridge University Press, 1990.

Lutz, Tom. *Crying: The Natural and Cultural History of Tears.* New York: Norton, 1999.

Lyman, Peter. "The Fraternal Bond as a Joking Relationship: A Case Study of the Role of Sexist Jokes in Male Group Bonding." In *Men's Lives,* edited by Michael A. Messner and Michael S. Kimmel, 86–96. New York: McMillan, 1995.

Lystra, Karen. *Searching the Heart: Women, Men and Romantic Love in Nineteenth-Century America.* Oxford: Oxford University Press, 1992.

MacKinnon, Catharine. *Feminism Unmodified.* Cambridge: Harvard University Press, 1987.

Madhubuti, Haki R. *Black Men: Obsolete, Single, Dangerous? Afrikan American Families in Transition: Essays in Discovery, Solution and Hope.* Chicago: Third World Press, 1990.

Mailer, Norman. "The White Negro." In *The Beat Generation and the Angry Young Men,* edited by Gene Feldman and Max Gartenberg, 371–94. New York: Citadel, 1958.

Majors, Richard, and Janet Mancini Billson. *Cool Pose: The Dilemmas of Manhood in America.* New York: Lexington Books, 1992.

Mariani, Paul. *Lost Puritan: A Life of Robert Lowell.* New York: Norton, 1994.

Marsh, John. *The Great Sin and Danger of Striving with GOD, A SERMON Preached . . . at the Funeral of Mrs. Lydia Beadle.* Hartford, Conn.: Hudson Goodwin, 1783.

Martin, Jay. *Harvests of Change: American Literature 1865–1914.* Englewood Cliffs, N.J.: Prentice Hall, 1967.

Martin, Randall B., and Susan M. Labott. "Mood Following Emotional Crying: Effects of the Situation." *Journal of Research in Personality* 25, no. 2 (1991): 218–44.

Martin, Randall B., Cynthia A. Guthrie, and Claudia G. Pitts. "Emotional Crying, Depressed Mood, and Secretory Immunoglobulin A." *Behavioral Medicine* 19, no. 3 (1993): 111–14.

Matthaei, Julie A. *An Economic History of Women in America: Women's Work, the Sexual Division of Labor, and the Development of Capitalism.* New York: Schocken Books, 1982.

Matthews, T. S. Review of *A Farewell to Arms,* by Ernest Hemingway. In *Hemingway: The Critical Heritage,* edited by Jeffrey Meyer, 121–126. Boston: Routledge and Kegan Paul, 1982. First published in *New Republic,* 9 October 1929, 208–10.

May, Larry, and Robert A. Strikwerda. "Fatherhood and Nurturance." In *Rethinking Masculinity: Philosophical Explorations in Light of Feminism,* edited by Larry May, Robert Strickwerda, and Patrick D. Hopkins 2d, 193–210. Boulder, Colo.: Rowman and Littlefield, 1996.

McCall, Nathan. *Makes Me Wanna Holler: A Young Black Man in America.* New York: Vintage, 1994.

McCartney, John T. *Black Power Ideologies: An Essay in African American Thought.* Philadelphia: Temple University Press, 1992.

McNeil, Helen. "The Archaeology of Gender in the Beat Movement." In *The Beat Generation Writers*, edited by A. Robert Lee, 178–99. London: Pluto, 1996.

Melville, Herman. "Hawthorne and his Mosses." 1850. Reprinted in *Herman Melville: Pierre, Israel Potter, etc.* New York: Library of America, 1984.

———. *The Confidence Man: His Masquerade.* 1857. Reprint, edited by Hershel Parker, New York: Norton, 1971.

Mercer, Kobena. *Welcome to the Jungle: New Positions in Black Cultural Studies.* New York: Routledge, 1994.

Messner, Michael A. *Politics of Masculinities: Men in Movements.* Thousand Oaks, Calif.: Sage,1997.

Michaels, Leonard. *The Men's Club.* 1978. Reprint, San Francisco: Mercury House, 1993.

Michaels, Walter Benn. " 'Race into Culture': A Critical Genealogy of Cultural Identity." *Critical Inquiry* 18, no. 4 (1992): 655–85.

Miller, Arthur. *Death of a Salesman: Certain Private Conversations in Two Acts and a Requiem.* New York: Viking, 1949.

Miller, Perry. *Jonathan Edwards.* New York: W. Sloane Associates, 1949.

"The Million Woman March Mission Statement," October 25, 1997. *U.S. News and World Report* 119, 15 (October 16): 58.

Minelli, Vincente, dir. *Home from the Hill.* MGM, 1959.

Mitchell, Juliet. *Women's Estate.* New York: Random House, 1973.

Mitchell, Stephen Mix. *A Narrative of the Life of William Beadle.* Hartford, Conn.: Bavil Webster, 1783.

Mizruchi, Susan L. *The Science of Sacrifice: American Literature and Modern Social Theory.* Princeton: Princeton University Press, 1998.

Moore, Sonia. *Stanislavski Revealed: The Actor's Guide to Spontaneity on Stage.* New York: Applause, 1991.

Mosse, George L. *The Image of Man: The Creation of Modern Masculinity.* New York: Oxford University Press, 1996.

Mottram, Eric. "A Preface to *Visions of Cody.*" *The Review of Contemporary Fiction* 3, no. 2 (1983): 50–61.

Muller, Herbert. *Modern Fiction.* New York: Funk and Wagnall, 1937.

Mulvey, Laura. "Notes on Sirk and Melodrama." *Movie* 25 (1977): 53–77.

Mumford, Kevin. " 'Lost Manhood' Found: Male Sexual Impotence and Victorian Culture in the United States." *Journal of the History of Sexuality* 3, no. 1 (1992): 33–57.

Neale, Steve. "Tears and Melodrama." *Screen* 27, no. 6 (1986): 6–22.

Nelson, Dana D. *National Manhood: Capitalist Citizenship and the Imagined Fraternity of White Men.* Durham, N.C.: Duke University Press, 1998.

New, Elisa. *The Line's Eye: Poetic Experience, American Sight.* Cambridge: Harvard University Press, 1998.

Newfield, Christopher. "Middlebrow Reading and The Power of Feeling." *American Quarterly* 51, no. 4 (1999): 910–20.

———. *The Emerson Effect: Individualism and Submission in America.* Chicago: University of Chicago Press, 1996.

———. "The Politics of Male Suffering: Masochism and Hegemony in the American

Renaissance." *Differences: A Journal of Feminist and Cultural Studies* 1, no. 3 (1989): 55–86.

Newton, Judith and Judith Stacey. "The Men We Left Behind Us: Narratives Around and About Feminism in the Lives and Works of White, Radical Academic Men." In *Sociology and Cultural Studies,* edited by Elizabeth Long. London: Blackwell's Press, 1997.

Nichols, Jack. "Men's Liberation: A New Definition of Masculinity." In *Home Is Where the Heart Is: Studies in Melodrama and the Woman's Film,* edited by Christine Gledhill, 70–74. London: British Film Institute, 1987.

Nowell-Smith, Geoffrey. "Minelli and Melodrama." *Australian Journal of Screen Theory* 3, no. 1 (1977): 31–35.

O'Neil, Paul. "The Only Rebellion Around." In *A Casebook on the Beat,* edited by Thomas Parkinson, 232–46. New York: Crowell, 1961.

Ongiri, Amy Abugo. "We Are Family: Black Nationalism, Black Masculinity, and Gay Cultural Imagination." *College Literature* 24, no. 1 (1997): 280–95.

Packard, Vance. *The Status Seekers.* New York: D. McKay, 1959.

Palmer, John Willamson. "For Charlie's Sake." In *A Library of American Literature,* edited by Edmund Clarence Stedman and Ellen Mackay Hutchinson, 8:261–62. New York: Charles L. Webster, 1890.

Pateman, Carol. *The Sexual Contract.* Stanford: Stanford University Press, 1988.

Patterson, Anita Haya. *From Emerson to King: Democracy, Race, and the Politics of Protest.* New York: Oxford University Press, 1997.

Paul, Sherman. *The Shores of America: Thoreau's Inward Exploration.* Urbana: University of Illinois Press, 1958.

Peck, Janice. "The Mediated Talking Cure: Therapeutic Framing of Autobiography in TV Talk Shows." In *Getting a Life: Everyday Uses of Autobiography,* edited by Sidonie Smith and Julia Watson, 134–55. Minneapolis: University of Minnesota Press, 1996.

Pfeil, Fred. *White Guys: Studies in Postmodern Domination and Difference.* London: Verso, 1995.

Pfister, Joel. "On Conceptualizing the Cultural History of Emotional and Psychological Life." In *Inventing the Psychological: Toward a Cultural History of Emotional Life in America,* edited by Joel Pfister and Nancy Schnog, 17–59. New Haven: Yale University Press, 1997.

Pinch, Adela. *Strange Fits of Passion: Epistemologies of Emotion, Hume to Austin.* Stanford: Stanford University Press, 1996.

Pleck, Joseph H. and Jack Sawyer. *Men and Masculinity.* Englewood Cliffs, N.J.: Prentice Hall, 1974.

Pound, Ezra. "A Retrospect." In *Literary Essays of Ezra Pound,* edited by T. S. Eliot, 3–14. New York: New Directions, 1968. First published in *Pavannes and Divisions.* New York: A. A. Knopf, 1918.

Priestley, J. B. Review of *A Farewell to Arms,* by Ernest Hemingway. In *Hemingway: The Critical Heritage,* edited by Jeffrey Meyer, 136–137. Boston: Routledge and Kegan Paul, 1982. First published in *Now and Then* 34 (Winter 1929): 11–12.

Primeau, Ronald. *Romance of the Road: The Literature of the American Highway.* Bowling Green, Ohio: Popular Press, 1996.

"Promise Keepers Poll Results." *Washington Post*, 5 October 1997, A19.

Prosser, William L. *Handbook of the Law of Torts*. 4th ed. St. Paul, Minn.: West Publishing, 1971.

Pullin, Faith. "Hemingway and the Secret Language of Hate." In *Ernest Hemingway: New Critical Essays*, edited by A. Robert Lee, 172–92. London: Vision Press, 1983.

Rachels, James. "Why Privacy is Important." In *Philosophical Dimensions of Privacy: An Anthology*, edited by Ferdinand David Schoeman, 290–99. Cambridge: Cambridge University Press, 1984.

Radway, Janice A. *A Feeling for Books: The Book-of-the-Month Club, Literary Taste, and Middle-Class Desire*. Chapel Hill: University of North Carolina Press, 1997.

Ramazani, Jahan. *Poetry of Mourning: The Modern Elegy from Hardy to Heaney*. Chicago: University of Chicago Press, 1994.

Rampersad, Arnold. *The Art and Imagination of W. E. B. Du Bois*. Cambridge: Harvard University Press, 1976. Reprint, New York: Schocken Books, 1990.

Ray, Nicholas, dir. *Bigger Than Life*. 20th Century Fox, 1956.

—, dir. *Rebel Without a Cause*. Warner Brothers, 1955.

Reisman, David, Reuel Denny, and Nathan Glazer. *The Lonely Crowd*. New Haven: Yale University Press, 1950.

Reisman, David. *Individualism Reconsidered*. Glencoe, Ill.: Free Press, 1954.

Renza, Louis. "Edgar Allan Poe, Henry James, and Jack London: A Private Correspondence." *boundary 2* 27, no. 2 (2000): 83–111.

Robinson, Sally. *Marked Men: White Masculinity in Crisis*. New York: Columbia University Press, 2000.

Robnett, Belinda *How Long? How Long? African-American Women in the Struggle for Civil Rights*. New York: Oxford University Press, 1997.

Rogin, Michael. *Fathers and Children: Andrew Jackson and the Subjugation of the American Indian*. New York: Knopf, 1975.

———. "Liberal Society and the Indian Question." In *Ronald Reagan, The Movie and Other Episodes in Political Demonology*. Berkeley: University of California Press, 1987.

Romero, Lora. *Home Fronts: Domesticity and its Critics in the Antebellum United States*. Durham, N.C.: Duke University Press, 1997.

Rosaldo, Michelle D. "Toward an Anthropology of Self and Feeling." In *Cultural Theory: Essays on Mind, Self, and Emotion*, edited by Richard A. Shweder and Robert A. Levine, 137–57. New York: Cambridge University Press, 1984.

Rosenfeld, Paul. Review of *In Our Time*, by Ernest Hemingway. In *Hemingway: The Critical Heritage*, edited by Jeffrey Meyer, 67–69. Boston: Routledge and Kegan Paul, 1982. First published in *New Republic*, 25 Nov 1925, 22–23.

Rotundo, E. Anthony. *American Manhood: Transformations in Masculinity from the Revolution to the Modern Era*. New York: Basic Books, 1993.

Rowbotham, Sheila. "The Women's Movement and Organizing for Socialism." In *Beyond the Fragments: Feminism and the Making of Socialism*, edited by Sheila Rowbotham, Lynne Segal, and Hilary Wainwright, 21–156. London: Merlin Press, 1979.

Rucker, Mary E. "Crevecoeur's *Letters* and Enlightenment Doctrine." *Early American Literature* 13, no. 2 (1978): 193–212.

Sadoff, Robert L. "On the Nature of Crying and Weeping." *Psychiatric Quarterly* 40, no. 3 (1966): 490–503.

Samuels, Shirley. *Romances of the Republic: Women, the Family, and Violence in the Literature of the Early American Nation.* New York: Oxford University Press, 1996.

Sánchez-Eppler, Karen. "Then When We Clutch Hardest: On the Death of a Child and the Replication of an Image." In *Sentimental Men: Masculinity and the Politics of Affect in American Culture,* edited by Mary Chapman and Glenn Hendler, 64–85. Berkeley: University of California Press, 1999.

Sattel, Jack. "The Inexpressive Male: Tragedy or Sexual Politics?" *Social Problems* 23, no. 4 (1976): 469–77.

Savran, David. *Communists, Cowboys, and Queers: The Politics of Masculinity in the Work of Arthur Miller and Tennessee Williams.* Minneapolis: University of Minnesota Press, 1992.

———. *Taking it Like a Man: White Masculinity, Masochism, and Contemporary American Culture.* Princeton: Princeton University Press, 1998.

Sawyer, Jack. "Men and Children." In *Men and Masculinity,* edited by Joseph H. Pleck and Jack Sawyer, 54–61. Englewood Cliffs, N.J.: Prentice Hall, 1974.

Schatz, Thomas. *Hollywood Genres: Formulas, Filmmaking, and the Studio System.* New York: Random House, 1981.

Schenck, Celeste M. "Charlotte Mew." In *The Gender of Modernism: A Critical Anthology,* edited by Bonnie Kime Scott, 316–20. Bloomington: Indiana University Press, 1990.

Schiesari, Juliana. *The Gendering of Melancholia: Feminism, Psychoanalysis, and the Symbolics of Loss in Renaissance Literature.* Ithaca, N.Y.: Cornell University Press, 1992.

Schwalbe, Michael. *Unlocking the Iron Cage: The Men's Movement, Gender, Politics, and American Culture.* New York: Oxford University Press, 1996.

Schwartz, Delmore. "Ernest Hemingway's Literary Situation." In *Ernest Hemingway: The Man and His Work,* edited by John K. M. McCaffery, 114–129. Cleveland and New York: World Publishing, 1950. First Published in *Southern Review* III (Spring 1938): 769–82.

Scott, Bonnie Kime, ed. *The Gender of Modernism: A Critical Anthology.* Bloomington: Indiana University Press, 1990.

Scudder, Horace Elisha. *James Russell Lowell: A Biography.* Vol. 1. New York: Houghton Mifflin, 1901.

Sedgwick, Eve. *Between Men: English Literature and Male Homosocial Desire.* New York: Columbia University Press, 1985.

———. *The Coherence of Gothic Conventions.* New York: Methuen, 1986.

Segal, Lynne. *Slow Motion: Changing Masculinities, Changing Men.* London: Virago, 1990.

Seidler, Victor J. *Recreating Sexual Politics: Men, Feminism, and Politics.* New York: Routledge, 1991.

———. *Rediscovering Masculinity: Reason, Language, and Sexuality.* New York: Routledge, 1989.

Sennett, Richard. *The Fall of Public Man.* New York: Norton, 1974.

Shamir, Milette. "Divided Plots: Space and Gender Difference in Domestic Fiction." *Genre* 29, no. 4 (1996): 429–72.

Shakespeare, William. *Hamlet,* edited by Harold Jenkins. London: Methuen, 1992.

Shepherd, Simon. "Melodrama as Avant-Garde: Enacting a New Subjectivity." *Textual Practice* 10, no. 3 (1996): 507–22.

Shipp, Cameron. "Men Are the Sucker Sex." *Nation's Business* 40 (October 1952): 32–33.

Sigourney, Lydia. "Death of an Infant." In *She Wields a Pen: American Women Poets of the Nineteenth Century,* edited by Janet Gray, 15. Iowa City: University of Iowa Press, 1997.

Silver, Allan. " 'Two Different Sorts of Commerce': Friendship and Strangership in Civil Society." In *Public and Private in Thought and Practice,* edited by Jeff Weintraub and Krishan Kumar, 43–74. Chicago: University of Chicago Press, 1997.

Sirk, Douglas, dir. *All That Heaven Allows.* Universal-International, 1955.

—, dir. *Magnificent Obsession.* Universal, 1954.

—, dir. *Written on the Wind.* Universal, 1956.

Slote, Bernice, ed. *The Kingdom of Art: Willa Cather's First Principles and Critical Statements, 1983–1896.* Lincoln: University of Nebraska Press, 1966.

Smith, Henry Nash. *Virgin Land: The American West as Symbol and Myth.* Cambridge: Harvard University Press, 1950.

Smith-Rosenberg, Carroll. *Disorderly Conduct: Vision of Gender in Victorian America.* New York: Oxford University Press, 1985.

Solomon-Godeau, Abigail. "Male Trouble." In *Constructing Masculinity,* edited by Maurice Berger, Brian Wallis, and Simon Watson, 69–76. New York: Routledge, 1995.

Sommers, Christina Hoff. *The War Against Boys: How Misguided Feminism Is Harming our Young Men.* New York: Simon and Schuster, 2000.

Spingarn, J. E. "Criticism in the United States." In *Criticism in America,* edited by J. E. Spingarn, et al., 287–308. New York: Harcourt Brace, 1924.

Stacey, Judith. *In the Name of the Family: Rethinking Family Values in the Postmodern Age.* Boston: Beacon Press, 1996.

Stammer, Larry B. "A Wife's Role Is 'to Submit,' Baptists Declare." *Los Angeles Times* 117, no. 192 (10 June 1998), A1.

Stanton, Kay. "Women and the American Dream of *Death of a Salesman.*" In *Feminist Rereadings of Modern American Drama,* edited by Jane Schleuter, 67–102. Rutherford, N.J.: Fairleigh Dickinson University Press, 1989.

Staves, Susan. "Money for Honor: Damages for Criminal Conversation." *Studies in Eighteenth Century Culture* 11 (1982): 279–97.

Stearns, Peter N. *American Cool: Constructing a Twentieth-Century Emotional Style.* New York: New York University Press, 1994.

———. *Be a Man! Males in Modern Society.* 2d ed. New York: Holmes and Meier, 1990.

Stearns, Peter N. and Carol Z. Stearns. "Emotionology: Clarifying the History of Emotional Standards." *American Historical Review* 90 (1985): 813–36.

Steele, Jeffrey. "Margaret Fuller." In *Encyclopedia of American Poetry: The Nineteenth Century,* edited by Eric L. Haralson, 165. Chicago: Fitzroy Dearborn, 1998.

Stern, Julia A. *The Plight of Feeling: Sympathy and Dissent in the Early American Novel.* Chicago: University of Chicago Press, 1997.

Stevens, George, dir. *Giant.* Warner Brothers, 1956.

Stimpson, Catharine R. "The Beat Generation and the Trials of Homosexual Liberation." *Salmagundi* 58–59 (Fall 1982/Winter 1983): 373–92.

Stoddard, Elizabeth Drew Barstow. " 'One Morn I Left Him in His Bed.' " In *She Wields a Pen: American Women Poets of the Nineteenth Century,* edited by Janet Gray, 101. Iowa City: University of Iowa Press, 1997.

Stone, Lawrence. *The Road To Divorce.* Oxford: Oxford University Press, 1990.

Stowe, Harriet Beecher. *Uncle Tom's Cabin.* 1852. Reprint, edited by Elizabeth Ammons, New York: Norton, 1994.

Strychacz, Thomas. "Dramatizations of Manhood in Hemingway's *In Our Time* and *The Sun Also Rises." American Literature* 61, no. 2 (1989): 245–60.

———. *Hemingway's Theaters of Manhood.* Louisiana State University Press, forthcoming.

———. "Trophy Hunting as a Trope of Manhood in Hemingway's *Green Hills of Africa." The Hemingway Review* 13, no. 1 (1993): 36–47.

Sykes, Charles. *A Nation of Victims: The Decay of the American Character.* New York: St. Martins Press, 1992.

Tan, Ed S. H. *Emotion and the Structure of Narrative Film.* Mahwah, N.J.: Lawrence Erlbaum, 1996.

Tanner, Tony. *Adultery in the Novel: Contract and Transgression.* Baltimore: Johns Hopkins University Press, 1979.

Thomas, Evan, and T. Trent Gegax, "It's a Bad Trading Day . . . and It's About to Get Worse." *Time,* 9 August, 1999, 22–28.

Thoreau, Henry David. *Journals.* Princeton: Princeton University Press, 1981.

———. *A Week on the Concord and Merrimack Rivers.* 1849. Reprinted in *Henry David Thoreau: A Week, Walden, etc.* New York: Library of America, 1985.

———. *Walden.* 1854. Reprinted in *Henry David Thoreau: A Week, Walden, etc.* New York: Library of America, 1985.

Todd, Janet. *Sensibility: An Introduction.* London: Methuen, 1986.

Tomkins, Silvan. *Affect, Imagery, Consciousness.* Vol. 2, *The Negative Affects.* New York: Springer, 1963.

Tompkins, Jane. *Sensational Designs: The Cultural Work of American Fiction, 1790–1860.* New York: Oxford University Press, 1985.

Traister, Bryce. "Academic Viagra: The Rise of American Masculinity Studies." *American Quarterly* 52, no. 2 (2000): 274–304.

Trowbridge, John Townsend. "The Old Lobsterman." In *American Poetry: The Nineteenth Century,* vol. 2, edited by John Hollander, 97–200. New York: Library of America, 1993.

Trumball, Benjamin. *A Complete History of Connecticut.* New Haven, Conn.: Samuel Wadworth, 1818.

Turan, Kenneth. "Triumph of the Ordinary." *Los Angeles Times,* 18 September 1998, Calendar, 1.

Twain, Mark. "Ode to Steven Dowling Bots, Dec'd." In *American Poetry: The Nineteenth Century,* vol. 2, edited by John Hollander, 338. New York: Library of America, 1993.

———. *The Adventures of Huckleberry Finn.* 1884. Reprinted in *The Unabridged Mark Twain,* edited by Lawrence Teacher. Philadephia: Running Press, 1976.

———. *The Adventures of Tom Sawyer.* 1876. Reprinted, in *The Unabridged Mark Twain,* edited by Lawrence Teacher. Philadephia: Running Press, 1976.

Unger, Roberto M. *Passion: An Essay on Personality.* New York: Free Press, 1984.

Van Fuqua, Joy. " 'Can You Feel It Joe?' Male Melodrama and the Feeling Man." *Velvet Light Trap* 38 (1996): 28–38.

Vidor, King, dir. *Stella Dallas.* Goldwyn, 1937.

——, dir. *The Champ.* MGM, 1931.

Vingerhoets, Ad J., Jorgen Assies, and Karin Poppelaars. "Prolactin and Weeping." *International Journal of Psychosomatics* 39, no. 1 (1992): 81–82.

Vogler, Candace. "Sex and Talk." *Critical Inquiry* 24, no. 2 (1998): 328–65.

Wagenknecht, Edward. *James Russell Lowell: Portrait of a Many-Sided Man.* New York: Oxford University Press, 1971.

Wagner, E. Glenn. *Strategies for a Successful Marriage: A Study Guide for Men.* Colorado Springs: NavPress, 1994.

Wallace, Michelle. *Black Macho and the Myth of the Superwoman.* New York: Dial Press, 1978.

Warner, Michael. "Walden's Erotic Economy." In *Comparative American Identities: Race, Sex, and Nationality in the Modern Text,* edited by Hortense J. Spiller, 157–74. London: Routledge, 1991.

Warren, Robert Penn. "Hemingway." *Kenyon Review* 9 (Winter 1947): 3–28.

Washington, Raleigh and Glen Kehren. *Break Down the Walls: Experiencing Biblical Reconciliation and Unity in the Body of Christ.* Chicago: Moody Press, 1997.

Webster, Daniel. "On the Death of My Son Charles." In *The Le Gallienne Book of American Verse,* edited by Richard Le Gallienne, 12. New York: Boni and Liveright, 1925.

Weinstein, Jeremy. "Adultery, Law, and the State." *Hastings Law Journal* 19 (1986): 215–29.

Weisberg, Richard. *Poethics and Other Strategies of Law and Literature.* New York: Columbia University Press, 1992.

Weisberg, Robert. "The Law and Literature Enterprise." *Yale Journal of Law and the Humanities* 1, no. 1 (1989): 1–67.

Welsh, Alexander. *Strong Representations: Narrative and Circumstantial Evidence in England.* Baltimore: Johns Hopkins University Press, 1992.

West, Robin. *Narrative, Authority, and Law.* Ann Arbor: University of Michigan Press, 1993.

White, E. Frances. "Africa On My Mind: Gender, Counter-Discourse and African-American Nationalism." *Journal of Women's History* 2, no. 1 (1990): 73–97.

White, James Boyd. *When Words Lose Their Meaning.* Chicago: Chicago University Press, 1983.

White, Kevin. *The First Sexual Revolution: The Emergence of Male Heterosexuality in Modern America.* New York: New York University Press, 1993.

Whyte, William H., Jr. *The Organization Man.* New York: Simon and Schuster, 1956.

Wicke, Jennifer. "Postmodern Identities and the Politics of the Legal Subject." *boundary 2* 19, no. 2 (1992): 11–33.

Wiegman, Robyn, *American Anatomies: Theorizing Race and Gender.* Durham, N.C.: Duke University Press, 1996.

———. "Fiedler and Sons." In *Race and the Subject of Masculinities,* edited by Harry Stecopoulos and Michael Uebel, 45–68. Durham, N.C.: Duke University Press, 1997.

Williams, Linda. " 'Something Else Besides a Mother': *Stella Dallas* and the Maternal Melodrama." *Cinema Journal* 24, no. 2 (1984): 2–27.

Williams, Raymond. *Marxism and Literature.* New York: Oxford University Press, 1978.

Williams, Tennessee. *The Glass Menagerie.* 1945. Reprint, New York: New Directions, 1970.

Wills, Garry. *Inventing America: Jefferson's Declaration of Independence.* Garden City, N.Y.: Doubleday, 1978.

Wilson, Christopher. *The Labor of Words: Literary Professionalism in the Progressive Era.* Athens: University of Georgia Press, 1985.

Wilson, Margo, Martin Daly, and Antoinetta Daniele. "Familicide: The Killing of Spouse and Children." *Aggressive Behavior* 21 (1995): 275–91.

Woolf, Virginia. Review of *Men Without Women,* by Ernest Hemingway. In *Hemingway: The Critical Heritage,* edited by Jeffrey Meyer, 101–107. Boston: Routledge and Kegan Paul. First published in *New York Herald Tribune Books,* 9 October 1927, 1, 8.

Wordsworth, William. "Ode: Intimations of Immortality." In *The Norton Anthology of English Literature,* 1st ed. edited by M. H. Abrams et al., 2:117–22. New York: Norton, 1962.

———. "Michael." In *The Norton Anthology of English Literature,* 1st ed. edited by M. H. Abrams et al., 2:98–108. New York: Norton, 1962.

Wordsworth, William and Samuel Taylor Coleridge, "We Are Seven." In *The Norton Anthology of English Literature,* edited by M. H. Abrams et al., 2:71. New York: Norton, 1962.

Yacovone, Donald. "Abolitionists and the 'Language of Fraternal Love.' " In *Meaning for Manhood: Constructions of Masculinity in Victorian America,* edited by Mark C. Carnes and Clyde Griffen, 85–95. Chicago: University of Chicago Press, 1990.

Young, Philip. *Ernest Hemingway: A Reconsideration.* New York: Holt, Rinehart, and Winston, 1952.

Zamir, Shamoon. *Dark Voices: W. E. B. Du Bois and American Thought, 1888–1903.* Chicago: University of Chicago Press, 1995.

Zeffirelli, Franco, dir. *The Champ.* MGM/UA, 1979.

Zelizer, Viviana A. *Pricing the Priceless Child: The Changing Social Value of Children.* New York: Basic Books, 1985.